PIECE OF MIND

My Journey to Peace Amid Seizures, a Tumor, and Brain Surgery

D E A N N A   M .   B R A D Y

ISBN: 1453734333
ISBN-13: 9781453734339

Author's Note

Out of respect for the privacy of people mentioned in the book, I have changed some names and some physical descriptions.

IN GRATITUDE

Many took part in getting this book published and to each I am grateful:

My family and friends for letting me step aside from our relationship and become a writer, interviewing them, enabling me to share a true story. I wasn't the only one experiencing it. I've been so blessed to have them through it all.

My early readers who helped fine-tune the chapters: Jasmine Purles, Kelsy Hinton, and my mother-in-law Cindy, with additional thanks to Race Alexander for his blunt opinions and helping me map it all out.

Sandra Dewar, RN, MS for verifying facts and spreading word and Dr. Steve Glyman for answering my medical questions. And thanks to both who encouraged me to spread word through a book.

While finding solutions, I have learned that I have a different kind of family, my medical family at UCLA and those who continue to be added in that line. Much credit for the science that makes surgery for epilepsy possible and successful is due to the life's work of Dr. Jerome Engel, Jr.—a pioneer of epilepsy surgery at UCLA and mentor to neurologists and scientists nationwide. The doctors, nurses, staff (specifically in my case, the teams of Dr. Engel, Dr. Itzhak Fried, Dr. John Stern, Dr. Brent Fogel, Dr. Tim

Cloughesy, Dr. Noriko Salamon, and Dr. Jessica Horsfall), and each contributor who makes it possible for UCLA to keep moving forward enables my family to have *me*. There are thousands of other patients who can gratefully say the same.

Marlyn Burleigh and Linda Teeter for their touching visit after my surgery and of course for opening my passion for writing. And then *my* students for reminding me.

My sister Shawna Doughman for helping in anything and everything to do with my epilepsy from the seizure drama up to book publishing.

Janet McKeon, my mom, for being exactly what my family and I need. I'm nuts about you.

Bridgett and Molly, my precious lively daughters, who keep giving me reasons to celebrate.

And finally my husband David, for being calm, encouraging, excited, giving, smart, and bold. He's what the doctor ordered.

FOREWORD

Sandra Dewar RN.,MS
Clinical Nurse Specialist and Clinical Director:
Seizure Disorder Center, UCLA

This book is a wonderful account of one person's experience with her epilepsy, the challenges of treatment and her later recovery from brain surgery. This is Deanna Brady's very own story. It is a personal expression of her experience of living with epilepsy for eleven years. She addresses the impact of uncontrolled seizures on her life during adolescence and young adult hood. Deanna tells her courageous story with humor and honesty.

She talks frankly about her earliest experiences of having seizures, her strange hallucinatory auras and the initial efforts to find a diagnosis. Is this asthma, a sleep disorder, low blood sugar, a psychological problem or something else?

This foreword is written to highlight some of the aspects of diagnosing and treating epilepsy that are discussed in the book. It is hoped that these few words will enhance the readers' understanding of this complex problem. Patient accounts are very important because they serve not only to inspire others in their journey towards achieving cure, but they teach important lessons about how people cope with ill health, their expectations about treatments, and particularly how the decision to have brain surgery is made.

For several reasons, epilepsy can be difficult to diagnose. It can be difficult to describe strange sensations and experiences in a way that they can be understood by others. Seizures are often not big, dramatic events which obviously affect body movements and consciousness. They can be very subtle and barely noticed by an observer. Seizures may appear as little more than brief lapses in concentration, and perhaps some strange behaviors. In the beginning they may occur sporadically with little pattern, and appear to have little impact on daily life. As such they can remain unreported, undiagnosed and untreated for a long time. Frequently, the condition predates the diagnosis by months or even years. Unfortunately these early untreated episodes frequently result in motor vehicle accidents, injuries and even larger generalized tonic clonic events. At this point, the problem cannot be ignored and this is when most people seek medical advice and a diagnosis.

Deanna had lived with uncontrolled epilepsy for eight years before she was referred to UCLA Seizure Disorder Center for evaluation. The current professional recommendation is for people to request a referral to an epilepsy center when seizures remain uncontrolled after trying two appropriate medicines at maximal doses without seizure control. In cases when an MRI and/or EEG tests are considered "normal," or when these tests reveal bilateral or diffuse problems, it is still important to request an evaluation by an epilepsy expert. Some doctors incorrectly consider these scenarios to be a contradiction to surgery, resulting in many people suffering for years, even decades, with an epilepsy problem that can be successfully treated. Doctors and nurses expert in dealing with epilepsy are mostly found at large academic hospitals. It is recommended that people seek an opinion early in the course of their illness. This way a range of treatment options can be discussed and people may avoid losing years of their lives to coping with the hazards and restrictions of uncontrolled seizures.

Part of Deanna's story includes her marriage and motherhood. This is a warm and touching part of her experience and attests to the fact that people with epilepsy *can* enjoy healthy parenthood. Medical guidelines for women planning pregnancies have been developed by epilepsy experts around the United States. Modern medical care assures a healthy outcome for at least 95% of pregnant women. Pregnancy for woman with epilepsy is certainly not something that needs to be discouraged.

Much of Deanna's story is about making a decision to have surgery for her epilepsy. There is a group of patients for whom surgery is a very good treatment option. This is true for epilepsy such as Deanna's which began in a temporal lobe of the brain. An evaluation for surgery requires a battery of tests that gives a comprehensive analysis of the brain and the impact of seizures on brain function. It is usual for the skills of people from several medical disciplines to be involved in the analysis of these test results: epileptologists (neurologist specialized in epilepsy), epilepsy nurse specialists, radiologists (specialized in looking at brain scans), psychiatrists, neuropsychologists and neurosurgeons. Surgery is almost always an elective decision. In other words, the final decision to have the operation rests with the patient.

The medical team will guide the patient and family as they make this decision. This is especially important as the risk - benefit ratio is weighed. The risks of surgery are relatively small. Most people recover very well when the operation is performed by an experienced surgeon who understands the electrophysiology of the epilepsy. The benefits of surgery for temporal lobe epilepsy are well documented. Patients can expect a 75-80% chance of seizure control.

Although epilepsy surgery is successful, many myths surround surgery as a treatment option. Deanna's story helps dispel inaccurate opinions about this very important option. Surgery for epilepsy is *not* experimental. Surgery for epilepsy is not unduly risky, nor does it leave people "missing pages of their dictionary", as one man put it. It really works for many people. It must also be remembered that untreated seizures pose a considerable risk to safety, and people can die from them. Surgery is a standard treatment for epilepsy in North America and around the world. It is considered the most underutilized modern therapy available to man. Why this is so, is a complex question. But many times people simply do not know that this is an option. Deanna's story illustrates this very well. Periods of good control may also delay the need to seek the expertise of an epileptologist. Unfortunately the net result is that it is possible for many years to slip by before the problem is adequately addressed. What is important is that patients seek the best care for their medical condition, and not settle for a life dominated by seizures and continual trials of new medicines.

In Deanna's case the cause of her epilepsy was a benign tumor in the front and deep parts of the temporal lobe. The pathology or tissue analysis done on the section of tissue removed, showed this to be a low grade glioma. It is suspected that this tissue change had been present for a long time and was not increasing in size. Besides the seizures it caused, it was important to remove it because some of these tumors or lesions can change in character and be harder to treat. There are several other causes of temporal lobe epilepsy besides low grade tumors. Deanna's MRI showed the mass very well. It should be remembered that sometimes MRIs are considered "normal." In these cases it's important that an epilepsy expert review the scans, or that a more sophisticated scan be done. In some cases previously unrecognized "trouble spots" will be observed.

Deanna documents her recovery from surgery with a humorous take on the various indignities she suffered in having to accept her role as a "brain surgery patient." Her tips for preparing for surgery will be very helpful to those thinking about surgery.

It is a great honor to have been asked to write this Foreword for the important account of Deanna Brady's journey with epilepsy and surgery. We know that this book will help others cope with their epilepsy and the treatment decisions they face.

INTRODUCTION
Seizures 101

I imagine it was difficult for old Mr. Webster to define seizure using so few words:

Sei·zure: \ˈsē-zhər\ *n.* **1** a sudden attack (as of disease); *especially*: the physical manifestations (as convulsions, sensory disturbances, or loss of consciousness) resulting from abnormal electrical discharges in the brain **2** an abnormal electrical discharge in the brain

Mr. Webster's confusion is not isolated; not even doctors today can completely explain the who, what, where, when, and why of seizures. I don't have a degree in medicine framed above my desk, so I've had to piece the accumulated information together and translate it into layman terms for myself. I have likened the seizure process in the brain to something I'm familiar with: a computer freeze. Have you ever been on a computer when an error box pops up? The program freezes. Then the screen turns black and odd computer equations in a 1980s font fill the page just before the entire system shuts down. I have felt like that computer many times through different levels of seizures; as if my brain had to be shut down and restarted after a moment of rest.

The error box is the *aura*. Some call it a warning. People's descriptions of auras range widely; mine started one way and then continued to develop over the years. At first it felt like a quick extra sense, similar to how it feels when you sense someone is looking at you. Over time, the intensity rose and the sense brought a feeling of fear, lodging a pit in my stomach. Often, if I took a quick deep breath and subtly shook my head, the problem would stop there. Usually, I wasn't fast enough.

The program freeze is the start of the actual seizure, any type. Control is lost in thoughts, emotions, and actions. Outside, the body can literally freeze into a firm position or make a repeated motion or sound. Inside, one's normal memory of anything can drop: relationships, discussion, location, language, actions, etc. To me it felt as if my computer could no longer heed the cursor's double clicks or drags.

The gibberish-filled black page is the phase that immediately follows the seizure. Confusion.

Shutdown is the body's last step in the seizure process. Sleep is craved. Energy has been sucked away and the weakened body needs rest in order to reboot.

Many are familiar with grand-mal seizures and petit-mal seizures, but there are many other types of seizures. Grand-mal seizures, are one of the most dramatic of all medical conditions and are more recently called generalized tonic-clonic seizures: "tonic" meaning stiff muscle contraction and "clonic" meaning rhythmic shaking. Petit-mal seizures are now called absence seizures. They easily go unnoticed as they are typically very fast and only manifest as a quick vacant stare.

The list of seizure types continues to grow as doctors pinpoint repeated traits; for example, how it makes one act. Most seizures are actually subtle and not obvious to those nearby. There are two main branches under the seizure category: generalized seizures and partial seizures. I've swung from both branches. Grand-mal seizures fall under the generalized seizure category—I had those. I also had complex partial seizures, which are under the other branch.

For my first five years of complex partial seizures I had no concept that what I was experiencing were indeed seizures. The five – twenty second episodes with a five second – thirty minute aftershock were frequent enough that I gave them a name: *flashes*. From the age of fourteen to nineteen, I thought the flashes were my fault because I was a busy person, wanting to be part of everything that was going on around me. I was involved in everything social, musical, and theatrical, all while trying to keep high grades. Being busy brings stress, and everyone knows that stress has side-effects. Some get tired, some get headaches, I got flashes. I decided that my busy schedule was worth it, so I kept it quiet. I never would have guessed there was a physical explanation. At the beginning, my seizures were similar to petit-mal/absence seizures, except the effects would linger. During a conversation I would try to play it off as if there was a word on the tip of my tongue. Then I would usually lose my train of thought and try to smoothly move the conversation along. I now appreciate that the brain has its own personality; a mind of its own.

Emotionally, my flashes took me through different stages as their frequency and intensity developed: *brush-off* stage, *pride/insecurity* stage, *seizure-holic* stage, *prisoner* stage, and then the *buck-up* stage. All of that led up to what I call my own *grand awakening*, when questions began to be answered.

Brush-off: They were usually a quick warning sense (aura) and then a moment of déjà vu. These were fairly easy to dismiss without explanation.

Pride/insecurity: I thought frequent flashes were a good sign that I was keeping active. At this point, the déjà vu had become more detailed and I felt there was almost a psychic side to me.

I kept it mostly quiet, though, because I also saw it as a sign of weakness or an inability to control myself.

Seizure-holic: I stopped ignoring the flash and began to study its process. The whole flash would include the aura, then a strange backwards yank feeling, followed by a strangling fear, ending with a utopian sense as the grand finale. I began to crave the flashes as a release—my nirvana. I was sure others would be jealous that I had so many moments to step away from life. While others around me were stressed, I was free.

Prisoner: The flashes began to happen at any time, regardless of my busy-ness. An illusion was added to my seizure. By now, during the happy part, I would see a party scene in the upper right corner of my eyesight. Despite the party excitement, I knew things were out of order with me and I got worried. Weariness was stronger and would linger longer. I felt like a freak and became withdrawn in depression.

Buck-up: I convinced myself that I was okay and used the flashes as an urge to rest.

The life of my seizures started when I was taking my eighth grade algebra final. Picking up my pencil seemed to immediately send a shock through my brain. Pressure rose, and everything I had studied suddenly rushed to my mind, no longer organized in my brain file. It was one big chunk of information; all rules, tricks, and terms were squished together.

I tried to clear my thoughts and studied the first question. It was difficult to read it clearly as I noticed the numbers slowly moving across the page. Nonsense thoughts came to my mind. *Why won't these numbers and words stay in the same spot?* I made a "that's not fair" pout instead of realizing how abnormal it was.

When my eyesight became surrounded by a thick, fuzzy ring, I began to recognize the oddity. It took a few moments for me to recognize that my brain was out of order. After trying to explain it all to myself, the only solution I could understand was to put my head down. Everything escaped my mind as I rested.

Rustling sounds brought my senses back, and my head whipped toward the clock. Thirty minutes of rest had zoomed past, seeming like five. Students were already done and turning their tests in. My stress was re-ignited, and I got right to work. Not wanting to go through the odd sensation again, I kept my thoughts on simply finishing the test before the bell rang. Why hadn't the teacher noticed? I had kept my pencil in hand and rested my head as if I were closely reading the questions.

On the bus ride home, I remember trying to make sense of what had happened. I felt uneasy, and I likened myself to a computer for the first time.

1

Powerless

It was after midnight when I finally found my sister's empty couch and curled up to sleep. *One more day until my wedding.* As if the stress of Christmas hadn't been enough, here I was two days later—practically a drifter—trying to get a few hours of shut-eye before another crazy day of anticipation and planning. I tried to calm my thoughts, and exhaustion won out.

My sister Erin was in the kitchen scrubbing at the sink when she heard a loud piercing sound. She turned the faucet off, listening. As she began to walk out of the kitchen, she heard the screech again. *That's not the baby.* She moved quickly to investigate.

When she rounded the corner, panic set in. She found me lying flat on my back, convulsing vigorously. The piercing sound had been coming from my throat. As Erin ran closer, she saw that my eyes were open and rolled back. My blue eyes were now white. "Joe!" she yelled to her husband. "Come! Hurry! It's Deanna!" My blood-curdling shriek made Erin drop any sense of control.

Joe, alerted by the loud shrieks, was already running up the stairs. Nausea set in as soon as he saw my blue lips. "Call 9-1-1!"

Neither had ever seen anything of this sort take place and had no idea what to do. They were mostly worried about doing the wrong thing. Usually Erin could instantly pull herself together, but this time was different—Erin felt powerless. Her fingers trembled as she tried to grip the phone and dialed.

The moment the operator answered, Erin lost it and began to scream into the phone, "Something's happening to my sister and I don't know if she'll be okay!" The flame of her fear rose when she officially stated her dread, "I think she's *dying!*"

The operator responded calmly. "Give me your address and your name …"

Her list continued, but Erin's thoughts were a tangled mess. *Address? Name? I…I… My sister is dying. I can't do anything about it.* Not one coherent answer could surface. She began to describe what her little sister looked like as I continued to shriek and convulse. *That's not our Deanna.* The pale, greyish flesh with white eyes was foreign to her.

The operator pressed on with an official firmness, "She will be okay."

Upon hearing the words, Erin managed to take a deep breath and slow her thoughts. The statement began to act as a declaration, helping her to pull herself together. The assurance enabled her to untie the knot in her thoughts and answer the operator's questions.

"Turn your sister onto her side." The information had been logged and emergency alerted.

Joe gently lifted my tense body onto its side. Instantly, the high-pitched shrieking stopped, and my caretakers felt a calm rush over them. A deep gurgling noise began to come from my throat as frothy saliva bubbled out of my mouth. Despite the odd sound and frothy extraction, my body seemed to be gaining control. My mind, however, was unconscious, in its own la-la land, and oblivious to the pandemonium.

Erin closed her eyes tightly and cleared her mind as she hung up the phone. The hysteria was being replaced by her motherly instincts. I laid motionless on the couch, with my eyes closed—my heart was beating and I'd started to breathe, but was not coherent. The two stood over me, guarding, waiting for help.

A prayer was said with a sense of determination that everything would be fine. Just as "amen" was uttered, lights began swirling through the windows. *They're here!* Erin rushed to open the door.

2

Flash

Three years earlier…

"Ah. Flash. Hold on a second." Three seconds passed and I was back to normal. Adam gave me a teasing "You're weird" look and Jordan seemed confused. "Umm, Dee, that's like your third brain freeze today."

We were standing in my front yard, enjoying the nice southern Utah April evening air. I didn't live in my native Southern California anymore. I was with new friends in a new area, living a life I hadn't planned. It was different and that can often be traumatizing to a teenager, but I didn't want to be the common drama-queen teen. I didn't want to regret changes. On notes that I wrote to my old friends and my new, I began to end them with, "Make it great!" At the time it was so simple, *make it great.*

I was currently living six hours from my hometown, attending a performing arts high school, serving as junior class president and Honor's Society treasurer, preparing for a state theater competition, hanging out with a whole new set of friends, and striving to graduate from high school a year early; all the while, enjoying every minute of it. Each day I was going to school at

6:15 a.m. and often didn't return until 9:30 p.m. due to theater or music rehearsals and a night class that I was taking. I had a full plate.

"Okay, boys, I need to go inside and get back to my homework. I think that's what my brain freeze was telling me. You two behave." As I walked inside, I thought about what Jordan had pointed out. *Third flash today.*

The flashes were another change to my life, but I sensed they were connected to the odd out-of-it spell I'd had two years earlier, when I was fourteen and concentrating on my algebra final. The flashes, growing in frequency, were now common for me. Each flash was quick and peculiar.

The day before had been busy like usual. I had rehearsed my scene for the state competition with my two new best friends, Katriné and Anna. After just two hours of practice I had already gone through four flashes. It was frustrating me and making me forget my lines. I felt that I needed to explain myself and, like best friends usually do, they sat and listened.

"I need a quick break, girls." The three of us sat back against the wall. "I tell you, I am out of it today!"

"Are you okay?" Katriné asked.

"Ohhh, I'm fine. I've mentioned my little déjà vu flash thingies to you before, right?" They both nodded their heads. "I've already had four in, like, the past two hours and they totally distract my thinking. It just throws me off." I ended with a sarcastic apology, "Sorry 'bout that!"

Anna took the moment to fill her curiosity. "So, what do you mean with déjà vu?" *Hmm, try and explain?!* I made a quick inner-debate on how much to share. "I guess I can't really think of a better word. It's kind of déjà vu because it's always the same thing and it feels like a 'been there, done that' sorta moment. Like, someone says two certain words and then it's like I know what they're gonna say next. I actually call the little blips 'flashes'

6

'cuz they're totally random, come really fast, and then are pretty quick. Weird, but I think it's just related to stress, 'cuz ladies, I'm busy!" Ending on that note, we laughed and got back to work.

Four yesterday and three today. By now I was tapping my pen on my English folder, not able to concentrate on Shakespeare's play, *Twelfth Night*. I was more wondering how my friends would react if I'd told them the details about my flashes. I closed my eyes and re-played the fresh memory:

Anna, Katriné, and I face each other in a circle while sharing character and scene tips. Katriné finishes her thoughts and I start to speak up when all of a sudden I phase out. My fingers and scalp begin to tingle and then suddenly my spirit jerks backwards with incredible force. The invisible power quickly surrounds my body, forcing all of my muscles to contract. I can't breathe!

Just as I reach a breaking point, my body is released from the turmoil and my fear melts away, releasing all weight and pressure off of my body. I become a cloud. My arms begin to slowly lift. Time stops. Every stress fades. I reach a state of peace and nirvana. The air that I am now freely breathing even seems lighter.

Then, as quickly as it started, it stops, and I re-join the conversation as if nothing happened. All the while, Katriné and Anna sensed nothing out of the ordinary.

I'd played it off as if there was a word on the tip of my tongue. It was obvious I had lost my train of thought and was smoothly trying to move the conversation along, calling it all a "blonde moment."

While chaos shook me on the inside more and more, I always was able to hide it from the outside. *No one is going to believe me.* I was sure the experiences weren't from my creative imagination, but kept it secret because listeners would probably say otherwise. I couldn't liken it to anything.

The next two months of school flew by. I was able to reach all of my goals, walk the bridge at graduation, and even received academic and artistic scholarships, all while keeping the haunting details of the growing flashes secret. As the grand hoorah of the graduation ceremony ended with a boom of fireworks, I didn't think about my dark side. I just happily grinned at my family in the audience: my mom, my dad, my four sisters, my three brothers, and every other in-law and niece and nephew who'd joined along the path. Since I was the youngest of the eight, it was my family's final high school graduation.

3

The Devil's Pull

The first semester of college swept by and I had enjoyed it, despite my lack of R&R. I was busy as usual, but the intensity of my flashes had been growing. By now, exhausted, I was forced into my prisoner stage—looking for answers, but feeling stuck and consumed. I tried to tell myself it was connected to my breathing, which was quickly strained by laughter or exercise. *I have trouble breathing during my flashes, but which comes first—the flash or the gasp?* I tried to ignore that it felt deeper, as if it were a physical weakness making my spirit vulnerable to haunts.

I fanned my bright red face with my hands as I walked from the dance studio. I wasn't acting as social as usual, but I needed outs—dance and exercise were the substitutes. I was trying to distract myself from the flashes, which were continuing to grow in effect and frequency.

I was determined to stay in action during dance, regardless of the breathing issues, and had pulled it off well enough during the last session. It felt good to have been able to keep up with the group, but I was wishing that my loud, strained breathing would loosen.

The dormitory main lobby was quiet when I entered. I took a refreshing drink from the water fountain in between one of my deep breaths and then headed up the stairs to my room.

Anxious to get back and clean up for dinner, I began to leap up the stairs, skipping two steps with each jump, still wheezing. Then, fear arose as a different sort of flash overtook me.

I took my third leap up the stairs and suddenly crashed down. Immediately my body seemed forced into fetal position. I couldn't move. The only way for my mind to explain to me what was taking place was to imagine the giant hand of the Devil himself pulling the insides of my body. I felt *possessed*. Everything I'd seen in movies or read in books that mentioned being possessed by ghosts came to my mind as I laid, stiff, on the stairs. I couldn't think of a different explanation. I was terrified.

The force physically made me continue to crumble into a tighter fetal position on the stairs and clench my eyes shut. It wasn't a physical pain that I was feeling; it was an unwilled pressure that was pulling my energy, my consciousness, and all of the organs inside of me down through the stairs toward the depths of hell.

While I laid there on the stairs with my body weighed down, it seemed as if the only thing holding me together from the Devil's forceful strain was my skin and bones. My entire body was being squeezed by the tingling fingers of this invisible hand. I could feel my oxygen being sucked away, and I had to fight harder for the air. My wheezing turned into rushing gasps.

Then, lights in the stairwell seemed to dim. My fears elevated to another level. I opened my eyes to witness the darkness only to see the room spinning around me. This felt different than the dizziness I would feel after a spinning fair ride. I felt stuck to one immovable spot as the walls began to spin around me. It was an intense vertigo.

Tears began to stream down my face. I couldn't tell if anything were taking place realistically, spiritually, or mentally.

Breathe! A moment later, my fear turned into a will to fight. I pulled my arms out from my fetal position and rolled from my side into crawling position.

Fight! Breathe! Move! These three words put me in motion as I crawled up the next five stairs, my nails digging into the carpet and the tears still spilling. With each move, the strain began to dissipate more and more. By the time I reached the top, the overpowering force that had just held me to the ground was gone. No traces were left other than the drying tears and tired body. *Gone.*

I sat there for the next few minutes pulling myself together before opening the stairwell door. *How do I explain what I just went through if anyone notices?* At the time, I didn't know anything about tonic seizures (muscle contracting seizures). I especially didn't know that *I*, a healthy person, could have been going through one. I took a deep breath, wiped my eyes and erased any signs of my dark side before I passed the door to a hallway full of girls—girls focused on school, boys, and enjoying college.

Or are they? Tossing them a few carefree laughs while I walked past, I wondered if they didn't have their own secrets they were covering.

That curiosity quickly flittered by, not letting me avoid thoughts about what I had survived the moment before. On the outside I had been able to erase any signs of my torment as quickly as they had started. On the inside it made me tremble.

The memory continued to play when I went to visit my brother Scott, whose house was up the street from the campus. The effects from that last flash had taken my normal energetic personality and will away—I was officially depressed, but I didn't want to be alone. Scott and his wife, Rachel, were both students as well and the time I spent with them had been growing.

I was about to tell them of my scare when a group of my friends came over and "kidnapped" me, insisting I join their campfire. I was so touched and tickled by their kidnap plan. The haunting memory was quickly forgotten and my liveliness returned. We spent the next few hours roasting marshmallows, burning old homework, and laughing at each other's jokes. I was genuinely enjoying myself.

As always, the fun had to end. The distraction began to fade as soon as we turned to walk toward campus. When the group separated, my mind was back to my issue. I had been wrapped in delight while there, but once again I reverted to my woe when I was alone.

I was usually one to organize get-togethers, but I had stepped back from that, extracting any of my friendship efforts; my flashes had been occurring more frequently. This brought on a case of gloominess, and my social involvement had been fading. The melancholy had been building whenever I had a moment to think about myself.

Kelsy, my trustworthy roommate, came up behind me after the group goodbyes. I could hear her humming a Broadway tune. She would start a line, and I would always finish it. I didn't tonight. She linked her arm with mine and started to pull me toward campus, but I insisted we visit Scott and Rachel before we returned to our dorm room. I was aching to talk about my stairs experience with the three who already knew about my flashes.

When we settled in with Scott and Rachel, I gave a mellowed description of the experience, even afraid to come across as crazy to them, but admitted that I had felt haunted and couldn't breathe.

The blank looks on their faces told me nothing while I spoke. That is probably what was going through their minds, actually: *Nothing.* They didn't have anything to liken my experience to.

When I finished my low key description of the flash, the four of us put our heads together. My difficulty breathing was the only problem that we knew might have a solution.

A week after the Devil scare, Rachel took me to a general family doctor down the street from the school. As the doctor did a basic check-up procedure, I mentioned my flashes, focusing mainly on the fact that I would get dizzy and feel pressure while trying to breathe. The doctor diagnosed my problem as exercise-induced asthma, and I walked away with a new inhaler. Asthma seemed likely enough. My dad and brother both had minor asthma. *What did I know?*

I put the inhaler to use during some of my exercises and it helped a little—only while I exercised. *Two different issues.* I knew the real problem still wasn't solved. I continued to have the flashes and the quiet pressure seemed to continue growing. I went on living my days as I should, enjoying moments here and there. Meanwhile, my dark side hovered over me, silently awaiting the next attack.

4

In Writing

"Perfect harmony, everyone. Now let's move on to the next few measures. Sopranos, we'll start with you." Our choir director, turning to face our small group, lifted his baton as the sopranos tightened their posture. Following his lead, the singing began. I listened from the alto section.

It was already 9:30 at night, and by the look of things we wouldn't be getting out of there anytime soon. In two days, we were to perform an Easter medley at the President's Cathedral in Washington D.C. We had a lot of work to do to get ready for such an important performance.

"All right ladies, that—"Our director's mouth continued to move, but suddenly something changed. It was another flash! They were continuously becoming even stronger, more grandiose.

I looked around the room at my classmates, but all eyes were on our director. No one had noticed what'd just happened. I began my repeated analysis. *What is going on?* As soon as I'd heard him say two certain words the chaos had erupted— the flashes had always seemed connected to a sentence that started with these particular words. The thing always was, however, that by the time my twisted senses would return from their la-la land, I could never remember what the words were. This time, however, I happened to be prepared. While the flash was progressing I had looked down and noticed the pencil and paper in my hand. *I can finally write down the words!*

Part of me, the side present in reality, had bubbled with excitement and curiosity. I felt as if I were solving a cold case crime or discovering the cure to cancer. The words came to my mind and were verbalized from the choir director's mouth. It was the same sentence that I had heard every single time over the past two years, only this time my brain could understand it enough to record it. To say I was excited is an understatement.

The singer next to me was Rachel, my sister-in-law. I quickly nudged her with my elbow. With a big smile on my face, I pointed to the words, which I had boldly printed on the piece of sheet music. She studied the sentence, but I noticed a look of confusion wrinkled on her face.

"Flash," I whispered, hoping that she would understand the importance of the words. When it still didn't register, I leaned toward her. "I just had a flash. This is the first time I've ever been able to write down what I've been hearing." *At least, I thought I was saying that.* Just as I was finishing the sentence, I looked down at the words to study them for myself.

What the…?!?

The entire phrase appeared grammatically correct, from the capitalization at the beginning to the punctuation at the end. But that was where the logic ended. The sentence was gibberish: Ynol sroic are i8cjs, iv shb2le het.

Before we could analyze it further, it was our turn to sing. We exchanged a look of surprise as we found the right measure and joined in. Needless to say, the shock of the whole event stayed with me the rest of the night. What I had expected to be a mammoth discovery ended up adding another dose of mystery to my life.

The next morning I stopped by to visit Scott and Rachel. I wanted to see if Rachel had any more thoughts about the incident.

"Deanna, I don't understand it and have no idea what it means, but I believe you." She was obviously flabbergasted and didn't know what to say. Despite the concern she felt, she couldn't think of anything specific she could do to help me. Clearly this was more than just a case of exercise-induced asthma. I'd known all along the inhaler wouldn't solve the issue that was now constantly riding me, dragging me down.

I got the typical response—"Whoa" and the concerned "That's really weird, Dee"—from Scott as I showed him the page and explained the experience. I still held back on flash intensity. What else can someone say when they're shown a bunch of gibberish that a sister swears she could understand while writing it down? That's where I left it for the evening. We didn't know what questions to ask or even whom to ask. What I was going through didn't feel medical. *It's always just a quick moment anyway and everything else is normal, right?*

5

You Need Help

That evening, Kelsy really began to worry when I showed her the sentence. Since she was my roommate, I couldn't hide the turmoil from her like I could my family or other friends. She always thought it was crazy that such big spells could take place with no one noticing. This one had taken place when she was a few seats away from me in the choir.

I had repeatedly confided in her about the recurring phenomenon and the way it tormented me. Her mind wouldn't rest until it had explored every possibility of what was causing these strange, dark moments.

"Deanna, something is taking control of your mind and it is torturing you, physically and emotionally." She had begun to get nervous seeing how I was getting more and more physically and emotionally drained.

Her statement made it official. I couldn't hide it from her, and she wasn't going to let me. It was beginning to affect too many things.

"Really, you should ask questions and maybe find something out. Maybe you are being haunted by something, or maybe it's something completely different. Regardless, it's something you need to find answers to." She was sitting up straight, telling me with as much authoritative tone as possible.

She was right. There were so many maybes in my situation, and that was beginning to scare me. I had already been to see that general doctor and his opinion hadn't helped. His diagnosis of asthma surely wasn't the cause of my issue as he had thought.

After the stairwell flash, I had also gone to visit with my religion class professor, who had just become my bishop—the local church leader for our denomination, *The Church of Jesus Christ of Latter-day Saints* (also known as 'Mormon' church or 'LDS'). He helped in our a cappella singing group, as well. He knew the everyday me, and I felt confident enough that he didn't see me as a freak. I had gone to him and described the flashes and the feelings. *Is it spiritual? Am I possessed? Whatever it is, it's freaky.*

I could tell he was baffled and at a loss for words as I'd described the torment. It was clear that he was new to his position; worried he might say the wrong thing. Part of me was embarrassed, but I mostly felt for him and how awkward he must have been feeling. I couldn't help laughing when I told Kelsy about his response, "Well, be sure to pray, read the scriptures, and oh, keep the commandments. Then you'll be fine." He'd paused and deeply pondered after each point.

Leaving a moment later, I shook his hand and gave a kind smile. *Poor guy. I sure threw him for a loop. Too bad I've already been doing everything he recommended.* I wasn't angry or put off that he didn't have a miracle explanation. I actually felt slight satisfaction because he was as confused by it as I was. I was at a point where I felt there was no solution to my problem, even though I was still looking for answers.

After that meeting I decided I could do each of the three a little bit better, which helped me feel more comfort. It didn't erase the flashes, but with the spiritual comfort, I was able to deal with them a bit better as I continued to search for answers.

Kelsy was the only one I had told about my visit to the bishop, and she took the visit as proof that I was desperate for answers. "Dee, what if you see someone about deeper things? I bet you could meet with Dr. Klein, the psychology professor. He's a licensed psychologist and might have some idea of what you can do to get rid of the flashes." She was excited that this could be a solution and that she may have helped.

The thought of seeing a psychologist made me a little uneasy. It had been a big deal for me to go to my church bishop, but I had known him well. Dr. Klein didn't know me. I couldn't stop myself from self-translating the doctor's Latin or Greek title to mean something like: "one who studies psychos." *If I meet with Dr. Klein, then I'm admitting that I'm crazy!*

After a little more discussion with Kelsy, I was able to recognize and even pique my curiosity that a psychologist is one who studies the mind and the reasons for the ways that people think and act. *Going to a psychologist doesn't mean I'm a lunatic. It just shows that I am trying to figure myself out—self-mastery. There are coaches for sports. A psychologist is really a coach for life. Right?*

6

Willing to Try

Kelsy's urge to ask questions came to my mind as I passed the psychology professor's office two weeks later and saw him sitting at his desk. I'd finally come to terms with the idea of meeting with a psychologist.

Won't hurt to inquire, right? Eight minutes until writing class starts. I stopped at the professor's door and slowly leaned in with a questioning smile, giving a quiet courtesy knock on his door.

Just setting down his phone, Dr. Klein looked over the frames of his reading glasses and welcomed me in. His forehead was scrunched from his raised eyebrows as he looked over the glasses resting on his nose. When he saw me, a gentle smile eased the wrinkles.

"Come in." He didn't personally know me, but the school was small enough that all professors had connection with the students simply because we were there.

"I've been dealing with some things, and I'm curious about your thoughts on all of it."

He leaned back in his chair and rested his chin on his index fingers, the other fingers crossed, just as I would imagine a psychologist would do. "Go ahead."

I spent the next five minutes quickly babbling about my flashes. Again, I put the information lightly, not admitting that it was enveloping my emotions and concentrations, driving me crazy. I told him how baffled I was about the writing experience I'd just had. I laid it all out in a very lighthearted manner. I gave my description with a sense of, "Aww, it's no big deal."

When I finished, he stayed quiet for a moment. He'd been studying my face and I could see that different possibilities were running through his mind. *What do I want him to say?* As soon as I had finished laying it all out I realized that I hadn't thought about the rest of the conversation. Awkwardness swallowed me. "Oh, I have to hurry off to class," I took an obvious look at my watch and stood up, putting my backpack on my shoulders. "Did anything pop out in your mind about all of this?"

Sitting back up, he moved his hands, folding them on his desk. "Well, first off, don't get down on yourself about it. It's something to figure out, but it doesn't say anything about who you are." *He must have read my awkwardness.* The professor continued as I took slow backward steps to his door, "I'm not yet sure what all of that is or what to tie it to, but I suggest that you journal your thoughts and feelings about it. That should help relieve some of your stress and maybe even bring out a few answers."

I'm glad you don't consider me whacked out or possessed, but this doesn't give me any answers, sir.

He finished with a cordial, "If you'd like, you can bring your journal over in a week and run some of your written thoughts by me."

That's a professor for ya. Just give me some homework and shuffle me along. I want an explanation, not another assignment.

As I hurried to class I shrugged my shoulders and mentally crossed out his assignment. *I just told you what I'm going through. So much for that.* With only two weeks of school left, I knew that I wouldn't be getting answers from him. He apparently needed time to study me out, but that wasn't available. *Oh well, at least he confirmed that I'm not a psycho.*

I spent the next two weeks of school avoiding the professor and the possible "homework" check-ups, which I figured would be useless. At the end of my freshman year in 2001, I was at a point of simply accepting that I was living a mystery and it needed to be kept quiet.

7

Change in Plans

I was leaning over the drinking fountain outside the classroom door when I saw David Brady. I was a new student at a different university for the summer and he was a member of my new study group—the member I had been interested in. Another year and a half had passed, and my issue was still trailing me—nothing had buried it. By now, however, I'd actually accepted it; I called it a quirk and a sign of needed rest.

I finished my sip and was quickly wiping my mouth just as he was passing me.

"Oh, hey. I didn't think you made it to class today!" David was surprised to see me. There also seemed to be a hint of satisfaction.

I had quietly slipped in and sat on the back row that day. Every other time we had sat next to each other in the front of the class room—the first two weeks by professor's requirement, the next two weeks by choice. I had wondered if *I* had anything to do with David's choice to continuously return to that seat. He had certainly caught my attention.

"Yeah. Late today." I chose not to explain that I had been on the phone with my counselor in Virginia, setting up my fall class schedule. All of that, by now, had actually moved to the back of my mind. What I was most curious about was what David planned to say next. *I've got a guess.*

"So, at our midterm study thing last week, you mentioned that you played tennis in high school. You up for a tennis match? You vs. me?"

He was asking me on a date! I guessed right. "Well, if you think you can handle my speed of light serves, I'm all in! Bring it on!"

He laughed, knowing I was being sarcastic about my skills.

Five months later, this memory and every other "David" memory was tickling my mind as we took an evening walk together, hand in hand, his fingers brushing against my engagement ring. It still felt new having only been wearing it for two months. We had quickly fallen in love.

My lips spread into a smile, tweaked up in the left corner, when I thought about the day we met. I had entered the classroom with no intentions of dating during that summer semester at college. When everything had gone so well after just a month of dating, however, I'd had to make a big choice. *Should I stay, or should I go?* I cancelled my Virginia plans and chose to stick around and try out our relationship. We had spent nearly every waking hour together since that first date and eventually decided that we never wanted it to end. The smiles on our faces and the ring on my finger were proof.

During all of this, flashes had moved to the back of my mind and had happened only twice when with David. I'd played off the first one, but then decided to explain the details when the second one happened.

David's reaction surprised me. I had expected him to find it spooky and unsettling, but his first reply was, "Okay. Just let me know if you need me to do anything for you." He tightened his arms around me and gave me a kiss on my forehead.

You aren't going to question my sanity? You don't worry that I'm messed up? Maybe he wasn't listening!

He had been listening—granted, part of his statement had been out of ignorance, but the larger part was out of sincere devotion. *We are engaged and getting married in eighty-six days!*

8

Survival Mode

Adrenaline from fear pumped through my body. Feeling the run of panic quickly rising, my eyes fluttered open to see a group of unfamiliar people surrounding me, reaching to grab me. *I am being raped!*

The men, getting ready to pull away the blanket covering me, were surprised when all of a sudden my face and arms jumped into alertness. I forcefully grabbed the blanket with my left hand and with my right hand I began swinging at them. They had no idea the sort of terror that was racing through my foggy mind.

When I panicked, over-powered by those surrounding me, I'd gone into survival mode. I didn't give the scene a second to explain itself and was instantly ready to fight. My wedding, family, and location were all gone from my thoughts.

I knew that my biggest fear was about to take place. It was the only explanation my thoughts gave me.

I knew that I was about to become a victim.

Fight! If they take this sheet away from me that is all the closer they are to my body. Hold tight, Deanna. I wasn't tempted to scream; I didn't want them to feel in control. Instead, I tried to think of a way to scare them. I continued swinging at them, delaying their actions while I tried to make a plan. I scanned my surroundings, trying to sum up their abilities and find anything I could use in my favor.

I suddenly felt dizzy. My determination turned into confusion when I saw Erin standing to the side, letting this assault happen to me. She looked scared. *Why isn't she helping me?*

I quickly blinked my eyes, trying to refocus and noticed that Erin was trying to explain something. I saw the stress in her eyes as she said the word "hospital." My thoughts turned to another issue. *She isn't scared of these people surrounding me.* I recognized the word "hospital" and instantly associated that word with my dad's recurrent trips to the hospital over the past nine years. His health was constantly getting worse.

Oh. It's my turn to ride with dad to the hospital. Okay. I calmed down. *I'll take care of him. Just tell me what to do.* I hadn't noticed that I couldn't articulate words or understand what was being said to me. I'd also completely forgotten that my parents were staying in a nearby hotel, awaiting my wedding.

Eventually realizing that my "attackers" were paramedics, I let go of the blanket and allowed them to lift me onto the gurney. I sensed that my inner explanation didn't fit the situation while rolling toward the ambulance, but I told myself, *Don't ask; just do.* After they shut the ambulance doors, I could see Brian, another brother-in-law who'd joined the frenzy, through the doors' tiny windows. He made a little smile of encouragement and gave me a thumbs-up. I hadn't completely understood people's words, but I understood the sign as meaning something good. It helped settle me as I "accompanied" my dad.

For the next fifteen minutes in the ambulance, I could feel my head relaxing. The siren had been turned on and I saw rotating lights flashing against the hills and buildings as we passed. My brain seemed to be thawing out, and as we sped along I began to recognize the town where I'd grown up. I could now tell that I was out-of-it and knew I didn't understand what was going on. It wasn't until the paramedic was sticking the last monitor sticker on my chest that I realized it was *me* they were caring for.

Embarrassment wrapped me. I instantly tried to play it off as if I were just catching a ride on a bus; a bus with loud sirens and people in uniforms. I saw the IV in my arm, not remembering when they had pricked me, and watched the paramedic snap wires to the stickers on my chest. As he reached under my shirt, I tried to ignore my usual comfort bubble.

I knew I wouldn't be able to completely understand the problem yet, so I didn't ask. I decided to keep attention away from me and began to ramble out questions to the nearest paramedic, "Have you guys been busy tonight? Do you like your job? What made you choose this? How long have you been in this field? Do you mind working nights? Are people usually nice to you?" I got tired even asking the questions. Noticing that I couldn't hold much of the paramedic's information, I chose to just look out the window for the remainder of the drive. I stopped trying to use my brain. *Why am I so tired?* I didn't connect any of this ordeal to my past flashes.

The paramedics rolled me into the emergency room, handing me over to a new group of nurses in hospital gear. I fell asleep on the way to the CT scan and didn't wake again until I was encircled by my immediate family.

Most had a look of surprise and concern on their faces. Erin had updated each one, and they were now bouncing their different ideas of a possible cause for the seizure. Hearing them talk about the issue was the first time I'd understood the word "seizure" as my problem. I was listening curiously, analyzing. All realized that they had very little familiarity with anything related to seizures.

They seemed to be ready for any sort of light-hearted conversation, and I felt all were waiting on me. Each wondered what I needed.

My mom sat at the end of the bed and rubbed my feet. It is a trademark she has when anything is awry. It may not always be the solution, but it helps anyway.

"Deanna, your feet are freezing!" She used her hands, rubbing quick friction along my feet to get some blood flow.

There it is. Let the humor begin. I jumped at the chance for humor. "That's it! The cause of my seizure! I'm getting cold feet!"

Welcomed chuckles were shared and the light-hearted humor began. Everyone began to feel more comfortable, wanting to believe the problem had successfully passed.

9

A Fluke

The ER doctor was surprised when he moved the sheet of dividers and entered the scene. My dad jumped into "father of the family" mode and reached out to the doctor to shake his hand.

My dad's health chaos had brought him to the ER enough times that most were familiar with him. His welcoming personality tended to be one that all remembered.

"Let me introduce you to some of my family that was able to make it here. You recognize my wife, Janet. Then these are three of my daughters: Shawna, Erin, and Deanna. And these are two of my boys, Jim and Jason. Two of my other chilluns, Scott and Nonnie, are on duty over grandkids and the last one, Heather, will soon be arriving for this girl's wedding, which is tomorrow." He pointed to me as he finished. The doctor shook the hand of each family member with a little smile and nod of his head.

"Wow. Eight children." The doctor looked impressed.

"Also, thank you for letting us all come and give Deanna support." He gave the doctor a wink, glad the doctor and nurses hadn't enforced the rule of one visitor at a time. My dad had been able to convince them that it was in their best interests to let all six family members be with me. He carried on, "So, what do you have to tell us?"

The doctor opened his folder and made a quick scan to double check the information he was about to share. He looked up, closed the folder and explained, "Well, Deanna, you had a grand-mal seizure. You mentioned the wedding tomorrow. Wow and congratulations! That can legitimately cause a rise in your stress level. Rises in any kind of stress, positive in this case, can lead to a random seizure. We've seen it before. The CT scan showed no reasons for concern. Nothing appeared irregular. You might call it a fluke occurrence. As it seems that this is her first seizure, it doesn't mean anything more than a random occurrence that can and does happen to people every day."

"Well, doctor, what should we do? When can she check out?" My dad put his hand on my hospital blanket-covered knee and gave a loving shake.

"She'll be out in the next hour." The doctor looked at his watch and saw that it was 4:37 a.m. "Just make sure she gets plenty of rest, food and water over the next few days. A relaxing honeymoon is probably exactly what she'll need. It also wouldn't hurt to get an MRI after everything settles." He turned to me, "Other than that, congratulations again and enjoy the celebration."

Then the doctor shook hands again, chatted with my dad about his family for the next few minutes, and walked out of the little sheet-lined area as we waited through the hour-long checkout process.

Shawna turned to me. "You should probably call David and let him know that you are in the hospital."

While this chaos was shaking my family, my fiancé David was still sleeping soundly in Las Vegas at his parent's house.

"Is it too early to call?" My thoughts answered the question as fast as it came out. "Can I use your phone?"

She handed me the cell phone and I pushed the keys. Enough memory was back to let me dial David's cell phone number without a delay.

10

Cold Feet

The rock beat sound of David's cell phone ring quickly woke him. He looked at the blurry, glowing numbers on his clock. *4:40 am*. I heard him clearing his throat as he answered the phone. I could tell he was too tired to react to the meaning of getting a call so early in the morning and had quickly grabbed the phone. His voice cracked, "Hel-lo?"

"Hi, honey. Sorry, it's so early, but I thought I should call you and tell you that I'm ..." I had to slow down. An awkward lump filled my throat, "I'm in the hospital." I wasn't prepared for the flood of emotion. I'd successfully held it back since realizing it was me with the problem in the ambulance.

I visualized David trying to focus his sleepy eyes as if that would help explain what I, his fiancé, had just said to him. "Are you okay?" He didn't know what else to say or ask and I knew he was making the occasional nervous run of his long fingers through his light blond hair—a quirk of his.

The lump hadn't left my throat, and it was beginning to push every form of liquid up to my eyes and nose. "Yeah ..." I made a quick, choppy breath in, "Yeah, I'm okay."

I blinked my blue eyes, determined to not let the tears fall and show any sort of weakness. I couldn't hold back the runny nose though. I glanced up at Shawna as she was quickly brushing at her own reddening nose. I noticed the ridge of water lining her eyelashes, about to flood over. That tipped me all the more.

"Here's Shawna." I knew that if I said another word, I wouldn't be able to hold back the tears. I quickly handed the phone to my sister.

Shawna didn't hesitate when coming to the rescue and jumped into action, "Hey!"

In that short instant of her taking the phone, she had debated whether to let him know how shocked and unsettled they were or to be calm and simply informative. This girl that he loved and wanted to have by his side had brushed shoulders with death, but he also was miles away at his parents' home in Las Vegas and couldn't do a thing to help. Shawna chose to focus on the current fact that I was getting back to my normal self and everything seemed okay, regardless of the quick shock.

David quietly listened, still trying to explain to himself that it was real. When the details were finished, Shawna was adamant that everything was fine and that there was nothing he needed to do. All he could say was, "Okay."

Shawna repeated my light-hearted joke about having "cold feet." The comment brought a calmed laugh from David.

The conversation soon ended after Shawna handed the phone back to me. I insisted that David go back to sleep and drive down in the morning like we had initially planned. "I'll be checking out any minute and will just go back to Erin's to sleep anyway." We shared our loves and "see you in twelve hours" regards.

David waited for me to end the call and set his phone down. *Go back to sleep? Who am I kidding?* He knew he couldn't close his eyes and turn off his thoughts for the rest of the night. He had to get it out.

After five minutes of sitting there on the edge of his bed, staring at the cell phone, he walked to his father and step-mother's room and quietly knocked on their door. He figured they would be willing to listen. As soon as they invited him, he gave them the little information he had.

Getting it all out helped to calm David. He'd frequently reminded himself that the doctor said it was just stress. *Our honeymoon cruise will be the perfect antidote.* He smiled that he'd been able to keep everything related to the honeymoon a secret.

He explained to me months later that while lying back down that night, he tried to convince himself that the seizure had been a fluke stress reaction and that everything was fine. He hadn't been able to settle, however, until he mentally noted that it may be the beginning of continued seizures and that he was ready to support me through thick and thin.

11

I, Deanna McKeon

I was checked out of the hospital soon after the phone call ended. Through the next day, I was forced by my family to follow the doctor's orders of rest. I felt burdensome, but was grateful and accepted the help of those offering. My sisters jumped into bridesmaids' action and finished the remaining wedding preparation details.

The next day, the wedding day, was beautiful and showed no signs of the seizure chaos. *I, Deanna McKeon, take David Brady* ... I spent every possible moment looking at my new husband, and the seizure scare didn't even cross my mind. Neither did my mysterious flashes.

Instead, I thought of our art history class at Brigham Young University when I saw him for the first time and boldly chose the seat next to him and when he proposed to me as he handed me a rose with the diamond ring. We had become inseparable after our first date.

That sincere devotion I'd noticed when I first told him about my flashes is what I saw when he bent to kiss me as I was called his wife for the first time. Seizures were now on my list of issues, and he was still strong.

The surprise seven-day cruise along the western coast of Mexico was the perfect prescription; just as the doctor ordered.

The only time the hospital experience was even mentioned was when we sat across from each other at our assigned dinner table on New Year's Eve, reflecting on the past year.

I shook my head. "Talk about a random twist to our year!"

David lifted his glass of sparkling cider and tapped the glass in my hand. "Here's to survival!"

We took a sip of cheer and then leaned across the table for another sweet kiss. Neither of us had any idea what survival would entail for us over the next six years. The two of us were a young naïve couple that would be forced to grow up fast.

12

First Appointment

Getting settled in my new life was all that I wanted to think about after we moved into our new apartment in Las Vegas, Nevada. My family, however, wouldn't let the seizure drama rest. The question, "Deanna, have you gone to a neurologist yet?" replaced the usual "hello" at the beginning of a conversation. After two months of persistence, I made a call.

With a referral from a family general practitioner, I made an appointment with Dr. Simon, a neurologist. I remember David and me walking into Dr. Simon's quaint office. As we entered, I looked to my left and noticed a variety of vending machines, lined under the TV, seeming to lead to the EEG and MRI testing area. At the time I didn't know what those letters meant, nor did I have any idea how familiar they would soon become.

The laughs of the receptionists brought my attention to the other side of the room. A clipboard full of papers for me to fill out was ready and gave me something to do over the next thirty minutes in the office.

A nurse called me in, measured my statistics, and then led us to a different room. She left to inform the doctor, leaving the door open. As I sat on the padded exam table, the lining tissue paper made loud crunching sounds no matter how delicately I tried to move.

While we waited, I looked through the doorway at the pictures decorating the wall. One picture was of Dr. Simon and his family. I tried to sum him up, studying the picture. His expression seemed mellow, making me hope he was an easy enough doctor to work with.

I gave a shrug of approval as the doctor entered the room. He looked no different from the picture, as if he had walked straight from the frame and witnessed my shrug. It felt like I had gotten caught. I felt goofy, and started to swing my legs back and forth, as if I were a four-year-old hoping to get a lollipop after the appointment. I realized that I had no idea what to say to this neurologist or where to even start.

Dr. Simon made a quick introduction and then began what I would later realize was a normal routine. "Remember these three words: chair, tiger, yellow. Touch your nose with your right hand, now your left hand. Watch my fingers. How many fingers am I holding up? Walk along this line." After opening a safety pin, he pricked different areas of my body, asking if I felt each one. I did. As he finished, he asked me to repeat the first three words.

He seemed to notice my discomfort and began to explain the little, seemingly pointless, tests he was quickly taking and then, while leaning back, he asked simply, "So, what happened?"

David and I explained the seizure details while he simply nodded his head and watched us. As he ran his fingers along his graying goatee and mustache he replied, "Well, I'll look through the hospital's CT scan, but we need to do some basic neurology tests: an MRI and an EEG." He went on to explain the two tests and what they would look for.

I imagined my brain modeling for a photo shoot, layer by layer, as he described an MRI. *Closest I'll ever get to modeling.*

As he moved on to explaining the EEG I visualized my head as earth, the seizures as earthquakes, and the EEG as the seismograph. I wondered where my epicenter was.

His next point was a shot between the eyes, a point I hadn't been prepared for, "It is Nevada law that a driver loses their license after a seizure, and must be seizure free for three months before getting it back. For the next five years, you will have to annually renew your license with a signed document of doctor approval." *What?!* I sent a mental curse to my family for their firmness on me seeing the doctor about my random seizure. I got sick to my stomach.

David and I stayed silent and gave a slight bob of our heads while the doctor carried on. I had no doubt that David's thoughts were driving down the same lane as mine.

The appointment ended after just ten minutes of discussion. I didn't mind the short time because I was more than ready to get out of the bad news zone.

13

Déjà vu

As we stood up to leave the doctor's office, a thought of curiosity randomly popped up and my "no license" issue was put on the back burner for a bit. "Actually," I asked, "I'm curious if you are familiar with something I've been going through the past few years. Probably not connected, but thought I'd throw it out there."

He sat back down on his rolling stool and gave me a look that told me to carry on. I decided to give a light report of the haunting feelings and illusions I'd been going through for the previous five years. "Well, it's kind of an odd sensation. I call it a flash. For instance, someone will be talking to me and as soon as they use a certain sentence—which I can never remember afterwards—I seem to go into this sense of …"

The doctor finished my sentence with the exact word that I was about to say, "Déjà vu."

My jaw dropped and I lifted my eyebrows, "Yeah."

"Anything else?" the doctor asked.

"Well, yes." As I explained the details I watched his face, hoping he didn't consider me a psycho. "What is the weirdest is that it seems to be getting longer and more wearing each year."

When I finished, I was surprised by his look. I expected him to scrunch his eyebrows and casually scoot away from this odd new patient of his.

Instead, Dr. Simon shrugged his shoulders and gave a simple, "Yeah. Those are seizures." He seemed to say it with an almost "well, duh!" tone and no surprise.

The look of surprise was, instead, on *my* face. *You mean you know what I'm talking about?! This hasn't been happening because I am possessed by some evil power? There is some legitimate explanation to all of this chaos!?*

He went on explaining déjà vu, and my mind drifted back to the stairwell experience. While standing there in my neurologist's office, the ton of bricks that had been weighing on my shoulders from these flashes over the previous five years seemed to be lifted up. I finished the memory and wanted to call Scott, Kelsy, and all who had witnessed any of my flashes to inform them that they were seizures and that I wasn't whacked out. My mind became a crowded pinball machine as thoughts, questions, and new answers bounced speedily through my mind, touching issues of the past five years. I was embarrassed I'd been so traumatized, but glad it all meant something. *And it all started during that Algebra test* (mentioned in Introduction, in case you skipped ahead.)

The doctor stood up and led us to the checkout desk. We made appointments for the beginning of the many tests to follow, and I got a pit in my stomach as I saw the doctor's assistant faxing my seizure information to the Department of Motor Vehicles. She saw me and with a sympathetic tone said, "They'll send you process details once they get this, but this information is unfortunately effective as soon as they receive it." *Ouch.* We left with the bill and next appointment information in my purse.

As soon as David started the engine his "get to the bottom of it" personality spoke, "All right. We'll just work it out." He would be driving me to and from work each day for a long time.

David had noticed the change in my demeanor when the doctor said my flashes were seizures and decided to not gripe about the hassle. I could tell he was being tactful about my license loss. Our conversation for the rest of the thirty-minute ride home barely touched on the doctor appointment. Both of us had to process the information on our own before we could discuss it. We mentally put it on the to-do list for our nightly pillow talk.

14

The Verdict

It had been fifteen months since the doctor visits started. Lately each visit to the neurologist was beginning to seem pointless. The only thing I was getting from them was a bill. My seizures were recurring rapidly. I was having repeated grand-mal seizures at least once every three months while sleeping, and my flashes were frequent. Both David and I had faced the fact: I had a seizure disorder. My situation could be considered minor by many who suffer from seizures, but it was a big deal to me.

I didn't know what to think or do. I liked the doctor's personality, each member of his crew was nice and attentive, and he appeared to be willing to give us every minute we needed. *What else could a patient hope for?* Now, it almost seemed like we were in a dating process with the doctor: good at first, but after a while of no progress the shine was wearing off.

I was on visit number thirteen and had the appointment procedure memorized. The conversation tended to follow a certain script.

Doctor: "How are you doing?"

Me: "Seizure."

Doctor: "Well, let's try another dosage of the medication."

At this point, however, I was getting nervous about responding to his first question. I had already reached what the doctor said was the limit for my current medication and was nervous to try others. David and I both were beginning to think more about adding to our family, and Lamictal was currently the pill with the fewest side effects on a baby during pregnancy.

I began to quiet down about my seizures. I tried to focus on anything and everything else, ignoring my problem. Meeting with other neurologists or looking down different health avenues hadn't crossed my mind. I was planning to keep quiet and deal with the reoccurring seizures. *It's just a disorder you deal with.*

Perhaps I stuck around with the same doctor because I didn't know any better and the first three visits with Dr. Simon had turned out to be more enlightening than I could have expected. The first appointment had informed me that the flashes were what he called petit-mal seizures and that I wasn't alone in the world. *Hallelujah!* (I later found out they weren't petit-mal seizures.)

The second appointment had involved my first MRI and EEG. Both were fascinating to experience. Lying, covered with a blanket, in the plastic tunnel during the MRI photo shoot, I felt like I was resting in a loud cocoon. Each picture included a noisy hum and knocking sound as its camera zoomed deeper into my brain.

Then, during the EEG, I almost felt nervous when they turned on the monitor and the needles began to shift up and down in waves as the paper rolled under the ink. It was as if I were taking a lie detector test sitting with a large light pointed at my face (which I soon found out was a strobe light),

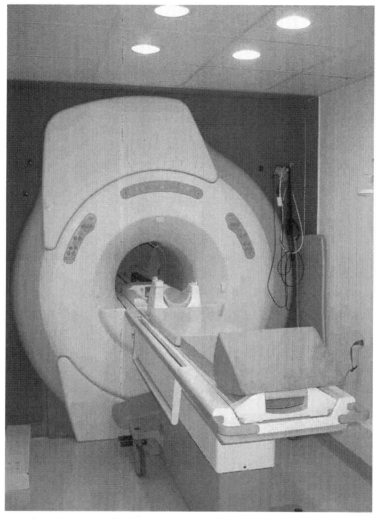

monitors strapped to my arms, and sixteen wires *sufficiently* glued to my head. I noticed that two of the needles were making lines that were greater and closer together than the rest. I could tell it wasn't normal as they marked areas of concern.

On the third appointment, the doctor casually walked into the room holding his Deanna Brady folder. How he plopped it onto the table seemed to make a "case closed" statement.

"Well?" David asked. He'd been by my side during each visit.

"Well, I sent the tests to a group of Nevada's top radiologists." Pointing to my forehead above my left eye he said, "You have a brain scar right here. It's dead tissue that disrupts brain waves and throws you into your seizures."

"A brain scar?" I was shocked; although, anything would have shocked me. I hadn't let the thought of reasons go through my mind; I didn't know there could be specific explanations.

I was ready to say, "Okay," and walk out the door, so I was glad that David was there as his questions began to roll from his tongue. "What do we do now? Can we get rid of it?"

The doctor leaned back in his chair. He was ready for an interview. "What's nice about it being a scar is that it doesn't change. We find the medication you need and stick to that. It keeps pretty quiet once the prescription level is figured out. For your second question, there really isn't anything that will get rid of it."

David battled the second answer. "You mean there isn't even any sort of brain surgery or something that could take care of her seizures?"

My stomach churned when David said "brain surgery." *Where'd that thought come from?! Creepy.*

The doctor made a laughing *humph* sound and replied, "She'd only be a candidate for brain surgery if there were something to remove, such as a tumor. Luckily, that isn't our issue. Taking away a scar will merely create a different scar."

David wasn't completely settled by that response, but let it stay at that. He told himself, *I'd say this neurologist knows more about what's available than I do. He's probably right.* He moved onto his next question. "Is there any future harm that's possible?"

"Not after we get the medication needs figured out for Deanna. We'll do the same testing procedures every three months over the next year and then once a year after that, of course, just to monitor the brain. It's routine."

I was still stuck on the brain scar fact. "I haven't ever had a head injury that sent me to a hospital. What could have caused this scar?"

"Any simple tumble or head bump could have caused it at any age. That spot is actually a common area for scarring. You may have fallen just right."

Just right?

The doctor lifted his right hand and slightly bent it in a crescent shape; I could tell immediately that his hand had just become the model of my forehead. With his left index finger he pointed to the model and explained, "Here is a forehead and right here are two small protruding bones. When the head is turned or bent to a certain degree and stopped with force from an accident or in some cases abuse, the brain can be pressed against one of these bones. The impact can cause an incision on the brain that then becomes a scar."

Wow, talk about bad luck. I could think of a number of trips and falls that I'd made as a child, but I could also think of others whose falls were much worse.

Following the doctor's explanation during visit number three I had left his office with a bittersweet taste in my thoughts. It was good to know the cause for the past five years of chaos and that it was a scar, not a tumor. A tumor hadn't been an issue as far as I was concerned until he mentioned it. So, in that respect, I agreed that I was lucky. The bitter part was that nothing could be done and I would be taking brain pills at least two times a day for the rest of my life. Growing up, my mom almost had to pin me down in order to get me to swallow vitamins. This was *twice* a day. That was a big deal at the time and took me a while to get used to.

Later, at the eleventh appointment I had gotten what I'd hoped for. After a year of being asleep during my grand-mal seizures, the doctor finally gave the okay for me to get my driver's license back.

Finally, thirteen appointments and three MRIs later, there wasn't anything more to do, as far as I understood. I decided to keep my mouth shut about my reoccurring flashes and grand-mal seizures. It had all been going nowhere. I scheduled my next appointment for a year later, when the routine testing, driver's license permission, and prescription refill would be given.

What I didn't know until four years later, when I got the doctor's records in my hands, was that the radiologists had pointed out a small change in the area of concern (the "scar") and that more testing should be done. There are two phases during an MRI: 1) without a contrast injection and 2) with contrast injection. No problems were visible during phase one, but the radiologists noticed something of possible concern during phase two. No extra testing was done by my neurologist.

15

I Love You

David turned on the washing machine and went back to the room to check on me. He had already cleaned me and changed me into a new set of underwear and pajama bottoms. Now I was lying on his side of the bed, still disoriented.

I had just gone through another seizure. We'd lost count of grand-mal seizures by now; 2004 was wrapping up and it had been nearly two years since the chaos started. This one, however, had been different than usual. I wet the bed.

A number of thoughts could go through one's mind after their wife pees in the bed while lying right next to you. Perhaps a thought of shock. *Mercy! You'd think I was tending to a rest home patient.* Or maybe disgust. *You've got to be kidding me. I can't believe my refined young wife just peed in the bed.* The thought could be sympathetic. *Oh, my poor wife. I want to make sure she doesn't get embarrassed. This is nothing she would have ever guessed she'd do.*

None of these thoughts went through David's mind as he tended to me.

I better change the sheets. That is the thought that sat in David's mind as soon as he saw that the seizure had squeezed every possible ounce of liquid from my bladder.

My seizures were routine for David at this point and he always stepped into his "take charge" mode. No worries, no woes, no drama; just take care of it.

This time he had made a silent blink of a wish that wetting the bed would not become part of my seizure routine, but the thought didn't linger. David quickly finished that wish with a *"But it wasn't a big deal"* and got right back to routine duty.

He successfully changed the sheets without having to move me off of the bed. By the time he was finished, I was starting to return from my la-la land. After a seizure, I was always very distant and incoherent for at least fifteen minutes. I had nearly reached that point, and he watched for my eyes to open. David's routine usually ended with him quietly staying alert until it was clear that I was okay. This time, as David got back into the bed, he cuddled up to me, wrapping his arms around me.

I blinked my eyes open and shut a couple times and looked up at David's face with a smile. I looked like a newborn baby opening its eyes for the first time. "Mmmm." I made a soothed cuddle sound as I burrowed even closer.

"I love you," David whispered. There was a slight tease to his tone.

"I uhhuvvuh oo," was my reply. I was startled by the sound and a look of confusion was stamped on my face.

David couldn't resist chuckling and did it again with an even bigger smile, "I luuuuvvvv youuuu." He moved a crusty chunk of hair off of my cheek. *She always looks so innocent after her seizures*, he thought. *I'll even admit that it is cute in a warped way.*

Even though I couldn't get the words out, I knew what was being said and that I was being teased. I couldn't hold back a smile as it slowly spread across my innocent face. I tried again more slowly. "IIII, uuuff, uhoooo," I squinted my eyes at my rascal husband and made a small giggle.

"Thhh-EEE-rrr?" I asked while trying to sit up.

David knew I was trying to say seizure now. "Yes. You're okay." With the quick process of interaction we'd just had, he could tell I was already more balanced.

I relaxed back into his arms and quickly fell asleep without another thought.

This time, David wasn't able to close his eyes as quickly as usual. He had gotten used to the seizures and usually could fall right back to sleep after monitoring me. As David lay there this time, however, picturing my innocent post-seizure look, he thought about the first episodes we'd gone through as a new-lywed couple.

He had surprised himself with his reaction while experiencing the first seizure. He knew the pre-wedding experience had helped to ready him, but when the second one happened he handled the entire situation much more smoothly than he thought he could.

Memory of the first seizure he'd witnessed began. He closed his eyes and the scene began to play through his memory like a movie:

The room is dark and David is sleeping soundly when he hears a long, loud shriek. He instantly sits up and whips around to look in the direction of the sound. He can barely see my body jolting and reaches to turn on his lamp. Alarm runs through David's veins when he sees my lips blue and fro-zen-looking and my eyes opened and rolled back. He jumps into rescue mode and turns me onto my side.

My convulsing soon stops, and my stiff body becomes limp. After feeling for my heart beat, he looks at my body. It looks like ice. No movements. He can't feel me breathing and thinks about the mirror trick he'd learned in Scouts, "Hold the mirror in front of victim's open mouth, if a film blurs the mirror then victim is breathing."

Just before David gets up to grab a mirror, I begin to gag and thick spit spews out of my mouth onto the pillow. David feels a rush of relief instead of disgust or fear. He knows that the saliva extraction is a good sign.

David begins a seizure clean-up routine as he leaps to the bathroom and brings a towel back to wipe my face and hair and then grabs a new pillowcase to replace the surprisingly drenched one.

Spooning close to my body, keeping me lodged on my side, David lays awake for the next hour listening to each breath that comes from me.

As this played through David's mind, he thought about the difference between then and now. The first few times made fear prick David's nerves despite his level-headed actions. Tonight, however, he'd been able to calmly and routinely handle the situation and even finish with a loving tease.

A moment later, David rolled onto his side with his back pressed up against mine and fell back to sleep.

16

Mind over Matter

The bed had stopped shaking from my seizure jolts. David leaned over me, pushing his pillow behind my back to make sure I'd stay propped on my side. The blue on my lips was fading fast and he took a breath. Although he felt used to seizures, he was never comfortable until the icy blue would fade.

He jumped up and hurried to the attached bathroom to grab a towel for me. *Next step.* The gushing saliva always followed the seizure and return of lip color. If he were quick enough, the spit wouldn't douse the pillow and my hair.

Just as David was walking back into the room, he looked up and quickly moved to the side, surprised. I had gotten out of the bed and walked past him shuffling my feet. I hadn't noticed him standing right there in front of me. I was only seeing the bathroom door in front of me.

Turning to watch me, David saw my body swaying side to side. He almost moved to catch me from falling when I extended my own hands to the walls on either side of me.

She looks like a drunk walking down an alley. David couldn't help, but smile, still surprised I was even awake.

I flipped the light on and heavily plopped down on the toilet. David's smile turned into a quick breath of relief. *Phew, I almost needed to change the sheets again.*

I sat in the bathroom and stared down at the tiled floor; my mind was empty. A long, wet, clear drop of something surprised me when it landed in between my feet. I awkwardly lifted my hands up to my mouth and felt saliva streaming out. I felt dumb, unable to control it. *What in Heaven's name is going on?*

A few moments later, David saw me come from the toilet area, moving my hands in a wheeling motion under my mouth. He noticed a long string of saliva and couldn't help but smile again. *Yeah, yeah, real funny*—I can say that now. He could tell that I'd been trying to stop the stringy flow of saliva and was now trying to break the strand with my hands. I had a look of determination mixed with confusion, still walking with a drunken sway toward David.

I looked up at David and he wiped my hands with the towel he'd been holding.

"Thhh-EEE-rrr?" I couldn't speak yet.

"Yes." David again knew I was asking if the river coming from my mouth was because I'd just had a seizure.

Seeing that I was still wobbly, he directed me back to the bed. He could tell I was at the point of understanding his words even though I still couldn't speak.

"That was crazy! Your seizure started, but mid-jolt you jumped up and got off of the bed." *Almost felt like I was walking through a Halloween spook alley where a "dead" person all of a sudden rises from the coffin!* he added mentally.

I made one of my post-seizure innocent smiles and rested back onto my still dry pillow.

The next morning while David got ready for work, I felt my wounded tongue and asked David to re-tell what had happened that night. I vaguely recalled the episode.

We were both still surprised that I'd been able to move after the seizure. It seemed like I had actually stopped the seizure before its normal routine finished. *Mind over matter?*

17

Awareness

It was April 2005, and for the past two years I had been a student at University of Nevada-Las Vegas. I was wrapping up my senior year, ready to receive my degree in elementary education. My seizures had been quiet for most of the two years during classes, but my body was beginning to feel the mixture of stresses: excitement to have earned my degree and apprehension about finishing everything.

I was very private about my bizarre seizure experiences. As I became friends with classmates, however, I thankfully began to open up.

It was my third class for the day, math education, prepping me to teach math to elementary students. I stood in the hall with my overloaded backpack on my shoulders and chatted with my table partner Susan while waiting for the classroom doors to open. Both of Susan's children were in school and she was "finally" getting her degree to become a teacher.

Her six-year-old daughter and eight-year-old son had put together a little club and she was telling me their rules, one being, "No parents." Some of their activities included figuring out how to sneak some of Mom's sweets from her candy drawer.

She went on with that twinkling eye, "Y'know, I wouldn't trade all of the motherhood chaos for anything." Susan paused for a moment and then turned focus over to me, "So, Deanna, when are you going to enter the door of parenthood? You've been married a few years right? I bet you'd love it."

"I don't doubt that! Y'know, if life had followed my schedule then we would have a child by now."

"Aw, yes. Life." She gave a look of invitation for me to carry on. I could tell she was expecting to hear about infertility or miscarriage. "Have you guys been trying for a long time?"

"Well, we've actually decided not to even start trying to get pregnant until some of my health stuff is figured out." Pregnancy hadn't been officially banned by anyone, but David and I agreed it would be irresponsible to get pregnant with my seizures in disarray.

This was not what she'd assumed, and her curiosity rose. "What?"

As far as she could tell I was fine, in fact a prime person for pregnancy. By appearance I had a healthy body, high spirits, and good energy. What could be the problem?

I started into my routine seizure explanation, and her questions flowed.

I hadn't noticed an eavesdropper leaning toward us. After explaining to Susan what the doctor had dubbed as the problem, the eavesdropper interrupted our conversation.

"I'm sorry. I couldn't help but hear you talking about your seizures. I had to come over and tell you to go to UCLA. What you are going through sounds very similar to my case."

Susan and I both turned toward her and raised our eyebrows in surprise.

She carried on, "I had a doctor here who told me that my seizures were from a brain injury that I'd gotten after a car accident. Nothing was solved though until someone told me to go to UCLA three years ago. My seizures have stopped, and I haven't had any problems since. I only have to go down for an MRI once a year now and that's no big deal. You really, really should go."

I didn't quite know what to say as I looked at this woman. She was well into her fifties. I could tell she had experience in the mom role as she looked at me with the motherly glare of insistence. I could only say, "Okay, I'll go." I was surprised at how strongly her insistence hit me.

I wanted to know more about her whole experience, but the surprise wouldn't let me bring the questions out. I gave a quick, "Thanks" as the professor opened the door and welcomed the class in.

Susan must have been logging questions in her mind during the entire class period because as soon as the professor closed her books and dismissed us, the questions started right back up.

Thoughts about that woman's urgings were put on the back burner. I began to explain more while we walked to our next class, history education. Two more peers joined the conversation, both having been quickly updated by Susan, and were very curious as well.

As we took our seats at the front table, the professor noticed the looks and reactions the three were giving as I spoke. She walked over and caught the last few moments of the interview. She heard enough to get interested, but looked at the clock and hurried to start the class.

The hour quickly passed and when the class ended, the professor called me over to her desk. "Deanna, I heard you guys talking about you having seizures. Are you okay?"

"Oh yeah, it's not a big deal; mostly just a hassle, actually." I hated appearing weak.

My professor went on, asking questions regarding my seizures and I informed her of the basics: doctor said they are caused by a scar at the front of my left brain; I have to take medication, sometimes mini seizures still happen while I'm awake, overall, no big deal.

Having never seen a seizure take place she became instantly nervous. "Umm, well, having you as a student I feel like I should get trained in all of this or do something!"

"Oh, you don't have to worry." I did an "It's fine" wave with my hands.

"Okay, but at least tell me what I should do if one ever happens in class."

With emphasis I stressed, "Do not call an ambulance."

I told her that there was nothing neither a paramedic nor hospital could do other than confirm that it was a seizure and give me a big bill. There was no need to worry; I would be out of it for a couple of minutes, barely noticeable, and it all would soon mellow out.

When I could tell that she'd caught my urgency to not call an ambulance, I said my adieus with a little added humor and left.

18

Casa Hogar

The professor's concern had spurred my memory of a grand-mal seizure that I'd witnessed in Quito, Ecuador, six months before my own grand-mal seizures began. It made me shiver. I went to my car and closed my eyes as I relived my Quito experience. My mind transported me to my memory; I was peacefully sitting in a taxi as it swerved through lanes of Quito. I was a volunteer for an orphanage support organization and on my way to "Casa Hogar," a government orphanage.

Following my freshman year in Virginia I had moved to Ecuador and spent six months as an orphanage volunteer. It was a program I'd learned about while at school and both Kelsy and I joined; it certainly helped my buck-up stage. Since my arrival, I had been spending three to five days a week at this specific orphanage, and my heart was in it. I was immediately attached. On my third day of duty I wrote in my journal with a new devotion:

> The people are so sweet and love to show that they can speak English. I started my first day of work with the kids yesterday. It was incredibly hard. The bedroom smells like complete urine and diarrhea. The flies are all over.

More are inside than out! Flies were covering the food in the kitchen, too. These kids are smart, but just have not been taught. … They are precious and so incredibly loving! They love to give hugs and kisses. … It's hard that there is no structure and things are kind of feeling out of control.

By now our time and money had paid off, putting the orphanage in order; education was now given, levels of cleanliness were raised, flies no longer swam in the soup concoctions, and daily routine was organized to include music, PE, art, play time, story time, etc., in between their meals.

Each morning as we arrived, the older children (ages two to ten) would be getting ready. They washed in the showers that only dripped cold water and then clamored to be one of the first to use the group towel. Then they would dress in the orphanage-labeled clothes and underwear that were marked with their size. As each one finished, they would line up, getting ready to enter the cafeteria for their watery porridge.

The morning routine hadn't changed over the five months. The behavior of each person had bloomed, however. At the beginning the workers, known as "Mama [their name]," were sour and un-caring toward the children. After a short time, they became the opposite. A smile was often on their faces, and they seemed excited to be helping the children. Laughter amongst the children and adults became a common sound inside Hogar walls.

I smiled as we pulled up to the gated area titled, "Casa Hogar." *Casa* means house; *hogar* means home. A few of the children were already standing at the gate with their eager smiley faces pressed between the bars. Each morning when I saw their faces, I silently recited my theme, *I am doing everything I can to make this house a home for the children and adults.*

As soon as I finished that thought, I ran in to be tackled by the giddy orphans. The morning hoorahs soon ended as the children were called in for breakfast.

I didn't follow the group of children this time. It was my turn to attend to the infants and the two children held back with mental handicaps. Their "house" faced the cafeteria.

My nose wrinkled as I opened the door. No matter how hard I continually tried to get used to the morning smells, I was still punched by the stench each time I entered. We had been able to change and better many things about the orphanage—this was not one of them.

My current nursery partner and I quickly got to work. All of the six children were lying in their cribs, wailing. There was no need to try and figure out their needs; they were "all of the above." Each was dirty, hungry, thirsty, and alone.

I picked up the first child, Diego, and began the routine. Take off his wet pajamas and drop them in the hamper to be hand washed and hung. Turn on the water hose and get over the fact that there isn't warm water. Untie and then rinse the grocery bag that was wrapped over the dirty makeshift cloth diaper. Hold your breath a little longer. Open, remove, rinse, and place cloth diaper in the other wash bin. Hand wash the mess off of each child—rags and wipes aren't used. Quickly use the common towel to dry child. Re-diaper and dress child. Scour own hands and move on.

I wasn't surprised that the children would continue crying during this cold process.

We were getting bottles and sippy cups ready in the kitchen when Mama Corrita called my name. Her normal sound of humor wasn't ringing; her voice was tired.

I saw her standing beside Manuel, caressing his hand as he was lying in the oversized crib. Manuel was a thirteen-year-old boy in a body the size of a six-year-old. His head, however, was opposite in size. As Mama Corrita bent over to kiss him on his cheek, it was obvious that his head was larger than hers. He had a major case of hydrocephalus, also known as water on the brain. He had been found in an outhouse as a baby.

He grunted and smiled when he felt her kiss. His view changed from the ceiling above his head to the area above hers. After much training, he was now able to make eye contact, but it was rare.

Mama Corrita moved her hand from Manuel's and I had to bite my lip. I could tell by the raw marks and flat blisters that Manuel had been gnawing on his bent hand.

I was glad I had forced myself to become fluent in Spanish because she started to ramble, telling me that Manuel had been through a lot that night. I didn't immediately understand when she used the word "*ataque*." I understood it for its literal translation of "attack," but knew he had not physically attacked anything or anyone.

She continued to explain.

I was about to have her slow down and start over until she said the word, "*convulsión*." A convulsion attack. Convulsion is part of a seizure. A seizure is an attack on the body. I had only witnessed two grand-mal seizures in my life and knew very little about them, but I was sure this is what she'd been referring to.

Just as Mama Corrita was warning me that another could take place, Manuel began to shake. His bony limbs jolted faster than I'd seen them move before. I instantly understood the marks on his hands as he pushed his fist in his mouth and his jaws clamped down.

I ached to pull his hand from his mouth and hold him, but I knew that I couldn't help him while the seizure was happening.

The therapist, Marta, ran into the room at the same time that a new "Mama" came in and reached for Manuel.

"*Paré!*" Stop! She put her arms between all of us and the crib until his convulsing stopped.

Marta climbed into the over-sized crib and wrapped her arms around Manuel's stiff, unconscious body and rested his large head in her lap. She kept checking his pulse and making sure he was breathing. Mama Corrita changed his wet diaper and put a new pair of sweats on him. The new Mama continued to stand motionless, still shocked from what she saw and could do nothing about.

Marta saw my look of helplessness as I caressed Manuel's closely shaven head. She told me he would be fine and sent me back to the other children where I could be helpful. There was nothing else any of us could do for Manuel.

Memory of this young boy had become branded in my heart. Two months after that seizure, I was back home in the States. I received an email informing me that Manuel had just passed away following a seizure. They were unsure if his death had been caused by the seizure or if it was directly linked to his case of hydrocephalus. Kelsy and I had mourned together, again unable to do anything.

Tears started to fall and I shook the memory from my head, carrying me back to my own car in Las Vegas. *And now I'm having seizures just like his.* I stopped that thought right there.

19

All Eyes on Me

Two days later, as I sat down for my history education class again, I certainly wasn't thinking about my seizure discussion with the teacher. Final presentations were being made that day and the stress was palpable in the room.

When the third pair of presenters stood in front of the class and shared their example of a creative history lesson, I read through their notes and—flash—what I thought was a petit-mal seizure began.

I decided to wait it out, resting my head in my hand. The pit in my stomach inflated, and all senses seemed to be swiped away as usual. I felt my "mind reading" begin and seemed to be thinking the presenters' words before they said them. My body became heavy and I had to concentrate on my breathing.

Then, it stopped almost as quickly as it started! Not even ten seconds had passed and I was already with it. *Phew!* I tested my brain's thought process to re-center myself: *I'm at UNLV, sitting in history education class, I have and feel my body and I can breathe.* In … out … in … out. As I took the last test, I raised my head to exhale, but my breath stopped.

Thirty pairs of eyes were on me. Instant embarrassment strangled my throat. I could feel the heat of their bodies as they leaned toward me. All of a sudden, I felt out of place. *Who are these people? Are they trying to speak to me? What is going on?!* Half of me was trying to explain my relationship to them through feelings, the other half of me may as well have been playing a tune of *Twilight Zone* because I was in my la-la land.

I knew I was breathing again, but I still felt strangled with pressure. I began to sense that I was familiar with those nearest me. I still knew I was at school, so when I felt the impulse to follow orders as one woman spoke to me, I could tell she was the teacher. I decided to concentrate only on her, hoping it would help make sense of everything around me. I watched her lips, sure she was doing more than just mumbling gibberish. Her voice was a roller-coaster moan that would end on a higher pitch. *Question.* I could tell she wanted an answer. I just didn't know to what, nor could I remember how to make a possible statement get from my mind to my mouth and past my tongue.

All the while, my body's air tube was still in a twist from the humiliation. It was getting looser as I began to recognize my surroundings more and more, but still keeping air from the rest of my body. The only solution that made sense and felt like it would solve everything was to laugh. *Laugh! Everybody loves to laugh and it makes people feel more comfortable. That'll work.* So, I laughed. Actually, it was more of a fake high-pitched "Hahaha," a pity laugh that one hears when they've made an unsuccessful joke and the listener is trying to be nice.

Hallelujah! It felt as if the oxygen snapped back into motion and wheels started to turn a little bit faster in my muddy brain. *Ohhh boy. They all just witnessed my flash and are probably weirded out.* Again, the only thing I could do was laugh. This time it was more of an "Oops" giggle, but I could see shoulders relax as the sound came out. I was relieved. *They're relieved. All better.*

The relief only lasted a moment, however. Those nearest me started back up with all of the questions, expecting more than just a laugh now. I could tell I was getting better, understanding the "test" questions that they were throwing at me: Where are you? What is the date? What class is this? How many fingers am I holding up?

I understood these questions clearly, however, I could not, for the life of me, piece together any of the answers. I felt a rise in pressure as soon as they started asking me their names.

Greeaat. Way to really put the pressure on me by expecting me to remember your name, of all things. I hope no one is taking this personally.

A part of me was feeling a bit more uplifted with the fact that I could understand what they were asking me, aside from the fact that I couldn't come up with the answers. This gave a momentary rise in comfort that was, however, swiftly erased.

Where I quickly became shocked a moment later was when they asked a question that even a two-year-old should be able to answer without thought. "What is your name?" *What is my name? What is my name?! I, I, I don't know! I have absolutely no idea!*

I heard the teacher say something. I recognized the three-syllable sound of it, but couldn't quite place it or repeat it. I knew that my name had three syllables and that a voice's pitch would rise at the middle syllable of my name. It annoyed me that I knew the syllabic layout of my name, but couldn't think of the letter combination and the sound. A smile of embarrassment was all I could do, and my insides mixed with irritation and fear. I was hearing and recognizing my name like a two-month-old baby.

I'm not sure what made me think of this next action, but it certainly raised my curiosity to what was taking place with my brain. I picked up the purple crayon in front of me and began to write, trying to answer each of their questions: my name, my address, my phone number, the date, my birthday, the school, the city, and the state. Everything was written very neatly with big letters; perhaps part of me felt that the neatness and size emphasis would help convince everyone, me included, that I was okay.

The teacher began to give me instructions and update me. "… wanted … ambulance … no … school president and university psychologist … discussion … talk with you … evaluate your condition." I could tell my brain was waking with each sentence she spoke. The pieces of her statement started to come together making me feel relieved, yet antsy at the same time. *Okay. She didn't call an ambulance because I had told her not to before. Phew. But, she isn't comfortable and so she called the College of Education president and the university psychologist to come and evaluate me! Oh boy. Embarrassment!*

I shrugged my shoulders and gave a deflated okay.

With that, presentations picked up and I did everything I could to prep myself. Definitions and the spelling of different words said by those up front raced through my brain. *Thematic. T-H-E-M-A-T-I-C. A unit taught integrating math, science, history, language arts, fine arts, etc, all focused on one theme. Hey, that's a big one. I'm snapping back! Bring on the assessors!*

A new group began and stated their topic. I understood that it was something about a trail that went across the country and ended up in a state far west. Vaguely recognizing the name of the trail, I began to go through my test process. I pinched my lips together and furrowed my brow. "_____ Trail." I didn't recognize the first word. I decided to try the writing method; after all, it had helped when I tried to remember my name.

This time was a bit more difficult. My lip bite went a bit deeper, hoping it would help give me the answer. O-r-g-i-n. *No.* I was pretty sure there was something wrong with the vowels. I began playing my own game of "Wheel of Fortune." *Can you give me a "U"?* O-r-g-u-n? *Nooo.* I wondered if the person sitting next to me noticed that I had been writing down random words, and that this time I kept crossing out whatever it was that I was trying to spell. *Psycho!* O-r-g-a-n. *Yes! Wait.* When I put the two words together, "Organ Trail," something didn't look right. I couldn't place what it was. It wasn't until I looked at their handout that I realized my mistake. O-r-e-g-o-n. It still seemed a little off, but I figured they had carefully spelled the word correctly, with it being a formal handout, and it just looked right sitting next to the word "Trail."

I continued with my personal test for another few minutes until the "judges" arrived. I was led like a prisoner to stand before the judges awaiting the sentence. *Life or death.*

The teacher quietly called my name and directed me to the hall with a tip of her head toward the door. The new presenters stopped their lecture and seemed to direct everyone's eyes toward me as I tried to slip away. As I closed the door and smiled at the two men in front of me, I wasn't sure which was worse: to be in a room full of sixty wide, curious eyes staring at me, or to be standing in front of these two high-ranked men there to authorize my release. I felt ready enough. Having had twenty minutes of recovery, I was plenty with it. The conversation was smooth and ended with us laughing about the whole situation. I passed the test.

An hour later, I sat in my car, awaiting my next class. With no signs of flash aftershock, I shook my head. *Test after test after test!* A half smile shifted my lips as a corny joke crossed my mind, "Should have studied." *Not funny.*

What was funny, however, was the drama that passed through the lips of my peers over the next few days. While getting a ride the next day, the driver, a gal from a different class, was excited to gossip with me and the two other carpoolers in the backseat, "Oh my gosh, did you hear about the girl in the history ed. class yesterday? My friend has a friend from that class and she told her all about it. Out of the blue, this girl started to have a total heart attack and just collapsed, hitting her head on the table!"

She carried on, telling us about the girl being completely knocked out and then the university president and school medical people rushing over to rescue.

Ohhh boy. I gave a little chuckle and cleared the story. I could tell the driver was mixed with shock and embarrassment when she found out it was me. At that moment, I decided it was safest to give people information. People are unfamiliar with seizures.

20

Eye Opener

After graduation and visits with other types of doctors in Las Vegas, homeopathic and chiropractic, I made an appointment with UCLA—I was finally following the classmate's command. My homeopathic doctor agreed that the seizures should be looked into more deeply at UCLA. It was nice to feel her support, which was very different than Dr. Simon's reaction—he'd given David and me a bitter look when we asked for his referral.

In January 2006, we entered the large medical offices at UCLA for the first time. My feelings were a nicely mixed salad of curiosity, nervousness, and excitement all covered in a dressing of preparedness as I walked from my first UCLA MRI. I had a folder full of my Las Vegas doctor's notes, the five Las Vegas MRI and EEG reports, my family health pedigree chart, four pages of personal health information starting from my first flu as a baby, and the new MRI report was waiting in the doctor's email inbox.

I rehearsed the meeting through my mind as we waited in the office and was surprised when a man walked in. The patient information mailed to me had given a woman's name as my assigned doctor and I'd done online research about her. The research had helped my readiness. I hadn't read anything about this doctor's background and had to shake off a moment of stress.

After a minute of conversation, I immediately liked the doctor and relaxed.

"Would you like to see the MRI?" The doctor showed us the computer screen.

Wow. I've only seen an MRI on film before, and my Las Vegas doctor never offered to show it to us. How handy that they get it immediately on the computer.

"First, tell me what you understand," the doctor insisted.

David jumped in, "Well, the doctor told us that Deanna has a scar from something on her left frontal lobe and that it's not epilepsy." He drew a line on his forehead to mark the area. "He said there is nothing to do about it and that it is a common area for a scar, but we are just double checking. We are anxious to get pregnant, but want to be more sure about the situation before we do. He also said that she is at the dosage limit for this medication, but we are nervous to change because of the pregnancy risks from other medications."

"Really? Frontal lobe, huh? Well, let me show this to you." The doctor picked up his capped pen and drew an invisible circle on the screen, circling an area amongst the many wiggles of my brain. "This is the area of concern, probably what he was talking about. We will, however, call it a lesion because it is most likely not a scar and certainly is not a scar from an injury."

The doctor moved his pen down an inch. "This here is your left ear." He gave us a look silently asking, *Do you get why I pointed that out?* "The lesion is not on your forehead or anywhere on your frontal lobe. It is actually lower on your temporal lobe, to the side of your head."

"Oh!" I was instantly surprised. *How could my nice recommended doctor who has been a neurologist for a long time and*

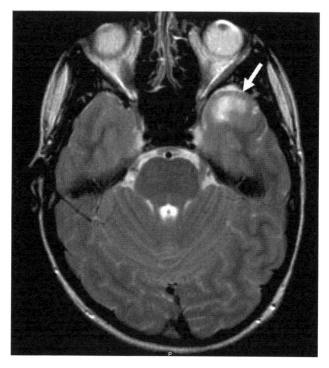

The arrow indicates the brightly enhancing *lesion* in the front part of the temporal lobe on the left side of the brain... A lesion that didn't belong.

seen my MRIs many times been so off, telling me it was above my eye? I had expected some differences of opinion, but not this drastic.

"You may be wondering why you are in the epilepsy department when your Vegas doctor said you weren't epileptic. Simply having a seizure disorder means you formally have epilepsy. It doesn't only identify a group that goes into seizures from flashing lights."

I gave another "Oh!" and continued with, "Well, that's good to know when I go to look information up on the computer. Now I'll stop passing up everything that reads 'epilepsy.'"

I got a laugh from him with that. "Also, you are not at the limit for this medication. The limit is 400mg a day. You are at 200mg a day. We want to do some different tests to find out more about what this lesion is. You can set them up as you choose. We'll also want to do another MRI here at UCLA in three months. We know our machines."

As the doctor went on, another doctor walked in the room. The moment I saw his name I remembered that he was the director of neurology in the department of epilepsy. *Hmm, can't hurt to have the top guy checking out my case.*

I could tell this doctor had read through my file. "I'm curious about the illusions you used to have during your 'flashes.' Explain those."

Illusions. This had been the biggest secret about my flashes. Though the flashes started in eighth grade, the illusions didn't come until three years later. They had started during my last semester of high school, and continued to grow through my freshman year of college. There wasn't a pattern to my flashes. Their occurrences were random: while with friends or alone, while hungry or full, while busy or bored, while watching a comedy movie or stressing to finish an essay assignment. I would go one, two or three days with repeated flashes and then one, two or three weeks without.

I shared the details and with my hand circled around the area in the outside corner of my right eye as I described it. "Umm. I'd be looking at you and a flash would start. Then a whole different and separate scene would appear. I only saw it in this upper right area of my eyes, yet literally felt like I was in two separate places at the same time. At first I only saw a woman in her forties with long brown hair, wearing a skirt and blouse and standing next to an antique phonograph. It felt like she would literally look right at me and give a 'hi' smile while putting the needle on the record. I would never hear the music, I just saw it all."

I continued my description from memory, yet recalled it plain as day. "So after seeing the lady's smile, the picture would turn to the right and I always saw a blonde boy in his twenties, wearing jeans and a T-shirt, who just looked like he was happy. Felt like we had a brother/sister connection, but I really don't think it was one of my brothers." I could tell that both doctors were fascinated by the fine points I was able to recall.

"A few months later during my freshman year at college, the scene got even longer. After seeing the boy it was as if my head would turn to the left and see a whole other room full of people; children and adults of all ages. In the doorway of that room would be a fairly slim, tall man, probably in his fifties, with dark blonde hair and wearing a collared button-up shirt. He would smile and then beckon me with his whole hand to come and join the party, and then that's where the illusion would stop. I don't know where it all came from. I didn't recognize the people or the location. The boy was the only one I felt a connection to."

I ended with a question, "Do you have any idea why I would have that?"

The director spoke, "As for eyesight, that region is actually connected to the same area as your lesion. That is why this is so interesting. If you were to ever have surgery, the view from that upper right corner of both eyes would be affected."

I felt that I was getting smarter by the minute!

"We're not sure where the specific scene would have come from. Very interesting that it isn't a specific memory. But it was somewhat of a visual explanation of what you were feeling at that point in your seizures."

Heavens to Betsy! You mean there is an explanation for these experiences that were driving me insane?! Many times I had wondered if I was foreseeing a future event and questioned the reason.

The doctors continued the explanations, "Also, your flashes have a formal name."

I wanted to feel smart so I answered before they could, "I know; petit-mal seizures."

I was wrong—and so was my Vegas doctor. "Actually, they are called complex partial seizures. The term 'petit-mal' is rarely used now because more detailed information has been gathered since the '70s. What is most similar to a basic petit-mal seizure is now called an absence seizure. Your 'flashes' are stronger than absence seizures and happen in one particular area. Absence and complex partial seizures can be confused, but first, absence seizures are never preceded by an aura— you have a distinct aura. Second, absence seizures are shorter—instead of two seconds yours are two to five minutes. Third, absence seizures begin frequently and end abruptly—yours happen in chunks and the effects linger for fifteen to twenty minutes. Last, absence seizures involve larger areas of the brain—yours always stem from your temporal lobe. You have complex-partial seizures."

I decided that term was too long, so I stuck with the name "flashes."

The doctors continued informing me of seizure details, "Also, you'll soon notice that your big seizures will now be more properly referred to as generalized tonic-clonic seizures. The term grand-mal is being phased out in the medical community, too. Generalized tonic-clonic seizures are the biggest they can get."

The two read through my list of visits with different doctors. A slight comment on my wasted time was made as they read through most of the procedures I'd been through.

"Hmm, sleep apnea and allergy tests. Bummer that you went through those unnecessary pokes and prods," the doctors and David chuckled.

I felt like they had stamped my forehead with a bold mark of "S-T-U-P-I-D" and defended myself, "Well, going to that doctor is what prepared me for coming here. If I hadn't met with that doctor then I wouldn't have even thought of questioning my Vegas neurologist." *Maybe you shouldn't make fun of my search!* I knew they didn't mean to irk me, but it still ruffled my feathers.

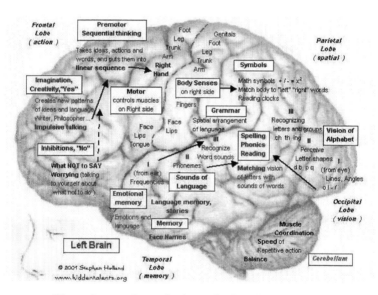

My seizure descriptions helped them nail the spot. Notice the temporal lobe: memory (emotions, stories, language, names).

21

A Bend in One's Road

I was on my third visit to UCLA, and this was different than what I'd expected. It was a long test. Phase I Telemetry Study was the test's official name. I had checked into the hospital for twenty-four-hour monitoring of my brain and body, an extended EEG that started on June 29, 2006. I felt like I was going through sleep apnea testing; ten hours was nothing in comparison to this. I had to have two tonic clonic seizures before I would be allowed check out. I had no idea that by the time I'd be able to pluck off the wires, my hair would be in such a tangled mess that I'd need to cut fourteen inches off. *Note to self: braid the hair.*

Five days had passed and I'd already gone through two roommates, one who'd undergone pituitary surgery, having a tumor removed through her nose. She went home two days after the surgery. The other was checked in for one night of post-surgery monitoring. A year earlier she'd gotten right-side brain surgery at a different hospital, so doctors were double checking everything.

I'd already had one tonic clonic seizure, but was bitterly anxious for another.

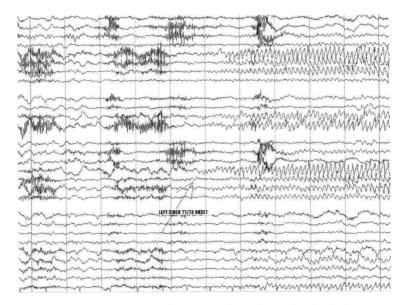

LEFT SIDED T1/T3 ONSET

An EEG showing the start of a seizure in the left temporal lobe. Notice the smooth flow of spikes on the right half of the picture. The EEG corresponds to the lesion in the middle and front part the left temporal lobe as seen in the MRI on page 85.

Katie Gramm was my third roommate. She was a younger woman I'd noticed who was in the UCLA hospital like me, while others were celebrating Independence Day. I'd seen her sloughing through the halls as I was being rolled to another room for a PET scan—a test they used that was similar to an MRI, but with radiation injections to verify my brain had no trace of cancer. The next day, I found out she was becoming my roommate.

Katie walked into the room with a "been there, done that" air about her. Very little emotion painted her face. The blue hospital gown was held together with tight plain knots along the side. The top wasn't knotted, however, and the gown hung sloppily over her braless shoulder. Her long hair was matted in knots; an extreme case of bed head. Her voice was monotone as she instructed her mom to put things in the chair and dragged her feet to the bathroom. Despite her current look, I could tell that if one were to see her at a social event, she would look very different and even pretty.

I couldn't overlook the large sunglasses on her face. It was clear that she hadn't picked them out for style. They were thick, dark black, and seemed to wrap around her, shielding her eyes from every possible beam of light.

I was instantly curious about her story.

After Katie's things were moved, she settled herself on the bed and shooed her mom back home. She laid herself down, bent her legs, and began tapping her feet side to side. I could tell that she wasn't trying to fall asleep.

"Hi." I wasn't sure how to start the conversation.

"Hey." (Pause.) "So how long have you been in here?"

Since she added a question to her response I guessed she was open to a conversation. "Seven days." I was about to use a dramatic tone to my number when something told me that she had seen more. "How about you?" It almost felt like we were comparing our time in a jail cell. *What are you in for? What's your sentence?*

"A long time, off and on. This marks day thirty of my current visit." Katie stopped her time information there, but gave me a look telling me that it was my turn to speak.

"Well, I'm Deanna." I gave her some of my basic information: from Nevada, grew up just north of Los Angeles, twenty-three years old, married for three and a half years, no kids, in for testing about my seizures ...

Katie met each point that I shared with her own information: from Idaho, twenty-five, married for two years, one seven-month-old daughter, and in the hospital because of her major headaches.

As we spoke, her shielded eyes must have been scanning the area around me. She pointed to the large card sitting on the ledge behind me, "Primary President, huh?" She had obviously read the "to" and "from" information, and the tone in her voice told me she knew what the title was. I was the leader of the children's church group in my area.

"Yup. It's only been six months so far. I've got a good group. The kids wrote some cute notes in there." I changed the topic back to her. "I gather that you are LDS, too?" Her familiarity with the church group and title were a good clue. "The fact that you're from Idaho doesn't make the guess too random."

She laughed. "Yeah. Born and raised."

This seemed to open her involvement all the more. She asked about the twenty-six wires "growing" from my scalp and what doctors were trying to find out.

"Well, I'm basically getting a twenty-four-hour EEG and have to have seizures so they can map everything out in my brain." I went on with more details. By the time I finished, she seemed ready to share her story. I prompted her, "So what about you? Why are you coming to LA about your headaches?"

At that moment, Katie's light switch of emotion was flipped off and she began her story.

For the past three months she had been suffering from headaches. She said that she hadn't yet come up with a word to justifiably describe them. Over the first two months her husband had taken her to their nearest hospital repeatedly, only to be sent home with pain medication. Doctors had not seen any areas of concern.

Her mom had finally put her foot down and forced Katie to get testing done at UCLA. Her husband was back at school and work, by her family's insistence. Her mom was helping with her seven-month-old daughter.

My heart sank as soon as she mentioned her daughter again. I felt for Katie and her little baby as I thought about her not being able to be mommy. Just as this was going through my mind, her mom walked back in with Katie's daughter.

This little one was adorable. She was in a cute outfit and her hair was pulled into a small ponytail on the top of her head with a coordinated clip. The baby seemed too familiar with this routine. Her reaction wasn't of grand excitement to see her mother; she gave more of a "Mommy's turn" lean when Katie's mom sat on the bed. This had been the little girl's usual pattern for half of her life now.

Katie's mother and daughter stayed for half an hour and then left. Our conversation picked right back up as I made a comment about her adorable daughter.

"Well, it's all hard because I don't know how long I'll be here."

This statement threw me for a loop. "What?"

"They've already done a lot of testing and I think they are debating on their next step. I'm now in here daily because of my headaches. They haven't officially decided what the problem is, but there are two possibilities."

Despite the casualness in her explanation, I noticed her swallow slowly and deeply before she went on.

"They can see a problem, or whatever, located in the middle of my brain. It is pretty much dead center and hard for them to get to. It is either a virus or a tumor. If it's a virus then they think they can take care of it. If it's a tumor, there isn't anything they'll be able to do. The mass, or whatever they call it, is spread out. They won't be able to successfully remove it."

I couldn't think of how to respond. She said it so simply, so plainly. This, however, was a big deal and worthy of a big reaction, but Katie seemed to want it to be low key.

So I said, "Oh my gosh. Talk about never knowing what to expect. Do you have any sort of feeling as to which it is? What are you going to do?" I could have added a number of words to that last question. *What are you going to do about the problem? What are you going to do about the time you might have left? What are you going to do about your new little family?* And so on. I chose to leave the question open, letting her carry it in whatever direction she chose.

"My headaches are a little more under control with different medications. They knock me out, but it seems to keep me on a nap schedule. I'm actually going to check out soon. My daughter and I will stay in town for a few days after that, and then we'll get back to my husband in Idaho. I'll be back in a few weeks for some more testing. It all depends upon what they decide in the next few days."

She took a few slow gulps from the large cup of Pepsi. "I don't have any idea which problem I've got, but I guess I've kinda mentally prepared myself for the worst; the tumor. My husband doesn't like me talking to him about it, but I told him that he should get remarried quickly if it is a tumor and I die. He won't be able to raise our daughter on his own. I know it. I want my daughter to have a mom."

Our conversation was abruptly ended as the nurse came in to check on me. Needing to utilize the nurses' visits, getting their surveillance for my bathroom breaks, I had to ask Katie to pause our discussion for a moment. "Shoot. Hold that thought until the nurse is finished."

When I came out, the divider sheet was spread between our beds. The nurse had sponge bath supplies ready for me. As I awkwardly cleaned myself and changed into new pajamas, I could hear Katie's breathing get slower and deeper. *I wonder if this nap is on schedule.*

The thoughts racing through my mind after our conversation got me wired. I tried to put myself in Katie's shoes. *What would I want if I were her? What if I had a tumor and questioned my time on earth? What would I tell David? Would I tell him to remarry like Katie told her husband?* The thought sent a shiver through me.

My thoughts went back to when I had read Nicholas Sparks' novel, *A Bend in the Road*, the year before. It was about a man whose wife, the mother of his child, dies. This book had unsettled me for a couple of weeks. The book flap reads, "Miles Ryan's life seemed to end the day his wife was killed in a hit-and-run accident two years ago. Missy had been his first love, and Miles fervently believes she will be his last." The book was told by Miles, so while reading it I put myself in the man's shoes.

Tears had streamed down my face as I thought about losing David. My shoulders shook from my sobs while I read the tragedy, imagining myself going through a similar situation—this was before I even had reason to worry. *Sheesh, good author.*

I was intrigued by the book. *His wife is dead, what is he going to do?* I got sick when I found the answer. *The man falls in love with someone else.* My stomach had churned as I read about this new fresh love that he had never expected. I was surprised by my reaction, realizing that it was perhaps immature.

I decided then and there that if I had children at home and David died, I would not marry someone else. My religious beliefs on marriage include being together forever and that life on earth is quick in comparison to the time that follows. I decided that I would keep that feeling and belief fresh in my mind if I had to live life without him by my side every day. I determined that I would find ways to tell our children about Daddy and raise them with him in mind. I planned how to monetarily support my family and how to utilize the time and influence of extended family. My mom would surely be willing to live with or near us, helping while I worked. We would stay near David's dad, so that he could give the Brady male influence in David's place.

After reading the book, it wasn't until I had chosen to plan everything out that I was able to calm down and sleep at night. I shared my plan with David after I had all my details figured out. He gave a casual "good to know" sort of reaction. Then his response to me was similar to my plan. He said that he couldn't ever see himself wanting to get remarried if I were to die. I couldn't convince myself that he wouldn't.

Again, while I read *A Bend in the Road*, I had only put myself in the character Miles Ryan's position. But now, after watching Katie, I reversed characters. I imagined watching David from Heaven and became sick. *I don't think David could be happy raising our children by himself and the kids wouldn't have motherly influence; but if he were to marry someone else then he probably would no longer hold me so dear.*

All of those book emotions re-connected as I laid in the bed thinking about Katie and her little family. *Her husband and child may have to live that story.* My stomach still churned as the cobwebbed thoughts re-entered. I had forced myself to put my emotions evoked by that book to the side since mine and David's conversation, but thinking about Katie's husband opened the creaking door again. I ached over having no control in something that meant so much to me.

At that moment, a new determination was lit for me as David's wife. I decided that I was going to do everything in my power to survive, regardless of what came my way. *Will power has the strength to fight anything, right?* I decided that I wouldn't "go" before David and because of that, I had a long path ahead of me. Health was strong on both sides of his family.

After making my self-promise, not even a minute passed before David walked into the room. I didn't mention a thing to him about my fears or my decision. I didn't want to know his response. Instead, I turned on the TV, scooted over on the bed, and had him cuddle with me as we watched the news.

The next morning, Katie was checked out of the hospital while I was taking a shower. We hadn't yet exchanged any contact information. I said a silent prayer for her, recognizing that I would probably never know which cards life would end up dealing her. After joining Facebook two years later, I looked up her name, hoping to see her alive and well, but her name never popped up.

22

A New Decision

"Rah-Rah- Rahrahrah! Rah-Rah- Rahrahrah! GooOOOO COU-GARS!" The Alma Mater song roared through the football stadium, celebrating another touchdown when the cell phone vibrated in my pocket.

Seeing the *3-1-0* area code I answered with a cheery, "HEYY-Yuh!" expecting the call to be from my brother and the following caravan letting us know of their arrival from California to Las Vegas for the Pioneer Bowl Game.

"Deanna, this is Dr. Stevenson." Realizing it was my UCLA neurologist, I tried to play it off as if I normally answer all of my calls with the same excitement. This crossed my mind before even realizing that my doctor was calling me at 6:30 p.m. on December 21 (2006), past normal doctor hours and when most doctors would be home enjoying Christmas break.

I figured there was a specific reason for this call; that it was not just a "How's it goin'?" phone call. I snuck away from the loud cheers, claps, and music to hear what he had to say. I could already feel that the crowd merriment was opposite from what the doctor was about to tell me.

Dr. Stevenson cut right to the point. "Our radiologists have looked through all of your MRIs again, closely comparing them. They have confirmed a slight change of the lesion in your head. This fact leads us to believe that it is a benign tumor. We have met again on your case and have, together, decided that with the form change and your continued complex partial seizures, that brain surgery is, in fact, necessary."

What? Are you serious? That doesn't make sense. Me? But, I thought it had been decided that this "lesion" area would just be watched over the next few years. So what does this mean?

Instead of sharing my dramatic reaction thoughts, I replied, "Okay. What is the process and when should we do it?" I acted as if it was a simple assignment given to me. *Let down my guard? No.*

My holiday-mode brain certainly awoke, becoming the German Autobahn with thoughts racing faster than my brain's usual "speed limit." *How is a person supposed to react to this statement? I can't believe I am standing here next to all of these people decked out in team spirit attire, who are all pumped for a good night of cheer, and I have just found out that I need to have brain surgery.* I wanted to stop one of the persons passing me and share the shock with them. *Maybe their reply will help me know how to react.*

My neurologist answered my questions with a light, everyday response, helping to keep my stress level down, "We'll want to start up as quickly as possible."

I asked that we at least wait until the holidays settled and he suggested that we wait no longer than February. "You will just need to do a couple more tests and then we can get right to it." This came across as, "Well, let's see. I'm sure we can pencil you in for February. No problem."

My reply was as untroubled as his information, "Oh. Okay."

As I started to say this, however, a different sensation buoyed me up, completely turning the rest of the doctor's words into a faint hum. A feeling came with the thought. This thought actually didn't even feel like a normal thought, more like a direction being told to me. I suddenly got warm and even my pink-tipped nose, bit from the cold, seemed to thaw. This thought excited me and overtook the thoughts of brain surgery, for a moment at least.

My thoughts jumped back to the phone call when I turned to see David coming down the stadium stairs to find me, not knowing why I had snuck away. At the same time, coming from a different direction, I heard my sister, Shawna, who having sat in a different area was looking for me, calling my name. I put my thought aside and gave them the news, somewhat in the same way as the doctor had given it to me. Simple and to the point, as if it was just another bullet point added to my day's To-Do list.

David had prepared himself for this call; I got a mental image of him as a soldier simply waiting for the commander's order. "Okay, we'll get it taken care of."

I could tell that Shawna wasn't sure how to react to this news. "Ummm," was all she could say.

David caught this and the comforter position swapped from what it had been four years earlier, after my first tonic-clonic seizure when Shawna had calmly informed David. It was his turn to soothe her. "It shouldn't be too bad. UCLA does over five hundred brain surgeries a year and have been doing this kind since the '50s. They know what they're doing, and we have the best surgeon. With all the tests they've done, I don't doubt that they know what they're getting into."

That's right! His reminder and assurance buoyed me up. *His confidence is not from ignorance, he certainly asked the questions!* I flashed back to our many doctor appointments and how he would drill the doctors. "What is the possibility of ..." and many other who, what, where, when and why questions. I'll admit to feeling like the damsel in distress being protected by her prince whenever he would raise his meticulous questions.

Much was in store for me from this moment, more than I had imagined possible. My comforting, aforementioned "thought" came forward to battle my dark side. The darkness would be tampered with and a new light would be moving me forward. It was a light that I wouldn't be able to confirm for another eleven days.

23

Happy New Year

Over the next two weeks of winter break, I thought about the surgery and wondered why I'd been so shocked by the doctor's call. *I got the information just like David did.*

I had mostly forgotten the issue. *I mean, c'mon, who actually goes through brain surgery?* After the two weeks of hospital testing in June and then a following five-hour neurocognitive memory and mobility test, the group of doctors had decided to only monitor the lesion on my brain over the next few years. I had let the worry rest.

Three months earlier, I had become a second grade teacher and brain concerns had settled. I hadn't even mentioned my seizures to any of the teachers or staff other than the principal, and certainly not my seven-year-old students. I'd gone through my normal flashes outside of the classroom and only one tonic-clonic in November, but they had come and gone without attention. They were normal to me now and everything seemed in order.

Even though I was certain the surgery would be okay, it was still unsettling to realize that I needed a change. I liked my everyday life, and one doesn't usually need change when life is good.

The other "thought" that had enveloped my mind and emotions during my conversation with the doctor had continued to linger as well. I chose to keep it silent until early New Year's Day, 2007.

I woke up early and started my year with a fib. I told David that I needed to run to Kristen's house and pick something up for school. Kristen was a classmate from UNLV and the friend who had connected me with the homeopathic doctor. We didn't have much contact after my graduation, but a year later we both happened to start teaching at the same school, and our friendship was reactivated. We did much lesson planning together, bouncing our ideas off of each other.

When I told David that I was going to her house, I rolled my eyes at my sneakiness. He was still in bed, too groggy to ask questions, but I had figured that he would be more curious about me getting up early and running to Walgreen's instead of going to Kristen's. I wanted the hoped-for results to be a surprise.

I walked into Walgreen's and headed straight for the aisle with pregnancy tests and picked the box with the middle price. *That's safe enough.*

I was certain about my pregnancy status and walked over to the card aisle. I picked out a "congratulations for the baby" sort of card.

The clerk smiled when I asked where their bathroom was located as soon as I paid for the card and tests. I wanted to know the answer immediately and didn't care that she knew exactly what was going on.

Not even ten seconds passed before a plus sign boldly appeared on the test stick. *I'm pregnant? I AM PREGNANT!* I hurried out of the bathroom and beamed a wide smile at the clerk as I left the building. I had never expected a store clerk to be the first to share the excitement.

When I pulled out of the parking lot my cell phone rang and I saw Kristen's number, I couldn't hold the news back. She too was pregnant and able to laugh about what I'd just done. "I'm trying to surprise David, so I told him I was going to your house! Ah!"

"Yeah, I was wondering about that," she replied.

"What?"

"Well, I called your house and was surprised when David said, 'I thought she was going to over to pick something up from you.' I couldn't think of anything to say other than, 'Oh yeah. Thanks. Bye.' You left me hanging there!" Kristen was laughing.

"Quick on the draw!" I joined the laughter that she had come to my rescue.

I was soon in my driveway, signing the card that read "Congratulations" underneath a picture of a baby's feet. Above my signature I wrote, "Happy New Year, Sweetheart. It will definitely be a good one. I love you. Congratulations!"

David was surprised when I gave him a card wishing him a Happy New Year. We hadn't exchanged New Years' cards before. He didn't catch on to the meaning of the baby photographs and "Congratulations" until I pulled out the test results. My mind took a picture of his tender reaction. He had forgotten that he usually hides emotion and instead became obviously surprised and elated.

"Do you feel okay about it?" His cautious side came forward after the big hug and kiss.

I went on to explain what I had experienced during the football game phone call, and I could tell he recognized the comfort and excitement it gave me.

Later that day I got online to instantly prepare for pregnancy and parenthood. I didn't want epilepsy surprises. I searched answers to every question I had. My worries were mixed between seizure risks and medication risks.

"Can the squeezing pressure from a seizure affect my baby? Will the umbilical cord get pinched during a seizure, cutting off the baby's oxygen? I can't breathe during a seizure. Will that stop oxygen for the baby? Are my seizures now hereditary, even though I'm the only one in my family with seizures? Will my seizure frequency increase? If I have a seizure during pregnancy, will my baby die? Can my baby be harmed by medication? What are the risks of fetal malformation to the body and brain?"

I saw a variety of answers online, but they all pointed in one direction—stay on the medication. Possible medication harm was less than possible seizure effects: cleft lip/palate versus miscarriage. Spina bifida was also a pregnancy risk if on the medication, but likeliness was greatly lowered when the mother took extra folic acid. *I can do that.* I couldn't always control my seizures on my own, however.

I quickly contacted a highly recommended perinatalogist, Dr. Bohman, and made an appointment. I went into his office, with David by my side and a list of questions in my hand. I can't describe the feelings that warmed my body as I looked at the ultrasound screen and saw the Gummy-Bear-looking fetus in my womb. *I'm becoming a mommy.* I'd played with so many children over the years, but now I was actually getting a child I could call my own. I wanted to be ready.

He strongly encouraged me to stay on my medication, Lamictal, verifying that it had very low risk of causing a cleft lip. He wrote up a prescription for 1mg folic acid tablets to be taken daily—the normal prenatal vitamin carries 0.4 mg of folic acid. My new doctor patted me on my knee, just like my dad, and while looking directly into my eyes instructed me to look after myself, to take it easy—as stress-free as possible—and to be consistent with my medication. (He'd been giving David the pressure look, too.) I left with a paper full of new information. Some women have more seizures during pregnancy, some have fewer; birth defect rate bumps from 2–3% to 4–8% for women who take seizure medications—very low, but still a fact; not all seizure cases are genetic—mine wasn't; tonic-clonic seizures can cause a variety of harm to a baby and mother, as I'd figured—a low chance, but a high risk; most medications have certain risks with different levels of possibility; and the number of perinatal doctor visits double, keeping a close eye on the baby and mommy; etc. I got into the car ready to become a mom.

I called my UCLA neurologist to inform him of the news. His continued factual tone was as smooth as it had been the call before, "Okay. Then we'll push the date back and resume testing after your pregnancy. Congratulations." It helped that he didn't gasp when I said I wouldn't be able to have the surgery in February. *Good sign.*

My football game "thought" had been confirmed by my new perinatalogist and was now official reality after the call to my neurologist. I felt good. I knew that I would be looked after and that my baby and I would be protected. All was in order.

24

"Mrs. Brady Was Silly Today"

The last week of school had already arrived and my heart was already aching; teacher syndrome. I had really devoted my thoughts, time, and love to these students, and it was already time for them to move on to third grade. Being a week of review, I used every last ounce of creativity I could squeeze out of me to go over the areas they had previously learned. Once again, the end of the school year stresses would take their toll.

I reserved the Wednesday math lesson for the end of the day. The students eagerly passed out the materials: Cheez-Its, graph paper, and orange crayons were on the list. As the materials were passed, the students became very curious. We discussed what topic we would be reviewing through this activity. They quickly tied it to area and perimeter. *Yeah! They've learned something this year!*

As I began to give the formal assignment guidelines my brain was hit by a flash warhead, scattering my planned words all around my brain. The words I started to speak to the children made no sense. If I hadn't been able to notice this myself, I surely could have figured it out by the looks of confusion on the children's faces.

I started to laugh and the students joined in. *All right, I can't think of the words, so maybe I'll just start to read from the page and pick up from there.* The instant I started to read the first word, I could tell it wasn't going to help. *Been there before*—I was remembering a time when I read something to David and only gibberish came from my lips. This was quickly turning into a game and the kids were getting a kick out of it with me. I was able to throw out my own silly remarks, "Wo, Mrs. Brady is definitely ready for summer. I've apparently forgotten how to read!" *Ha-ha-ha.*

I still could not put together any words regarding the activity. I turned to the whiteboard. *Well, I can't say it, but maybe I can write it. It's been that way before.* I recalled back to my UNLV class when I had written down my personal information even though I had not been able to speak it.

Before I even took the top off of the dry erase marker, I decided it wasn't necessary. I turned back to the group and with a chuckle said, "Aww, you guys know this stuff. Read through the instructions and you can figure it out for yourselves. Making sure you follow directions will be part of the score." The last bit was an extra addition—an excuse for my lack of assistance.

The students laughed with a new sense of determination to succeed, and I walked to my desk for a sip of water, hoping this would buy a few extra seconds for my brain to settle before needing to answer any questions.

As I set my water bottle down, two students walked up to my desk. I couldn't think of their names or the details of their questions, but I knew the answer. I knew the two needed help and I knew where to direct them. I took the shoulders of one, turned him to face a boy seated nearby and said, "You and you"—part of my brain still knew the two of them worked well together. I did the same for the other student, directing her to a partner I knew would be willing to help.

My vocabulary soon returned. Before I knew it the day was done, and it was time to clean up. The last thirty minutes of class had swept by. After I walked the students outside, I made a quick phone call to my sister-in-law, who was the mother of one of my students. I told her about the incident and asked her to get details from her son.

She called me back an hour later with a report. "I asked him how the math activity went today and he said it was really fun. After he told me about it, not mentioning a thing about you, I asked him if he noticed anything silly about you. He giggled and said, 'Yeah, she was being kinda silly. It was really funny.' I then went on to inform him about seizures and that it was what had made you act a little silly, but told him not to tell the other students. He definitely went wide eyed from this and after a big, 'Ohhh,' he just went on to tell me about the rest of the day."

"Phew. I was nervous that these kids thought I had turned into some whacked out teacher. I figured that if it made any of them question, then they would probably blame it on this baby in my belly," I joked. I loved being able to bring up my pregnancy every chance I got. Everything with the pregnancy had so far been in my favor. I was eating right, drinking a lot of water, sleeping as soon as I got home from work, and I'd only thrown up once. Frequent visits kept my worries settled—the baby was healthy. I regularly acknowledged that I was being taken care of and was enjoying my days.

She chuckled, "Ha. Yeah. Apparently, you kept it all running smooth enough though, and it's nothing they'll think to ask their parents about. How did the rest of the day go?"

As she said that, I remembered my episode earlier that same day, "Oh my gosh, I think I made myself look stupid this morning! We were walking to class and a teacher behind me either asked me a question or threw out some 'good morning' greeting, and I could not understand what she was saying. I just looked at her, gave her my normal little laugh, and quickly turned back to my students as if one of them were asking for my attention."

"So you tried to play it off, eh? You think it worked this time?" she replied with an "aw, bummer" tone.

I rolled my eyes at myself having tried to be clever. "Geez, there's another one who has probably raised their eyebrows at me. I better go explain myself to her." We ended our conversation and said our goodbyes.

I entered the classroom of the teacher that I'd inadvertently snubbed, and with an "I'm so sorry" expression I began the conversation with an embarrassed, "Hiii," as she looked up from her desk.

Kind of surprised she gave a quick, "Oh, hey!"

"I just wanted to say sorry for not responding to you this morning. I was out of it for the moment," I said with a light resonance in my tone.

"Yeah." As she said that, a look of speculation was in her eyes and I could tell she was curious, guessing there was more to the story.

I decided to give a bit more information than I had originally intended. *This may be useful for her in the future as a teacher,* I told myself.

"Have I ever told you about my seizures?"

She pulled her head back quickly with a look of shock on her face. I took that as a "no" and carried on.

"Well, I've been having seizures for a few years. Sometimes I'll have random small seizures that throw off my thought and verbal response process. They usually aren't noticeable unless you are trying to have a conversation with me, like this morning."

She nodded with a "that makes sense" satisfaction. "Oo-kay. It really seemed like something was up with you. I figured something stressful was on your mind. I thought I'd distracted you mid-thought and wondered if there was something going wrong. This makes more sense." She went on, "So, is everything all right? Things had seemed in order for you with the kids, so I let it be. How do you get out of it?"

"It was certainly nice that the students had music class first, today. They knew the morning routine and I didn't need to do a thing." I let out a breath of comfort and finished, saying, "I was able to really just chill and get that last minute of rest that I'd needed. It helped not needing to think."

The usual box of questions was opened, and I spent the next half hour informing her of my situation and the crazy things I'd experienced through all of it. These conversations never got old; I always liked to hear different people's responses and their stories of people they knew with seizures.

The conversation ended casually as I answered the last question regarding how we were going to make it all better, "My pregnancy has given a little break from all of the testing, but we'll pick up where we left off after the little one comes. They think that surgery may be the route to take, but I'm trying to get my brain to kick out the naughty area itself. Not sure that's too likely though." I finished with a light-hearted wink and chuckle.

25

Puppy Love

There was no other way to explain the ease of my pregnancy, and my doctor agreed with me. "You must be getting some extra care from above."

Thirty-seven weeks of pregnancy had breezed by with my body in its best condition ever. Aside from the embarrassing moments while teaching, the seizures had slept.

During week thirty-eight, I felt ready and willing for my baby's arrival. *Any day now, little one.* My body seemed to agree. My blood pressure had stayed consistently high for the previous week, showing readiness for delivery. I finished all the last pre-baby details and had my hospital bag packed, waiting by the door.

"Hey, Mom, I just wanted to give you a heads up." I went on to explain the possibility of induced delivery due to my high blood pressure. She had tried to leave her schedule open so that she could come to my aid when I beckoned. "I have my doctor appointment tomorrow, and I'm guessing they'll have me go to the hospital the next day. It's a guess though."

My mom chose to come down early so she could go to my appointment with me. "I'll play it safe."

"Oh, okay. That works. But I really may be fine, early delivery is just my guess."

The next day my mom and I pulled up to my doctor's office, anxious to hear his decision. After the first reading of my blood pressure, which was high, the nurse kept my arm in the monitor cuff and they watched closely for the next forty-five minutes.

My blood pressure didn't settle, however, and the doctor made his decision. "Well, Deanna. This is exciting! Your baby is fine and at a sufficient point for delivery, so in our concern for you, we are going to have you go in for delivery."

I expected to hear *tomorrow* as his next word. Didn't happen.

"I've just started the labor process, so go on over to the hospital from here. We've called them and they will be ready for you. If you have a hospital bag ready, just have David bring it."

"Right now?!" I had not expected that. "Oh my goodness. Wow. All right."

Yeah! I called David a moment later and shared the information with an enthusiasm that I wouldn't have been able to hide if I tried. I could hear his "new dad" anxiety tipped with eagerness. I checked into the hospital, and as I looked around the room I laughed at my bed, or rather my cradle. Every bar was up, surrounding the mattress and wrapped with blankets. Because of my seizure possibility, the nurses had taped four blankets to the bars to lower possible bruises. I knew seizures would remain in their hibernation, however, and aside from the blood pressure spike, all was well.

August 24, 2007, became a day to celebrate. *It's a girl!* Five hours after they broke my water, a new baby entered the world and was placed in my arms. *Just right.* The baby was strong, healthy, and beautiful; cuddling in my arms. *7 pounds, 14 ounces. 21 inches.*

My heart melted when she was wrapped in a blanket with a small cap on her head, being slowly rocked by her new elated daddy. *She's an angel.* Her pink skin was pure newborn and her big eyes and chubby cheeks melted the heart of all who saw her. She rested on her daddy's shoulder, content and happy. *Bridgett Brady.*

I'd been excited to see my baby and to imagine her future: her learning to walk, read, dance, ride a bike, and then making friends, going on dates, going off to college. But actually, none of that came to mind. I was caught in the moment, the here and now, having forgotten the delivery process, and could only think of the little toes, the still white fingers, and the perfectly shaped lips. Her eyes were still blinking slowly as she too was taking it all in. She was perfectly satisfied, and the mommy/daddy/daughter bond was sealed.

I was happy to be a new mommy.

A week quickly passed. I was all alone on Mom duty, as ready as ever. My mom had returned home, and David was attending a business appointment. Bridgett already had her own eat, play, sleep schedule, and I was loving it all.

I checked the clock, counting how much longer she would be asleep for her third nap of the day. I'd been busy doing laundry and had just put a batch in the dryer. *2:00. Sixty minutes left ...*

Without another thought, I headed to my bedroom where my comfortable mound of pregnancy pillows still awaited me. My lab/pit-bull mix dog, Scout, read my mind and followed, walking slowly to his own fluffy pillow bed, next to our queen size bed.

As I laid my head down, ready for the shut-eye, I was surprised when Scout jumped up on the bed, pouncing on my stomach. I was instantly mad. He continued to pounce on me and with his teeth quickly grabbed my blanket and sheet, pulling them off of me. He wasn't being playful. Warnings that I had read regarding dogs and a new addition to the family sped through my mind. *Scout is trying to get my attention right now. He's mad that I have been holding Bridgett more than him. Blast!*

My inner nap clock was ticking loudly, and all I could think of was taking a nap before Bridgett was ready to get up. I yanked the sheet from his mouth and reached down to pull the blanket over me. As I pulled it under my chin, Scout bit at my fingers, getting one hand and then the other. He was serious. He knew he had crossed his boundaries, but didn't care.

I shoved him off of the bed, but he jumped back up faster than he had gone down and got right back to harassing me. Worry started to build. Thoughts of a pit bull's mean reputation came to mind. I didn't know much about pit bulls, but I knew they could get aggressive if they wanted to.

The only solution I could think of was to distract Scout. I yanked the sheets off of my feet, where he had dragged them down to again, and left the room. Scout seemed satisfied and calmly hopped off of the bed, following me with a happy wag of his tail. When I sat at the computer to do a quick email check, Scout settled himself on the couch. After just a few minutes, I could hear his deep breathing, telling me he was sound asleep. I crept back into my room, locked the door, fixed the sheets and blanket, and then fell asleep as I calculated that I only had forty-five minutes until duty.

The next time I opened my eyes, I couldn't tell if I was tired or well-rested. I looked over to the clock to see where I was in my day's timetable and saw a vague impression of red blurry lines on the clock. I squinted my eyes to focus and realized that I didn't even know what the clock would tell me. I laid my head back on the pillow and looked up. The only thing that was clear to me was the white ceiling above my head.

Thoughts slowly snaked through my mind. *Why do I feel pressured to know what is in my schedule? Is there something I need to get done? Why am I sleeping even though it is bright outside?*

The thought pace picked up with each question, and then a command came to mind, "Touch your tongue." I moved my tongue through my mouth. A section felt raw and a bump was protruding from my tongue. As the shot of pain zipped through my nerves my brain waves seemed to jump back in place. *Seizure.* My confusion made sense now. *I must have had a seizure while sleeping.* During a seizure, my jaws would always clamp shut with a bit of my tongue sandwiched in between. From the resulting pain in my mouth, seizure realization usually took place and made sense of my disoriented sensation.

My next thought made my heart sink. *Scout hadn't been jealously fighting for my attention; he was trying to protect me!*

Memory raced back to 2005, just a couple months after we had adopted him in front of a Petsmart. I had laid down for a nap when he rushed into the room, found a way to pull the door handle down, opened the door, and tried to get me out of bed the same way he had just done. It was one of the first times that I slept without my husband nearby, and my dog put himself in caretaker mode, senses awakened. That time I had followed his warning, having just seen a Discovery Channel show two weeks before about different dogs' senses on seizures and cancer. As I had gotten out of the bed, I could tell I was woken just in time to stop it, noticing my disoriented state of mind. Following his warning that same day, I had three flashes, proving my body was in a weak state.

Reflecting on this made me kick myself. I'd been so tired and worried about not getting a bit of rest that I had ignored Scout. Now being able to read that the red lines on the clock read 2:45, I got myself out of the bed trying to ignore the pains clenching my muscles together and cuddled Scout with a big hug on the couch. I calculated the minutes and decided that I must have had the seizure fifteen minutes after I closed my eyes and then took another fifteen minutes to get back with it.

As we laid there on the couch, I thought more about Scout's warning. Many seizures had jolted me in my bed since the first time he had warned me. Why did he warn me this time and not the others? Two thoughts came to my mind. Maybe having been a year since he'd been near one of my seizures, his awareness was renewed through this last one. Yet, David was gone, so perhaps he only went into security mode when David was away. I brushed my raw tongue along the inside of my cheek, rubbing it in that, whatever the reason, we should have gone into the training with Scout that we had seen on that Discovery Channel episode two years earlier.

After the fifteen minutes of giving Scout the loves he deserved, I heard a rustling in baby Bridgett's little crib. She was like clockwork. Just before I entered her room, feeling my strength return, I said a quick prayer of thanks. I couldn't help but notice that I'd had no tonic-clonic seizures during my pregnancy, and just a week after delivery, they started back up. Was this proof that I'd been taken care of from above during the pregnancy as my "thought" had relayed at the football game nine months before? Or was this seizure an urge to get back to the business of finding the solution to my seizure problem? Both.

26

Mother's Care

It was a calm October morning and I was comfortable with the "mommy" routine. I was tired, of course, but I took care of that, resting during Bridgett's naps. I didn't have any stresses riding me. However, that day my brain chose to prove that it had its own plans in mind.

First ... Casual phone conversation with my mom and ... *FLASH!*

One hour later, I was folding Bridgett's laundry and ... *FLASH! Second.*

I tried to take a deep breath and shake the seizure nerves off. *There's nothing to stress about.* These flashes were quick and the effects weren't lingering, thank goodness.

Bridgett soon woke up from her morning nap, and I was able to put myself aside. Apparently, however, I only told myself that.

After feeding my two-month-old Bridgett, I needed to rush to get her bathed and ready for her next nap. I quickly filled the little blue tub for a short bath. She was happy to be in the warm water and her infant body was adorable as she splashed—she hadn't always been a fan of the bath. Her giggle melted my tensions.

All of a sudden, the ease turned into alarm. I felt an "aura" and knew I only had a second left to prepare for the flash. My body seemed to kick into Mom mode, and I immediately readied myself for the effects. One hand immediately turned off the running water spout, the other pulled the plug from Bridgett's plastic bath, and then both hands rested on Bridgett as I tried to take a quick deep breath.

Just as my hands touched Bridgett, my head began to spin ... FLASH! Third.

I suddenly became disoriented, forgetting my daughter's name and barely recognizing my own home. The flash carried itself out as if Bridgett were speaking "the words" to me. I understood the meaning of lightheaded when my head suddenly felt empty, held up only by my deep breaths. The one thing that was clear to me was that I needed to take care of the little girl who was smiling at me, whoever she was. I knew she would be fine, but I still took every care to make sure no harm was possible.

When my strength returned after just a couple of minutes, I wrapped a towel around Bridgett and held her as I slumped down in the nearest chair, taking energy precautions.

After another five minutes, the seizure session was done and I jumped right back into my day's schedule. Simple as that.

The day progressed and soon enough David was putting Bridgett in the car, while I prepped her outing bag. A friend of ours was in town and we were joining him for a house hunt.

"Hey Jordan, come up front. Deanna's going to feed Bridgett her bottle. If you sit up here and look through these house pages then I can explain the areas as you go along," David said.

Before we made it out of the parking lot, David already had Jordan discussing his plans with him. As I started to join the conversation, asking Jordan a question, I silently suffered another flash. It seemed like my body was singing lines from a kids' song that goes: *Second verse, same as the first. But a little bit louder and a little bit worse.* I was on verse four and each was getting a little bit louder and a little bit worse.

"What?" Jordan asked, confused. My question had not been clear and my breathing was already getting loud—an awkward flash reaction of mine.

"Ohhhhh. Ummm. Goshhhh. Uuuhhh." I started to speak very slowly, trying to make it sound like I was thinking of the right word to use. I was certainly trying to find a word. *Any word!*

David caught right on and lightheartedly informed Jordan, "Aw. She's going through a seizure right now. She'll be out of it for a bit and won't remember what we just talked about. She'll snap back though; give her a few minutes." He made Jordan laugh.

I giggled and bobbed my head up and down agreeing with David. I understood that, but I certainly did not catch the next few minutes of their conversation. I silenced myself, knowing some time needed to pass before I could speak clearly.

David's sarcastic, *aww, no big deal* tease had warmed me. *That's what I needed.*

Ten minutes later as we neared a Denny's restaurant for lunch, I was mostly back with the conversation, "So, what happens in *blah-blah-blah* sort of situations?" I forgot most of the sentence the moment it left my mouth.

Jordan turned around and looked back at me with a *where have you been?* question on his face. I was sure that I had just become a freak of nature in his book … And that *was nothin'.*

David piped up, "Like I said, she misses most of a conversation after a seizure."

"Oh, did you guys already talk about that?" Apparently they had.

Hearing David casually explain the routine helped ease my senses, letting me regain control of my body. The remainder of the house hunt actually carried on smoothly. My seizures stopped—it was as if they'd gotten feisty with me covering them up, but now there was nothing to hide, so they mellowed out. That night I slept soundly and was justifiably tired the next day. David was simply used to it, and it didn't cross his mind again.

27

Inform and Move On

It was November 15, 2008, and a year had passed since my last UCLA appointment. It was time to check in. I'd had my MRI done in Las Vegas before driving the four hours to UCLA. The Las Vegas radiologist didn't see any area of concern.

My enthusiasm was soon quieted when the doctors disregarded their reading. "Not true. We need to move forward with our plans. The lesion is still there, and we still believe it is a benign tumor. Your PET scan showed no evidence of cancer, but it is still best to remove." Both David and I agreed. The surgery preparation process was resumed. My confused emotions still rose. I felt nervous and shocked, but I also felt comfortably confident in my UCLA doctors.

After a discussion with the surgery team about timing, we decided to hold surgery off until April, when Bridgett would be seven months old and using the bottle instead of me; the doctors believed six months of nursing was worth the wait. Aside from the nursing reason, I also knew it would be an easier stage for people other than her mommy to take care of her—no crawling, more independence, and easier to entertain. I welcomed the extended preparation.

One week after my update appointment at UCLA, I had told very few people about the decision my doctors had made. I wanted to spare others the awkwardness of thinking how to respond to one saying that they are getting brain surgery. Keeping the news from the thoughts of others, however, made it drag all the more in my own thoughts, building nerves each day.

That following Sunday morning at my church council meeting, the surgery was on my mind as I sat down. Being the president of the children's organization, Primary, I attended this monthly meeting with the leaders of the other men's, women's, and teen's groups in our area.

At the beginning of each meeting, before our opening prayer, we would discuss various needs of our church members. These needs varied in all degrees, one getting ready to take the bar exam, others' pregnancies and newborns, financial issues, and one having gone through knee surgery.

The group's genuine concern for each of these situations seemed to hit me, making me face the fact that brain surgery was a big deal. This realization would hit me a few other times, but this was the first, and in front of fourteen people. The gal sitting next to me, president of the women's group, was about to say the prayer for those we had spoken of when I whispered in her ear to include my health situation.

When I was pregnant with Bridgett, I had been included in these prayers, but this time was so different. It had been exciting then. This time it was daunting and awkward. It felt that with including me in others' prayers the situation was made official. *It's time.*

"Dear Heavenly Father … please bless Sister Brady that she will get the proper care and comfort for her health…" As she included my name, I bit my lip trying to keep the tears from falling. It was official, I was in need.

As soon as she finished saying her closing *In the name of Jesus Christ, amen*, all eyes turned to me. *Geez, did I have to make it so dramatic!? Well, I guess there really isn't a way to justifiably put it lightly.*

Most knew something about my seizures, but others had no idea that there was any issue of concern. You could tell by the looks who knew what. If there were thought bubbles above each of them, then they'd read a variety of, "Oh darn, it's really gonna happen." Or, "Whoa, I thought these were just little shakes she had while sleeping. Don't a lot of people have seizures?" Others' bubbles would have read, "This normal girl, half my age, who laughs a lot, has to get brain surgery?"

Knowing that if I said a word within the next five seconds then I would surely cry, I gave a look to the bishop, our area leader.

Seeing my edge, he spoke up and gave a few details. "Most of you know about Deanna having dealt with seizures and how they were a great deal of concern to her pregnancy. Well, seizures have started back up, and Deanna met with her doctors last week."

Having had a moment to calm my near flood of tears, I spoke calmly, "The doctors have found an area of concern on the left temporal lobe of my brain and want to remove it. This is the area causing the seizures. They said that the effects of my seizures are worse than removal of the mass or lesion would be. We're going to wait until April so that Bridgett is a bit older." I took out the part *oh, and it might be a tumor*. I wasn't ready to say that in front of them, in front of anybody outside of my family.

I was glad we had a meeting agenda so that attention on me could be quickly re-directed. They all said their, "Keep us posted," and "You'll be in our prayers," and we jumped back into leader mode.

As I took my notes and shared different activity ideas, I knew that with the surgery being in motion, this would be one of my last meetings as the children's leader. Another person would be asked to serve in the position. I was glad I could make some emotional preparation for the ending of my two years of service for these 130 children.

The experience from the meeting helped prepare me for the rest of the notifications to take place. "Inform and move on" became a motto. Still, who I told, and when I told was very random. I didn't tell some because of the doting worry they would portray, or I kept it silent if they didn't seem to want to care. I would tell some in a plain and basic update way and others in a "who'd-of-thunk-it" manner. If it seemed like it would be awkward, then I kept it to myself.

After the meeting, my history ed. classroom experience at UNLV came to mind—when I'd told the teacher about my seizures and then happened to have one the next day in class. This gave me a reason to explain it all to others who were bound to eventually find out.

I still wasn't completely comfortable with talking about the information as December quickly rolled in. A war was taking place in my brain. *Seizures are one thing to tell others about, but brain surgery?* I reminded myself that I would be hurt if even a distant friend of mine had brain surgery and didn't let me know. *Christmas card, there we go.*

I decided to put the info on a Christmas card. Others would know without me feeling awkward. It had been a busy and exciting year. I had taught second grade, and I was a new mother of a perfect daughter. I didn't want to lessen that. I decided to make it as upbeat as the rest of the update, leaving it as light-hearted as I could. It came out lighter than the reality of the situation, but at least it was there. My bit read:

Deanna: To say that teaching second grade was a delight for Deanna would be an understatement. She enjoyed all of her time and effort to make it the best for them. What an opportunity. She just so happened to have the best class ever! She is happy to be a full-time mother now and still gets to work with children in Primary. Deanna's brain lesion (cause of seizures) is not holding her back. Since delivery, tests have resumed and her UCLA doctors are ready to remove it, finding more evidence that it is a low-grade tumor (Benign. Phew!). Surgery is planned for 2008 unless it happens to disappear! ☺ It is a common surgery with very little risk.

There we go, "Inform and move on." Simple and to the point, went through my mind as it had the first time I told David and Shawna at the football game. I put the notes and the photo cards in the envelopes and sent them off. *Done*. I was actually able to set it all aside as I prepared for my four-month-old daughter's first Christmas.

As Christmas got closer, more and more mail arrived. The notes of prayer and moral support that arrived meant more to me than I had expected. It was touching to receive the support from all sorts in ways they saw were best. It became a crutch to keep me standing, no matter what happened. It was a surprising eye-opener, making me even more determined to succeed as best as I could. I continued to be surprised by the effects of others' help upon me.

28

Levels of Family

It was late, but I wanted to be sure that I logged information about the busy Saturday in my journal. The journal gave only four lines per day, so I had to pick and choose through my days' happenings. I replayed the exciting events through my mind, deciding what to write.

We had just spent Saturday at the San Diego Zoo with the families of some of my former students, celebrating one's birthday. Then we put a cherry on top, flying back to Vegas just in time to attend a comedy show with David's parents that same night.

Talk about a busy day!

I finished my small print entry and set my journal on the night stand. I hadn't mentioned my stresses. My rush of pleasure was about to be pushed back.

As I turned the lamp off, the room became dark and my thoughts changed. Dread settled itself. Concentration on my dark side often turned on when the lights went off. It was time for me to face the facts. I hadn't mentioned to anyone on the trip what my next month held. I'd put my dark side on the back burner because I wanted to enjoy the good.

But now it was late Saturday night and I couldn't avoid the bad any longer.

As my family and church friends went to bed that night, they were also thinking about my dark side.

David and I would be returning to southern California in two days to meet with my doctors. This visit was a big deal for me. It included tests that would determine the final decision of surgery. *Yea or nay.*

Those friends and family were thinking about this because they were all praying for me. They also had chosen to fast—no water or food as Jesus did in the bible—for me as they held the prayer in their minds and hearts through the day. All those who cared came together for me. Together, they decided to pray for my well-being and ask that everything turn out successfully.

As I thought of everyone's care, I began to say my own prayer. My prayers usually include points of gratitude as well as various requests. Tonight, however, my prayer was focused on one thing: my brain. I began to plea that my brain be healed and that my tumor would miraculously disappear. I begged that my brain would be perfect when I had my MRI two days later. I promised that I had no doubt of God's ability to do this. I let myself repeat, "Please, please, please," over and over. *That would make things so much easier.*

I kept pleading even after I finished my prayer, until I fell asleep.

My brother, Scott, was tossing and turning at this same time in his own bed, hours away from me. He was thinking about me going through the surgery and recuperating. He felt helpless.

"My little sister is five hours away. I will be here, helping others and keeping busy with regular life, while Deanna is suffering without support from her family." Guilt weighed on his chest as the thought kept going through his mind.

He was very quick to be of service to those in need around him and in his church area, "But family is the most important. When it really counts, I'm not there for her." Scott couldn't erase the ache. It was very different than it'd been while we were students together in Virginia—he now had a full time job and was a father of three.

The next morning, as he sat in church, thoughts of my health came to his mind again.

Just a moment later, a man that he didn't recognize walked to the pulpit to speak. On this particular Sunday, the first Sunday of each month, no one was assigned to speak and people were able to go to the pulpit to share their personal testimonies of our gospel and Jesus Christ.

Scott raised his brows as the white-haired man leaned toward the microphone to speak.

Hmm, I don't know him, thought Scott.

The man soon introduced himself as Arden, the father of one of their church members, visiting from Las Vegas. He went on to share his testimony of prayer and shared a story.

Interest was immediately perked in Scott as Arden spoke.

"Today is a special day of prayer for my church family in Las Vegas. Over a hundred of us are fasting and praying today for a young mother in our area. She has a seven-month-old daughter and is about to go through brain surgery." Arden went on about this girl and her situation. He ended by commenting on the union made as they prayed for her and the comfort he had felt through the day.

Scott noted that every detail matched his sister, and he could hardly blink from the surprise he was feeling. The night before this he had been lamenting that his little sister was alone, without her family to help her. His eyes were now opened, *She has a different kind of family all around her. Just as I help people here, others will help her there. She won't be overlooked.*

As soon as the meeting ended, Scott and Rachel hurried over to Arden and his wife Carolyn. Scott stuck out his hand to shake theirs as he introduced himself.

Scott jumped right to the point, "I couldn't help but notice the similarity of our prayers today. I am also fasting and praying today for a young mom in Vegas who is soon going in for brain surgery at UCLA."

Arden was surprised, "Really?"

Carolyn, "Deanna Brady?"

Scott had to hold back his appreciation. He wanted to tackle these people he hadn't ever seen before with a bear hug. "Yes! That's my little sister!"

"Wow. That's a coincidence! Oh yes, I can see the connection now." Arden was commenting on Scott's light blond hair. "We all sure do love Deanna and have been praying so much for her. We are ready to help."

Scotty's heart was melted, "I can't tell you how much it means to me. You guys are an answer to my prayers. Hearing you was an eye opener to me, and I can't thank you enough." He skipped over common courtesy rules and gave these people he'd just met a hug.

My prayers have been answered and she will be okay without me there. His thoughts and heart were reassured.

29

A Sales Pitch Prayer

I could tell that work was silently running through David's mind as we drove to downtown Los Angeles. It was dark outside, and we had just left Erin's house; we were getting closer to my next MRI by the minute. Bridgett's usual backseat sounds were gone. She had stayed behind at my sister's house for a fun sleepover. I was missing her, but knew that it was best to not drag her along. The silence was letting health thoughts reactivate themselves.

A plan of a grand miracle was building in my mind. I thought about my prayer and the possibility of healing and began to imagine reactions. *So, I will go in for the MRI and the radiologist won't find a thing. He or she will call in some others to double check. They won't see any trace of a lesion. They will claim it to be a miracle and that the pregnancy of my child had healed me. The remaining tests will be cancelled and surgery will no longer be considered. Then I will go home and spread the word of miracles.*

The thoughts had been stirred up after hearing about a family friend. During her pregnancy, she had been having odd pains. A tumor was found in her stomach, being compressed by the pregnancy. They could do nothing while the baby was in her uterus.

Quickly after her delivery, the tumor problem was addressed. Doctors were stunned when they could not find any trace of the tumor she'd had just months before. It was decided that the change of hormones during her pregnancy had deteriorated the tumor. *That could happen to me, too! I am more than willing to experience a miracle.*

This led me to thinking about my own pregnancy. My body had certainly been comfortable during the pregnancy. I'd always felt in the back of my mind that I was being taken care of. *My body was definitely different during those nine months. Anything is possible.*

I managed to ignore the fact that I'd had a tonic-clonic seizure just one week after delivery, as well as a number of complex-partial seizures.

The remainder of the drive went by fast; almost too fast for my comfort. Nervousness for my miracle had lingered. I kept thinking, *Maybe a few minutes longer*, as if a few extra seconds would make the mass more likely to disappear.

I had one last moment alone as I changed into a hospital gown for the MRI. I decided to throw in one more plea to God. *Yes, our fast and prayer had been that I'd be okay through everything, but I want more.* I sat on the shiny wood bench and began to pray—to beg. In this one, I started to give all the reasons for me to be healed and things I promised to do if the lesion was erased. I went through the miracle plans I'd thought of in the car. My prayer was sounding like a sales pitch.

Just before I said my *Amen*, I let myself take a deep breath. This pause from my sales pitch seemed to allow another stream to join my river of thoughts. *Oh Deanna, who are you kidding? You, trying to convince God, our Heavenly Father, and His son, Jesus Christ, that your idea is the best? You really think so?* My conscience was talking to me.

An image of my daughter's innocence popped up. I couldn't count the times that I'd had to stop her from doing something that she saw no problem with. I smiled when I thought about trying to explain to my baby why she shouldn't bite wires, stick her fingers in outlets, or roll right over some hard toys to get to her destinations quicker. It was clear that my seven-month-old didn't understand the reasons why I would restrain her from different things. *Aww, she'll eventually understand.*

It didn't take long for me to realize why this thought of Bridgett's innocence came to my mind. I likened myself to Bridgett when it came down to my miracle plan. *Who am I to say what's best?*

An excerpt from the Bible came to mind, "And he said, Abba, Father, all things are possible unto thee; take away this cup from me: nevertheless not what I will, but what thou wilt" (St. Mark 14:36). I agreed with Christ as He prayed to our Father in Heaven. I knew that through God, the miracle I wanted was possible, but I decided that I had even stronger trust in His will.

At that moment, I felt that I knew what the MRI outcome would be.

I made a personal decision right then and there. *I am going to make whatever happens be* right. *I am going to find and carry out all of the good that can possibly come from this experience.* While thinking this, a warm comfort settled me—the comfort one feels when they've done something right; religiously spoken, the comfort of the Holy Spirit. (In my religion, we believe in three separate beings: God, the Eternal Father and His son, Jesus Christ and in the Holy Ghost—a spirit that confirms truths, urges good choices, comforts, etc.) I was ready to walk out of the changing closet and receive my fate.

Nevertheless not what I will, but what Thou wilt.

The comfort I was feeling seemed to help my thoughts move along while lying in the MRI tube. The earplugs numbed the knocking and buzzing sounds that were surrounding me. Some find the whole experience uncomfortable; being belted to a table and stuck in a tube as thunderous sounds encircle you. I, crazily enough, seemed to have talked myself into seeing the forty-five minute MRI session in a brighter light. As I laid there I felt like a fetus with nothing to do and nowhere to go. No pressures. The numbed knocks were a mother's heartbeat and the hum was her voice. The tight tube was actually the warming surrounding of a mother's womb, or perhaps a butterfly's cocoon. *Just close your eyes and let the machine do its job.*

Time quickly passed and the results were even faster. A radiologist was waiting at the door as I left the "womb" room. I knew that the only reason this woman was there at ten p.m. was to write up instant results by my request. *Thoughtful doctors.*

"Thanks for coming over here so late and reading the MRI!"

She could have looked it up on her computer and sent the doctor results from her office the next morning.

I was surprised that the radiologist didn't make any jabs about her being there so late. I could tell this was something she loved doing. "Well, Deanna, everything looks great! I don't mind coming in."

"Everything looks great?" *On whose terms? If my terms, that means it has disappeared.*

"Yes. There are no signs of growth or change. Your team can go forward with the plans."

Oh, doctors' and everyone else's terms. "Great! Thanks." I sounded genuine.

Nevertheless not what I will, but what Thou wilt. I walked back and redressed myself. I admit a lingering feeling of somberness, but a blaze of spiritual strength was growing—warming me from the inside out.

30

WADA You Know

I woke up early with little time to ponder about the night before. The sleep helped me accept reality while it settled in. After a quick wash and rush back to the testing areas, having to skip breakfast, WADA test preparation began. After the gluing of the usual EEG wires, my head was wrapped and I was put into a wheelchair. I felt quite odd as the tech wheeled me through the halls—it was as if I was *weak*. David was left behind.

The oddness of the experience grew as a man entered the room and explained the entry of the catheter into the carotid artery at my groin. I made a silent mental groan of discomfort as he uncovered part of my lower body and shaved around the area of incision. That being the start should have helped me guess that it would be an experience that would make me shiver each time it was mentioned.

The anesthesiologist came in when my groin was "ready" and made a few pokes. To me, a visit to the dentist is nothing in comparison to these pokes. I had to bite my bottom lip and take deep breaths. *Oh Betsy, I'm getting this pain so that I don't feel the other pains?*

The party began as more entered the room, wearing thick vests to block the different rays. My artery became a tunnel as a tube was inserted and pushed through my entire body to the base of my brain. A video camera was attached to the wire, showing my clean tunnel. *This sort of thing only happens on the Discovery Channel!*

I was surprised to feel a wet warmth at the area of incision as the doctors gave me an angiogram on my left side, checking for any blood clots in my brain. I was glad one of the doctors leaning over me had warned me that it would feel like I was wetting my pants. I could barely tell that urine was staying inside my body as the warm fluid streamed through my body. When it reached my brain, attention on the wet-pants sensation was distracted. Firework flashes erupted, blocking my left eye's view of the room. Everything inside my head, on the left side, warmed up, awkwardly feeling like hot cocoa; my skull was the cup.

No blood clots.

Following this angiogram, the WADA began. It would turn out to be a test I was glad would never be repeated. The pain was mostly from the surprise of the whole process; I hadn't asked questions or collected any WADA information.

Lying on my back, one neuropsychiatric doctor had me raise my arms, reaching toward the ceiling. "Don't pay attention to me. Just keep hold of my fingers and squeeze whenever I tell you to."

That's easy enough.

With a few more brief instructions, I was ready for the next step: injection of the "truth serum." Apparently the brain would answer questions without controlled thought. The doctors had joked with David, asking if there were any questions he'd ever wanted to ask me; questions that he could get honest answers to and which I would forget after the test. I instantly felt nervous even though I didn't have a box of buried secrets. I still made a quick mental note of my life making sure there wouldn't be any surprises. *Phew.*

I was still flat on my back, with no view of the "port of entry" for the injections when the next fluid, sodium amytal, went through the long tube. I began to feel its effects the moment it reached my brain. I immediately felt stunned, like I was just coming out of a seizure; far from my normal with-it-ness. I still *felt* in control, however, and couldn't understand why it was called a "truth serum."

My thoughts quickly shifted again as a new sensation followed the injection. I began to experience blindness in my left eye. My view didn't seem to disappear, instead it just turned black. I blinked and then tried to stare with my left eye as if that would help bring eyesight back. No luck.

Those surrounding me didn't seem concerned. The doctor to my left instantly got to work with the test procedure. She asked me to look at her without moving my head, and I felt as if I was stretching vision from my right eye as far to the left as possible.

She began showing me items: watch, pen, sunglasses, scissors ...

The thought, *Random stuff, did she just pick these out of her purse?* went through my mind after the first few items. I felt a little annoyed thinking that she obviously hadn't taken much time to choose items.

I went to name each silly object, but when I began to say "watch" a battle with my tongue arose. *Blind and now dumb.*

All I could say was, "Huhh hhhuooo" each time she showed an item.

The doctor named each piece when it was clear that I couldn't verbalize the answer. It felt so strange to have a locked tongue, yet to still be able to understand her words. I knew what she was saying was correct. I was now Ariel from Disney's *Little Mermaid* after the wicked Ursula had taken her voice.

This same experience carried on as I went through the next step, naming pictures: mouse, shoe ... Being surrounded by neuropsychologists, I had almost expected to see ink blot pictures like I'd seen used in movies. Instead I was apparently a kindergartener and figured I should be saying, *Mouse. Mmm. Shoe. Shhh.*

No matter what they wanted me to say, however, I couldn't.

"Squeeze. Reach higher." The other doctor whose fingers I was holding had continued to have me squeeze and then stretch my arms up more and more. I wished I could see her fingertips; *they have to be purple by now.* My back began to ache as she made me reach higher and higher. *I sure hope this has a purpose!*

The only time I was allowed to let go was when the quiz doctor had moved on from item and picture identification to having me copy movements. She had me tap my fingers to my thumb. That was the second action. The first action had been more embarrassing. The first action included me sticking out my tongue like an upset four-year-old.

I hadn't understood what the doctor was saying about the step in the test, but as soon as she stuck out her tongue I figured she wanted me to do the same. I had put this together mainly based on her facial expression. *Why else would a highly trained neuropsychologist stick out her tongue? I am on foreign land here.* I stuck out my tongue.

The doctor stopped sticking her tongue out at me as soon as I copied. I figured I'd passed the test and pulled my tongue back in. I was surprised when she quickly started to talk. The sound seemed rapid. *Oh shoot, I think she's telling me to keep my tongue out. Dang it, a point lost.* I didn't understand her words, but her haste made me feel like she was correcting me. I quickly stuck my tongue back out.

I had guessed wrong. She started to chuckle. *Now I've surely lost a point.*

I felt like men probably do when they are trying to "read" women.

After the pictures and motions tests, it felt as if they began to put me through interrogation. The fluorescent lab fixture above my head turned into a single swinging bulb.

"What is your name? Where do you live?"

I still couldn't say the answers. I smiled and moaned.

Her third question was multiple choice, "Are you in a school, a hospital, or a cafeteria?"

I repeated the words to myself. *School, _____, or cafeteria.* I couldn't remember the second option, but was immediately sure that it was the answer. *How can I help myself remember that word?*

I recognized that the sodium amytal was wearing off. I could finally speak and I really wanted to say something, anything.

I jumped into action and replied, "I used to teach at a school." That is all I could get out. I let out a quick laugh with a hint of embarrassment, knowing it had nothing to do with their question.

The doctors that surrounded me joined in with a small laugh as they jotted information in their notes. They became witnesses of the "truth serum" effect as I blurted out my personal remark.

I was soon instructed to rest for thirty minutes, letting the "truth serum" completely lose effect. I fell asleep on the metal table within five minutes and had to be woken when it was time for the memory check.

I felt a relief when I was *finally* able to verbally answer their questions. I listed the items and pictures, which I hadn't been able to name before. My memory was strong, my eyesight was back, I could speak, and I had self-control. I was surprised that

I'd felt so imprisoned by the handicaps and was now cherishing my simple abilities.

The procedure was repeated for the other side of my brain. After another similar angiogram, amytal was injected through the same carotid artery corridor, but directed to my right brain lobe. The lobe quickly lost its life as the left side had. I noticed that I didn't go completely blind in my right eye, but my vision was very blurry. I valued even the simple ability to see light.

The process was all similar, but the effects were very different. My tongue spoke fluently. I easily named the items and then the pictures; each was different from the first round. I moved slowly with the actions, but answered questions smoothly. I was no longer on foreign land. I felt smart.

When the recall time arrived, however, my memory had erased.

They asked if they had shown me any items or pictures. "No." *Hmm, why did they only have me do an action and then answer questions?* I only remembered the last two parts of the entire process.

It still shocks me to have absolutely no trace of memory.

When they were done asking their last questions, getting ready to unhook me, I asked my own questions. My arms were now sore and made me think about the squeeze and reach process. I was curious.

I had figured that when they put the left side of my brain to sleep that the right side of my body would be paralyzed and feel like a bag of sand. *The left brain controls the right side of the body, right?* Therefore, I had been quite surprised that during the test I was not only able to squeeze the doctor's fingers with equal strength, but that there was no difference in my strength from normal. I hadn't felt any muscular difference with either side during the tests.

I commented on this and asked how I had kept strength.

I was stumped, however, when she informed me that I had, in fact, lost most of my strength during the tests. My arms had kept weighing down. While under the influence it felt like the doctor was making me reach higher and higher. She informed me that she'd only been telling me to reach so that I would get my arms back up to where they had started.

My mind had been tricking me. I had been sure that my arms were stretching nearly high enough to touch the lights. I shivered at the thought of "phantom limbs," when the brain feels legs or arms, but they don't exist.

After the three hours of testing, a doctor removed the long catheter and gave me one stitch on the artery—it hurt. That was the only thing that could go through my mind. *Pain.* I was rolled to the recovery unit, and David was able to join me as I laid flat for the next two hours.

Pain continued to grow and tears started to flow. I had done so well at hiding health-related emotion from David ever since that first phone call from the hospital before our wedding. I couldn't hold back from this, however. The numbing meds began to wear off. My whole right leg began to cramp up, sending pain from my foot all the way to my neck.

My labor came to mind. I tried to concentrate on my breathing, hoping it would help. It didn't. During my labor I had been able to move; now I couldn't. I couldn't change positions because too much pressure on the artery would easily make the stitch pop. They gave me some Tylenol. It took too long to take effect, in my opinion. I was a stressed-out woman in pain.

Sympathy was written on David's face as he watched me. He felt helpless. His inability to solve the problem made him uncomfortable.

"Will you rub my feet?" I was begging.

He was glad to do it, even though it wasn't a past time of choice for him.

My heart melted as he jumped to my rescue. I quickly realized that the only thing that helped me was his rub. He continuously rubbed for nearly two hours.

Once I was able to walk around the recovery unit, I was given the okay for check-out.

As David slipped my shoes and socks onto my feet, the nurse came over with the check-out list. *And I thought nothing else could possibly make this experience worse.*

This is when I found out that I couldn't lift or move anything over ten pounds for one week—including my daughter! Panic set in: feeding, changing, bathing, playing, bedtime, naps, picking her up, laying her down. *What?*

The nurse expressed the importance of the rule and suggested I get help for the week. *Lesson learned: get information beforehand!*

The surging pain continued with each move I made to the car and then during the forty-five minute drive back to Erin's house. Never before had I ever noticed so many cracks and bumps on the Los Angeles freeway. David had to push on the brakes very gently because the pressure would hurt. He stayed in the right lane; the slow lane. I held the seatbelt away from me so that it wouldn't rub the incision. I couldn't hold back the whining.

The moment we had gotten into the car, David and I had realized that we were in a bind. We had initially planned on making the four-hour drive back to Las Vegas that evening. Before the test, I had assured David that we'd get back that night, so he'd made work appointments for the next day. We now knew that I was in no condition to be sitting in the car and caring for Bridgett in the back seat.

Once again, I called my mom to the rescue. "Mom, I need your help." I made the call to my mom as soon as we returned to my sister's. My mom was two hours away, at Scott's house.

Rachel had given birth to their third child just a week earlier and my mom was there to help them.

My mom knew I was serious when my request involved making her leave Scott's a day early. Putting myself higher on the priority list was very unusual. "Wow, yes. I'll make my way up to Erin's tonight."

I was glad that Erin, David, and my mom were able to talk because I could not put enough thought together to come up with the solution. David soon drove back to Las Vegas alone while Bridgett and I stayed the night at Erin's, waiting for my mom's arrival.

My next seven days were spent with me cringing in pain to any movement, shocked by the effects. Going through this test opened my eyes to how much help I would soon need and how much I didn't know. This is when my surgery preparations began. *I have one month and I'd better get to work.*

31

On Your Mark, Get Set ...

Time before the surgery was running short. I needed to know things and I needed to know them ASAP. Ignorant recuperation from the WADA test had stimulated me in getting ready for the actual surgery. As I did my studies and interviews, I was shocked by how much I needed to arrange.

I was now determined to get as prepared for the surgery as possible, and I had exactly one month to do so.

Where do I start? Find someone.

I emailed my surgeon's assistant, Brooke, "Would any of Dr. Fried's patients be willing to chat, giving me recuperation tips and maybe answering some of my questions?"

The assistant was very quick to reply. "I've spoken with one of Dr. Fried's patients from six months ago whose situation is similar to yours. She'll be glad to speak with you."

I wrote down a bullet point list of questions to ask and made the call. "Hi, I'm Deanna Brady. Brooke from UCLA gave me your information and ..."

The conversation flowed from there. The thirty-three year old woman gave me her story and I took notes. *Surgery on right side, benign tumor behind her eye; bad headaches; be sure not to bend down or lift things; slept most of the day for the first three months; has thirteen-year-old son, he's okay, but having hard time every once in a while, he's very helpful though; she is single and her mom had stayed there all six months since the surgery, couldn't do without; personality seemed to change after surgery, but was just withdrawn with less energy, much better at six months point, even better than before.*

When I hung up the phone I could already feel the comfort that knowledge was giving me. Over the next three days I happened to connect with five other people who had undergone different types of brain surgery. The list included my neighbor and my mom's neighbor, and the rest were friends of friends. This was my first realization that brain surgery is becoming more common.

None had surgery in the same area as I soon would, but I still took every piece of information. When I finished the interviews I typed up a list of twenty-eight personalized final questions and emailed them to my surgeon.

Again, I was quickly helped.

"Hello, Deanna. This is Dr. Fried's nurse, Sandi." I had met Sandi at the past two appointments, so it was nice to have a face with the voice. "We received your questions, and Dr. Fried is letting me get back to you over the phone. Now, let's see …"

When she called I had happened to be sitting at my computer and quickly opened up my questions file. I typed her answers in as she spoke:

Questions for Dr. Fried from Deanna Brady:

1. Is there a diagnosis for my condition? A name for my low-grade tumor? *Not yet.*

2. Will I be awake during the surgery? *No; always depends upon amount and type of tissue taken.*

3. What is the size of my lesion/tumor? *About size of a nickel* (I hadn't realized how small brains were until later

going to a body exhibit on the Las Vegas strip and seeing an actual brain; a nickel wasn't a small size).

4. Are there any signs as to what has created the tumor and when? *Long time ago, variety of possible causes ranging from birth to viruses. Will be decided once it's in their hands.*

5. Will stitches or staples be used to close my incision? *Both, mostly staples.*

6. If staples are used, what will be done about removing them? Do I need to stay in LA until they are removed? *Can be taken out in Vegas, ask my local neurologist to or have him suggest. UCLA will give me a staple remover when I check out. A primary care doctor can do it, or even urgent care.*

7. Do you have any suggestions for soothing itchiness on the scalp? *Itchiness is from nerves growing back; itchiness is a good sign. Keep fingers away from scar. Run warm water over wound after staples removed. Ointments aren't good; can stop "breathing" for wound.*

8. A patient mentioned keeping my head out of the sun, even from a house window. How long? *A few minutes in the sun is fine, but until hair grows back wear hat if outside for a while.*

9. What will my speech be like during my recovery? Problems with verbal memory were mentioned, what will this be like? *Local swelling can interfere with language. Just slower in coming up with words, only half have problem—don't expect. Improves over six weeks, if not by then, therapy may help. Names of objects and people are difficult. Trend is improvement because will no longer be bombarded with seizures.*

10. Do you suggest any sort of speech therapy? *After six weeks if not healed.*

11. You had mentioned that poor memory of lists and loss of my upper right peripheral vision are the permanent deficits likely to take place. What are the temporary cognitive, emotional, and physical deficits that I will most likely experience? How long? *Will have same memory problems or improvement. If choose speech therapy, neurocognitive testing will help direct. Continues to improve over first year. Peripheral vision is usually not noticed. Watch for bumping head on cupboard or ball coming from right. "With it" in six weeks to three months. Could even be three weeks. May be very tired due to blood loss and anesthetics. Emotional relief makes one tired. Fatigue for about six weeks. Rest, rest, rest. Not many cognitive problems—difficulty to read or concentrate is usually from fatigue. Will find improvement in thinking. Because my seizures haven't been daily I will improve at good pace.*

12. What sort of pains will I probably feel following the surgery? Chewing? Impaired vision? Earaches? *Headache likely but not definite. Stay efficient with pain meds and aggressive with them at beginning. Often pain with jaw; depends upon how low incision needs to go, often worse than headache. Two to three weeks until jaw muscle heals. Earache possible for a bit, sometimes swishing noise for a bit until fluid is absorbed, mostly just annoying.*

13. Should I plan on headaches? About how long? *By second or third week, headaches are usually gone. Usually just where incision is. Sometimes certain times of day.*

14. Will my balance be affected during recovery? *No.*

15. I understand that Vicodon is the regular pain killer. I've been prescribed Vicodon before and it made me vomit. Should I chance Vicodon again? *May have been given Vicodon too soon. Will get morphine for first while because not taking anything orally.*

16. When will I be able to drive again? *Six months after surgery is normal. May need to wait full year. California law is from six months after last seizure.*

17. When will I be able ride on a boat? *Fine at the beginning. Six weeks after surgery is recommended for any activities.* (Boating activities were common during our Vegas summers)

18. When will it be safe for me to water ski or do similar sports? *Three months*

19. How long before I can hold/carry/lift my child? (Almost eighteen pounds.) *Six weeks. Can hold on lap while sitting down. Usually increases headaches. Will not harm brain.*

20. When will my body be strong enough to be pregnant? *Wait one year. Possibly six months. Own health is still returning. Depends upon step-by-step recovery.*

21. When can I swim? Pool? Lake? Ocean? *Okay in pool after six weeks. Wait until wound is well healed. Suggest three months for lake, ocean, etc. Possible infection in dirty water. If no seizures within three months, good sign of no more in future.*

22. When can I resume exercising? What types? *Walking good once I get home from hospital. In six weeks I can run on treadmill. No weight lifting, sit-ups, push-ups, etc., until three months.*

23. I've seen that some surgeons shave the entire area of surgery and others only shave along the incision. What is your reason for shaving more than just the line of incision? *Sometimes need to cut more than just the initial incision. Shouldn't stop surgery to re-shave. **Tip: Put all hair in ponytail except for shave area before I go in.* (I didn't. I chose to leave it up to them and they were considerate.)

24. I may get hair extensions in the area shaved. Is this okay? When is the soonest that my head can handle it? *Three months. Good hair growth by six weeks. May be surprised how hair hides area.* (I didn't get extensions. She was right.)

25. Other than yearly MRIs, what other tests should I expect in the future? *Every six months for MRI. If seizure, then an EEG.*

26. What symptoms may arise that I should make you aware of after the surgery? *In early weeks, call if have a seizure, increase headaches/severity or big change in headache character, any vomiting or sensitivity, and light sensitivity.*

27. Are there any sort of dietary needs or changes I should make? *Watch for dehydration! Nourishing soups, fresh veggies, and moderate exercise each day.*

28. How long will I be on medication? *Stay on meds for at least two years.*

32

Checklist

Repeatedly, I read through the Q&A pages and reflected about others' experiences until I had almost created a visual of the worst possible recuperation scenario. I imagined myself with a constant pounding headache and no energy, lying in a bed, and trying to remember who, what, where, when, how, and why.

Prepare for the worst, but make it the best. I'd used that line before in all sorts of situations. I would have never guessed it would be used in thoughts about brain surgery.

Deciding to make it the best it could be, I began my To-Do list for surgery preparation. *What will I need?*
-   *Place to stay in California.*

I got online and found a perfect rental house through vrbo. com. That was quickly solved. *Check.*
-   *Help for Bridgett and me.*

I had lamented over this many times. *Be needy?!* It was hard enough asking someone to fill my role as mother for six weeks, but to add myself to the list as one with the same needs as an infant was not easy.

I set up six weeks' worth of twenty-four-hour assistance after calling my mom, Shawna and David's dad and step-mom.

With having doctors' order to not hold Bridgett for six weeks, I set that as my recuperation goal. *Mom: weeks one and three. Shawna: week two. Bill and Cindy: weeks four and five. Split week six with David's parents and my mom. Check.*

- *Get Bridgett ready.*

Bridgett was naturally a happy girl, but there were a few things to teach before surgery. Two included stopping normal clinginess and creating a routine. For routine, I read the book *Babywise* by Gary Ezzo and Robert Bucknam and followed their orders. As for clinginess, I made a point for Bridgett to be held by others, getting her used to being out of Mommy's arms. I had started to prepare Bridgett months earlier. *Check.*

- *Make a Mommy's Manual.*

In thinking of Bridgett's care I had to, again, act as if my memory was going to be absent. *What sort of questions could possibly come up?* This led me to make Bridgett's personalized "Instruction Manual."

The "manual" started with a brief outline of Bridgett's schedule in fifteen-minute increments. It was of course written similar to how I'd written teaching schedules for substitute teachers. Following this was a detailed description of Bridgett's activities, needs, and even her common behavior routine. While putting the information together, I couldn't help but chuckle about my details and formality. *Hey, I put a lot of effort into getting her onto a routine. It won't help if they don't know how to use it!* I couldn't resist making a thick cardstock cover page with a formal instruction manual title and a picture of Bridgett.

Before I knew it, others began coming to the rescue. I'm certain that their help meant more to me than they realize. Relief raised my shoulders when I was able to put a check on the last two points on my list. They'd weighed on me and I felt awkward just thinking of them. My daily To-Do list didn't only consist of caring for Bridgett, but also cooking and cleaning. These were both things that needed to be done, and I felt sick needing to ask.

- *Meals.*

My sister-in-law, Breann, and I were chatting, and she asked how preparation was going.

She interrupted me as I was telling her about my manual for Bridgett, "Deanna, what are you going to do about food? Has anyone offered to bring a meal? I'm sure Michelle and Laura [other sisters-in-law] would be up for joining me in bringing you guys some meals."

"That's currently something on my list without a check mark, actually. I'm thinking I'll try and make some meals ahead of time and just freeze them. I'll probably be buying some frozen TV dinners, too. David, my mom, and my sister are already going to have to do a lot over the first few weeks, and I just hate having to add that to their list. It's been stressing me out." I'd had a secret worry that I would go hungry. I worried that I would wait until I was on the verge of starvation before asking anyone to make me a meal.

Breann continued, "Seriously, don't worry about it. I'm going to make some calls and I'll get back to you."

"Really? Are you sure? That's just so hard to ask for!"

"Think of it this way. We are already making dinners for our own little families. It's just adding a few extra cups of rice or noodles. Not a big deal." Breann actually seemed excited to put it together.

Our conversation ended a few minutes later. I was already feeling the relief of three dinners being taken care of.

The next day, Breann called to update me. "Put a check on your list regarding meals. I made a few calls and some have even called me. Your meal calendar is full. There are two weeks' worth of dinners when you get back and then every-other-day lunches in that time, too." She read through the list of names.

I didn't know what to say. I was shocked that so many were willing to come to the rescue. "Are you serious?! I can't believe it. Amazing! Thank you, thank you, thank you." *Check.*

- *Clean.*

I knew David could handle laundry and that my mom and Shawna were willing to pick up, but I knew I wasn't going to be able to relax if they were doing all of the work. *Each of you is already doing so much!* I was afraid to burn them all out and then burn myself out with the worry.

Another came to my rescue. She was my neighbor friend who'd also been through brain surgery, Elizabeth. I have since dubbed her as an angel because I am not the only one she has come to the rescue for. "Deanna, I've been through all of it. I know there is a lot that you won't be able to do and shouldn't do. I am going to help." She didn't give me the option to turn her down.

Elizabeth went through a checklist of everyday home responsibilities. It felt nice to be able to tell her that meals were taken care of.

When she got to house care and laundry, she noticed a moment of delay in my response as I thought of how to answer that. *Truth? David and my "nurses" are physically able to help in those areas, but it is making me sick to think of putting even more on their shoulders.* I didn't want to say the truth, but I think she read my mind. *After all, she is an angel.*

"David and those attending to you and Bridgett will already have their hands full. If there isn't anyone else already taking care of the cleaning and laundry, will you let me take care of that?" She honestly asked as if I would be doing her a favor! "I have a couple of friends looking for a job and I would like to take care of that. Would you be okay with them coming for about three months? I'll cover it. That should help a little, we can see from there."

I couldn't hold back the tears. *Check.*

Having made my list and then been able to put a check next to each bullet point, I was able to calmly go to California for my surgery.

33

The Five-Star Butcher Shop

It was April 15, 2008, and my cell phone alarm vibrated at 4:00 am. I was already awake, having caught very little shut-eye through the night.

When I turned the alarm off, I hastily got out of bed and acted as if I were following a practiced emergency routine; quick, but calm. No thoughts of the scary surgery went through my mind, only the steps I needed to follow so that I could be ready in time. I told myself that I wanted to concentrate on getting everything in order so that I could check in with ease. Perhaps, however, I was trying to avoid any last chances to panic myself about the surgery. Distraction can be helpful at times.

I hurried to the bathroom for a quick shower, the last I'd be able to effortlessly enjoy for the next six months. I was not thinking about that, however. Instead, I was only concentrating on my next steps: dry hair using no chemicals, double check medical files and suitcase, triple check that Bridgett's things are in order, take pills with very little water, and leave by 4:30 a.m.

We arrived at the check-in desk at 5:00 a.m. *Right on schedule.* What we saw when we walked into the office surprised both David and me. We'd expected very little noise in the room, and it was quiet when we entered, but clearly not for the reason we'd figured. We both thought the office would be quiet because of a small number of people. It was 5:00 a.m. However, nearly every seat was taken in the large office. We lost count after we got to thirty. *And this is just the first round of patients for the day.*

I walked to the registration desk. The host handed me a card with a number and then pointed for me to take a seat. It reminded me of jury duty check-in with everybody taking their numbers and then sitting down to read, hold quiet simple conversation, or simply stare at anything until their number was called; no one excited to be there, but fulfilling their duty. *You do what ya gotta do.*

A variety of emotions painted the faces of the patients as I studied their looks. I had expected more fear to be evident, but it was only visible on a few. Most sitting in the room seemed bored. The early hour could have spurred that effect, but I was still surprised. Most were probably like me at the moment, purposefully avoiding pre-surgery fret.

When we sat down amongst the others, I looked at my number ticket and smiled. *I am now one of the branded cattle, waiting to face the butcher.* I quickly erased that thought, leaving it on its note of humor. The fact that my "butcher" was highly recommended and that UCLA rankings were soaring helped me to smile versus shiver.

David pulled out his cell phone and started what he would end up doing for most of the following eight hours: mastering cell phone games.

I bit my lip. *What about David?* I'd put so many things in order for Bridgett, but I hadn't thought of David, sitting there, alone, for at least six hours.

Looking around, I noticed that some had two others sitting with them. The two visitors would be there for each other while the patient was under the scalpel. *Dang it.*

David later insisted that he was fine being alone because he was confident with the surgeon, but I'm sure it certainly would have made time move faster with someone there to talk to.

"Numbers 523 through 530, please come to this area." The cattle were being prodded into groups of seven.

As we began to move deep into the seemingly secret underground tunnels of the hospital, the numbers grew smaller. Patients were being quietly slipped away as we passed random unmarked doors. The thought almost made me shiver. I looked down at my medical folder to find something to distract me, and a moment later we stopped in front of our unmarked door. I was one of the last three, David still at my side.

After just one step into the mystery room, a cheery nurse walked up to me and handed me my blue and white hospital gown and disposable booties as if it were an honor for her to do so. With her welcoming smile, I almost expected a little baggie of homemade cookies to be on top of the folded gown. This room was her own little bed and breakfast, minus the breakfast.

When I laid down on the gurney, decked out in my hospital attire, I noticed that I was much younger than the two patients on either side of me. In fact, I had been younger than most of the cattle in the waiting room.

Is it better to do when you are older? A chart of compare and contrast points formed in my thoughts. After laying it all out in my mind, I made a final decision. *It's bittersweet, no matter the age: a bummer that it needs to be done, but a blessing that it can be.*

The next thought to string through my mind was a comparison of the three of us, lying on the gurneys in our unisex gowns. The lady to my left, probably in her fifties, was clearly nervous. Her four surrounding family members were making efforts to comfort her like a newborn baby. To my right was a man in his forties almost twiddling his thumbs as his wife mentioned a conversation she'd had the day before, obviously trying to pass the time by. Then there was David and me. We both bobbed our heads and silently studied the room; noticing the same things, but staying quiet and ready.

It was an awkward moment when the anesthesiologist walked in and, after asking what area would be shaved, pulled out an eyeliner-like pencil.

"We all know the area of surgery, of course, but we still take all precautions." He raised his hand to the left region of my head.

Aw, yes, good idea. That would certainly be unfortunate to wake up and find that I've had surgery on the wrong side of my head.

I double checked the information for myself. *Left side, correct? Yes, undoubtedly the left side.*

Then he drew a thick blue "X" on my head and hair. *"X" marks the spot.* I was curious what treasure they would soon find under that "X."

Before the anesthesiologist walked away, he commended me for choosing to do the surgery. That felt good.

He explained, "Everything that we continue to learn about seizures shows all the more reason for brain surgery. Your brain gets used to seizures. With each year of 'practice,' the brain gets better and better with seizures." He was certainly being sarcastic as he described the brain getting better at creating seizures. "We also continue to see that the more seizures one has, the sooner irreversible amnesia comes in."

I certainly agreed with him regarding his first point. I'd seen that! My brain was an example of seizure mastery, comparing the differences over my eleven-year seizure period. Practice had certainly helped my brain to make the seizures more and more "grand."

The last point was new to me. *Amnesia?* I noticed David cringe when the doctor mentioned that. *Oh, mercy.*

As soon as that doctor left, the bed and breakfast nurse escorted David out. It was my turn to enter the butcher's shop.

As they pushed the gurney along, I was surprised with my emotions. I felt at ease. I figured my comfort was stemmed from a correlation of my studies, confidence in my doctor and the crew, and the many prayers by me and others.

I was surprised with how similar the surgery room looked to a restaurant kitchen. Silver! I was lying flat on my back, but most everything I noticed was stainless steel. That gave me one last smile before they placed a mask over my mouth. My eyes darted around the room, taking in every detail that I could before the anesthetic gas tank was turned on. I wanted to see the doctors, nurses, and, nervously, the supplies before I lost my senses.

The last thing I heard before my sense shutoff was, "We are giving you this pain killer so that you don't have to feel us giving you the main anesthesic for the surgery."

A pain killer for a pain killer? I've been there before. I thought about the WADA pain killers. *Heavens to Betsy.* They had me count down from ten. I made it to eight and fell asleep, ready for the surgery.

David was led from the underground hallways up to an area of natural light. The sun had risen, and all around him life was carrying on like normal … *and my wife is getting brain surgery*. He later informed me that he left that thought, surprised he wasn't worried, and evenly looked at the guide who was handing him a pager just like one he'd gotten a few nights before when we'd waited for a table at Olive Garden.

"We'll page you when we have different updates through the surgery and then afterwards when it's okay for you to see Deanna. When you feel it, just take it to the information desk and they'll give you the information." Then the person turned and walked back underground.

"Thanks." David got a quick wave and then sat down and pulled out his cell phone again. He would end up reaching the highest level in the game by the time he felt the pager's third buzz. With each buzz he walked to the desk.

First buzz: Surgery had begun. He looked at his watch and saw that one hour had already passed. *Five more hours to go.*

Second buzz: The surgery would be longer than six hours. Four hours had passed, and he was slightly uncomfortable as he left the information desk this time. He'd just been informed that the doctors needed to cut deeper than initially planned, removing the entire hippocampus area in order to avoid the possibility of re-growth. (I didn't personally understand the reasoning until later.) David felt overall at ease about this change. *The doctors know her brain.* He'd been referring to the mapping done through the WADA test.

Third buzz: Surgery completed successfully and he would soon be able to visit me. I was still asleep, but the drug was wearing off. He gave a small nod of his head as soon as he received the information and gave my mom a call with the update.

Eight hours had passed before David saw Dr. Fried walking up to him, still in his scrubs. The doctor had been by my side since the moment I was put under, and David could see that. He looked tired, yet satisfied and calm. *Good.* David was glad to get the report straight from the doctor himself, although the only point sticking with David was the fact that I was okay.

34

A Hoped Visit

Something had secretly excited me since surgery had first been mentioned by the doctors. It is a surgery possibility that some fear, but I welcomed. It was a threatening desire. I wanted a swift taste of death.

I thought of the many stories of people getting a quick visit with death who then see a loved one who has already passed away. Four years, six months, and four days before my surgery, my dad had passed away. I wanted to see my dad. I thought of him being without any of his health weaknesses, nothing like he was the night he died.

Before my surgery, I had seen interviews and read books about different people's near-death experiences. I fearlessly hoped to have my own experience of it so that I could re-taste my dad's love. I imagined that I would wake up after one of my many naps in the hospital, being disoriented, and then see him come over to me with a sense of control over the whole situation, making sure everything was just right. Just the way he always had. He would hold my hand, and this time I would feel his warmth.

I yearned to see him near me while I lay in the hospital bed. Just before my surgery, I had thought much about this man who had been with my family, doing the best he could, every step of the way until October 11, 2003, just two hours after I had kissed him goodnight and left to go sleep in my mother-in-law's extra bedroom.

John David McKeon, my dad, had been part of the baby boom. His life began at the same time as the life of WWII was ending, on April 25, 1945. This was the same day that Russia and America shook hands as comrades, and just five days before the life of Adolf Hitler ended. His dad, my grandpa, had been amongst this all as a soldier.

My dad grew to be a man strong with character and love, opening the hearts of many along his path. As a child, I never thought it possible for the life of my dad to end at the young age of fifty-eight. At his funeral, I was touched when I walked into the chapel, following his coffin, to see over three hundred people there to mourn the loss. In the eulogy, his younger brother talked about the rheumatic fever that had infected him as a young baby. This ended up opening him to many other ailments in his life. He went on to say that my dad's ambition, however, was never slowed down.

Being the youngest of eight children, I saw my dad's health become a roller coaster when he came down with type II diabetes. I saw when his body became greatly affected by his efforts to go and do until he would get wiped out. He would only slow down enough to regain a bit of energy before he would jump right back into his busy life. High blood-sugar levels from the diabetes then damaged the blood vessels and nerves in my dad's legs and hands; this lead to neuropathy. Numbness, cramping, loss of reflexes, weakness, clumsiness, loss of balance, and dizziness were some of the symptoms my dad suffered daily. It was a form of painful anguish each day and night.

As he endured the spreading neuropathy, his legs always felt on fire. I remember him describing how he would often awake from nightmares with a jolt and cry, expecting to see dirty alley cats clawing at his legs. As the nerves flamed, his feet were unable to recognize different pains. His senses were numbed, and his feet would easily blister. My mom would frequently monitor him to check for infections. I remember when my brother Jason, my mom, and I would take turns cleaning and bandaging the nickel-sized holes. He eventually had to have two toes amputated because his feet were unable to heal.

The poor senses had affected my dad's balance, and he began to easily fall more and more. Doctors told him to stay put, but my dad desired independence, like simply to walk. At this point of my dad's health, all of us eight children had left home and were in the next phases of life. Tripping and falling became very frequent if my mom was ever out of his sight. His falls led to his shoulder surgery, which led to his death. It was hard to hear that after his years of fighting through the torture of the neuropathy, a simple popped surgery stitch took his life.

Three hours before my dad's death, I had no idea that I would soon be receiving his last hug. Earlier that day, David and I had been invited by his mom, who lived ten minutes from my parents, to visit for the weekend and see the play, *Fiddler on the Roof*. Our schedule was clear enough for us to join them, so we made a last minute two-hour drive to the red hills of St. George, Utah. My mom and grandma joined us for the play, but my dad was in no condition to leave the house. I was bummed because my sisters and I had a tie to our dad with this play. At our weddings, our dad had danced with each of us to the song, "Sunrise, Sunset" before walking us over to dance with the new husband.

Just a few hours after the play, I received a call from my mom and rushed to the hospital only to see my dad's body. His life had left while David and I were trying to find a way into the emergency room and past the check-in receptionist.

With our first try, the receptionist told us she was busy and to sit and wait until she had a minute. I knew deep down that time was running short— David and I ran to the doors that the ambulance had taken him to, trying to get them open. Unable to immediately do that, we rushed back to the waiting room, ready to beg again. Sweat was beading down my neck as we rushed with anxiety.

As we neared the receptionist's desk again, I was determined to get into the ER. All I could think about was when I had been in the emergency room after my first tonic-clonic seizure. My dad had been great at explaining why it was in everybody's best interest to have the family at my side. I was determined to do it as he had ten months earlier.

Anger soon boiled under my skin. As soon as we made it back to the desk, the same receptionist gave me a look of annoyance, "We've spent the last while searching for you. I paged you! They want you in the ER." She acted as if I was late and being a hassle.

Did I not just beg you to check? I wanted to grab her arms and while shaking her, remind her that I had been in front of her three minutes earlier and she had refused to give me attention. I bit my lip and turned toward the double doors. She made a slow push at the button on her desk and the ER doors spread open.

As the doors opened, I noticed that the hall was full of a team of nurses and doctors exiting what seemed to be a closet. Looks of remorse stained their faces. Everything in my body seemed to sink when I then saw my mom standing at the closet door. She looked stiff, and I could tell she'd been standing in the same spot since their arrival. I didn't have to ask any questions.

I hurried my arms around my mom and squeezed firmly, as if I were trying to squeeze any pain out of her. She broke down, having tried to hold back emotion since she'd called 9-1-1. Her shoulders shook back and forth as she sobbed, more sobbing than I'd ever witnessed before. My hug now seemed to be the only thing holding her up. She seemed disoriented and was clearly in a state of shock. My dad had been so close to dying so many times that one might think it to be easier. Nothing, however, can prepare for the actual loss.

I thanked God that I had happened to be in town. I didn't want to imagine my mom having to experience the trauma alone.

David stood there, not knowing what to do and wishing he could say, "Don't worry, everything is going to be all right." He couldn't bring himself to say that though. A tear rolled from his eye. It was the first teardrop I'd ever seen from him.

After a couple of minutes passed on the clock, time having otherwise seemed to stop, my mom stepped aside and let me go to my dad.

I cringed. The nurses had covered his body up to his shoulders, but I could still see a line of crusted blood coming from his mouth and noticed that more blood had been sloppily wiped from his neck and chest. The towel under his neck was red.

His eyes were still open. *Why hadn't the nurses closed them?*

Using my thumbs, I slowly and tenderly closed his eyes. While doing this, I actually felt grateful that I, a member of his family, was the one to do it. It was a loving goodbye and show of respect. This is when I held his hand and gave his cold cheek a gentle kiss. His hand had still been warm, but was quickly getting colder and firmer. I said a prayer of thanks for even the little time that he had been in my life and wondered if he were watching from above.

One of the nurses came in to give her regards and explained what had just happened. She had me touch his stomach, and I realized it had expanded. I could feel the firmness. She then informed me that it was full of blood. The nurse went on to say that the blood had gotten to his brain, causing him to feel disoriented and act oddly. She noticed the bloody towels and then explained that blood had rushed from his mouth when they tried to revive him. She finished her explanation by informing us of the popped interior stitch.

The past week, my mom had called the surgeon's office many times, concerned with some of my dad's behavior. The doctor told her it was reaction to the pain medication— assured her that he was fine. Apparently, the doctor had been wrong. At the time, none of us knew to screen and shop for the right doctor.

35

All Is Well

As I looked at my dad, I thought back on my past few hours. While watching the play, *Fiddler on the Roof*, I wouldn't have guessed my night would end as it was. I had been thinking about our dance, not about his death.

We had given my mom and grandma a ride to the play, and when we dropped them off at their house, I had followed them inside to say a quick goodnight to my dad. It was late and I guessed he would be asleep. His shoulder surgery had been just the week before. It was taking a toll on his energy.

As we walked to the door, my mom, a rock for our family, stopped me and gave me a little update, "Let me warn you, Dee. Dad is pretty out of it. He may not recognize you. I've called the surgeon about this a couple times, but he said it is from the high dosage of pain medication he has him on. He's been having hallucinations; kind of seeing things and, a few times, has held conversation with people not even in the room. The doctor said it is fine, but I just wanted to let you know so that you don't get shocked."

I pulled my head back and wrinkled my forehead in surprise, "Really? What kind of medication do they have him on this time?" Doctors had put my dad on a variety of pain medications for his neuropathy, but none had seemed to have this effect. "All right, thanks for the heads up. I'll see if he's even awake," I said, tip-toeing toward his bedroom.

I instantly recognized my mom's warning as I peeked through the door. A mumbling moan was coming from my dad's mouth. As I leaned in, the door opened, making a noisy *creak*. My dad jolted awake and made a loud, "Huuh?!"

I walked closer, "Hi, Dad, its Deanna. How are you?"

He slowly reached for my hand like an old man and held it tightly. "Ohhhhh," he said as he let out a breath of relief. Then he narrowed his eyes, looking closely at my face and tilted his head. With a tone of concern he asked, "Deanna, why is there tape all over your face?" He let go of my hand and reached toward my face with pinched fingers, ready to pick at something.

"Umm, what?" I asked. I wasn't sure if I should play along, acting as if he was making sense.

"You have strips of clear tape all over your face like a mummy," he said. I rubbed my face, trying to think of what could have made him think that.

It was interesting to see his next reaction. He seemed to quickly jump back to his real self. A glaze over his eyes disappeared, and he became aware of his surroundings. He shook his head with more frustration than embarrassment, "Ohhh, I'm sorry. I don't know why I was seeing that. I'm kind of going in and out of it. Never mind all of that."

Hearing this made me relax a bit more. I bent down to give him a kiss and he wrapped his arms around me with a big hug, making me sit down on the bed. He seemed to choke back on his voice as he said, "I love you so much. Always remember that." He let go of me and held me back a little. He looked at me and brushed my bangs from my face. I smiled, thinking about his many reminders to move my bangs to the side, keeping my "welcoming" face visible. Then, he locked eyes with me and held my arms tightly, seemingly wanting to press his thoughts into my mind. "Deanna, always remember that you are beautiful and that you are priceless."

The power in his voice stunned me. "Okay, Dad. I love you, too! And—thanks," I said with a giggle, trying to lighten the pressure his tone made. I reached down to give another hug, being gentle around his bandaged shoulder.

As I started to move back from our long hug, his head shifted to my side, looking at something behind me. "Is that Erin?" he asked. His eyes were pinched as he stared toward the closet only four feet behind me, thinking he was seeing my sister.

I looked back, trying to figure out what made him think that. "Nope. She's at home in California. Do you want me to call her though?" I tried to answer with casualness; as if there was nothing odd about him being sure my sister was standing right there.

He seemed confused with my statement, but brushed it off as he changed the subject, "Well, did you have a good night? Where's David?"

I welcomed this change and quickly replied while standing back up, "We had fun at the play tonight. I thought about you, of course. David's mom drove with us, so David is waiting in the car with her. We've officially reserved you guys tomorrow. David's mom got us up here with the play invite and some extra tickets. I was glad we brought Mom and Grandma home because I got an excuse to come and say goodnight to you!"

"We get you for tomorrow? What are your plans?" His eyes seemed to light up at the thought.

"We will be at your beck and call!" I said with a beaming smile. I took a moment to think about the next question. I knew that the sort of answer he would want to hear from the "plans" question would include a lot of activity, but it was obvious that he wasn't up for it. Not wanting him to appear as the reason for low action, I tried to take blame for the stay inside plans. "It's supposed to be pretty cold tomorrow. We plan on staying indoors and keeping it mellow. Work's been crazy for David and he's pretty welcoming of the idea to chill out here."

My dad's eyelids were beginning to get heavier as I spoke. I could tell sleepiness was putting more fog through his mind. I bent down to give him a kiss and he whispered, "I love you and David. Be sure to come tomorrow."

After we said our goodnights, he instantly closed his eyes. As I shut his bedroom door I could hear that his breathing was already deep. My mom was standing near the door and walked outside with me. Her voice had a nervous tone as she asked, "So, what do you think?"

I figured she had heard most of the conversation. "It was weird seeing him jump in and out of awareness. He would make sense for one moment, and then the next sentence would be bizarre. When he was with it, though, he was totally there."

Her nodding head told me without words, "I know exactly what you mean."

We walked the remaining steps to the car quietly. Before I opened the car door, I gave her a hug and whispered, "Hey Mom, if you need anything at any time, call us at any hour. David has his cell phone." I opened the car door, grabbed a pen and then pulled a receipt from my pocket. I began to write some numbers on the backside of the receipt, "Here's the phone number to David's mom's house if you can't get us through his cell phone. She and Don won't care what hour you call." I was grateful that I could mean that about his mom Virginia and his stepdad not caring what the hour was.

She said her "yes" with a slow nod of her head as I got in the car and pulled my seatbelt on. She said her quick goodbyes to

David and his mom before she closed my door and walked back to the house. Her walk was slow, as if she was weighed down from the stress.

I didn't say a word as we drove the ten minutes back to Virginia's house. Both she and David seemed to recognize my feelings and didn't pry. I immediately walked to the guestroom and got ready for bed. David followed me in. I could hear tenderness in his voice as he asked, "How did it go?"

Realization of my dad's condition had settled during the drive back. "He's not doing too great. Mom's thinking of taking him back to the hospital again, even though the doctor said it isn't necessary. I told her to call at anytime if she needs anything." I continued telling him about the conversation.

He looked at the clock on the nightstand next to the bed, "Try to get some rest. I'm going to be upstairs talking with my mom for a little bit. I'll keep my phone with me in case she calls."

After lying in the bed for ten minutes, I couldn't settle myself. I wanted to talk to somebody who could feel my same pain. I wanted to openly express the fear racing through my thoughts and heart. I thought to call Erin—this sort of call was part of her role as the oldest. I looked back at the clock, "12:02 a.m." I figured she was still awake and wouldn't mind the call even if she were asleep. However, I let my etiquette lessons keep me from making the late call.

The only solution I could think of was to pray. I had done this many times before with a similar ache for comfort. I got out of the bed and walked into a different room, not wanting to be walked in on. As I got down on my knees, I thought about the fact that 90% of those pleading prayers had been related to my dad's health. This wasn't new.

I took a deep breath, trying to clear my thoughts, and tears immediately broke through. I felt like a kindergartner as I pulled my sleeve over my hand and wiped at my nose, but I didn't care about that. Taking another deep breath, I bowed my head, folded my arms, and began to beg.

A variety of begging thoughts regarding my dad's well-being raced through my prayer. I began to tell what I had just experienced with my dad, the nervousness I felt from my mom, and the fear that was running through my nerves. I was still like a five-year-old, babbling on and on. Tears were now rushing down my face, and my breath became choppy as I would breathe in and out.

As soon as my heart felt like it couldn't get any more out, I went silent in my prayer. I felt as if I was saying, "Okay, your turn," asking for a response from God.

My own will stepped up and I began to remind myself that we had been through this many times. On my fifteenth birthday, the doctors had the family come in to say our goodbyes to my dad, but a few hours later his health snapped back. That was just one example. I insisted to myself, *This is sure to be the same.*

My crying had mellowed into small sniffles, and my breathing was becoming smooth as I began to end my prayer. Before I said my "Amen," my thoughts became alert. I had expected to be bitter, but I instead felt a comfort; it was a comfort—again, I believe to be the Holy Spirit—saying that perhaps my family should let my dad go. I began to see his suffering in a different way. As if, perhaps the only reason he had hung on for so long was because none of us would let him go. Doctors readily admitted that his determination was the only thing that kept him coming back. His health condition had held him back from his true self, from living a "go and do" life, and would only continue to get worse.

My beliefs of life after death began to bring a comfort to me in a way I couldn't deny. I bowed my head down again and continued to pray. My thoughts were different. I began to pour out specific thanks for my dad regarding memories, qualities, and lessons that involved him. This time, just before I ended my prayer, I prayed that the best thing be done by God's standards and expressed gratitude that my family could handle it together.

I walked back to the bed. Before I fell asleep I had a mix of feelings. I hoped that what I had felt about my dad's health wasn't the case, but I was also confident that the right thing would happen and I could handle it even if it wouldn't be easy.

An hour later I found out it wouldn't be easy, but the comfort I'd had from that prayer returned and lingered as I called each of my siblings from the hospital ER to tell them of our dad's passing.

Going into my surgery, four and a half years after my dad's death, I still felt the prayer's comfort and imagined my dad being busy and happy in Heaven. *Sheesh, he's probably too busy enjoying Heaven to even come and visit!*

Hours later, after the surgery, I opened my eyes and saw David, my mom, and Erin—the feeling was bittersweet. Having been able to quickly recognize them had proven that the surgery went well and that I was fine. It also made me realize, however, that I wasn't weak enough to have a near-death experience. I wouldn't get a glance at my dad. I welcomed even a hallucination to make me think I could see him. I rolled my eyes when I noticed that I was even alert enough to analyze all of it. *Still good ol' me.* Bittersweet for the moment, I moved on as I saw the smiles on their faces. I sent a quick prayer of gratitude that I had my memory bank and that my dad was in there. I still knew exactly how he would have acted through the surgery process, and just the thought warmed me. *All is well.*

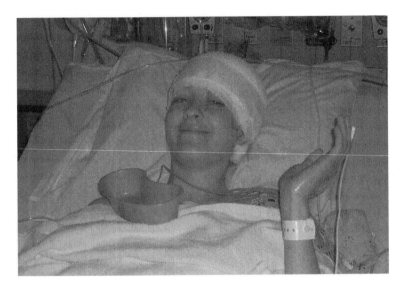

36

Earning Points

I woke up and immediately looked at the mini whiteboard in front of me with the date, "Thursday, 04/17/08," written along the bottom. Above it was the nurse's name with a smiley face drawn next to it. I wasn't sure if, in my thoughts, I was pronouncing the name correctly, but I didn't care at the moment; I just wanted to know the date and the time. I noticed the darkness against the windows and tried to figure out if Thursday were just beginning or almost past. It had been two days since my eight-hour surgery.

My flickering thoughts began to battle my next actions, turning into two voices: physical versus emotional.

My weak physical side pouted: *Who cares what time it is, just go to sleep. I'm tired.*

The emotional side seemed ready to fight: *Stay alert and figure out what time it is so that we can know how much closer we are to leaving. We are close to Friday, but how close?*

The check-out date had been set for Friday, and I was anxious for its arrival. The battle of my thoughts alone was beginning to wear me out when a nurse entered the room. Her composition matched the smiley face next to the name. It brought a breath of comfort to my stressful mind.

While I watched, the nurse measured my blood pressure. My eyes slowly opened and closed as if they were full of a heavy lead. Once the finishing beep sounded, she handed me a mini plastic cup full of a variety of medications in one hand and in the other hand, a plastic cup full of cold water. *Oh noooo.* Every few hours the nurses would bring in cups of medications, and each time I had to fight the little sandpaper pills down. Even water was difficult for me to swallow. A mental image of my throat being red ground beef was painted by the raw pain I would feel every time I swallowed. I hadn't expected the surgical throat tube for air and wires to leave so much pain.

When I finished the dramatic gulp, she removed the icy cup from my hand and with a smile said, "It is time to take your gauze cap off. This means you are one step closer to going home!" As she said this, my emotional side felt lifted.

Mixed feelings rose as I thought about seeing what was under this pillow of gauze, but I reminded myself that the removal simply meant I was getting better. With that thought, I was ready to hand her the scissors myself.

The thick numbness of my head put a distance between my sense of touch and the removal of the gauze. The sense of sound, however, was strong and seemed to be making up for my poor touch senses. I thought that hearing the scissors tear through the taped cast would gross me out, but as the nurse worked in slow motion it gave me a little twitch of humor inside.

As the scissors ground through the thick gauze, it sounded as if she were preparing for a grand presentation. I thought about the TV show, *Extreme Makeover*, where people are transformed through plastic surgery, dental cosmetics, etc. I felt as if I were one of their works of art, anxious to see my new "beauty" from plastic surgery. I got a kick out of thinking what reaction I would give if I thought they were beautifying me, only to then look in the mirror after the gauze is removed and see a new Frankenstein with staples on the side of the head. That would be an attention grabber for viewers!

By the time the two-inch-thick gauze cast was removed, I was too tired to carry out the grand entrance with a look in the mirror. Before the nurse even finished, my eyes had already closed; just thinking about the humor had sucked my energy. As I fell back asleep, I didn't notice the wide area of smooth baldness on the left of my head or the bun of blonde and bloody hair on the right side of my head.

When my sense of sound alerted me next, my eyes fluttered open and my thoughts immediately began to beg, *No medication, no medication, no medication*. This was stopped when I recognized the person bending next to me, quietly setting down a card, obviously trying not to wake me. My brain jumped into action, recalling random details of this person in my thoughts: Angie, one of my very first friends, grew up on same street, July birthday, had lunch last time she was in Vegas, caring, didn't expect her to come, so thoughtful.

I surprised her with my quiet, "Hi, Angie." When I said her name, I ran a double check through my mind to make sure I was right.

She seemed a little nervous about what she should say, "Oh my gosh, I'm sorry, I didn't mean to wake you!" I could read her embarrassment, thinking she had thrown my recovery off.

I chuckled, "No! How fun to see you. Sorry I'm not quite dressed for visitors though. I'm probably quite a sight." I didn't realize how true this was until the next time I awoke.

"No, you look good. It's not too bad," she said trying to make me feel more presentable. I had to make another little chuckle at her efforts. "Dee, I totally didn't mean to wake you up. I just wanted to bring you a little card while on my way home from work. David told me where your room was."

Home from work? That means it's the evening now! Yeah! She recognized that I could barely keep my eyes open and quickly slipped away after the adieus.

When she left, I opened the card and smiled at the bulldog picture on the front, reminding me of their dog from when we were in first grade. Setting the card on my side table, already decorated with flowers from David, I gave myself a "point" for another successful use of my memory. I closed my eyes faster than I had opened them and quickly fell back to sleep without another thought.

37

Brain Surgery Patient #24601

The next time I woke up was once again due to my feelings. My body couldn't sleep through this feeling. *I need to go to the bathroom.* I called the nurse in to release me from the bed's constraints and hurried in my wobbly manner to the restroom at the other corner of the room. I was already, thankfully, no longer in need of the bedpan or the extremely uncomfortable urine catheter.

After the bathroom relief, I shuffled over to the sink to wash my hands and a reflection in the mirror caught my attention. My stomach dropped when I saw that the nasty reflection was me. I was sure that if any children were to see me, they would have nightmares with me as the monster. I quickly thought of Angie's visit and her sweet, "It's not too bad," comment. *Maybe she was comparing my head to chopped liver, in which case my head isn't that bad. But it is still bad.* Angie *is going to have a nightmare.* I was worse than Frankenstein with his green color. I was red, and red is scary.

Seeing myself in the mirror opened up every sense of awareness I'd been missing. I wasn't going to go back to sleep until the "mess" was taken care of. I knew that the longer I sat looking like a bloody Frankenstein, the longer it would take for me to get back to my family.

This led to the next thought: *How to get clean?* It was at this moment that I realized I was a bit limited in my abilities of personal care. *How am I going to clean myself without getting the IVs and staples wet?*

I weighed out the pros and cons of getting help and soon realized that there was only one option—get help. I debated waiting for David to arrive and get his help: having him bathe me. *That is just going to make the wait longer, and I don't know if his stomach can handle getting all of this hospital gunk and blood out of my hair.*

I took a deep breath and thought the other option through. I can have a nurse come help me. My teeth clenched. *Get naked in front of a nurse?* I'm not one who would pose for *Playboy* magazine or spend a day at a French nudist beach. I prefer modesty. The nurse option didn't correlate with that. I took another deep breath and ran a pep talk through my thoughts. *This is not me, Deanna Brady. I am UCLA hospital brain surgery patient #24601.* I gave myself the ID number following Jean Valjean's prison number in the play *Les Miserables*, finding it very fitting at the moment. *The nurses are trained to do these things and will not find anything odd about seeing me stark naked.* I began to repeat this, and each time seemed to help a little more.

I pressed the button, and a new nurse entered the room. Thoughts of discomfort started to go through my mind. I could tell that if she were to write her own name on the board, she wouldn't include a smiley face next to it. *Is she new? Is this going to freak her out and make her wish she wasn't a nurse?* I had only thought about my side of the awkwardness. I hadn't thought of her having to do it.

This realization made my mentality change from nervousness to a state of command. *I've talked myself into this, and there is no way it isn't going to happen now.* I sat up and said as smoothly as I could, "I need to take a shower and get this stuff out of my hair. Can you help me right now, or do you need me to wait a few minutes?" I didn't even give her the option of turning down my request for help. I was determined and had used a common parenting technique of giving one option in two different ways.

Her discomfort was easy to notice as she stumbled on an answer. I could tell as she looked up and down, then wall to wall, that she was trying to come up with an excuse. But there wasn't one. She was there to care for patients and I was a patient. "Umm, well, yeah. Uhh, let me get you a towel, new dressing gown, and other bath things first." It was obvious that she was trying to find ways to push back the "meeting."

"Okay, I'll go in and bathe for about five minutes. I think I'll be fine for most of it, but I need help with my head and hair since I can only use one hand and can't get water on the staples. So, it would be good if you could come in for that." I tried to end it with a mixture of showing that I was in need, but also show that I was not requiring as much from her as a person in my situation could. Whether she put herself in total nurse mode or if what I said helped her, she got right to work with less awkwardness.

I hadn't realized how tightened my muscles were from the stress and lack of movement until I felt the warm water streaming down my body, seeming to ease the knots. The five minutes slipped by. When she knocked on the door I asked for a few more, my caution and lack of energy were making me move very slowly.

The nurse had placed a plastic chair in the tub, and I was glad to have it to sit on. I noticed each movement reducing my energy even more. The shower head was one with a hose attached to it, making me able to hold onto it while I sat down. I would soap myself up, set down the cloth, pick up the shower head and rinse myself off; one handed for just one more day.

The next time the nurse knocked, I was beyond ready, mentally and physically. *I am a patient and I could care less if when she is out with her friends tonight, she tells them all about the young freakish Frankenstein whom she had to help bathe. If she hasn't already seen many patients' bodies, then she should start getting used to it.*

As the thought went through my mind, I realized that this wasn't the first time my body had been exposed to others in a hospital. *Hey! That's right. Plenty of nurses and doctors saw me during the delivery and nursing of Bridgett just eight months ago!* This seemed to make me a little more ready for the interaction. I chose not to point out that perhaps the delivery was easier because I was then a delivery machine and attention was all on my baby's arrival and health. This time, it was all me. *She's a nurse, I'm a patient, and I really don't care.*

As she walked in, I noticed her putting gloves on her hands. I agreed that "playing" with my hair wasn't going to be pretty. I tried to make the dense feeling in the room lighten a little, "All right, let's see if I am still a blonde or if I have become a permanent redhead."

Her simple, "Yeah," with a small puff of "ha" laugh wasn't much, but I told myself that I got an A for effort. A thought of embarrassment went through my mind. I looked to check how many towels she had put in my pile. I hadn't thought about covering myself up with a towel while she cleaned me. Judging the size of the towels, I guessed they were the size of hand towels. *I would have had to go mummy style with putting those on.*

Instead of one wrap, it would look like layers. At this point in the thought process I decided I didn't care if she had expected me to wrap myself before she entered, getting the bundle of towels soaking wet. *She's a nurse, I'm a patient, and I don't care.*

Just as that inner argument was closing I felt the warm water running down the right side of my head. I had to close my eyes as it trickled down my face. I wiped the water from my face, and when I looked down, blinking to clear my eyes, an unavoidable shiver gave me goose bumps. I was in my own scene of the horror movie *Carrie* when she got the bucket of pig blood dumped on her while at her senior prom.

The water, dyed from the chemical they had used during surgery, was washing down my body leaving blood red streaks. *This is sick.* As she moved her gloved fingers through my hair, chunks of, now gooey, dried blood joined the dyed red water. I couldn't help snickering more about the horror movie. *So which is worse: Pig blood running through your hair and over your body or your own blood doing the same thing?* It was kind of nice to be able to lament in my drama with a little humor.

After nearly ten minutes of scrubbing and the use of two entire bottles of hospital provided shampoo, I was able to dry myself off with the many towels provided, get into a new gown and return to the bed. For the next while, I planned to comb out the many knots in my leftover locks of hair. My hair was blonde again, but the nurse hadn't been able to get all of the sprinkles of blood chunks out, which would slow down the process. It would take another week of washes to get the clots out. I reminded myself, *Hey, it's better now than it was before the shower.*

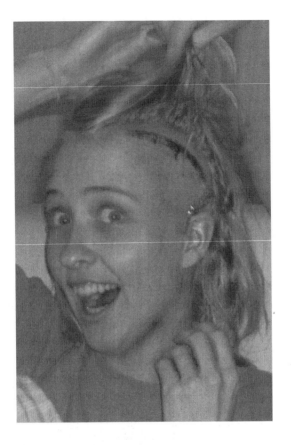

Despite the "Carrie" movie experience, the shower had been delightful, easing tensions in my body. I was glad to have had one and to now have something to do, because sleep was not an option at the moment. Having shared hospital rooms during my many visits for testing before the surgery, I felt used to it and chose to not pay extra for a private room. I didn't realize that this time, any commotion would add to my recovery discomfort.

A roommate had joined me that morning for testing, and she did not like to be alone. I soon got used to her many phone conversations, sleeping through her sounds after the fourth call, but over the next two hours, as I was picking through my hair, a party began to arrive. One by one, ten of her relatives came in, each with a grand entrance of surprise and joy. My emotions were mixed between my surgery patient side and my normal everyday me side.

Surgery patient side: *Quiet down, please! Can you not see that I am trying to recuperate from brain surgery? I should be sleeping.*

Regular side: *Oh, how sweet, they are making sure that she is okay and trying to bring some cheer to the whole situation. Keep her company as long as you would like!*

I was glad I wanted to be awake, because aside from the bustle of the family bringing in chairs and the shuffling around, other sounds were heightened. Her hearing wasn't very good and she would tell each one, upon entrance, that she left her hearing aid at home. So, aside from the activity going through the room, the conversation volume raised a few decibels. Each visitor seemed to realize the sound level at different times, but felt bad because they also knew that she wouldn't be able to hear them if they lowered their voices. I kept to myself while picking through my hair.

David arrived by the time all ten visitors were bunched like sardines in the room. The moment he entered the room, I could tell he was noticing the probable discomfort from the loud noise and commotion. I gave him a little smile and wink, a silent, "Don't worry, I'm fine." He looked at my washed hair and nodded his head as if saying, "Not too bad." While he updated me, telling me about what he and Bridgett had been up to and what was in the cafeteria, the group seemed to mellow as the number of visitors tapered down. When only one was left, I was able to close my eyes.

David saw my weariness setting in and sat back to read while I slept. He had gotten used to this over the past few days, but was getting more and more ready for me to be released. *Soon.*

38

The Escape

As soon as my eyes opened on Friday morning, I noticed the difference from the day before. So far, my recovery had been wonderful and smooth. My awareness and common sense had jumped, and I was ready to get to the next step: leave the hospital. The hospital had been as comfortable as my body and the location allowed, but when my doctor had said that a Friday check-out was possible, I had become determined to make that happen. To me, staying past Friday meant I wasn't getting well, and I didn't want that to be the case.

I got out of bed and immediately got myself ready for the day. I packed my things, wanting to be able to leave as soon as they gave the okay. When David walked in that morning, he had to smile when he saw me sitting there in my own clothes, my disfigured head covered in a hospital-made hat, and my bag on the chair, ready to be grabbed. "How soon can we go?" he asked.

"I'll have Dr. Fried's nurse, Sandi, contacted, so that she can come check me out. When she says I'm in a good enough condition, then they can release me. Soon enough we will be in the car." As soon as I finished this explanation, he pressed the hospital nurse's call button.

Unfortunately, the process wasn't as fast as we had hoped it would be. After forty-five minutes of waiting for the surgeon's nurse to be contacted, I wished that I hadn't let myself get so eager to leave, having rushed to get myself ready. Sitting there and seeing my bag zipped and my area tidied up made the time drag even longer.

When Sandi arrived, she gave a close evaluation of my wellness. Both David and I were nearly holding our breath until she signed the "check-out" sheet. As soon as her signature met the paper, she put the remaining procedures into action.

Soon after she left the room, Jennifer, the nurse whose name had the smile next to it came in with a folder of information. I quickly signed every line at which she pointed. She gave David a handful of prescription order forms, suggesting that we get the order filled at a lower price in the lobby pharmacy.

Seeing that I was already packed and ready to go, she called the wheelchair valet. David told her he was fine pushing my wheelchair. The nurse went into an explanation she seemed to have well rehearsed. "It is hospital obligation that she be wheeled to the exit by our people. A patient is in the hospital's care until he or she is out of the building. Sooo, we have a handy valet system that will pick you up and take you right to your car."

Being from Las Vegas, I expected the valet crew to arrive within five minutes. As soon as the nurse made that call, I took a seat and held the large vase of flowers from David in my lap. David had my belongings hanging from his shoulder and the files in his hand.

After ten minutes passed, he moved to the doorway to make sure we weren't overlooked. We were irritated that the crew kept saying, "In just a couple of minutes," whenever David would ask the status of valet for me. He could have run the prescription to the pharmacy if we had known the time this would take. He hung around though, not wanting to go and then come back to find me gone.

We both just waited.

After a long hour passed, the "valet" finally arrived and led us to the pharmacy. The man pushing my wheelchair was very cordial. I could tell that he had been rushing around all day. This thought helped a little; I felt bad for him, but it had been three hours since I had readied myself and I was past my wake-time limit.

David hurriedly took the prescription orders in before six others entered. When David walked back, the valet informed us that he had to leave and that he was sure it would take them at least thirty minutes to fill the order. He suggested that we have the pharmacist call fifteen minutes before the order was filled. He assured us that this would make perfect timing. *Ugg, here we go again.* David shook his head, sat down, and pulled out his cell phone to find some games to play. I set the vase of flowers next to me and shut my eyes in an effort to rest. Any onlooker would notice that my body was melting. *Another waiting period.*

It was a relief when after only ten minutes of waiting in the pharmacy, our order was filled. We begged the pharmacist to demand a prompt arrival of valet, but could tell that he had as much power as we did. He made the call and we waited.

After twenty minutes passed, feeling like another hour, David looked at me with a little slyness in his eyes, "Hey, let's sneak out. I know how to get to the car from here. I'll push you outside of the entrance, run to get the car and then pick you up. They'll find their wheelchair the next time they valet."

I immediately agreed with his plans and we took off. I was surprised with my guilt, feeling like I was a child, sneaking out of my house to go play at my cousin Mare's house. As David pushed me through the hospital, we chuckled at our bonding moment of rebellion.

David left me at the side of the sliding glass doors and ran to get the car. I welcomed his quick arrival, having felt nervous that I was going to get caught by one of the security authorities in the hut, just feet away. David gently helped me slide into the car and made sure I was comfortable.

As soon as we left the underground parking area and I saw the bright sunshine of the day, everything seemed odd. I felt distant, even separated from life around me as we moved along the roads that I had traveled many times before. After five minutes of watching all around me with glazed eyes, I fell asleep for the remainder of the twenty-minute drive back to the rental house.

The fresh salty sea breeze that kissed me when I opened the car door eased me for a brief moment as I walked toward the house. I couldn't help but feel a slight nervousness as we walked through the side door of the rental. This was the longest I'd ever been away from my daughter. With the separation having been four nights, I was nervous that she would feel distant from me. *Will she remember that I am "Mommy" or has she moved on? Is she mad at me for having been gone for so long?* I'd heard different stories of children's reactions to Mommy being gone for a while and had tried to prepare myself.

As my mom brought Bridgett to me, I wanted to reach out and grab her. Following doctor limitations, I hurriedly took a seat and opened my arms.

When she saw me, Bridgett's body and aura seemed to relax. No grand reaction took place. She didn't lunge toward me or pull away from me. Instead, the eight-month-old child simply settled herself in my lap and played with the toy in her hands.

My mom laid her down for her scheduled nap a few minutes later, and Bridgett quickly and calmly fell asleep. My mom later informed me that this turned out to be the longest and most peaceful nap my daughter had taken since I had gone in for my surgery. On my first day in the hospital, Bridgett had suffered from a random fever. My mom had wondered if there had been a connection. *Was baby Bridgett feeling the stress?*

I could tell that my mom had stepped into nurse mode when she brought me a snack after laying Bridgett down. As I sat, slowly swallowing the yogurt, a knock came to the door.

Melody, the owner of the rental, entered with a vase of handpicked flowers. *How tender.* Her jaw dropped when she saw that I was able to sit up, smile, and talk.

Thoughts raced through my mind as I tried to remember her name. *Name? Starts with M. Mmmm? I like her name. Melanie? No. Has something to do with music. Harmony? Same name as a girl from high school. Melody!* This was the beginning of the name search I would go through for the next few months.

After that quick visit, I was ready to take a break. My whole body felt sore and the only thing that seemed relaxing was a nice hot bath. I hadn't even finished the requesting sentence before David had the warm water running. He spent the next forty-five minutes keeping a guardian eye on me as my aching body soaked in the warm water and probably realized he would be doing much of that for the next three days we stayed in the rental.

When my skin couldn't handle anymore soaking, I started to get out of the bath and lifted my shriveled hands from the water to stabilize myself. *Well done.* I got a chuckle from the thoughts while I dried myself off.

The only thing that I did consecutively through the following three days was to change positions every few minutes as I rested on the beds and couches. I was too tired to think of the many things I still couldn't do. It was settling enough to simply have my little family and my doting mom nearby as I let myself be lazy.

39

Lack of Communication

David was doing work on his computer when I walked in to the room. We'd returned home from California the day before, and he was catching up. He saw the look of need on my face and I could tell he was not anxious to find out what was on my mind. Not this time. My mom had taken Bridgett with her to the grocery store and David knew he was on duty.

What now? He wanted to be the good caring husband that I'd subtly hoped for, but the stress was getting to him. Without saying a word to me, he looked back at his computer and began to open a file.

When David didn't ask if I needed anything, I felt a little sting. *You force me to beg now? It hasn't even been a week and you are already sick of caring for me. Is that it?* I knew that he was preferring work over me for the time being.

Both of us were on an edge.

"David, um, I need to take a bath and wash my hair." I was sure any sort of bed head bacteria was getting too close to the incision.

He looked up at me with a hint of irritation in his eyes, "Okay, go ahead."

"Can you come help me?" I became the beggar. *Why else would I come tell you?*

"Umm, I guess. Give me a minute." David took a deep breath and it said enough. I knew he didn't want to help.

I started the water and got into the bathtub, waiting for David to come wash my hair. A feeling of frustration boiled in my emotions when I saw him walk into the room with his laptop and some paperwork. *Serious? You've been working all day and can't give five minutes to wash my hair? Is asking you to wash my hair too much?*

David sat in the corner and opened his computer. He didn't notice my *you're kidding me* look, but I certainly noticed his *I'm annoyed* look.

Embarrassment for my helplessness pushed me further into the tub of warm water. *I try to take care of myself, but I still have limits that I can't beat.* My frustration turned to hurt. *If I could do it all alone, I would. Trust me.*

I hadn't realized that David had no idea I needed him to actually wash my hair to the roots. Every other bath had only involved him making sure I didn't drown. It had been four days since the nurse had washed my hair, but he thought I had to wait until the staples were out before washing it again.

Our simple lack of conversation was leading to pain.

David sat in the corner, doing his work, without saying a word. He was looking more irritated by the moment. He kept his eyes on the computer screen. I knew that he was avoiding any other possible requests from me.

Tears began to silently fall from my eyes as I cleaned my face. I turned away from David's view until I was able to regain my composure.

A moment later, I needed my hair done. He clearly wasn't anxious to be there, but I needed his help. "Okay, can you wash my hair?" My eye redness was obvious.

He was surprised that I wanted to do my hair. "You really want to wash it?" I could tell a silent punch line followed his question; probably something along the lines of me taking care of myself.

I just looked at him without saying anything. He took my glare as a silent, "Don't ask; just do," and he was right. I was too tired to defend myself and remind him of the nurse's instructions to wash hair, but steer clear of staples. With a slow exhale, he closed his computer and scooted over to the bathtub. He figured it would be better to get it done and over with versus riling me up with his opinion.

David's main issue at this point, he later mentioned, was not regarding the mess on his hands or the time it would take. He was actually and genuinely worried about hurting me, his currently frail wife, and somehow affecting my recuperation. I didn't realize that. Even though his hands were on the opposite side of the surgery, he still felt that any wrong touch or pressure would damage my skull or my already bruised brain. He squeezed shampoo into his hand and spread it over my hair as if he was spreading icing on cake.

Already feeling hurt, I read David's soft spreading as half-hearted help, as if he was making an "I don't want to be here" statement. I didn't recognize his worry—I was still stuck on his frustration.

"David, spreading it on there is not going to wash it." The strained attitude in my voice didn't help get my message across. I started to demonstrate with my fingers. "The shampoo needs to be worked in. Use your finger tips or something. Pretend like it's your own head."

David's sensitivity rose and he immediately slipped into resistance mode, pulling his hands off of my hair. "Well, then why don't you do it yourself?" I'd been right about his mental punch line. "I can't tell if it's being done right. Plus, if you can't tell, I'm busy and this doesn't help me."

David's reaction brought my tears back. I was hurt, and I curled into a defensive ball. My body seemed to shrink as I pulled my knees to my chest and wrapped my skinny arms around my legs. My shoulders melted down, and I rested my chin on my knees. "You think I like having to be so dependent?" I felt broken.

David made a quick eyebrow raise as he glanced at the ceiling. He still didn't understand why I wouldn't do it myself.

"I hate having to obligate you. Don't worry, I get your point. You have no desire to be doing this right now. I know. But I *have* to get your help. I would do it on my own if I could."

By this point David had rinsed his hands and was drying them as he stood near the door. He welcomed my next response.

"Nevermind. Just get back to what you were doing."

He didn't hesitate. David picked up his computer and walked back to the office, closing the door behind him.

I put my head down and my body shook as I began to sob. *I ask as little as possible from you. Why does it have to hurt to ask for your help? I'm sorry that I am such a hassle to you; not what you expected.* I wallowed in the pain instead of thinking how I could have done it all differently. I could have started by simply explaining to him why I needed his help. Perspectives certainly would have changed.

Why don't you care that if these staples get wet or messy then an infection can arise? Possible infection is what the doctors are most nervous about. My head is numb, and I can't tell where the hair ends until I actually touch the staples.

David didn't recall any of that. He sat back in the office chair and opened his files. Unable to focus, he later expressed having to take a moment to pull himself together. *I'm trying, really I am. Aren't I a good husband? I've made sure everything is done right, I'm taking care of Bridgett a lot more than most dads do, and I'm trying to do everything you ask. It's just hard when I'm in the middle of something else… like earning money to pay for the medical bills. I feel like I'm constantly running around, but no matter what I do, I seem to still be getting something wrong.*

He got back to work.

Now leaning close to the water, I tipped my head to the right and guardedly dipped my hair into the water. I used my right hand to stabilize myself and the other to carefully measure the distance between my head and the water. A moment later, I stepped out of the bathtub with my roots still covered in shampoo.

Few words were shared between the two of us for the rest of the evening. By morning, however, we both chose to genuinely get over it and kissed each other good-bye as David left for work. Not another word was said about the bath until it came time to write this chapter.

"David, do you remember when I asked you to wash my hair?" I had closed the laptop and pulled out a pad, ready to jot notes. I became the interviewer, not his wife.

After I mentioned a few details he nodded his head and a more calm discussion on the topic began. We soon realized that it'd started with him thinking I'd wanted his company while I relaxed in the tub and then me feeling like he was sick of caring for me. Things started to make sense. *Oh, that's why he brought the computer in. He thought I just wanted him to sit there so I wouldn't be lonely.* He'd walked in already frustrated, so he then couldn't laugh at the misunderstanding and explain himself. Realization tugged at my heart strings. He thought I'd been asking for forty minutes instead of only five, but he still came.

I took notes and knew right away that it was going to take a lot of work to share both sides to this story. It all came down to the fact that, thankfully, we recognized reality of the situation and neither of us took it personally. We'd both accepted that emotions would be fiddled with through it all.

40

Changes Inside and Out

As soon as Shawna, who was in town as mine and Bridgett's caretaker, saw the nurse laying out the staple removing supplies, she could feel herself getting sick. She had worried that watching staples pulled from my scalp would twist her stomach. It already was.

"Here Deanna, lay on your side with your back toward me and I'll start at your ear." The nurse, Misty, wasn't only paying attention to me; she saw the questionable look on Shawna's face and invited her to sit.

Shawna took a seat, but her curiosity would only let her miss the action for a moment. After the nurse successfully pulled the first two staples, Shawna stood back up on the other side of me and slightly leaned over. "Not too bad."

She later described the image of an unlaced baseball which had come to Shawna's mind as more staples were removed. "Shoot, we didn't bring a camera! This is photo worthy." I tried not to move, but she made me laugh.

She thought of her phone camera and took it out of her purse. "Low grade, but it'll get something." (I would have included one of the photos, but in my opinion they were a bit too graphic for my average reader.)

"Sorry, don't mind me. Just tell me to move if I get in your way at all," Shawna said to the nurse leaning across from her.

Queasiness continued to brush Shawna's stomach as she watched, despite her interest. Each time she felt her stomach turn, she would look around the room trying to see anything other than my bald head, which was looking meatier as each staple was removed.

As she saw the plastic 3-D model of a baby in a uterus, she smirked. *I would have never guessed that we would come to Deanna's OB-GYN to have her brain surgery staples removed.* I'd explained my reasoning, "This doctor and his nurses probably remove surgery staples more often than a neurologist's crew does, even if the staples are usually from the stomach instead of a head." I'd made her laugh.

I'd grown attached to my perinatologist and his nurses, having visited the office over the past year twice as often as women with normal pregnancies. Having been warned by past patients, I had not been anxious to experience the removal of the staples and wanted to be sure it would be done with care.

Shawna looked at me and had to smile when she saw the nurse taking such care. She could tell I'd been right.

"Number twenty-three. How are you doing, Deanna? We look like we are just over halfway. Let me know if you have any discomfort." Misty kept pep-talking, and all three of us were surprised to only be halfway after that many staples had been removed.

"I'm fine … Can't feel any … of it; … just pressure … on my numb- … numbness … I'm hearing grinding sounds … or something." I laid there showing no signs of discomfort other than my breathing. When I spoke I was having to take a deep breath after every few words; my breathing was more strained in week two than it'd been in week one.

The nurse had gotten to a patch of scabs that had crusted over some of the staples, the cause of the grind. "Hmm. We have to work with this."

As Shawna took more phone pictures, she figured that my discomfort was low only because I wasn't watching. *Yuck.*

My OB-GYN, Dr. Bohman, walked in to check on me while the nurse was gently liquefying the scab with moist towellettes. "Well, hello patient! We are all glad to see your smile and that you still know who you are." He bent closer to inspect the incision. "I'd say it is all a job well done from start to now, and I'm sure it'll continue to be good through the rest of the healing process."

Looking at the scabbed region, he commented, "Hmm, they used stitching under the staples in this little area. Those ones will just disintegrate."

That explains the extra mound in that spot. Shawna had thought the area was raised too high to be only due to the scab, but later said she'd been nervous to bring it up to me.

"Last, but not least—forty-one!" Misty made a dramatic drop of the last staple on the tray.

The previous metal question mark was now a raised thick red incision with forty-one dots on either side.

I had not expected to have forty-one staples and looked at Shawna with a look that said, *Pretty impressive, eh?*

Shawna had to smile and slowly shake her head. *Yes, Deanna, that is something you may certainly brag about. Go for it.*

As the nurse cleaned the area, Dr. Bohman made his complete inspection of the entire incision region and then of my breathing. I had mentioned my difficulty breathing, but my lungs were clear. "Seems to be an effect on your throat, but not down to your lungs. It may be due to the tube that was down your throat during the surgery. Time will heal it." He went on with a few recovery tips.

Soon enough, I was gently putting my hat back on and we left the office, which was full of pregnant women instead of brain surgery patients.

We made a quick stop at a drive-thru for a Tommy's Chili Cheeseburger, a family favorite for as long as we both could remember. The related family dinner memories added extra flavor to the already good taste.

A thought went through Shawna's mind as she enjoyed the lunch. It had recurred many times since she'd arrived. "Deanna, you need a close friend." Shawna got right to the point with her opinion.

She'd been watching me and purposely bringing up questions about my "after surgery" plans. The plans sounded great, but one big thing was missing: a close friend to carry my health, mothering, and girly plans out with.

"I have friends! Lots! Sheesh, you know Annie and I chat on the phone or do emails almost every day!" I was in defense mode, defending myself and my friends.

"No, Dee, I mean you need a friend here in Vegas."

Annie and I had become friends while both volunteering in Ecuador and time continued to build our friendship. However, it was a seven-hour drive to Annie's, and the visits were few and far in between.

Shawna continued, recognizing that I felt like my friend plate was sufficiently full. "I know you have a lot of close friends and you want to keep them close. That's fine. But none of those friends are here in Vegas. Getting a best friend here doesn't mean that you'll put others on the back burner."

A song I'd learned as a Girl Scout was humming through my mind, *Make new friends, but ke-EP thee-e oool-ld. One is silver and the other's gold.*

Shawna could tell that I hadn't caught on to her reasoning. "I didn't realize the benefit of an everyday 'down the street' sort of friend until I got one and became one. I enjoyed being busy as a mom, but a friend added to the cheer. You need a nearby friend who doesn't care if you randomly stop by or who feels comfortable telling you the truth—a friend who doesn't take advantage of you or who only gives you time when nothing else is on her plate. Someone who makes sure you baby yourself every once in a while with her at your aid." A list of friendship qualities was coming together as Shawna spoke.

With each point, I could feel their weight settling on my shoulders. I wasn't so much the social butterfly anymore. I hadn't really thought about being a mom *and* social.

"Plus, having a friend physically involved with what you're working on, or whatever, happens to make your success all the more likely! How can you resist that?" Shawna ended her argument with a note of benefit and a teasing smile. "It's just a thought."

Shawna left the conversation at that, and it left her thoughts at the same time. *Said and done.* She'd given me some advice and moved on. She couldn't help but notice that the wheels were already turning in my head. She casually took a big bite from her burger.

By the time we returned to the house, the advice was certainly lingering. *What? Am I supposed to show up to someone's door and say, "Hey, you and I should be best friends."?* I rolled my eyes and quickly fell asleep.

Although it was something I had rolled my eyes about, two months later it was something I actually did.

"Hey, Kristen, how are you doing? What are you and your little crew up to?" I made a phone call to the friend of my choice, the one I'd taught with. We had tried to get together two times before over the past six months, but both of us had let everyday things delay a get-together.

"We just finished making our Monday Muffins, which I connected to a cute book that I got from the library."

This was something I had already put on my mental list of things I valued about Kristen. *That is right down my alley.* Neither of us were full-time elementary school teachers anymore, but we both wanted to keep up the passion in the home. *Good influence and a fun one to bounce ideas with.*

"Now, however, my kitchen is a mess, but I'm about to get ready for our next activity. How about you?"

"First off, the mess is just proof of the kids' involvement. And second, Bridgett and I are standing outside your front door." I was holding a plate of cookies I had made with Bridgett's "help." I'd figured that bringing something would ease the surprise arrival, even though I knew that my baking skills didn't match Kristen's.

"Are you kidding me?! Umm, okay, give me two seconds and I will open the door. B…!" Kristen hung up before she even finished her goodbye.

I smiled. *I'm sure this is a bittersweet visit; she's tickled by the surprise, but notices her messy kitchen all the more.*

When Kristen opened the door, neither of us had any idea that the door was being opened to what we would later dub as a soul sisterhood.

"Peter, you're not going to believe what happened today." Kristen had tears in her eyes. Three months had already passed since my surprise visit, and the two of us had been spending more and more time together with the kids.

It was Kristen's birthday and earlier I had left Kristen's house with a giddy smile on my face and tears in my own eyes. I was sure Kristen would get a kick out of the gift, but was still touched by her reaction when later that evening, she replicated her and her husband's phone conversation.

"Deanna made me this gift, and she has no idea what it means to me. There's nothing to compare it to. She insisted that she made it because of her personal benefits from it; that if I start carrying out my ideas and achieving my dreams, then it is going to get her to do the same. But I can't even explain how excited I am right now!"

"Honey, what are you talking about?" Peter was at work, in the middle of a project, but he could tell Kristen wanted his attention.

"She has made a file of each of my book, Internet, and creative ideas. Then she named each one, wrote a project outline including details I've mentioned as far back as while we were at UNLV four years ago, and then some even have a budget and income outline. This had to take her hours to put together."

Peter couldn't help, but chuckle. "I like this friend."

Later, I sat at my computer beginning to organize my own list of ideas. Kristen's excitement had already inspired me. *That's what friends are for.*

While typing, I thought of Kristen's comment. Hugging me just before I left, Kristen had said, "Deanna, I can't begin to express what your surprise visit a few months ago has since meant to me."

Ditto.

41

Party Pooper

I was starting my third week of recuperation and things were consistently getting better. Watching movies was no longer spurning headaches or giving dizziness. My body was getting a little more used to limited sleep positions. My throat pain was settling. My breathing was returning. The incision was sealing. It was all reason to celebrate.

The neighbors who lived four doors up behind us apparently had reason to celebrate as well. Their party music began at 8:00 p.m. I enjoyed the variety of music; everything from 1950s to now.

I was glad that I liked the music because the small ravine behind our house was acting like a pipeline bringing the music straight to our bedroom window; otherwise, the sound would have been irritating. It sounded like we had our own stereo on.

This music mixture was used until 10:00 p.m., and then it all began to quiet down. *Perfect timing.* I was closing my eyes, ready to fall back to sleep.

Just as my thoughts had completely settled, however, the music picked back up. My body instantly noticed a difference in the music. I couldn't hear the words or different instruments used. Instead, the main sound going through the ravine pipeline was low and heavy. I figured that the party group had changed from adults to teenagers.

My head began to ache, and after ten minutes of not being able to block the sound, my head was pounding to the harsh beat. BOOM, BOOM, BOOM, BOOM.

Being tempted to call security with a complaint was against my nature, and I couldn't bring myself to take everyone down to my level of momentary gloom.

I slid out of the bed and popped a small Motrin into my mouth. The irritation mixed with the delayed medication effect kept me lying awake for the next forty-five minutes; the pounding in my head was still moving to the music thumps. I decided to keep quiet and pushed the pillow against my ears.

It wasn't until two weeks later that I had another headache—my last one related to surgery. It was my fault this time.

We were staying with David's dad and step-mom, Bill and Cindy, a five minute walk from our own house. I hadn't wanted to overload my mom, despite her limitless offer, so when they expressed willingness to help out I'd grabbed it.

I've had a good relationship with David's parents since the start, but the reliance was still nerve-wracking. I felt comfortable and knew their offer was genuine, but I didn't want to push the unknown limits.

My in-laws were prepared. Every item on my "Bridgett checklist" was stocked. Cindy had taped each page of the manual onto their refrigerator for her to see.

Routine ran smoothly from the start. David's dad doted on Bridgett each morning and both of them readily took responsibilities from David—he didn't mind that one bit. That, however, raised my stress level, and I let myself put more effort in taking care of myself and Bridgett than I should have. I had been feeling well and decided to ease up as much of our burden as I could. It was week five.

My First Mother's Day

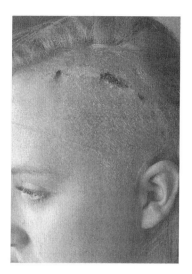 

Now you see it   **Now you don't**

A week of too much effort successfully passed regardless of his parents' assurance that they would gladly do more. My frustration with David's willingness to put so much weight on his parents' shoulders didn't fade, however; it grew. Part of me knew that he needed the break, another part of me wished that he would show more care. I battled between thoughts of gratitude for the time David gave versus feeling like he only helped because he saw me as his responsibility.

my husband and Bridgett

I repeatedly reminded myself of his frequent "helper" moments

I could feel it gnawing at me that his new routine involved going to work and then going down to his own world to play *Rocky IV* on his parents' X-Box when he got back.

On the night marking week five, I sat on his parents' patio and let thoughts bombard my brain. *This has been stressful to him. He needs a break. But he hasn't even come to say, "Hi," or see how my day went. We are in this together, but he's signed off on helping me and Bridgett. Does he care what I'm going through? Is he considering me as a burden? Am I right? But he's tired and it is impossible for him to understand what I am going through. Of course, this is wearing on him. Is he right?*

All of this, added to my effort strains, gave me a pounding headache and a night of choppy sleep. The next day I renewed my mothering limits and let myself rest even if Bridgett was awake. After a week of the refreshing rest, I quickly recognized that everything was fine.

42

The Verdict

"Oh good. I'm glad you had fun. … All right. I'll let you go then. Have a good day and keep up the good spirits! … I love you, too. Bye." *Click.*

I had laid down for a nap when David called to tell me about his fun time with a group of his clients at a fundraiser golf tournament. *Finally, he got a break.*

Setting my cell phone on the nightstand, I let out a long breath. I could tell that David was getting more and more worn out each day. We were at the end of week five in my recuperation. *Certainly all work and no play. I may have doctor's orders to do nothing, but David has needs, too. By now he probably feels like there is no end in sight for him having to fill my role and his, all the while I seem to be fine. Even the thought of it is stressing him out.* The bald area hid under my leftover hair and I was generally cheery through the day—my limits weren't as visible, but were still there.

Despite my sympathy for David, part of me stayed the victim. I still wished that he would dote on me more willingly and that I wouldn't have to repeatedly ask for his help. This is a normal womanly trait—wishing the man would "read" her. It had also been having the normal effect: a shutdown on meaningful conversation as both of us bottled our emotions.

I shook my head. My brain was too tired to think of a simple solution, yet too wired by the stress to fall right asleep. I reached over to pick up the book I'd been slowly reading through, but instead picked up the stack of cards that various friends and family members had sent.

Reading through the cards had repeatedly given my spirits a quick lift. I smiled when I came upon the handmade card from a young girl that I had taught at church three years before when she was eight. *How sweet!*

I felt mellowed out enough by the time I looked at the last card. Ready to close my eyes for a nap, I laid the cards back on the table and got comfortable.

Just as my thoughts were starting to turn into dreams my phone rang again. I was almost too worn to reach and answer it, but my curiosity got me to grab the phone.

I saw the 310 area code. *UCLA?* "Hello?"

Sandi's smooth British accent answered me. "Hello, Deanna. How are you feeling?"

The nurse. Is she checking up on me or does she have something to tell me? "I'm doing well and lying in bed right now. It's hard to get myself to do nothing! I have to keep reminding myself."

"I wanted to call and tell you that we got the results back from the biopsy made on the mass ... " As she continued to speak, I made a quick draw toward the nightstand for something to take notes with. I knew there was no chance of me remembering the information at this point of recuperation.

The nearest piece of paper was an envelope from one of the cards. I flipped it over and immediately started to jot down the long words she was using:

- Type of surgery: *Left Anteromedial Temporal Lobectomy;* removal from deep structure area of the left temporal lobe
- Confirmed tumor; low grade glioma
- Mass was very hard and deeper than expected
- No clear time of or reason for tumor growth
- If it hadn't been removed, there would have been possibility of tumor growth and change
- Low grade for re-growth "proliferation" or likelihood
- Seizures seemed to be caused by tumor growth
- Will stay on Lamictal for two years. Time lowers risk of brain going through seizures and picking up as a habit.
- Tumor and thin area of surrounding brain removed during surgery. Silver dollar sized area.

After another few moments of conversation the phone call quickly ended.

Well there it is. A quick and simple explanation of what has been tormenting me for the past eleven years. I, Deanna McKeon Brady, officially had a tumor.

When I was fourteen, just after my first flash, if anyone had come up to me and asked if I saw any likelihood in me having a tumor, I would have laughed. *That's absurd!*

But no, it's not absurd because it happened to plain, old everyday me. Wow. A tumor.

Those last thoughts moved my energy to overdrive and my brain slipped to off mode. Before I could dial David's phone number to share the information, I fell asleep.

Riiiiiing.

My eyes flickered open, batting open and shut to fight the sleep. I reached for my phone and saw David's name on the Caller ID. An hour had just passed.

It took me another two rings before I pulled my thoughts together. *Oh yeah, tell David!*

I made a quick throat clearing cough and answered the phone. "Hey, hon, Sandi called me today with information about the lesion!"

I continued, sharing the bits of information as I read the envelope notes.

As soon as I got off the phone with David, I repeated the same process many times as I called my family and some friends with the information. With each conversation I realized more and more how matter-of-fact I was about the situation whenever I shared it out loud. "Yeah, that thing my first doctor said was, y'know, 'a scar.' Turns out he was wrong."

For the following few days I was still in shock that my brain had been home to a tumor. Even though the UCLA doctors predicted that it was a tumor, I hadn't officially "bought" it until they gave the results. Now, there was no question.

43

Why Him and Not Me?

"Should I call her tonight?" My phone was in my hand. I had asked myself that question many times since the surgery. I'd decided to hold off the call until I got the surgery results back and now I had them. I wouldn't consciously admit my delayed phone call reasons, but the reason was there. I was well, but her husband wasn't. I felt bad having good news for myself.

A few months before my surgery, I had read my sister-in-law's family webpage and saw a comment from a mutual friend of ours, "Hey, we don't know if you already know but Cody is in the final stages of brain cancer and isn't doing really well. His wife just started a blog (website) and we are contacting everyone who knew him and asking them if they could just take a minute to send a message. In one's final days, simple, meaningful contacts mean so much. If you could take a minute, that would be great."

Cody? Final days? I was shocked. I knew Cody from college and adored him and his constant cheerfulness. I quickly found their blog and read the details his wife of three years had written.

Nine months earlier, Cody had undergone an emergency brain surgery from which a cancerous tumor was found. The tumor had grown "legs" and spread like a spider web through the nooks and crannies of his brain. There was nothing the doctors could do, and they guessed that he had a year to live. I immediately thought of Katie Gramm, my one night roommate at the UCLA hospital.

Thoughts raced through my mind. *Brain tumor. Cody, too?* The fact that Cody had gone through brain surgery was a shock to me. *But only, like, one in a million goes through brain surgery! And the reason is a tumor, too?* I later realized that brain surgery is a lot more common than I'd guessed, but still couldn't believe it was someone I'd known.

I left a message of memories, admiration, and support and mentioned that I'd be having surgery, but that my situation was much lighter.

Cody's wife contacted me after I left that message, offering her help in surgery preparedness. As she described what Cody went through during recovery, it reminded me of my limits just after my seizures. It was very interesting to hear her perspective on all of it. She was a lot like David and his level-headed temperament.

When Sara told me the area in which the tumor had started a lump filled my throat. The spot was the same as mine—hippocampus. *Cody is almost six years older than me. What if my tumor stayed silent until I was his age? Each year can make a difference.* I knew there was no answer to the question. There is a lot to be learned about brain tumors.

She continued with details about his experience. For the three months leading up to his surgery, he had been quiet about "flu" symptoms he'd been having, trying to be his normal tough self despite the fast development. The flu had been floating around, and Cody just figured it was his turn. He, like many, had no idea what it could all mean.

It wasn't until he vomited and then passed out during a class that anyone noticed his symptoms. He was rushed to the hospital. After a CT-scan, the doctors quickly administered brain surgery. What he'd thought were flu symptoms were actually the body's reactions to pressure on his brain from a tumor. They were only able to do a biopsy of the tumor, finding that it was malignant.

Cody had now reached "one year," the point to which doctors said he would be lucky to live, but Sara said he was dwindling. "It's hard. I haven't gotten a full night's sleep for the past few months because he can't sleep. He's also gotten ornery, which is tough because it is so opposite his real self. He can't control it though. But we are just taking it all as it comes and glad for each day we get." I could tell that last note was genuine, both parts. 1) He was still alive. 2) They didn't know if each day was his last.

I was taking notes as she brought up different points. "Cody had a difficult time remembering names. He didn't even remember mine and that stung, but I know it didn't mean anything. He remembered our daughter's name, though. Let's see, his other most difficult things were reading, memory, following a conversation and energy. They put him on steroids for swelling and that put him in a sore mood for the two days, so head's up on that." She was being honest, like I'd asked, and I thanked her for that. I had wanted to be able to prep David for the worst, avoiding any surprises.

We carried on with our conversation for the next hour going into more details of his situation and surgery recovery. She ended the conversation insisting that I call and update her after the surgery.

Twenty-one days later, while staying at David's parents, I was sick to my stomach with gloom and walked outside for a deep breath of remorse. I had just finished reading a funeral announcement—a funeral for Cody. Cody's life had ended because of his brain tumor; on a day I had picked up the phone to call, but didn't. I was dazed by it.

But he was so young! He was such a good person! He was just about to start his career. What about his young family? Sara had said they'd openly discussed it at the start.

Whoa, wait a second. My thoughts went back to a discussion Cody and I'd had— I'd told him about my mysterious flashes. I'd told very few people about them, but he was one that others always found themselves sharing their darkest secrets with. I felt a shiver down my spine.

I had described them as odd things taking place before I knew they were the small seizures from the tumor. He had sat there, listening, while his brain was being silently attacked by the same thing. My body ached with sorrow, and the tears silently fell as I sat alone in the dark. *But he brought good to so many people.*

I quickly called Kelsy, my old roommate, and we cried together.

That night when I had cried outside after learning of Cody's death I had felt so guilty. The question, "Why was mine found and his wasn't?" repeatedly shot at me.

An answer eventually followed once I took a moment to stop lamenting and to think: *There may not be a reason, but regardless, you need to take the time to live.* So, from that moment I decided what living meant to me.

To me, living meant building: building myself and my family and then using that to help others. For the next month my thoughts silently remained stuck on the entire situation. I couldn't settle until I decided to learn new things, take new steps, and be ready to grow.

44

Now What?

It was September 15. Five months had already passed, and every day I felt even better than I had the day before. Stresses had melted. I was able to laugh more. My energy was revived, and I felt like I was on a new trail.

I was lying in bed and reflecting, my head resting on David's shoulder as he had his arm wrapped around me. All sorts of thoughts were crossing through my mind. They all led to one point: *I feel good.*

That morning I'd visited my new local neurologist for a check-up and medication renewal. I was still on a high about the answer I'd given to one of his questions, a question I hadn't expected to hear.

"So, you are a seizure and brain surgery survivor. What are you going to do because of it?"

What? I was surprised to be asked such a deep question.

I made a small grin. "Actually, doctor, I have been quite busy."

He put my folder on his lap. "Oh?" He invited me to go on.

I listed my new passion on developing talents and practicing my old, allowing me to grow in all areas. "You might say that I am celebrating who I am."

The spark of personal growth had been spurred after showing up at Kristen's door and then putting together her birthday gift. She had definitely turned out to be a friend I needed.

I had since written an article and was preparing to send it to a magazine. Writing was a hobby that I'd had and played with since kindergarten. It wasn't until this experience that I decided to follow through and do something with it. *At least give it a try.*

Then I decided to start sewing and designing. Something had caught my eye and an idea grew. After encouraging Kristen to get on her projects, I decided to move on mine. *Why not?* I began spending hours at my craft desk with a measuring tape draped around my neck and using my mother's twenty-year-old sewing machine, building calluses on my fingertips. Kristen and I were then able to have a table at a shopping expo selling items we'd created. *I never thought I'd be able to do such a thing.*

In July, I had started tutoring three children, awakening my teacher creativity. I enjoyed utilizing my education, but still getting to be Bridgett's full-time mommy when she awoke from her naps. I was surprised how helpful the tutoring became in relation to my recuperation. I was certainly putting my brain to work and glad that it was in a way I liked.

And that is all just a start!

Then I told my doctor about Cody. My high spirits sobered to a sort of determination and respect when I then told the doctor about Cody's death and the drive it had given me to "do."

When I drove home from that appointment I'd thought about that decision again. I thought back on the time I'd told Cody about my spooky flashes and how much I wished they would just stop. Then my thoughts moved to after his death when I had realized our tumors were probably in the same spot, at the same time. This realization had brought a change to my perspective about having to deal with the seizures and brain surgery. My flashes that I had thought to be dreadful and haunting had actually been a blessing.

My perspective opened. In the article I had written the week before my doctor appointment I'd stated,

Because of those unplanned bricks in my road, I am still able to have a path. I can reach the future points I mapped out years ago. While grieving the loss of my friend, my heart fills with a new gratitude for my experience. I have a new determination to live life to the fullest.

I wonder if the woman who pulled me aside, whose name and looks I don't remember, had any idea what her insistence would mean to my life. When she chose to step out of her comfortable social boundaries to share her experience, she made a longer path available for me. I hope that by sharing my story, her urge to find out more will be passed on to others who have lingering gut feelings about their own health.

As I reflect on this entire experience, I look for lessons I've learned. Perhaps my biggest personal lesson from this experience is on life focus. Well known pastor and author Rick Warren described life as the two rails of a railroad track, with good and bad events happening at all times. I agree that it is a personal choice as to where we focus.

This all tied into the question the doctor had just asked me: "What are you going to do because of it?"

My new focus is on enjoying my journey, using whatever time I have left to live life to the fullest. I am utilizing time and opportunities to personally grow, to enjoy and cherish my family and friends, and to recognize and build good in my life.

I had found more opportunities to serve others. I no longer entered my church doors for only me; I now recognized even the simplest needs of others and found ways to help my "other" family members. I started taking more walks, pushing Bridgett in her stroller, and stopping to chat with those we passed. Each effort had already seemed to add to my life. I was in a position to do these things, so I did; things which are so easy to ignore.

Now, with the moon in the sky, I reached up to David's cheek and gave him a soft kiss. *And I have time to do even more.*

After the kiss, a secret idea the doctor happened to agree with came back. It would turn out to be an idea that wouldn't leave my thoughts until I acted on it. Before leaving the doctor's office, he had given me a surprising response. "Deanna, have you thought of writing a book about your experience? You really should. You've documented so much and recall everything else. Your story matches bits and pieces of so many people's lives. Patients, doctors, and many others would find it helpful."

I hadn't mentioned the thought to anyone, but the urge to write a book had been pushing pressure points in my consciousness. Hearing the doctor's encouragement sealed the urge. *I can, I should, I want to—and so I will.* I had walked from his office already making book notes.

45

Celebration of Birth

"Hi, sweetheart, how's your day going?" David had been at work and it was near lunch time. I couldn't resist calling him.

I could tell that David knew there was more to my call than just small talk. "Good. Do you need something?"

I suddenly felt awkward. *Am I doing this the right way?* I had an early Christmas surprise for David and wanted to give it to him right away, but I was getting nervous that he would be too wrapped up in work to really enjoy the moment. "Are you busy right now?"

David would have preferred that I cut to the chase, "Kind of." That was him saying it depended upon what I was about to say.

I decided to go for it. *His office is only five minutes away.* "Is there any chance that you could grab a pregnancy test for me at the grocery store? Then you could have lunch here. Bridgett's asleep."

David's reaction was perfect. "Wait, what?" He'd caught on to my nonchalant request. "Really? You think you might be pregnant?" He was already excited.

"I think so," I chuckled. "I need to double check though." I was beaming.

"Okay. I'll run to the store and be home soon." David had already grabbed his keys and was getting up from his office desk. *Click.*

I walked back to my bathroom sink and looked at the pregnancy test stick. *Two bars. Positive.* I was very surprised. That same month I'd convinced myself that I didn't need to be in any rush to be pregnant. I'd been hoping for the last two months that we'd get pregnant, but with the way my body had no routine I figured it would take a while for it to happen. Two weeks earlier I had decided that the first two kids being three or four years apart was just as good as being two years apart. I still had my preference though and was now stunned that it was actually working out! *Right down to the month!*

Just before I called David, I had been on the phone with Annie. It was because of her that I even took the test. If she hadn't told me to then I probably would have gone most of the first trimester not knowing, especially if the pregnancy continued to be anything like my pregnancy with Bridgett.

Annie had called me, sure she was pregnant, but it was driving her crazy because it was too early to test. She started her symptom list. "I'm getting hungry, actually starving, but usually nothing sounds okay to eat. Or if there is something then I feel like I need to eat it 'A-Sap.' I feel like I'll throw up or pass out if I don't eat something fast enough."

She continued, and I told her I was feeling her pain—as any good friend should. After my fourth time of saying, "Oh totally! Last week …" or "This morning …" or "A few nights ago …" and then sharing a similar experience, Annie stopped me.

"Deanna, you have to take a pregnancy test. Where are you on your calendar?"

"Oh, don't ask. Ever since I did the birth control shot method, I haven't been on any sort of woman calendar."

"Do you have a test? Go take it right now! Put the phone down. I'll wait." She'd become a drill sergeant.

Laughter was pouring out of me. "Oh my gosh, Annie." Ha-ha. "Sheesh! I've been going through those symptoms for a little while and I'm understandably wiped out. People have told me they were tired for two years after brain surgery. It's only been eight months for me."

Each time I would feel the different symptoms, I figured they were side-effects from being so busy with my "new life." *I'm doing more, so I need more. I'm just in the process of adapting and figuring out my new need. Right?*

"Do you have a test?" She persisted.

"Yeah, just one," I admitted. I was beginning to see her reasoning the more she insisted.

"I'll wait." I knew she was silently doing a *tick-tock, tick-tock* for me.

"Heavens to Besty. You've got to be kidding me. Really? You think so? All right, hold on." I set down the phone and took the test.

Results showed positive in less than one minute.

I rushed back to the phone. "Annie!"

"Already?" She screamed. "Ahh. We might be pregnant at the same time! And we're both having girls!" She had quickly sat at her computer while I was getting the test stick and looked up her trusted Chinese Pregnancy Calendar.

"I cannot believe it!" I was bubbling and couldn't describe my excitement. "I've gotta go. I have to figure out how to surprise David."

"All right, keep me posted."

"Hey," I paused, "Thanks." I laughed, feeling silly that she was the one to make the connection.

"Yup. Now, that's what friends are for, pointing out the truth. See ya!"

"Ha. Bye." *Yes, friends are good.*

Now it was time to tell David. He'd made record time, getting to and from the grocery in just twenty minutes. He paced as I went in to give it another try.

"Wow." I walked out with the test. "Talk about positive!" The results had taken less than ten seconds to show and gave a bold positive.

"We are pregnant." David felt good being able to state that. He gave me a tight squeeze and stared back at the test results.

I didn't let myself completely believe that I was pregnant until I went in a week later and saw the precious embryo through the ultrasound. I hadn't gone through the same motherly sensation moment as I had with Bridgett, so I was nervous to get my hopes up. *It would almost be too perfect to be pregnant.* Over the past year, things hadn't exactly happened as I'd wanted them. This was a breath of fresh air. *I'm really getting a baby.*

46

Neuro-Oncologist

After getting the official results from my OB-GYN, I figured I should call Sandi. *MRI?* I knew I needed an MRI a year after the surgery, but wasn't sure how an MRI would affect my pregnancy. *Do I need to take it during the first trimester? Do I take one at all during pregnancy?* Christmas and New Years quickly came so it wasn't until January that I made the call. The second trimester was three weeks away.

"Hi, Sandi. I'm pregnant!"

She was surprised and had to think for a moment, probably counting the months since my surgery. *Eight.* "Wow. Congratulations!" I smiled again at her accent. I hadn't spoken with her since she'd given me the biopsy results.

"So, I'm wondering what I should do about the MRI. I'll be at the end of my second trimester and beginning my third trimester in April, the one year mark."

"Hmm, let me get back to you about that. I'll speak with Dr. Fried and see what he would like. You can probably wait until after the baby is born."

We spent the next five minutes talking about my health and what I had been up to.

"Actually, Deanna, I am writing a book for brain surgery patients and compiling information from past patients. Would you be willing to write an entry for the book?"

"Absolutely!" I felt tickled that I was somewhat able to help others. *Yeah! I'm doing something!*

A few days later I looked at my cell phone and saw a message. I quickly picked it up and listened. Immediately recognizing Sandi's voice, I grabbed a pencil and took notes. "Hi, Deanna. I was looking through your file and don't see that you got an MRI six months after your surgery. I also wanted to make sure that you have met with Dr. Bedke. Call me back please and we'll go from there."

I was instantly nervous. Six months? How did I forget that?!

And make sure I've met with Dr. So-and-So? Who? I hadn't heard of that doctor before. *Did I miss that part of our conversation in May?*

Hurrying over to the computer I typed up the doctor's name in Google. A pit filled my stomach when I read his title. "Dr. Bedke, Neuro-Oncologist." *Oncology?* I knew that cancer patients went to oncologists.

Did I misunderstand the biopsy results she gave me? Is there something that they missed then and are trying to double check? Is my brain damaged because I haven't met with Dr. Bedke and gotten more care? Do I have cancer?

The logical side of me knew that everything was fine, but the emotional side of me rushed through my body like a tsunami.

I called Sandi and left a message trying to sound cheery, "No and no are the answers to your questions. No MRI and no appointment with Dr. Bedke. Just let me know what I should do! Thanks!"

When I hung up the phone I looked back at the doctor's webpage and saw that every link on his page had to do with cancer. Nothing had to do with simple benign tumors.

Deanna, you know you're fine. My logical side kept insisting that, but I was still letting my emotions take control. I was trying to make myself be realistic—*but what's realistic when it comes to the brain?*

Did I wait too long?

47

Where Did Pollyanna Go?

Sandi and I played phone tag again as I missed her call the next morning, "That's fine. Call Tina and set up an appointment with Dr. Bedke for next week. As for the MRI, we'll go ahead and do one without the injection before you meet with Dr. Bedke."

My emotions took over again. *Wait, yesterday, she said they'd probably wait until after the baby was born before doing the MRI. Is there now some particular reason they need one sooner?!* I hadn't noticed concern in her voice, but I still let panic crawl into my nerves.

I wrote down the information in her message and then made a call to "Tina," a new name on my UCLA list. When I told Tina I was from Las Vegas and needed to set up a first time appointment with Dr. Bedke, she calmly started her new patient routine. "Okay, no problem. What kind of cancer do you have?"

I instantly cringed. "Oh. Umm. I don't." *At least I don't think I do.* "I actually had brain surgery last April and a benign tumor was removed. I don't really know why they have me seeing Dr. Bedke."

She didn't answer, just moved on with her routine. "Hmm." She sounded confused. "All right. When would you like to come

in? He meets with newcomers on Mondays and Wednesdays."
ASAP?

By the time the appointment was made I was sweating with anxiety.

I started to cry as soon as I hung up the phone and, unable to think clearly, I took a bath hoping it would clear my emotions. *What is going on with me?* My usual Pollyanna attitude was gone—I couldn't help but reflect on Katie's and Cody's experiences. Then I thought of different people's famous tragic stories, those who held on with positive attitudes—their messages about leaving with a smile, to complete your bucket list, to be happy. I couldn't do that. I was acting against my nature. *I've been through a lot and handled it all well, so why is this piercing me?* Despite worries, I'd always felt confident that everything was going to be okay—always. This problem wasn't following the pattern. *Why?* My worry continued to boil.

I thought I already chose to take the positive road. I was referring to the conversation I'd had with my new Las Vegas neurologist. After the surgery, my eyes had been opened to the fact that the seizures had been a blessing in disguise. I'd learned a lesson after looking back at what I'd gone through, and now that perspective was being tested. This time I was being challenged with my attitude toward specific possibilities—my future. I couldn't find Pollyanna.

After soaking in the warm (usually comforting) bath, my brow was still scrunched and I began to pace through the house entry. My thoughts became stale. I finally called Erin, wanting to talk to someone who would let me express my unnecessary fret—hoping it would clear my mind. As I let all my worries out I was already feeling better. Two hours of worry were momentarily calmed in five minutes. *I'm such a woman.*

Just before ending my release call, I brought up a different reason for contacting her, determined to end it on a cheery note.

"Let's go to Disneyland!" Disneyland visits had become a tradition for us after UCLA appointments at this point, always adding good memories. This would be the first time for Bridgett. *Why not take the opportunity to have some fun?*

"Awesome! We're in!" I knew they'd be on board.

"All right, put it on your calendar." Deciding to include Disneyland in our plans made my focus change from thinking about a daunting appointment with a cancer doctor to preparing for an exciting visit to Disneyland. *How fun! Right?*

That evening while David and I watched TV, a Disneyland commercial happened to come on. They were advertising birthday celebrations. In the ad, people of all ages were in the park wearing the birthday buttons. *It's your birthday? Come free! It's a reason to celebrate!* I thought about that ad while falling asleep. *I agree; a birthday is something to celebrate. Life is priceless.*

48

Check-up

On the morning of the appointment, David and I left early to get to UCLA with time to spare. Bridgett didn't mind getting to stay back with her doting older cousins. I had prepared for my appointment, pulling together a new list of questions for my first visit with the new doctor. The first question being, "Why are you my doctor?"

I couldn't avoid the odd feelings that arose when we pulled off the freeway and entered UCLA Territory. I was still baffled that my seizures had been taken care of in just eight hours. Flashbacks of everything rushed through my memory. I had mixed feelings. *It's so great to return to the place that opened my mind* (pun intended) *and released me from my dark side,* versus *My eleven years of confusion, anxiety, and pain is connected to this place.*

Despite the comfort and joy I was feeling, I also began to feel weaker as we neared the buildings. My usual confidence was void. It was almost as if I felt exposed. *I have been seen at my weakest here.*

David must have sensed my frailty because as soon as we parked the car, he led the way without double-checking where we were to go first. I quietly held his hand and followed his lead to the MRI. Being pregnant cut the MRI in half. We quickly rushed to the next appointment—to the cancer room.

Before going into the new doctor's office, I stopped by Brooke's office, my neurosurgeon's assistant, to get a copy of my file. When I walked into her office she welcomed me with a hug. "Yeah. We finally meet!"

Brooke and I'd been on the phone with each other various times over the previous three years, but we'd never met. I'd only seen her photo in the UCLA directory and she'd only seen photos of my brain. Her welcoming personality matched her friendly voice.

I left after a few minutes of talking and smiled. *That felt like an extended-family reunion!* I thought for a moment and added, *Well, a family usually protects each other. My UCLA team certainly protects me. Now I'm about to meet the new member of my team.*

After checking in and filling out the stack of health history paperwork, I sat and looked around the room. It was full of people from my age up to some at least in their eighties.

Curiosity and wonder moved my eyes from person to person. Most weren't alone. *Who is the patient and who is the guest?* With some the patient was obvious: a visible scar, a wig, or noticeable weakness. *Do they all have cancer? Who will live? How long do they have? Can they fight? Will they fight? Are they pleased with their lives?*

My thoughts moved along. *Each of these patients in here certainly has a deep dark side of some sort, but it looks the same as a group waiting to board an airplane! Casually waiting.*

What about me? I had been sitting there, assuming they all had cancer until I put myself in the group and realized that maybe I wasn't the only "misfit."

What might that person over there guess is my problem? Anybody would have noticed that I was the one with the issue as I filled out the paperwork and David read a magazine. I felt a quick chill through my spine. *Is what I'm about to learn something others in here have already guessed? Why am I seeing a cancer doctor?*

Just as I'd picked up a magazine my name was called.

"Would you like me to show you the MRI?" The doctor had barely leaned into the office and introduced himself. My new neuro-oncologist was immediately likeable and ready to get to work.

He led David and me into the room with a large computer screen and explained the different pictures.

"Oh my." I instantly noticed the difference. The affected area was larger than I had expected it to appear. Instead of normal brain squiggles through the entire brain, there was a circle of blur on the left temporal lobe.

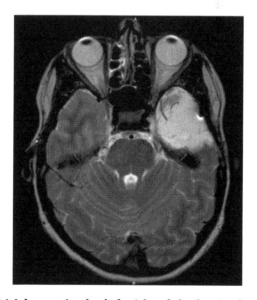

The whitish area in the left side of the brain shows the extent of the brain tissue removed. Only the front and middle structures of the temporal lobe were removed. A large part of the temporal lobe remains even though on the scan, the surgery looks impressively large. (The right side of the picture is the left side of the brain)

David pointed to a thick scar that was missing texture just below his knee, "So basically it looks like a large area of this?" It reminded me of the stretch marks I was already getting from this second pregnancy.

"Yes, that's a way to describe it." The doctor seemed to like David's thought.

I stared at David's knee and was glad to put some sort of mental image, but I still felt a quick shiver when I looked back at the MRI clips. *There really is a chunk missing!*

The doctor took us back to the office room and asked if I had any questions.

I let it out, "Actually, we are not quite sure why you are my doctor." I was dreading his response, but holding a calm front.

He immediately laughed. I wasn't sure how to take that at first, but he went on, "I can understand that. I'll admit that I made a double-take when I saw your information. It is just your other doctors being very cautious." He continued to explain the tumor, "Your tumor was made of two different cells. The middle of your tumor was made of one group that has extremely little chance of re-growth, but the outer area is of more concern for re-growth and then becoming cancerous. They removed a great deal of area that could have been possibly affected, but they are playing it as safe as safe can be."

As he spoke I began feeling more at ease about everything even though he was talking about the chance of tumor return and possible cancer. *I'm under watchful care.* I reminded myself that having had seizures and then finding a benign brain tumor and then going through brain surgery—all of which were burdens for a while—had put me under the watchful care of specialists who would join me in keeping my body well.

I'm okay.

49

Hip-Hip-Hooray!

As we drove back to Erin's after leaving UCLA, I made phone calls to spread the word that I was okay. When the calls ended I began reviewing my past eleven years. I still felt a bit uneasy from the scare I'd gone through emotionally. *I am out of control. I wish this had never…* I made the thought stop there. It almost felt that if I finished the sentence, my attitude would be set in stone. *Do I really want to feel that way?*

A line I frequently repeat, "It is what it is, now deal with it," went through my mind. *I do still have* some *control.* As I sat there, making the choice of attitude, it was as if I were seeing a new light. *So, how am I going to deal with it?* I began to evaluate my situation—my past eleven years. Positives versus negatives.

If I hadn't silently endured the haunting complex partial seizures (flashes), then I wouldn't have gone through the depression and sorrow during college. However, now I am able to empathize with others and be a support to them when life has them down. I like being able to help.

My body's seizure suffering delayed parenthood, but it forced me to take time during which I chose to develop and practice a passion—teach children. I still smile from the memories.

I was weak for months after the surgery and in need of others' help, but it taught me another level of service for those that surround me each day.

The trauma brought me pain and worry, but has inspired me as a woman, a mother, a daughter, and a wife.

Those are negative experiences that have brought (and may continue to bring) positive results, but not everything connected to my health situation brought benefits. It was expensive. Unexpected stresses were forced on me, my marriage, and other relationships. Pains were suffered. Limitations were mandatory. I had to be babysat. Yearly driver's license renewal was a hassle for over five years.

Yet, all the while unrelated good things still took place as well. I was never held back. I reached personal goals. I shared my love with orphans. I traveled through the Amazon jungle. I fell in love with and married a wonderful man. I earned a degree and use it daily. I became a mother. I created a good home.

I realized that the dark side, everything related to my tumor, simply made me more of who I am. My dark side never entirely enveloped my life. I didn't allow it to. It was only part of me, so those good things I listed (and more) still happened.

I recognized the good that the entire experience brought me. I cringed when that thought came to mind, but I knew the truth.

I am smarter now than I would have been without the entire experience, in a way that can't be replaced. I have a new perspective on life at a young age. I value my days in a better way. I've made new friends. I understand and respect life and people more. I realize that there is so much more to learn. Most importantly, I am so glad that I can do it. I have today and can use my time as I choose.

I once asked myself, *Has it made life better? Has it made it worse?*

At that moment I knew that I could say that it has added more to who I am. It has made me grow in ways I never expected.

It has forced me to look at myself and decide who I want to be. It has brought me pain, but also opened my eyes to joy.

I started to beat myself up that I'd even pouted, and then I realized how it helped me reach a new level. It was all a process. The short moment of pouting was good. It made me stop, think, and make a decision. It made me look at both paths of attitude.

Pains will continue to meet with me along my path of life, pains that I won't be able to control. What I will always have control of, however, is my attitude.

I now value more of what my mother taught my family. While raising us, my mom was a stress-management counselor. We were her most prized clients, and daily she would use her training on us. We usually rolled our eyes when in the early morning before getting ready for school she would have us cheer, "Hip-Hip-Hooray for another great day!"

Now, fifteen years later, I value and understand her concept a little bit more. Yes, today is a day to celebrate. Now when I get up in the morning I'll repeat, as my mother always made us say, "Hip-Hip-Hooray for another great day!"

So, next stop—Disneyland!

50

One Year Mark

I woke up on Wednesday, April 15, 2009, very differently than I had the year before. It was the one-year anniversary of my brain surgery. I was busy, but in very different ways. Kristen's kids were coming over, and I was preparing our day's activities. I watched her children on Wednesday, and she watched Bridgett on Thursday—my time to write.

As each hour passed, I couldn't help thinking what had been taking place at the same time the year before.

Before Bridgett awoke and the two children arrived, I measured my hair. *This is a creative method to finding out how long my hair grows in a year!* I held up the ruler and measured. *Four and a half inches. Hmm.* It didn't seem very long to me, but it was better than the smooth skin that had shined a year ago.

A moment later I jumped into my Wednesday routine. *Waffles today!* Bridgett had joined me and was excited to help mix the ingredients.

I looked at the clock when the doorbell rang. *8:30. Hmm, exactly a year ago they had already sliced my scalp and muscle in the question mark and were maybe now removing parts of my skull. Good thought.*

"Welcome, welcome!!" I quickly pushed the thoughts away and answered the door with reason to celebrate. *I'm alive and well!*

Mostly well. Allergies had begun to tickle my sinuses and due to my low immune system from the surgery plus pregnancy, it quickly turned into a cold later that evening. Odd as the thought may be I couldn't help telling myself, *Isn't it nice that I can handle getting sick?*

There was now an extra cheer about being sick, because two weeks earlier I'd found out I was pregnant with another girl. Bridgett was getting a sister! I knew the pregnancy would stretch out my recovery process, but it was worth it and the pregnancy was treating me nicely.

Wellness was strong when it came to my brain. For the past year there had been no signs of seizures. I hadn't even felt the warning "auras" that the doctor had said were possible. The surgery side effects were very few, being mostly continued weariness. I still relied on, even cherished, my daily naps. I wasn't sure which side effects were tied to my pregnancy and which were tied to my surgery.

Names, vocabulary, and details were back in my memory as much as before the surgery; I was still remembering things better than others tend to.

Through my year of recuperation I had noticed changes in memory. My memory of hours, days, and years, in fact, returned stronger than it had been before they removed the tumor. I began to recollect more details. Aside from instant recall, I would picture myself in the scene, almost recreating the event.

Now, today, I'm still under watchful care of doctors who will jump at the trace of anything, getting to know me and my body. With cautious doctors and nurses who love what they do, I know I won't be overlooked.

I feel good and whole. Each day, when I give my husband a kiss or play tea time with my daughters, I replace thoughts of negative possibilities with gratitude. "I'm so grateful I can do this today." It makes a difference.

May this book always remind me of that.

APPENDIX

Dig for the Answers

- Log your health information (and your parents' information if there are particular issues) with detail even if you don't think they are related. If your doctor laughs, reply by reminding that it is better to be safe than sorry. You'd be surprised!

- Plan from the get-go that you will get multiple opinions. Tell your doctor, "I'm asking for different doctors' opinions on _____. What is yours?" That sets the stage. Then, if your doctor seems offended, take that as a sign—get a new doctor. When we asked Dr. Fried about meeting with other doctors, he welcomed it and even gave a list of others with high credits—that said something. If you are like me and don't want to hurt feelings, take someone with you.

- Check out websites (ex: EpilepsyFoundation.org), talk with friends, and listen to others with situations similar to yours, etc. This helps with connections, information, guidance, tips and noticing what your body is telling you.

- It is okay to try different methods of medicine if there is time. Get an MRI first.

- If you have a hunch, follow it. Don't let others' expertise override your sense.

Surgery? Be Prepared

- Get contact information of past patients from your doctor and make some calls. Have a pen, paper, and questions ready.
- Write specific questions for your doctor (see mine on pg. 112).
- Make recuperation plans: housing, food, self-help, family help, books, exercises. It helps to assign someone else to officially organize the care for your needs.
- Buy thank-you cards and stamps. I made goody baskets for my caretakers (my mom and sister) and it felt good to see them smile—nice to give a little something when you are getting so much. I included activities for them to do, slippers to wear, and things to read while staying with me.
- Get a friend.

Recuperation: The Aftershock

- Set goals.
- Find reasons to get better, or something that'll give you an extra *umph*. Mine was my daughter; I wanted to be able to play with her.
- Make a saying for yourself or use an ancient proverb. Repetitive reminders help.
- Set limits and stick to them. Don't overdo it—it's not worth the pain.
- Shut your door, close your blinds, and turn off your phone—you have to sleep.
- Become active step-by-step (ex: daily exercise).
- Read—it's interesting to notice the different cognitive levels as you recuperate.

- Find an activity that will stimulate you—mine was to tutor past students.
- *Sleep!* (Repeated to show its significance)

10474761R0

Made in the USA
Lexington, KY
27 July 2011

Praise for *Shanghai Love*

"Author Layne Wong transported me to another world that is both familiar and distant. Great job!"
—**Amy Hill**, actress, writer

"Peilin and Henri's is a love story that spans cultures and eras, making Shanghai Love *truly one for the ages."*
—**Michael Feldman**, radio host of "Whad'ya Know?"
Public Radio International

"A beautiful, touching love story set against one of the most tragic times in history. Layne Wong deftly takes us on a journey to forge our own identity beneath the weight of war, culture, and family ties. A captivating read."
—**Amy Hatvany**, author of *Best Kept Secret*,
Outside the Lines, and *Heart Like Mine*

"A timeless journey for the soul . . . the quiet yet bold Peilin casts her fate into uncharted waters. Peilin cultivates her own identity with the caring help of the Good Luck Lady. May we all be so fortunate to find such a wise and loving ally."
—**Patricia Miya**, writer

"Layne Wong breathes life into the fascinating yet little known history of the Chinese people and Jewish refugees during World War II. Rich in detail, romance, and tradition, Shanghai Love *is an amazing novel that deserves much recognition."*
—**Professor XuXin**, writer and director,
Glazer Institute for Jewish Studies at Nanjing University,
People's Republic of China

SHANGHAI

love

SHANGHAI
love

a novel

LAYNE WONG

SHE WRITES PRESS

Published 2013
Printed in the United States of America
ISBN: 978-1-938314-18-6
Library of Congress Control Number: 2013930136

For information, address:
She Writes Press
1563 Solano Ave #546
Berkeley, CA 94707

For my husband, Jay

*Thank you for your patience with my late nights
and early mornings at the computer.*

With love

NOVEMBER 9, 1938: The Good Luck Lady dipped a large wooden ladle into the hot water and poured the steaming liquid over Peilin's naked body. Wiping away the sweat in the deep lines of her brow, the attentive old woman then carefully peeled a fragrant pomelo and squeezed the sweet nectar into the deep wooden bathtub to chase away any evil spirits from the bride-to-be.

Peilin was just seventeen years old. Her long torso glistened. Her silky black hair cascaded around her oval face and down her slender neck. Peilin's beauty and exquisite physique eclipsed every other young woman's for miles around. Even the dark round beauty mark just above her upper lip added an aura of mystery—like a rare pearl. It was only fitting then that Peilin would be marrying into the pearl farmer's house. She breathed in the steam.

"*Nah, nah, nah,*" cooed the Good Luck Lady, whose own life had played out as well as any Chinese woman her age living through the 1920s and '30s could have. As she had done countless times before, the gray haired matron purred auspicious words to the new bride—many sons, a happy mate, much prosperity, a life of obedience to her new family.

Bubbles rose to the surface of the oak washtub. Peilin sank into its depths. She felt a tingle on her skin as the Good Luck Lady rubbed the fresh-smelling sandalwood soap over her taut belly. "Bath purify body, bring happy fortunes to new bride and groom," continued the dignified woman.

The Good Luck Lady grabbed a bronze mirror and rubbed her hand across the reflective glass. She angled Peilin's head so that she could gaze at her own reflection. The young maiden could not believe the moment had finally arrived.

"Become woman today," the caretaker smiled.

The wizened matron glided Peilin's left foot out of the water and began kneading the sole with her gentle hands. Searching for the center point in the soon-to-be bride's heel, the Good Luck Lady pressed firmly into the area. "Fertility point," she announced.

"Soon you will be growing with baby inside."

Peilin could only muster a sad smile, gazing down at her belly and the region below it. Her mother had told her about the secrets a husband and wife share in bed, secrets that were forbidden and sacred until marriage. Peilin wondered if she would ever experience the love she hoped for.

"Obeying, hardest part for me," continued the old woman. "Even though wife to obey husband, new bride must also obey mother-in-law. Always be polite. Always do best. Best embroidery, best tea serving, best bowing. Then, no reason for mother to retaliate, make your life miserable. Always serve husband, mother, elders first. Pick smallest fish portion for self. Be sure to leave tiny morsel in bowl, even if still hungry. This way, they know their new bride not greedy, not wasteful." The Good Luck Lady prided herself in sharing her intricate knowledge. "Never show anger. Never complain. If you must, whisper only to the wind, which will carry your thoughts safely away. Best keep unkind words to self."

The woman continued on with her monologue as Peilin graciously took it all in. "Me, when I was married, I make sure my husband always see me smile, always see me happy. Then, he think of me that way all the time." The wrinkled-face caretaker smiled into the mirror to demonstrate for Peilin what she meant. Reluctantly, the young miss smiled back.

"I have prepared many girls for this, their most important day. All beautiful, all look forward." The Good Luck Lady softly stroked Peilin's hair. "You, though, have *inward eyes*."

Peilin turned to the gentle lady with piqued curiosity.

The matron continued. "You not know *inward eyes*? I think you do, but don't say. That is your nature."

Peilin gazed up at the woman before her, who'd only met her for the first time that morning.

"You see the truth others ignore. You feel it here," said the Good Luck Lady, pointing to Peilin's heart.

The wise woman smiled and held out a large plush towel for her bride-to-be. Peilin gingerly stepped out of the tub and into the warm blanket.

She wondered about her new beginning, her future, her destiny, but didn't dare voice her nagging concerns.

Peilin had lived with her parents and younger brother Ping in Chuan Tian, a small farming village along the Yangtze River in the Jiangsu Province. For generations, Peilin's father, and his father before him, tilled the hard claylike soil, nurturing its callous and unforgiving density in hopes that it would give birth to new rice crops each summer. The Du family lived by the land that determined their future. Some years were fertile, while others barren. Regardless of the blessings or hardships, nature and man lived in a precarious balance.

Some of the peasant girls Peilin's age were sent to Catholic orphanages. The ones who remained in the village spent their days at home cooking and cleaning or threshing, winnowing, and grinding the rice in the family fields. Illiteracy for lower-class women was considered a virtue.

Peilin, however, was born into luckier circumstances. Grandpa Du, an herbalist and a farmer, had spent most of his life tending to the rice fields. But his true calling and passion was his herb garden. Around the time Peilin was born, her father was coming into his own as a farmer. The family was finally self-sufficient, and Father Du had encouraged his father to pursue his true love—his healing garden. And so it was that Peilin's formative years were spent absorbing her grandfather's knowledge. As he nurtured his garden, he was also securing Peilin's future by cultivating her mind. Although this type of knowledge was generally reserved for sons, neither Peilin's father nor brother possessed an interest in medicine. Peilin, on the other hand, showed an early aptitude for remedies and formulas. As Peilin grew, it was clear to Grandpa Du that she was not only smart and talented but that she was also going to be a great beauty. That's when he realized that he could change his granddaughter's future. She would not be destined for a lifetime of hard, backbreaking labor. She was going to have a different life than the one her family was bound to.

Peilin's father, like most men, did not value his daughter, but rather focused on his son. But Father Du's only boy had been handicapped at an early age. Instead of being daunted by the physical deformities that befell his son after the accident, Father Du seemed only to redouble his efforts to help Ping thrive and become self-sufficient. In later years, Peilin often wondered if her father blamed himself for what had happened but never dared voice her musings for fear of being reprimanded.

Peilin was only seven when it happened, Ping five. She had looked on from the open porch as her father directed the family's lumbering gray-coated water buffalo. Her brother assisted her father with plowing the rice fields that morning and she noticed that the animal dug its hooves into the muddy water. At first Peilin thought the oxlike beast with its swept back horns had stopped for a drink of water. But as she continued to watch, she realized that the animal

4

was oddly still, not making a move. Her father yanked abruptly on the wooden yoke that harnessed the water buffalo. Suddenly the massive animal reared up, choking. Her father quickly released the yoke, but it was too late. Ping's young body stood no chance against the trashing animal, and a heavy hoof came crashing down on her helpless brother. It all happened so fast. Peilin stood stunned as Ping continued to be pummeled into the rice fields, her father screaming and thrashing in a vain attempt to control the animal's reckless behavior. By the time Father Du could finally calm the animal, the tender boy lay severely wounded. Finally, Peilin heard herself cry out, and seconds later Grandpa Du was running toward her. He grabbed his granddaughter by the hand and the two rushed out to the field where Ping lay lifeless on the ground. Blood gushed from a gaping hole in his cheek; Peilin was paralyzed with the dreadful feeling that her only sibling was surely dead.

With Grandpa Du's help, Peilin quickly applied pressure to stop the bleeding from the deep gash in Ping's cheek. Then she stood back as Grandpa Du used silk thread to sew up the open wound. As he repaired his grandson's face, Grandpa Du instructed Peilin to rub a strong smelling liniment—*zheng gu shui* (bone-setting liquid)—to Ping's broken ribs and crushed foot. After Peilin wrapped his chest and foot, the elderly man instructed her to combine several herbs, including *gu sui bu* (drynaria root), known as a strong healer of shattered bones; *mao cao gen* (teasel root) for its ability to knit together ligaments and bones; and *bai shao* (white peony root) to move the blood and relieve pain; and boil them into a healing tea. Peilin worked quickly and soundlessly, barely aware of her brother's moaning. She and her grandfather made a good team. The boy was carried back up to the house to recuperate.

After a year, the wound on Ping's left cheek formed a long, jagged scar that was hard to miss. The boy finally learned to walk again, but his foot was never the same. Slowed by a pronounced limp, Ping nonetheless continued to tend the rice fields with his father. He was as determined as his father was for him to grow strong. By the time he was twelve, his bull-like torso and massive arms allowed him to haul a truckload of coal on his own.

It seemed to Peilin that her father overcompensated for his guilt, and his conflicting treatment of Ping, which alternated between immense pride and embarrassment. Their father concentrated on ensuring that his only male heir could till the land and run the farm, even though his severe limp often made it difficult for the boy to cultivate the land without modified plows. Peilin was also aware of the way her brother constantly tried to prove himself to their father. Since Peilin's father was engrossed with his son, and because he did not see worth in a daughter, he indulged Grandpa Du in his tutelage of Peilin. Father Du, like all children, respected his elders and therefore allowed his father to shape Peilin's destiny, perhaps as penance for past sorrow. Much later Peilin would learn that Grandpa Du carried his own shame, having sold his daughter into slavery many years before Peilin's birth.

Grandpa Du was a large, balding man with an easy smile, even though he had lived through drought, famine, and flood. He often sat cross-legged on a large pillow. When Peilin was little she enjoyed poking his belly, which often invoked a deep-felt laugh.

Grandpa Du had introduced her to his herbs, like ginseng root, lotus seed, and peony bark, while she was still quite young. Tending to the garden with him each morning, she plucked seeds, flowers, and roots and dried them in the sun under the careful guidance of her beloved grandfather.

Peilin's mind recorded every leaf structure, seed casing, and root. The *hong zao*, a tiny red date, was her favorite and she would plop them one by one into her mouth. The sweet herb fortified the heart and in her later years it would prove to aid Peilin through heartache and trouble.

By age six, Peilin could already trace the meridian lines across her body, from the heart to the liver and all the way back. At seven, largely because of her calm presence and good instincts at the scene of her brother's accident, she started traveling through the village with Grandpa Du as he delivered babies, cured fevers, and set bones. Peilin was in charge of the medicine bag. The doctor taught her to identify each herb by smell and sight. He encouraged her to memorize all of their properties. So she learned, not only how to prepare the healing formulas, but also to have extra insight into each one's cooling or heating properties.

Each spring, Grandpa Du would leave Peilin and set out north for Dragon Lake. The year Peilin turned eight, her grandfather left for his annual journey with his walking stick and wide-brimmed straw hat. He hiked ten miles through several villages and ended up at a bus station. There he boarded a rickety vehicle en route to his final destination. The few seats were filled with others traveling with crated chickens, goats, and pigs, so Grandpa Du squeezed into a corner and stood, clutching the handrail overhead as he braced himself for the one-hundred-and-eighty-mile trip.

Dragon Lake was nestled high in the mountains, surrounded by cypress and pine trees. The blue fog that blanketed the lake each night fortified the tale of the Pearl Dragon who protected his precious treasures within its deep black waters. Local legend had it that lake bandits often became confused and lost their way as the heavy mists shrouded their view.

Few doctors traversed the region for their medicinal ingredients, but Grandpa Du found that the Kwan family pearl powder provided excellent results in his healing formulas, especially to help renew the skin.

When the physician arrived at the pearl farmer's gate, the shouts of Kwan Taitai echoed from behind the door. Grandpa Du hesitated, not wanting to intrude.

"You are to blame for our son's misfortune!" he overheard her cry out.

"How can that be?" wailed her husband. "I do everything you say."

"You were not home when I gave birth to our son."

"I was on the lake attending to the pearl harvest. I came in as soon as I heard."

"Not fast enough. I was without you, my husband, alone on that most important moment. The ancestors saw. Now the Matchmaker cannot find him a suitable mate."

The Kwan's only son, Yao, was born four years before Peilin. Tall and lean like his father, young Yao, nonetheless, took after his mother—outspoken, brash, and headstrong. Kwan Taitai had no brothers and had, therefore, inherited the pearl farm from her family. She had been raised with treatment traditionally reserved for sons, and all the spoils that went along with it. Still, being a woman, Kwan Taitai's feet had been bound as a young girl, for her perfect golden lilies would assure her a good marriage partner.

The morning Grandpa Du arrived, Kwan Taitai had just finished conferring with the Matchmaker, who had informed her that none of the twelve girls available in the nearby village came close as a proper match for her son.

As the voices faded into silence, the kind doctor made his presence known. A servant greeted him at the door with a nod and led him into the Kwan's receiving room. Grandpa Du stood waiting. He admired the tall cloisonné vase filled with fragrant chrysanthemums. The house was lavishly decorated with zitan furniture made from the purple-brown wood once reserved for royalty. The sitting room was adorned with chairs that had smoothly curved arms and a pair of armoires whose doors were intricately carved with dragons. As Grandpa Du studied the boxwood carving of a large frog, Kwan Taitai emerged, lightly treading across the floor on her bound feet. She was trailed by Father Kwan, who was dressed in a coal gray Western-style suit.

"Don't mind my husband," said Kwan Taitai dismissively. "He's just returned from Shanghai."

"Business?" questioned Grandpa Du.

Father Kwan shook his head. "Visiting my elderly uncle," he replied while loosening his tie.

"Uncle is also an herbalist," Kwan Taitai interjected. "So you see why we respect your profession, even though you come from a lower class," she continued, waving her hand through the air.

Grandpa Du ignored her slight. "I am humbled by your regard."

Opening the armoire, she pulled out a heavy sack and presented it to their guest. "Our finest for you, Doctor Du," bowed Kwan Taitai, whose statuesque figure was tastefully clad in a high-collared celadon-green dress.

The agreeable old man bowed and handed her a good sum of money in return. "I am always grateful for your generosity." He studied her appearance.

"Good lady, your face looks very flush. May I take your pulse?"

Kwan Taitai nodded. The gentle physician took her wrist and felt for the three points just under the skin. She scrutinized the doctor with an intense gaze.

Grandpa Du released Kwan Taitai's hand. "Your pulse is weak and thready," he concluded. "Liver energy rising must cool."

The petite but fiery woman softened as she watched the old man pull out his healing bag and measure the dry herbs to remedy her heat condition. "You have known me for a good number of years now, Doctor Du. Please tell me, is our house cursed? Our Matchmaker cannot find a suitable bride for our son."

Grandpa Du observed the rapid flash of anger darting from Kwan Taitai's stern gaze as she glanced at her diminutive husband before turning her attention back to her visitor. Father Kwan retreated farther into his inert repose. It was largely known that Mother Kwan demanded the best, and everyone at Dragon Lake and its surroundings scurried to meet her demands—best pork for feasts, best silks, and rarest teas. And while she was admired and feared by all, her father had arranged for her to marry not the most handsome or wealthiest boy, but the one young man who possessed more knowledge of the pearls than any other, much to Kwan Taitai's disappointment.

Grandpa Du cleared his throat. "Perhaps young Yao's future bride is like a rare pearl—one must dig deeper to discover it."

Kwan Taitai smiled for the first time. "Of course! My son is very special. He deserves someone equally precious. If you come across such a girl, Doctor Du, I would be most grateful."

The astute physician studied the commanding woman. "I have a granddaughter a few years younger than your son. I am teaching her the way of healing and she is well-versed in the importance of the pearl."

Mother Kwan's interest piqued. "I have always liked you," she confessed. "Because of your superior skills, I will overlook your unfortunate inferior family status."

Grandpa Du nodded toward the imperious matron. Leaning in, she clutched her hand around his arm.

"Tell me more about this young girl with your talents."

He smiled. "She is a quick and studious disciple with beauty that outshines the sun."

Grandpa Du spotted Kwan Taitai's pencil thin eyebrows elevate with heightened interest.

"If you please, may I offer her eight characters for your inspection?" he inquired.

The enthused mother nodded. The doctor carefully wrote down Peilin's *ba zi*, the eight characters describing her birth year, month, date, and time. Kwan Taitai took the information and placed the rice paper on the Kwan family altar.

When Grandpa Du returned to Chuan Tian, an identical ritual was carried out at the Du household with Yao's eight characters. Three days later, no disasters, not even a broken chopstick, had befallen either home. Word was sent to Dragon Lake and a date was set for the Matchmaker to visit the Du family a few months later.

Peilin watched as news of the impending Matchmaker's visit set her mother into a flurry of preparation. At eight, Peilin was not quite sure what all the commotion was about but knew that it was important by the way her mother swept their small dwelling with the new straw broom and tended to the ancestors' altar, burning fragrant ylang-ylang incense and leaving offerings of barley, sorghum, and fresh plums. All this so the gods watching overhead would send blessings from above.

The day before the Matchmaker was to meet the Dus, Kwan Taitai had instructed her cook to purchase the largest pig possible and roast it with the finest basting of ginger, lemon, and honey. The succulent gift was securely wrapped for the journey and delivered to the Du family by the Matchmaker upon her arrival. At the day's end, Kwan Taitai hoped her marriage emissary would return bearing the pig's head and rump, a signal that the nuptial process had an auspicious beginning with promises for an equally fortunate end.

Peilin, hidden behind the door, caught a glimpse of the Matchmaker when she arrived the next day. A stocky woman missing several front teeth, she presented the roasted pig to Mother, Father, and Grandpa Du. Peilin noticed that her mother wore her best acorn-brown jacket and trousers as she led their guest to the large bamboo mat in their small sitting room.

The elder Du had advised Peilin's mother not to serve tea. Should even a drop spill on this important day, Peilin's future family would withdraw their intentions, interpreting any mishap as a bad omen.

11

The Matchmaker kneeled as she pulled out a heavy and well-worn almanac—the Ten-Thousand Year Calendar. Generations of matchmakers had referred to this definitive text when predicting future marriages. Once the visiting woman was ready, Mother Du officially presented her with Peilin's *ba zi*.

Peilin's father, with his long straggly beard, paced the room. He turned to Grandpa Du suddenly and announced, "Father, my own sister did not receive such an opportunity. She was sold as a servant at a very young age."

"*Aiiii!*" lamented Grandpa Du, his heavy eyes cast downward. "And I have regretted that decision so many times. I should have sold the animals, the land—anything but my own flesh and blood."

Peilin gasped. Prior to that point she hadn't known she had an aunt. She had heard of other girls in the village being sold off, but she'd believed it was because they had done something wrong. Even at her young age, Peilin knew in her heart that her adored grandfather would never do such a thing unless he was forced.

"It was the drought," Peilin's father reminded him. "It was for survival."

"Still," Grandpa Du sighed, "I should have figured out another way."

Father Du grunted. As the second son, all he had known was hard work. Peilin could sense the pain on her father's face. His older brother, Quong-Yiu, had been groomed to be the herbalist, while Father Du tended to the labor-intensive rice fields. But when the boys were still young, a plague hit the village. Grandpa Du and Quong-Yiu did all they could to treat the sick. Quong-Yiu was in constant contact with the disease and soon fell ill. He died as a teenager and Grandpa Du never fully recovered. He abandoned his herbal garden for many years, choosing to join his second son in the fields. In the years after the plague it was critical to their survival. Grandpa Du put his passion for herbs, remedies, and helping others on permanent hold.

It wasn't until all these many years later that Grandpa Du was finally ready to return to the garden. It was partly about having the stability to do so, but it was mostly because it took that many years to heal from the loss of his first son. By the time Ping was born, Peilin was already spending the majority of every day in the garden with her grandfather. He had already claimed her as his little apprentice. When Ping came along, he was naturally consigned to join his father doing the hard labor of tending to the family's fields.

Peilin continued to think about her aunt. She wondered how old she had been when she'd been sold. Peilin shuttered to think, *What if it had been me?*

Lost in contemplation, she didn't detect Grandpa Du approaching her. He must have sensed her distress because he reached over and gently patted her on the back. The Matchmaker spoke up. "Destiny cannot be changed."

With her oversized magnifying glass, the stout matron returned to the pages of her large book, flipping back and forth between several charts. Grandpa Du studied the Matchmaker as she toiled with her calculations. Peilin sensed that her grandfather might have once agreed with the intense woman's assessment of destiny's immutable quality, but here he was changing hers. A lifetime of toiling under the hot sun and years of studying the healing power of herbs taught him a new way of thinking—while destiny may be impossible to change, it was possible to refine.

Working with Peilin's eight characters, the Matchmaker drew lines between the symbols, forming four columns. The venerable time-honored system took years of training to master. Although it was not customary, the sharp-witted woman attempted to explain her calculations the best she could.

"The Four Pillars of Fate are anchored by the prospective bride's year, month, date, and time of birth," she explained. "This first column is called the Earthly Branch. Peilin was born in the year of the rooster."

Mother Du nodded. "My daughter rises each day with the morning sunlight."

"There is more," continued the Matchmaker. "The calendar is a sixty-year cycle. Therefore the rooster appears five times—each with a different Heavenly Stem—wood, fire, earth, metal, or water." The toothless matron returned to Peilin's chart. "Your daughter's stem is metal—power energy. Her confident bird sign is supported by two elements of wood." The visiting matron smiled. "Kwan Taitai will be pleased to hear this."

Grandpa Du grinned as Peilin's fate continued to grow more positive. Peilin sensed that his heart was forever burdened with his own children's destiny. Anything he could do to change his granddaughter's might ease the difficult memory of what he'd allowed to happen to his daughter.

"And Master Yao?" queried Peilin's anxious mother. "What does his chart reveal?"

The Matchmaker held up her hand, pulled out young Yao's calculations, and closely compared his to Peilin's. "Kwan Taitai's son is a fire snake, supported by elements of earth," she revealed. "Much ambition, much power—fire must be kept under control," she advised, "For excess heat energy can be lethal."

Mother Du twisted her hands together, plagued by this possible cloud in her daughter's future, but the Matchmaker assured the family. "This is a small caution, not a big concern."

Turning back to her almanac, the concentrating woman continued, "The rooster and snake fall into the triangle of success." She looked up. "This is an excellent match."

Now Peilin's father turned to the Matchmaker. "But how can we ever provide enough dowry for such a prosperous match?"

"Not to worry," replied the confident fortune-teller. "The Kwans will supply all that is needed, including the bridal dress. And due to the distance, Peilin's wedding preparations will take place at Dragon

Lake. The fact that Peilin's eight characters match Master Yao's will be more than satisfactory for Kwan Taitai."

With the session completed, the Matchmaker packed up her belongings. As Peilin watched her mother wrap the pig's head and hindquarters for Kwan Taitai, she noticed her grandfather alone outside.

Digging his walking stick into the ground, the elderly man seemed to be murmuring. Peilin observed Grandpa Du turn his head up toward the sky, but she was too far away to understand his words.

And with that, Peilin's fate had been sealed.

Peilin sat in front of the small dressing table in her new family's home. The Good Luck Lady took her time performing the combing ritual on Peilin's long hair. "The first combing symbolizes beginning to end," the old lady recited. "Second, for harmony all your life," she continued. "Third—"

The bathing room door flew open; the Matchmaker entered with a flourish.

"What is taking so long in here?" she wailed. "Kwan Taitai is nearly in hysterics—the entire family waits for Peilin's entrance."

But the attentive woman continued to stroke Peilin's locks with care. "Almost done. Third combing blesses this bride with many sons and grandsons. Fourth—"

"Give me that comb," snapped the Matchmaker, but the Good Luck Lady held on tight.

"Fourth and final combing brings wealth and long-lasting marriage," she persisted. The Good Luck Lady finally put the comb down and smiled at Peilin.

Coiling Peilin's hair into a tight bun, the caretaker declared, "The proper hairstyle for a married woman." She held up the bronze mirror. Peilin stared at her reflection, surprised by the change she witnessed in her own features. Prior to this day, like all unmarried women, she had only worn her hair in a long ponytail against her back.

"We must hurry," said the Matchmaker, holding out the new bride's outfit.

Peilin slipped on the two-piece red silk *hong qua*—a dress adorned with golden phoenixes, chrysanthemums, and peonies. Red shoes decorated her tiny feet. This was the day she had been waiting for for many years.

Finally, the ornate phoenix bridal crown was carefully fitted atop Peilin's head. It was embellished with numerous kingfisher feathers and pearls. A red veil covering the bride's face represented her loyalty to her husband. As she rose for the first time, the elegant headdress caused Peilin to balance herself against her kind caretaker.

The Good Luck Lady smiled. "Beautiful bride," she cooed.

"Yes," agreed the Matchmaker. "Like none I have ever seen."

Continuing the customs, the Good Luck Lady turned so that Peilin could climb upon her back and be properly presented to her new family.

But Peilin stood, unable to move. A tear trickled down her cheek.

The old matron turned around and saw the sadness in Peilin's eyes. "*Wah!* Why is my pretty bride crying?"

Peilin bowed her head, unable to contain her heartache any longer.

"Good Luck Lady, you have shown me much kindness, but maybe you do not know," whispered Peilin. "My future husband is already dead. I am marrying a ghost."

2

NOVEMBER 9, 1938: Tossing his cigarette aside, twenty-eight-year-old Henri Neumann adjusted his thin woolen cap in a feeble attempt to shield himself against the bitter cold. The brisk wind kicked up the crimson-hued Nazi banners that lined Berlin's Unter den Linden thoroughfare. Henri shook his head. Century-old trees, some towering as high as a hundred and thirty feet, had been chopped down to make room for the offensive flag display. He shoved his gloveless hands into his coat pockets. Hitler's presence was impossible to ignore. Earlier that morning he'd seen a vulgar sign posted at the public park entrance—*KEINE HUNDE ODER JUDEN ERLAUBT* (No dogs or Jews allowed)—which not only raised Henri's ire, but reminded him of his helplessness. He'd wanted to kick the flagrant notice down, but with the growing number of storm troopers patrolling the streets, he'd restrained himself. He had a mission to accomplish after all. At his uncle's request, he'd been sent to purchase more insulin, aspirin, and camphor from the old pharmacist. He'd set his sights on that and forged on.

It had been a few months since Dr. Danziger had been forced to close his business. The chemist continued to sell what medicines he had left to Jewish doctors, but the very thought of the restrictions made Henri's hands clench. He was outraged over Hitler's unjust laws, and equally outraged that there seemed to be nothing he could do about it. Nothing anyone would do about it. This certainly wasn't the life he'd envisioned for himself while in medical school. Just this past July, Henri, his Uncle Viktor, and all Jewish doctors, had been stripped of their licenses. They could still see Jewish patients, but even that concession was becoming more dubious. The Third Reich now required Jewish doctors to get special permission from the government, approval that Henri considered preposterous. He punched the air with his fists. Feeling no relief, he turned north and headed farther into the Mitte district.

He lit another cigarette. Maybe the nicotine would calm his growing irritation. Along the way, Henri spotted the stark pale exterior of the Jazzkeler. For the last couple of years, the club had practically been Henri's second home; he was there at least four nights a week. Sam Arkin, the club owner, had been Henri's close friend since their days at the gymnasium. The two had bonded over their shared passion for musicians like Benny Goodman, Louis Armstrong, and Stefan Weintraub's Syncopators. Jazz's black and Jewish roots infuriated Hitler, who had immediately banned the *entartete Musik*—degenerated songs—when he took office in 1933. But the prohibition proved hard to enforce, even after the tunes were officially taken off the airwaves in 1935. Jewish musicians, like the Syncopators, were exiled. Others incarcerated, all for the love of music. But unlike cities such as Frankfurt and Stuttgart, Berlin was a sprawling metropolis. Here, the regulation was hard to impose and the scene had easily thrived underground. Places like Sam's were doing well, with regular clientele, both Aryan and Jewish alike.

Henri surmised that Sam's half-Jewish, half-Aryan heritage combined with his outgoing nature enabled the club owner to maneuver easily among the patrons who frequented the Jazzkeler. Sam often brought in new talent and liberally claimed bragging rights whenever someone took off. In fact, Sam had introduced Henri to one of his favorites, Wiener Zwerin, who sang many of Louis Armstrong's tunes, including "I'm in the Mood for Love."

Henri wasn't used to seeing the club in daylight and now its glaring white exterior stared back at him. Somewhere inside himself, he felt the stinging vulnerability of the harsh light cast upon his own skin: the flesh of a Jew. He shivered.

Yet, down in the Jazzkeler's boughs, Henri had found a warm and inviting atmosphere. The music, as well as the deep-walnut-hued walls and velvet-red stage curtains, created another world to him. The Jazzkeler alleviated the pain and sorrow of the real world—his mother's death, his father's depression, the constant worries about an uncertain future, if only temporarily. Here the music had opened Henri's heart and exposed it to love.

It was in this dark, smoky bar that Henri had been first captivated by Sophie's voice, too. Sophie. Her name alone evoked feelings of longing and sadness.

It was a year ago, the summer of 1937, when Henri had forged through the packed room toward his dapper friend, dressed in a sharp, charcoal pinstriped suit.

"Business is good, no?" Henri had bellowed above the clamor.

"Lucky for me," Sam had replied.

He had nodded toward a couple of young Nazi officers sitting in a back corner.

"I don't see them, and they don't see me."

Henri stiffened when he spotted the brownshirts out of the corner of his eye. Their presence had grown much worse this past year. Before, Berlin Jews worked around the uncomfortable situation. Now with more and more outbreaks of random arrests and beatings, they were feeling less and less secure.

"Wait till you hear this next act," he said, poking Henri's rib with his elbow.

Henri glanced at the stage. A microphone and stool were

being set up; a pianist rehearsed in the corner. Henri felt a rush of anticipation.

"Where's the new singer from?" he inquired.

"Sophie's a local," Sam answered.

With that, the room went dark. A bright spotlight pierced through the blackness.

And there she was.

Sophie's long silver-sequined dress shimmered as she softly crooned "Smoke Gets in Your Eyes." Henri stood enthralled. Her long blond hair and cherry-red-stained lips would have been intriguing on their own, but Sophie's deep, sultry voice enveloped Henri like a warm, lingering caress. As he continued to listen, Henri felt as if he was entering a wind tunnel--her voice pulling him toward her. Other men whistled, but Henri barely noticed. Sophie's smoldering eyes seem to stare only at him. He wondered if every guy in the place felt that way, or if she really was looking at him. When the song ended, she stood and bowed. The applause was deafening, and Henri noticed that everyone had risen to their feet. Standing ovations were rare at the Jazzkeler. Immediately at least a half dozen young men, including a couple of SS guards, surrounded her. Sophie moved to the edge of the stage while the next band set up to play. She gracefully shook the men's hands and accepted the red roses offered by one brave fan. Clearly this wasn't the first time she had been showered with attention. Henri was sure his chances with her were next to nil.

A bouncer hailed Sam from across the room.

"Stick around," he called back to Henri. "I'll introduce you later."

It was nearly midnight when the crowd finally thinned. Henri sat alone nursing a brandy when Sam appeared, leading Sophie.

"Sophie, I'd like you to meet my dear friend, Henri Neumann."

Henri stood. He extended his hand.

"Pleased to meet you," she replied.

Henri was suddenly tongue-tied. She was beautiful onstage, but even more stunning in person.

"Your voice," he stuttered, "I felt myself surrounded by its sublime, gentle breeze."

At first Henri wasn't sure if he had said too much. But after a moment, she broke out into a wide smile.

"My," she said. "I don't think anyone's described my music like that.... Tell me more."

Sophie took a seat next to Henri and with her elbow supporting her chin, she immediately became his audience.

"Well, it sounds like you two have a lot to discuss," Sam mused.

He quickly called out to the bartender.

"Couple more boilermakers over here," he said, pointing to Henri and Sophie. He placed his hands on Henri's shoulders.

"Take good care of my girl," he winked. "I've got to close out the cash register."

The two sat silently as the bartender plunked down a couple of whiskey shots and beers. Henri picked up one of the small goblets and noticed his hand tremble.

"To your beautiful voice—" he stammered. "You're absolutely mesmerizing."

She smiled demurely.

"I mean, have I gushed too much?" His cheeks felt hot.

"Actually, from you, I take it as a high compliment."

He placed his glass back on the table.

"Oh yes, only from me?"

She picked up her shot and downed it with a gulp.

"I sense your alligator ears," she said, plunking the empty glass on the table.

Henri didn't know how to respond to her praise.

"I do have an ear for music," he agreed.

"Sam told me you knew your jazz," she continued. "And he was certainly right. You're not just some bull looking for—shall I say—free milk."

"I've collected records of all the greats since I was a kid," he conceded. "Duke Ellington, Louis Armstrong, Ella Fitzgerald. Maybe you'd like to hear them sometime."

Sophie smiled and he immediately wondered if he'd gone too far.

"Jazz infuses the soul," she said. "When you get it, you get it deep down here—" she touched his heart.

Henri nearly quivered. He hadn't believed women like Sophie existed before that night.

"Jazz frees the spirit like no other," he'd added.

"Amen to that," she'd said, staring deeply into his eyes.

Henri now headed down Oranienburger Strasse in one of Berlin's older shopping districts to the northeast. *Engel Apotheke*—Angel Pharmacy—was located at the bottom of a once-grand eight-story red brick apartment building. Henri rounded the corner. Even though he knew about the plywood that boarded up the apothecary, it still took him by surprise. Once pristine, the complex was now marred with offensive graffiti—swastikas, "*Juden sind hier unerwünscht* (Jews not welcomed here), and "*Untermenschen* (subhumans)." Angel Drugstore had been in the Danziger family for generations. Henri had been coming here as long as he could remember. Slipping around to the back of the building, Henri furtively snuck down a narrow back alley and through a side door leading to the dwellings above. The dark interior hallway would have made it difficult for anyone else to make out the numbers on the doors, but Henri knew exactly where he was going. He could've found the apartment with his eyes closed. He had to knock a few times, but he was eventually greeted by his uncle's dear friend.

"Come in, come in," Simon murmured.

The hunched pharmacist ushered Henri inside. Henri hadn't seen Danziger since he'd been released from his arrest back in June. According to Uncle Viktor, Danziger was just leaving the Jewish cemetery in Weiβensee when guards seized him for jaywalking. Henri had been home the night his wife, Naomi, had banged on their apartment door, seeking Uncle Viktor's help. She hadn't known what had happened to him—only that her Simon was never late. Then as they met up with others roaming the Scheunenviertel area near the Neue Synagogue, it became clear that many Jews had been apprehended that evening.

Naomi had pleaded for her husband's release at the notorious police station on Grolmanstraβe. She was unable to pay the hefty fine—150 Reichsmark, when the Aryan fine for the same offense was a mere 1 Reichsmark. Naomi was finally united with her husband after nearly a month. By then, he'd been badly beaten. Henri and Viktor had helped her take her frail husband home.

Now Henri barely recognized the chemist whose dark hair had turned stark white.

"My uncle sends his regards."

Danziger cracked a faint smile.

"How's he feeling these days?"

"Better. We open the windows each day so he can get fresh air."

"I've something for him," the old man replied. "It'll help his breathing."

Henri nodded and the pharmacist disappeared into a back room. As Henri waited, he noticed the chopped up remains of the Danziger piano; its wood sacrificed for a fire to keep them warm. In another corner Henri spotted the rusted sign that used to hang in front of Angel Pharmacy. It was marred by angry red paint: "*Achtung Jude! Besuch verbotene* (Beware of Jew—Consultation Forbidden)." Danziger was right to have removed it from public view, but now, to keep it in his home? Henri's blood roiled at the indignity. The Nazis spared no one the disgrace of their hatred.

His uncle's friend returned with two bulky brown parcels bundled with twine.

"The smaller one's for Viktor," Danziger explained. "The larger one contains the medicines he asked for."

Henri tucked the parcels inside his wool coat. Simon rubbed his face and Henri couldn't help but stare at the dark lines etched along the elder man's forehead. When Simon turned to look out the window, his hand quivered. Henri was struck by the sad, faraway look in his eyes.

"My wife begs for rotted beets at the grocer's back door. Others yell names and spit at her while she's walking. With my business gone, I don't know how much more we can take.... "

Danziger buried his head in his hands.

Henri felt his own anxiety rise. Seeing the chemist's desperation scared him. He had known him since he was a young boy. Danziger had always been a strong, robust man, a proud and upright citizen. Now his gaunt figure cast a defeated shadow, a mere silhouette of what he had once been. There'd been so much anguish in their community these past years: family businesses confiscated, men beaten, arrested, and taken away. More recently the population endured hunger and increasing coldness. Henri wanted to believe that they would overcome, that the torment couldn't last. But seeing Danziger, he realized that even the most resilient struggled. It seemed no one was spared.

Feeling he could no longer take it himself, Henri bolted for the door.

"Everything's going to be okay," was all he could say as he closed Simon's door behind him.

Henri wanted to believe it, but he knew he spoke empty words.

On his way home from Simon's, Henri stopped by the Jazzkeler again. The club was closed, the front door locked. Henri looked around; no one was in sight. Sam should have been in by now. He needed to talk to his old friend, to find out if he knew anything about Sophie. It'd been over a week since Henri had heard anything from her. He knew her family hadn't been supportive of her dating a Jew. Now, with tension escalating, he worried that it had finally been too much for her to resist their urgings that she stop seeing him.

Henri knew better than to try to contact her at home. He had never met her father, but from what he gathered, Herr Schweitzer was a rigid, intolerant man. Sophie tried to keep her affairs to herself. As far as her father knew, Sophie sang opera.

Henri thought longingly back to the last time he'd seen her. She'd been at the Jazzkeler with her brother, Gerd. Henri had liked Gerd instantly, and the young man had taken to him. The twenty-three-year-old shared in their passion for jazz and was especially proud of his sister. But the last few weeks, Gerd had become increasingly cool toward Henri.

Henri couldn't help himself. As much as he feared it was over, he allowed his mind to drift back to the night of their first kiss.

It was on one of their early dates. He'd taken her for a stroll along the Spree River on a warm summer evening. Sophie had worn a rose-colored dress with chiffon laced sleeves. Her long blond hair flowed freely.

"You're as pretty as an angel," Henri sighed.

She glanced up at him and he felt the smothering flame within his heart grow more intense.

"*Ich glaube, dass ich mich in dich verliebt habe* (I think I've fallen in love with you)," she said coyly.

"Ah, you say that now," he volleyed back. "But it's still early—we're just getting to know each other."

"That's just it—you already get me—my music. All that I am is on display in the Jazzkeler. That place is like my refuge."

Henri looked up.

"Mine, too."

Sophie placed her hand on his.

"When I'm on that stage, it's like I'm a songbird let out of its cage. I'm free to express myself."

They kissed. A cascade of sparks ignited within him; Henri's whole body awakened with a fervor new to him.

He again considered whether it might be her father's influence that was keeping Sophie from him. He couldn't believe it. As if everything that was going on around Germany weren't already hard enough, the one person who gave him hope had disappeared from his life. *Was the world he knew conspiring against him? How much more pain could he take?*

What was ironic was that Henri himself barely acknowledged his own Jewish heritage. Except for observing the major holidays, he and his family barely kept any of the traditions.

Not having heard from her was frustrating, and frightening. He couldn't imagine what it would be like not to have any contact with her. The past week had been excruciating. He looked at his watch: twelve-thirty. Henri knew he had to be on his way. He'd stop back later and inquire when she'd be performing next and ask Sam to intervene on his behalf if he had to.

Henri rushed down the street. Across the way, a vendor flashed a newspaper emblazoned with the headline: "Polish Jew murders Nazi Leader!" Henri stopped, tossed a mark at the young boy, and grabbed a copy. Others huddled around the kiosk, catching up on the latest.

"*Verdammt* (damn)," he heard several men utter under their breath.

Henri read while making his way toward his father's bakery.

A shooting occurred a few days ago. A teen angry over his parents' abusive treatment by the Nazis had forced his way into the German consulate in Paris and shot the undersecretary.

Now that one of Hitler's own was dead at the hands of a Jew, who knew what might happen next? Henri looked around. For the moment, his fears were alleviated by the relative normalcy surrounding him. He was grateful for Uncle Viktor's foresight in having solicited Henri's help to move more medical supplies into the cellar underneath the family bakery.

Neumann's Bäckerei occupied the bottom level of a Neo-Renaissance-style three-story building. A beige structure with repeating windows reflected its simple, stern environment. Henri's paternal great-grandfather opened Neumann's in 1849 and it had supported the family for nearly a century. Through the bakery window, onlookers could view baskets full of fresh *Brot*, bread baked the night before by Henri's father Georg and older brother Otto. Otto took after their father—stout and robust. Henri had never seen his father without a beard, which had turned gray some time ago. Georg and Otto's stamina suited the long hours and vigorous labor it took to manage huge ovens and bulky sacks of flour. Delicious smells of warm *Weßbrot, Schwarzbrot, Bauernbrot,* and *Salzstangen*—white, dark, coarse rye, and pretzel sticks—wafted outside into the morning air, making it nearly irresistible not to step inside.

It'd been over a year now since Jewish shop owners had been mandated to display nameplates above their doorways. A sign now identified their Hebrew heritage to all who passed by. To Henri, the placard was as demeaning as the one Dr. Danziger had torn down and discarded in his apartment. It upset Henri that his father had complied without emotion. Henri had heard from other Jewish friends that their mothers were urging their husbands to emigrate, but Georg had been widowed for eleven years now and Henri knew he would never make a move to abandon his home country. Georg had grown accustomed to living without a wife. That coupled with his unwavering allegiance to the country he had fought for, affected Georg's ability to see what was happening around him. Henri couldn't blame his father for the way he was. It was his character to ignore the growing signs of anti-Semitism around him. That's how he coped. Otherwise, Henri was sure the existing circumstances would shatter his melancholic father. But with all that Henri was hearing and seeing, he worried. Only Uncle Viktor seemed to take the threats seriously—or at least he was the only one willing to talk to Henri about what was happening. It disturbed him that his father was so naive, and it was partly why Henri lived with Viktor on the third floor while Otto and Georg lived on the second.

At least the bakery provided a modicum of concealment. Since last summer, Henri had been sneaking down late at night when he knew he'd be the least likely to be detected. He'd push the worn carpet scrap aside and slide the floorboard open over the hidden bakery cellar. He'd then make his way down the narrow cement staircase and into the cool concrete enclosure where his father stored grains, flour, and salt. Georg was carrying fewer supplies now, with only their fellow Jews as customers. And even they couldn't afford very much. Georg often ended up giving away more bread for free than he was able to sell. Now most of the space that used to be filled with ingredients had been stuffed with syringes, needles, iodine swabs, compresses, and other medications. Henri had even squeezed a small cot between the rusted water pipes and handmade shelving. With each clandestine mission to obtain supplies, Henri's secret medical room was becoming more complete.

The first time Henri had brought Sophie to the cellar was on a night after they'd seen the popular American movie, *Swing Time*. Henri had enjoyed sitting in the darkened theater with Sophie's head nestled on his shoulder. He'd loved watching Fred Astaire and Ginger Rogers dance across the screen.

But it was Sophie's wandering hands that ultimately captured Henri's attention. At first she lightly brushed her fingers across his forearm. He kissed her. Taking in a whiff of her sweet-smelling hair, he smiled. As he relaxed, her moves became more daring, grazing his hips and then running down his thighs. Henri shuddered as he felt himself press against the pleasing sensation. When the movie ended, it was all he could do to walk straight.

She agreed to come back to his house. Upstairs a light was on. Uncle Viktor was awake. With Henri's physical longing reaching a fervent pitch, he immediately thought of the converted basement.

He slipped his arm around her waist.

"Where are we going?" she asked.

"*Shhh*," Henri said softly.

He led her inside the unlit bakery. He deftly moved aside the floorboard that led to the basement entrance. In complete darkness, he held her hand and kept her steady as he guided her down the stairs. Once he had replaced the floorboard above, he struggled to find the light.

When he finally found the switch, Sophie let out a small gasp. "Henri, what is this?"

"It's our secret medical alcove," he whispered.

He could see her eyes widen as she took in all the supplies and medicines stuffed into the tiny basement.

"Henri," she whispered. "Couldn't you get in trouble hiding all this—"

He quickly cut her off, holding a finger to her lips. "Not if no one knows it's here."

She began stroking his hair. "I love you."

As her lips moved closer to his, he felt himself rise again.

"I love you, too," he said softly.

With her body now pressed against his, he quickly grabbed her by the waist and guided her to the cot hidden in the corner. He locked his insisting mouth onto hers and another gasp escaped her lips. Through her blouse, he could feel her taut nipples. She loosened her braided hair and then quickly removed his shirt.

"Come closer," she murmured as her hands loosened his pants button and pulled down the zipper. Henri groaned as he eagerly tugged at her clothes. Her blouse easily slipped off. Her body was more beautiful than he had even imagined. Henri's heart pounded as he caressed her breasts, so soft that he had to resist his urge to examine them more closely. Sophie quickly removed her skirt and tossed it aside. Henri had wanted this for months but he'd held back—he wanted to wait for her to be ready. She glided his pants off. She gently bent down and kissed his thigh, her hair grazing his stiff member.

"I want you," she whispered into his ear.

His excitement rose to a frenzied pitch. Now, more than anything, Henri wanted to feel what it was like to be part of her, to be inside her. Before he knew it, their two naked bodies had entangled, each of them groping hungrily for one another as they made love for the first time.

When it was over, Henri wiped the sweat from his brow. He looked over at Sophie, who was also catching her breath. She smiled and buried her head into his chest. As they lay beside one another, Henri knew more strongly than ever that he was deeply in love.

Now Henri entered the family bakery alone. Georg appeared, refilling the breadbaskets. Henri grabbed a roll and bit into it.

"One of your English students is already waiting," Georg told his son.

Henri nodded. He was expecting his first patient, and this was the code they'd come up with to discuss what was going on underground, beneath the bakery floorboards.

Yet as Henri prepared to descend the stairs, he couldn't get his mind off Sophie. Recalling their first time together, he felt a renewed hope that not all was lost, that she loved him as much now as she did then. Their commitment was strong; it would weather this unfortunate time of their lives. He was sure of it.

P EILIN STEADIED HERSELF under the heavy bridal headdress as the chamber door opened to the throng of people waiting in the evening's cool air. The Good Luck Lady and the Matchmaker nudged Peilin forward onto the outdoor terrace. Peilin was overwhelmed by the bursting lights and noisy firecrackers. She shielded her eyes as she made her way across the garden to the Kwans' ancestral hall.

With her crimson-hued shoes, Peilin stepped over the carefully placed *ma an*, a horse saddle, in a gesture meant to bring tranquility to her marriage, and into the packed building. Red banners emblazoned with gold characters for "double happiness" adorned the walls.

Kwan family and friends, some of whom had traveled days to attend, crammed the large inner sanctum. From beneath her veil, Peilin scanned the crowd, searching for her natal family. But by the time she neared the altar, she still hadn't spotted her parents, Grandpa Du, or Ping among the throng. She knew they wouldn't miss this for anything. After all, the whole family had been invested in this day since she was eight years old. And while she had long fantasized about what it would be like, her dreams never accounted for what this day would look like without Yao.

Peilin had heard the story of Yao's fate from Grandpa Du. As Kwan Taitai's only child, he was even more special to her. She doted on him, shielding him from bad weather, insects, and even other boys whose rough playing caused her great alarm. Mother Kwan pampered Yao like a delicate royal prince. According to Grandpa Du, Yao went along with his mother's wishes, but as he grew older he began to feel increasingly stifled.

When Kwan Yao turned twenty, he decided to join the Kuomintang army and battle the Japanese, as well as the communists. Despite Kwan Taitai's pleas, Yao liked the idea of wearing a uniform and fighting for a cause. It gave him a sense of purpose. Mother Kwan could not believe that Yao needed a purpose beyond becoming head of the Kwan household. It was only when Mother Kwan seemed like she might actually prevent Yao from leaving Dragon Lake that Father Kwan took a stand and insisted they let him serve in the army, for family honor. When Peilin had first heard this, she recalled how admirable she thought Father Kwan's gesture was and ever since then he had a special place in her heart.

Yao was convinced that his service in the military would elevate his status when he returned to Dragon Lake. Despite Kwan Taitai's pleas, Yao was immediately deployed to Nanking. That December of 1937, Japan invaded the capital city. Yao died fighting off several mighty Nippon attackers. Hearing of her precious son's death, Mother Kwan demanded details. A well-connected friend revealed Yao's violent beheading.

At first Peilin thought the Kwans would call off the wedding. But Kwan Taitai insisted that her son not leave earth an unmarried man. So it was that the marriage arrangements stood firm. Peilin, her legs heavy with fear, nearly froze at the festive sight of her nuptial celebration, grateful for the protective veil that hid the depths of her despair.

As the ceremony continued, Peilin made her way to the Kwan family ancestral altar. Peilin stopped before Yao's newly painted picture and felt calmed by the serene portrait. But when a straw mannequin was suddenly placed beside her, she gasped. Her ghost husband. She bowed her head to the figure, but inside she trembled.

She had met Yao only once, when she was ten and he was fourteen. She'd accompanied Grandpa Du on one of his visits to Dragon Lake to purchase pearl powder. On the long bus journey there, Peilin's curiosity and fear about her betrothed grew. She wondered if he would be ugly or spoiled, or if he would even take notice of her.

It was raining heavily when Grandpa Du and Peilin arrived at Dragon Lake. The servants took their wet belongings while grandfather and granddaughter sipped tea at the dining room table with Mother and Father Kwan.

While Grandpa Du talked with the Kwans, Peilin looked around the large house, wondering where Yao might be. Then a slight movement caught her attention near the rear door. Taking a closer look, she spied him peering through a narrow crack. Peilin could see that he was no monster, but rather a handsome young teen. She smiled. The door opened ever so slightly. Yao quickly flashed an impish grin in return before darting off into the vast household.

It was the only time Peilin had ever seen her husband-to-be alive.

Through her veil, she viewed the crude representation of Yao that stood nearly six feet tall. With its thick straw sticking out through the soft silk of his black overcoat, the soulless spectacle seemed to goad her with its surreal manifestation. Peilin hoped that the figure would at least be faceless, as faceless as the bizarre ceremony around her swirled with empty, meaningless love. With one swift glance, though, Peilin saw that Yao's face had indeed been roughly sculpted from clay. The frozen expression was a ghastly grin. The head that had been topped with the groom's red-tasseled black hat caused Peilin to hastily turn away. She wanted to run, but abandoning her arranged marriage, no matter what the circumstances, would bring much shame to her family.

Together with her phantom husband, she paid homage to Heaven and Earth, the Kwan family ancestors, and *chu shen*, the kitchen god. With her new in-laws seated nearby, Peilin then placed two red dates, her favorite *hong zao* herb into cups of warm water. She picked up the cups and turned to serve her new in-laws, stopping to bow before them. After a few moments she realized that the tea had not been received. Peilin looked up just as the quick-tempered woman swatted the cups out of Peilin's hands and onto the floor.

"*Aii-yah!*" shouted Kwan Taitai, her fiery eyes blazing with rage. Peilin could only guess that Kwan Taitai was suffering in the aftermath of Yao's death. Peilin studied her new mother-in-law. She had not seen Kwan Taitai since she was a child. She now stood before the matriarch as a woman. Peilin could not understand why Mother Kwan was so agitated.

"You offer your new husband's parents *cold* tea?"

The room went silent. Peilin felt her heart overcome with fear. She hurriedly retrieved the dashed cups, replacing the red dates and filling them with fresh hot water from the kettle.

When she re-served the tea, Peilin avoided direct eye contact with Mother Kwan. But as she presented Father Kwan with his cup, she felt a hint of compassion. She understood that he, too, often endured Kwan Taitai's imperial wrath.

After the tea ceremony, everyone moved out of the ancestral hall and walked back to the main house to the dining room. Peilin took her seat next to Yao's straw mannequin at the expansive banquet table. Generous platters of roasted duck, baked lobster, and honey-walnut prawns circled the room, but Peilin sat in silence, barely able to eat. She glanced at the cheerful crowd, avoiding her in-laws nearby. Peilin politely smiled as more guests entered and took their seats. She scanned each face, hoping to see her family, but she was disappointed by each renewed attempt to locate them. Her stomach churned, but she continued to smile, telling herself that she needed to make it through the celebration without becoming sick.

When she was finally able to retire, Peilin entered the bridal suite. She sat on the large four-poster bed decorated in red and gold. Her straw husband had been brought in before her and was propped up with pillows. A servant had already lit the double crimson candle decorated with dragons and phoenixes. It cast a soft and romantic glow in the room. Two goblets filled with wine and honey, linked by a red string, sat on the stand nearby. Peilin's mother had instructed her young daughter that the bride and the groom were to pick up the goblets together and drink in unison. Peilin sat staring at the large cups. Not knowing how to proceed, she decided it was best to leave them untouched.

Peilin sat frozen. Glancing around the large chamber, she pulled a thin blanket around her to keep her warm as the mannequin stared at her grotesquely. She laid it down and herself beside it, wondering what bodily wonders she would have experienced had Yao lived. Staring once again at the terra cotta head, Peilin reached out to touch its lips with her hand—then pulled back quickly as the clay's cold, corpselike hardness confirmed the harsh reality of her situation.

She sat up, her hopeless plight once again filling her with terrifying fear.

Then she remembered a story that Grandpa Du told her when she was very young:

Water, standing in an elephant-shape vase, froze after being in it for so long. It stood so long in that vase that the solid water grew to believe that it was an elephant. But one day, the vase broke. The ice melted, suddenly realizing that it was not an elephant. Discovering it was actually water, it had to learn who it really was again.

As Peilin peeled off the layers of her bridal outfit, she felt herself melting into a puddle of tears. Exhausted, she lay down next to her ghost husband, uncertain of her new future, and fell into a restless sleep.

Peilin's slumbering eyes fluttered as the morning sun streamed through the window. It took a moment for her to remember her new circumstances—she was now a married woman living in her husband's house. She immediately looked around for the straw mannequin, but it was gone. Peilin breathed a sigh of relief. The servant must have removed it while she slept, she thought, feeling grateful.

Warmed by the sun's light, the new bride knew that she could not continue to stay in bed. A weaker person would, or worse, run away or kill herself. Any of these choices would bring shame to her natal family, especially her beloved Grandpa Du, who had arranged the marriage so that she might have a better chance in life.

Peilin sat up. Even though Kwan Taitai was difficult, Peilin knew that she must do as the Good Luck Lady instructed and please her new mother-in-law beyond reproach so that Kwan Taitai would have no reason to become angry.

Peilin vowed to accept her circumstances. After all, she was bound by duty—the obligation and conduct arising from one's position in life. She recognized that women in her situation did not have many choices. As she rose from bed, Peilin knew that a combination of patience, loyalty, and courage were needed now.

Noticing a desk under the window, Peilin discovered what were known as the four treasures: a writing brush, ink stick, paper, and ink stone. To clarify her new resolve to herself, Peilin sat down, grinded the ink stick into the stone, and began to write the words mindfully onto a piece of paper.

Ren nai, the Chinese word for patience, also stood for tolerance. As she drew the Chinese character, she could see that the symbol for *knife* was written over the notation for *heart*. Patience would require endurance despite any threat that may be looming overhead. Peilin studied the character. She was proud of her accomplishments, again thinking of Grandpa Du and all the opportunities he had provided her by teaching her so many skills normally reserved for boys. She would not allow fear to strike her down.

Next she wrote the Chinese character for loyalty—*zhong*—another heart-based word. Above the heart she drew a box with a line through the middle, the symbol for *center*. Peilin could see that a loyal person was someone who had their heart in the right place.

Lastly, Peilin drew the figure of a person standing with arms outstretched, the symbol anchoring the word *yong*—the Chinese term for *courage*. She gazed at the figure and saw that it stood alone in the wide-open space. Enduring nature's wilderness—symbolized by the tiny marks of wild-looking grass around it—the person braved the unknown.

Peilin put the brush down and drew strength from the three written words. Then she carefully folded the paper and tucked it into a hidden pocket as she dressed. *Just as every river finds the sea*, she thought to herself, *so, too, would she find her path in life, her destiny.*

Fully dressed in a long azure blue silk cheongsam dress, Peilin emerged from the bridal suite to find Kwan Taitai already seated at the dining room table. Peilin politely bowed as she took a seat next to the imposing house matron.

"There you are. I would have thought being born under the sign of the rooster you would be an early riser," said Kwan Taitai. "Obviously your family operates differently than ours," she finished curtly and then mumbled under her breath. "Especially one that doesn't even show up to their daughter's own wedding."

Although Peilin, too, wondered why her family failed to attend, she immediately set out to calm Kwan Taitai's disapproval. "Many apologies, Mother Kwan. I was exhausted from last night's festivities. It will not happen again."

"I should say not," the elder woman reprimanded.

Kwan Taitai clapped her hands rapidly. "Bamboo!" she called out. Within seconds, a young female servant appeared with a plate of steaming dim sum and a hot pot of tea. The girl looked to be about thirteen years old. She swiftly set the food before Peilin and disappeared just as quickly as she had materialized.

"Eat," ordered Kwan Taitai.

Peilin picked up the white bun *bao* filled with sweet *cha shao* pork and bit into it. As Kwan Taitai continued to peruse a fashion magazine, Peilin perceived the beauty that must have once been beneath the fine lines of Kwan Taitai's paper-thin skin. *Like a fading chrysanthemum,* Peilin thought to herself.

Yet of all Kwan Taitai's features, her three-inch lily feet, most prized by men for their beauty, still commanded admiration. Peilin clearly remembered the first time her own mother explained the procedure in which a very young girl's toes were broken and tightly bound for years to inhibit their growth. At one time, the women in Peilin's village had bound feet, but a hundred years before she was born, there was a terrible flood. With so many people and crops lost, the village women needed to start working alongside their husbands. They needed to walk and haul heavy objects so bound feet became obsolete.

It was obvious to Peilin that the stately woman understood their allure, for she displayed her tiny feet whenever possible. But Kwan Taitai was constricted to the most confined movements, and occasionally wobbled unsteadily or winced when she walked. Peilin wondered about the price her mother-in-law paid for the honor of her beauty. Kwan Taitai lacked mobility and freedom, two things Peilin treasured most. And Peilin supposed that the constant pain added misery to Kwan Taitai, which she took out on everyone around her.

As Peilin was finishing her sticky rice cake wrapped in lotus leaf, Kwan Taitai erupted with a deep hacking cough. Bamboo appeared and launched into a series of strong whacks on Mother Kwan's back. Peilin reached in and stopped the young girl.

"A dry cough cannot be helped in this manner," said Peilin without delay.

The servant's eyes went wide as Kwan Taitai's coughing turned violent. The muscles of her neck suddenly expanded, causing Kwan Taitai's pearl choker to burst into pieces. Peilin urged her mother-in-law to take small sips of tea. But between spasms she continued to gasp for air.

"I have just the herbs you need to quiet your cough, Mother Kwan." Peilin turned to Bamboo. "Quick, get my medicine bag in the next room."

The scared servant did as she was told. Once she had her supplies, Peilin immediately entered the kitchen and added sweet almonds and rock sugar to a pot of boiling water. The almonds had a neutral nature that tempered coughs. Peilin promptly returned to Kwan Taitai's side and urged her to drink the almond tea.

"This will soothe your throat, Mother," said Peilin.

The wheezing woman grabbed the cup and gulped it down. Feeling its calming results, Kwan Taitai demanded more. Peilin continued to fill her cup with the medicinal tea until Kwan Taitai had consumed it all.

Peilin reached down and gathered the ruptured pieces of Kwan Taitai's necklace. Placing the loose pearls into a rice bowl, Peilin handed it back to her mother-in-law.

"Think you deserve my gratitude for your little trick?" Kwan Taitai sneered as she caught her breath.

Peilin was at a loss for words. As her mother-in-law recovered,

Peilin sensed that she was incapable of revealing any sense of vulnerability.

"Stupid girl," hissed Mother Kwan. "Do not underestimate me. My ghost son asked for you to be his bride even though he has traveled to the next world. It was my duty to honor his request. But how your life plays out from now on is up to me. You think you saved my life and now you want my pearls. Those are mine."

"Mother Kwan, I would never think such—"

But Peilin was cut off with a sweeping dismissive arm as Kwan Taitai stood upright. The old woman's eyes glanced over toward the picture of her son resting on the ancestral altar. Peilin perceived the pain lurking beneath the anger. But it was as if Kwan Taitai willed her eyes to dry up and the old woman, raw on the inside, lashed out one more time.

"Since you think you can repair my throat, repair my pearls, too."

Taking Bamboo's arm, Kwan Taitai hobbled out of the room. Peilin stared at the rice bowl full of pearls, not knowing how she was going to fix them. Mother Kwan expected her to mend the necklace, yet Peilin had no experience stringing pearls. She turned to the window, wondering what to do. She spied a rudimentary shed near the dock. It was built from raw wood and thick mud, and it seemed like a good place to escape until she could figure out what to do.

Peilin made her way up the squeaky stairs leading to the lonely structure perched over the lake's placid waters. Inside, Peilin saw several large tables filled with oyster shells, pails of harvested pearls, and an assortment of magnifying glasses, metal pliers, and instruments. Peilin clutched the bowl filled with Mother Kwan's pearls. Looking around, she was grateful for the reprieve supplied by the secluded surroundings and dim light. Peilin laid her head on the table and closed her eyes.

She woke up some time later and shook off her fatigue. With her eyes now adjusted to the shed's dark shadows, she was surprised to discover Father Kwan quietly huddled in a corner of the room. Peilin had never seen him without Kwan Taitai at his side. He seemed lighter and less burdened. He removed his glasses and looked up at her.

"I didn't mean to fall asleep," stuttered Peilin, "I just have no idea how to salvage Kwan Taitai's necklace—" Peilin held out the bowl of loose pearls.

Father Kwan nodded. "Not to worry. I, too, like to rest here." He held out his open hand. "Here, let me show you how to restore it."

Peilin handed the bowl to her father-in-law. His fingers quickly sorted through the tiny white spheres as he nimbly strung them with a knot tied between each precious pearl. Father Kwan said nothing as he worked. Peilin admired the ease with which he repaired the strand. After he had strung several pearls, he handed it to Peilin. "Here, you try now."

Peilin cautiously took the filament. Father Kwan gave her a bead and helped her thread and knot it onto the necklace. With each pearl, Peilin grew more confident.

Peilin was so caught up that she was surprised when she noticed her father-in-law staring down at her large, unbound feet.

"You must think mine ugly," she said, hiding them beneath her long dress.

But instead Father Kwan smiled. "I do not understand the lure of broken feet bound together until they are no longer useful," he said.

Puzzled, Peilin stared at him.

"My mother had feet like yours," he continued.

"How could that be?" Peilin gasped aloud.

"My parents were Hakka—nomadic people who roamed this country. Father found employment here at Dragon Lake as Number One Worker for the Kwan family. We are common people. But Kwan Taitai's father saw my worth and betrothed me to his only child."

Peilin nodded. She could relate to the concept of having worth and parlaying that into a better life. Silently, she fretted about her family's absence from the wedding the night before. She had heard nothing of their delay or inability to attend. The lack of communication caused her to worry even more. When the necklace was finished, Father Kwan walked outside and looked at the sun overhead.

"Just enough time to check on the oysters. Do you want to see?" he asked.

Peilin nodded, grateful for any time away from her mother-in-law. Father Kwan untied the small rowboat. Peilin climbed in. She gazed ahead over the lake as he paddled them out to his farm beneath the water.

The boat glided along the glassy surface. Peilin studied her father-in-law. His lean physique complemented his simple, effective movements.

Father Kwan surveyed their surroundings, as if he himself embodied the lake bound by land on all sides. Like the water beneath them, Father Kwan stood perfectly still. Yet Peilin sensed a raw strength hidden below the peaceful surface.

He paddled to a row of floating bamboo poles and stopped. Tugging on the rope attached to the slender shaft, Father Kwan pulled up a wire cage that contained large oyster clams pregnant with their precious gifts. Peilin watched as he gently tapped the shell. When satisfied, he pulled some oysters into the boat while re-immersing others back into the lake.

"Some say the pearl comes from the brain of a magic dragon. Others talk of a pearl so brilliant they could cook rice by the heat of its rays. Certainly, the precious pearl contains powers of luck and fortune."

Peilin nodded. Father Kwan plied open one of his harvested shells. Fishing through its meaty interior, he pulled out an iridescent white pearl and offered it to Peilin. At first she declined, but he insisted. She took the gift thankfully.

Peilin examined the treasure. She recalled that Grandpa Du also treasured the pearl. Rich in calcium, it was an effective remedy for many illnesses.

As they continued to check the cages, her father-in-law lowered his voice. "Kwan Taitai is very hot, full of fire. Best to stay out of her sight as much as possible."

Peilin nodded, grateful for his acknowledgment of this adversary.

As Father Kwan rowed back to shore, he continued to speak softly. "You must not ever tell her what I have told you today. My duty is to protect the pearl."

As she returned to land, Peilin, too, felt protected.

Right away Peilin learned how to maneuver between Kwan Taitai and Father Kwan. Peilin spent most of her time tending to Kwan Taitai's every whim—cooking, cleaning, and even washing her soiled foot bindings. But whenever Father Kwan had work to be done with the pearls, Peilin volunteered her services and instantly became adept at sorting and stringing the spherical treasures. Peilin hoped one day to give her natal mother a strand.

A few weeks had passed since the wedding and Peilin had yet to hear news of her family. Under Mother Kwan's ever watchful and wary eyes, Peilin felt like she was in prison at her new home. Homesick, Peilin longed to go back to her village.

While Peilin kept to her chores as a dutiful daughter-in-law, she was torn inside about how to ask the Kwans if she might return to her village for a visit. Kwan Taitai seemed to grow more and more agitated with her each day, and although she found a protector in her father-in-law, it seemed too big a request to ask so early on in their arrangement. Peilin often caught Kwan Taitai's eyes darting back and forth from the ancestral altar, as if her dead son's portrait watched his mother's every move. If the elder matron pricked her finger while sewing, she would jump up and call out to the servant girl to add more offerings of oranges in front of Yao's picture. Some mornings Peilin sat alone at the breakfast table as the elder woman tried to shake off a fitful night's sleep. But despite Kwan Taitai's distractions, or perhaps because of them, she grew increasingly unsatisfied with Peilin's work. No bowing or cooking or cleaning could please her haunted mother-in-law. Only Father Kwan's silent understanding saved Peilin from going crazy herself.

Each night as she fell asleep, Peilin reminded herself of the promise she made to fulfill her role with patience, loyalty, and courage.

Twenty-four days since the wedding had gone by and Peilin was growing ever-more perplexed and concerned about not having heard from her family. She started to plan out how she might ask for permission to go home for a short visit. That night, a letter arrived. At first Peilin did not recognize the writing. She quickly scanned down to the bottom of the page. It said it was from her brother Ping, whom she knew couldn't write. As she scanned its message, it dawned on her that he must have found someone to pen the letter for him.

My dearest Sister,

I hope this letter finds you well and thriving as a new member of the Kwan family. I continue to miss you daily, but am warmed by your improved circumstances. I'm sure with all the activity and celebration you may have missed that we were not able to attend your wedding. An unforeseen situation prevented our attendance.

As you know the last two years have brought little rainfall. This year was no different. Grandpa Du wisely instructed Father and Mother to plant sorghum, which did not require as much water as the rice. We worked diligently to grow and nurture the sorghum, which produced a sizable crop. As soon as it was ready for harvest, I hooked the cart to our trusty water buffalo. Together the beast and I headed to town for the two-day trip. As I waved goodbye to Mother, Father, and Grandpa Du, I had no idea that would be the last time I would see them alive.

On the morning of my return, the cart broke down. I was delayed an additional day in order to fix it. If only I had known the fate back home, I would have abandoned the cart and run all the way back to our village! For as I grew closer to our farm, I could smell the bitter wind of burning, and then discovered that our farm was lit up as bright as a firecracker. I shouted and ran from one end of the land to another, but there was no answer. They had torched our straw roof and destroyed the house. Then I spied Japanese soldiers—too many to count. At first I hid. Then I spotted them—our family, and oh, the things I saw—they are too horrible to describe, dear sister. There is nothing left. Father, Mother, and Grandpa Du all perished. As I sat crying, our neighbor from three farms down arrived. His own property suffered much loss as well, although no family members died. He helped me bury Mother, Father, and Grandpa Du and they now rest under the weeping willow tree.

The scorched ground will no longer support the life we once lived. Our neighbor offered to take me in, but I cannot stay. There is nothing left for me here.

I am told there are good jobs in the city and so I leave for Shanghai in the morning.

Know that you are in my thoughts daily.

Your brother,

Ping

Peilin wept. She folded the letter and tucked it into her pocket along with her three special characters and her precious pearl. Thoughts of ever returning to see her family, especially her beloved Grandpa Du, now vanished. She hid in her room, telling Bamboo she was sick and would not be attending dinner. Peilin was distraught, not only about losing her elders, but also about her only brother's well-being. He was disabled, and the farm was all he'd ever known. Her father had spent a lot of time adjusting the equipment so that Ping could till and harvest the land himself. *How would Ping find work in the city with such severe limitations,* she wondered.

By nightfall, Father Kwan entered with a pot of tea.

"Heavy sorrow for such a young woman to endure," he said.

Peilin looked up at her father-in-law, surprised that he knew the real reason for her confinement.

"Kwan Taitai insisted we open your letter before it was delivered to you. I'm very sorry for your loss."

Father Kwan poured Peilin a steaming cup of warm ginseng tea. She sat up and drank it gratefully.

"*Xie Xie,*" she whispered, thanking him.

"But much about your future can be derived from your past," he continued.

"I have no past now. It has been destroyed."

Father Kwan gave her a compassionate smile. "Kwan Taitai's father, Old Man Kwan, recognized my family as a descendant of Lao Tzu. Legend has it that his offspring were the keeper of the pearl. That was also why, despite my humble background, Old Man Kwan selected me as his son-in-law. It was my destiny."

Peilin studied Father Kwan's gentle and reflective manner.

"*Hao,*" she nodded. "I can see that."

He studied her closely. "Just as I can see that you are written on water—*liuyan*."

Puzzled, Peilin looked more closely at Father Kwan.

"Sometimes you are caught between a sense of despair and a desire to emerge," he explained. "Water converts to steam and condenses into ice. It flows between states of being. Your life will be ever-shifting. A river flows through many landscapes."

"I'll remember that," Peilin replied.

He now stood at the door.

"Take as long as you need," Father Kwan said. "Don't worry. I'll take care of Kwan Taitai."

Peilin nodded, grateful for his understanding.

"*Wan an* (good night)," she replied softly as he closed the door.

From that point forward, she worked to hide her grief from Mother Kwan, who would erupt at any sign of Peilin's emotions. While she had an ally in Father Kwan, Kwan Taitai's behavior was intolerable and ever-more abusive. With no family heritage left to betray, Peilin began to scheme ways in which she might escape from the Kwans and leave Dragon Lake forever.

4

BEHIND THE LARGE OVENS in the rear of his family's small bakery, Henri pushed the loose floorboard aside while his father stood watch. Henri scanned their surroundings, too. For him, fear lingered heavily in the air. He felt it wasn't enough to keep watch; it was also important to think ahead.

"We must be extra careful these days," Henri whispered. "There are more spies than ever."

Georg nodded; Henri slipped into the cellar. Though few of their patients had the means to pay, neither Henri nor Viktor had turned a single person away. They were dedicated doctors, and times like these were unprecedented. Henri enjoyed helping people; it made him feel useful during this dire time. But now, Henri kept the practice going alone while his uncle recuperated from his recent bout with bronchitis.

Frau Weinberg sat perched on a narrow cot that had been set up as a makeshift examination table. Her short legs dangled above the cold floor as she shivered in a thin cotton gown. Henri dug up a blanket from one of the cupboards and placed it around her shoulders.

"Always did like to keep me waiting," his old schoolteacher snorted with an air of authority.

"Me? I think you're confusing me with my older brother," teased Henri.

Frau Weinberg grunted. "I never forget a student. Otto cringed at the thought of raising my ire. You, on the other hand, constantly challenged my patience. If it weren't for that twinkle in your blue eyes and the fact that you could add numbers so fast, I would've sat you in the corner the entire school year."

She paused and smiled. "Now look at you."

Henri wanted to feel lighthearted, but he knew her spry humor was a way to mask her recent hardships.

"Your eyes are heavy, Frau Weinberg. Have you been sleeping?"

She shook her head. Henri knew his former teacher had been fighting for her husband's release for the past five months. Unlike Simon Danziger, Herr Weinberg had been sent directly to Buchwald. Ever since the Nazi roundup in June, rumors had been swirling about beatings and hard labor at the camp.

"I've filed applications to Switzerland, Denmark, and Sweden. I've sold all the family heirlooms, including my mother's gold necklace and our own wedding rings. As soon as I can prove we have emigration papers, they'll let him go. I know Bertie won't like the thought of moving across the Atlantic, but I'm looking into the United States and Mexico."

Henri placed the stethoscope on the back of her chest and noted its uptick as she spoke.

"Deep breaths, Frau Weinberg. You've many options."

"What about you and your family?" she asked.

Henri froze. He didn't want to cause her any more worry.

"You're so kind to think of our safety," he began. "It's a long process, as you know. Otto's been working on papers to get us all out of here," he lied.

"I'm glad to hear that," she said, patting Henri's hand.

The truth was that Otto was doing no such thing. Neither Henri's brother nor father seemed to feel the panic shared by their fellow Jews. Whether they refused to see or were just living in denial was unclear, but it frustrated Henri. He'd discussed the situation on many occasions with Viktor, and both had agreed they needed to try something. Viktor had been writing friends in the States, but so far no one had responded. They weren't even sure if their letters were making it to their intended recipients.

"For now, concentrate on your husband," Henri replied.

He finished taking her blood pressure and pointed to the scale crammed under the basement stairs.

"May I?"

"Only for you."

She stepped up gingerly and Henri did a double-take. She'd lost too much since her last visit. Many of his patients had. He wrote the new number down.

"What can I say, dear teacher? Please eat and rest as much as possible."

The familiar feeling of helplessness rose in Henri as he turned his back so she could get dressed in her street clothes.

"You know," she said, "my neighbor has a boat ticket to Shanghai."

"To China?" Henri hadn't even contemplated that some of his countrymen would flee to China. "Why there?"

"Someone gave it to her. They welcome Jews without visas."

"When will your neighbor be leaving?" Henri asked.

Frau Weinberg sighed. "A single ticket does her no good. She, too, has a husband. Neither of us can use it." She paused. "I'm finished dressing now, Henri. Thank you."

Henri turned to face her.

"You're single—you should take it. I'll get it for you. It's not often that these openings come along." The words seemed to tumble from her mouth and Henri didn't know what to say.

"China?" he repeated. "My uncle has had a strong interest in Chinese medicine for as long as I can remember, and I've even studied some Chinese. I've wondered what it would be like, but—"

Frau Weinberg grabbed Henri by the hand.

"All the more reason. You must go."

Henri smiled at his old teacher, yet his mind drifted back to Sophie.

"I—it does sound like a good opportunity. But I have—business I need to attend to."

Frau Weinberg huffed.

"Very well. It is short notice. But it'll probably go to waste."

Henri knocked on the floorboards to let his father know that Frau Weinberg was coming up. The teacher ascended the stairs. On her way out, Georg handed her a loaf of bread. She quietly thanked him as he closed the door gently behind her.

Only a little more than a year ago, in the summer and fall of 1937, Henri's anticipation grew each time he met up with Sophie. With the safety of the hidden basement, the two lovers threw themselves into wanton lust, their naked bodies pressed tightly against one another. Both discovered that the more forbidden it became, the more exciting it was to be with one another. Damn the Nazi laws that made an Aryan-Jewish relationship illegal—for Henri, it was heaven.

When not in the basement making love, they often hung out together at the Jazzkeler. Sophie's popularity was growing; Sam had booked her for weekly gigs. Henri often sat with Gerd, the two of them cheering her on.

One night in December, after Sophie had performed a rousing rendition of "A Tisket, A Tasket," the two of them were alone at their regular table enjoying their usual boilermakers. Henri had slipped a small silver box tied with a red ribbon into her hands.

"Henri," Sophie's eyes beamed.

"It reminds me of you," he had said tenderly.

But just as she was opening the bottle of rose-scented perfume, a lanky young man caught Sophie's attention.

"There's my favorite cousin!" The young man swept Sophie into his arms.

"Dietrich!" shouted Sophie.

Sophie turned to Henri. "Cousin, this is Henri Neumann."

Dietrich shook Henri's hand. With his deep-set eyes, he seemed to be studying Henri and the box still in Sophie's hand.

"I'm just opening my Christmas present. Let's see what it is." She finished unwrapping the gift and held up the perfume bottle. "Oh, isn't it beautiful, Dietrich?" Sophie murmured.

"A Jew celebrating Christmas?" Dietrich bellowed.

"Dietrich, what does it matter?" Sophie admonished.

"My family isn't very religious," Henri admitted. "In fact, since my mother died, my father has given up on faith."

"Still... ," the wary man let his words linger in the air.

Now Henri felt the hair on his neck rise.

"Dietrich's a history buff," Sophie interjected, anxious to change the conversation.

"Political science," her cousin added.

"You must read a lot," said Henri, trying to be cordial.

Dietrich nodded and pulled a book out from under his arm. *Mein Kampf,* Henri read, feeling the heat in his neck threatening to overwhelm him. Sophie's cheeks reddened.

"Let's get some fresh air," she said to Henri.

When they were outside, Sophie spoke up. "Don't worry about Dietrich; he's never been good with his social graces."

Henri was relieved to see how Sophie had reacted, and to be away from the dour young man. Yet, though she didn't speak of her uncouth kin the rest of the evening, Henri couldn't shake a nagging angst. He had watched as Dietrich seemed to delight in showing them the autobiography of the dictator who wanted Jews extracted from Germany. Between Sophie's father and now Dietrich, Henri feared the worst.

When they hit the river's edge, Sophie grabbed him by the arm and stopped him.

"I haven't given you your Christmas present yet," she said softly.

"The evening was more than enough," smiled Henri.

But before he knew it, Sophie handed him a small gold-wrapped box.

Henri's eyes glistened.

"Open it," she encouraged.

Henri tore open the paper and lifted the lid. Inside was a silver pocket watch. He held it up.

"You're missing the best part—turn it over."

Henri did. "My everlasting love—Sophie," it read.

Henri clutched the timepiece and held it up to his heart. They kissed.

"It's been a long time since I've felt this happy."

"Me, too," she answered as they continued to stroll through the darkness.

The next day, after a morning full of patients, Henri decided to go up and check on his uncle. He found Viktor dozing on the sofa. As he gently reached to open the window, the ailing man stirred.

"What time is it?" Viktor asked.

"It's early afternoon. Time for tea," Henri replied.

Henri turned on the gas stove. He watched as the water heated.

"How're you feeling?"

"As well as can be expected considering the bronchitis," his uncle responded.

Henri took his stethoscope and listened to Viktor breathe. He could hear his lungs laboring to process the oxygen. Remembering, Henri retrieved the small brown package that Danziger has given him earlier.

"Simon sent this to you. He said it would help."

Viktor opened the package.

"Epinephrine," he smiled. "He always did take good care of me. Did he also have the drugs we needed for downstairs?"

Henri nodded. "I've already stored them."

"Good boy," Viktor said.

Henri sat down with the pot of weak tea between them. He poured two cups.

"Frau Weinberg came in today."

"Oh, how is she? Any word on Bert?"

Henri shook his head.

"She's still trying to secure immigration papers. The stress is weighing on her health."

Viktor nodded.

"I'm sure it is."

"She did know of a single ticket—to China. She asked if I wanted it."

"China?"

Henri nodded. "Apparently you don't even need a visa."

"Take it," the older man implored.

"What? Why?" Henri asked, surprised at his uncle's urgent tone. "Everything and everyone I know is here."

"That's not the point. It's not safe anymore."

Henri could see Viktor's genuine concern for him.

"What about you?" Henri asked.

"Me? I'm an old man. I've lived my life," he smiled. "You—you have too much ahead of you yet."

"I'll think about it," Henri offered.

"What's there to think about?"

Henri didn't want to tell Viktor about what was happening with Sophie. He couldn't depart before seeing her. He wasn't even sure he could leave once he'd seen her.

"I appreciate what you're saying," Henri finally said. "I just need some time."

"Don't wait too long, my boy," Viktor said, picking up his teacup and taking a long sip.

Uncle Viktor had longed claimed that his great-grandfather had an eighth of Chinese blood in him, and portraits reflecting his ink-black hair and almond eyes convinced many that he was telling the truth. Because of this, Viktor had always been curious about the ancient herbal remedies administered by Chinese doctors. The more he studied their principles and theories, the more convinced he'd become that these unfamiliar yet simple medical treatments worked in ways Western medicine could not.

When Henri's mother, Anne, fell ill with diphtheria eleven years prior, Viktor announced that the condition called for him to clear her lungs with an herbal combination that included *ad qing ye,* used by Eastern doctors to dispel this upper respiratory infection. Although Viktor contacted everyone he knew, looking for a way to obtain the formula, Anne eventually fell into a coma. He'd never been able to secure the herbs, and she died a week later.

Losing Anne was devastating for the entire family, but Henri's father and brother returned to their daily routines and never spoke her name again. Only Viktor was available to show Henri the concern and attention he'd needed back then. He was barely thirteen at the time.

After Anne's passing, Viktor dove deeper into his studies of Chinese medicine, searching for more books to help him better understand Eastern remedies. Henri joined his uncle's quest as a way to deal with the pain and loss of his mother. They both devoured the few German and English texts available on the subject. When Viktor had exhausted those, Henri imagined his interest might subside. Instead, the intensely driven doctor rooted up an old herbal text from a used bookstore. He also hired a Chinese student from the nearby university to help them learn to read the strange-looking characters that graced the pages. After several lessons, Henri surprised even himself as he began to recognize and pronounce the pictographic characters with their peculiar high-pitched sounds.

It wasn't too many months after his mother's death that Henri announced to his father that he was moving upstairs with Viktor. Georg had barely acknowledged Henri's pronouncement and the living situation had been the same since.

As the years wore on, Uncle Viktor began trying out herbal concoctions on himself and Henri. Henri appreciated what they'd learned from books but started to feel that without someone who really knew about herbs, someone who could mentor them, they could only go so far. He didn't feel competent practicing Chinese medicine. Now China was showing up in an unexpected way, piquing his curiosity once again.

After making sure Viktor was comfortable, Henri checked the time. Two-thirty. Surely Sam would be at the club by now. Henri made a quick excuse about needing to stretch his legs and was out the door in a heartbeat.

On his way to the club, he passed the newsstand he had stopped at earlier. A larger crowd had gathered along Oranienburger Strasse. News of Ernst vom Rath's assassination continued to echo through Berlin. Some shouted aloud, "Murder! Murder!" Henri lit a cigarette and kept to himself. Hitler was in Munich that very day for the annual Nazi celebration. Many had expected him to issue a radio speech, but so far they'd heard nothing.

The Jazzkeler door opened when Henri pushed on it. He climbed down the familiar steps and found his friend hooking up a new beer keg behind the bar.

"Hey, you're here early," Sam said looking up.

Henri mustered a smile as he approached the bar.

"I just stopped by to see if you'd talked to Sophie lately," he said, not wasting any time.

"She called and canceled this weekend's gig."

"Is she sick?"

"She didn't say. I had the impression it had something to do with her father."

"Really?" Henri responded a little too fervently.

Sam took a look at Henri. He rested the keg on the counter and walked around the bar to sit with his friend.

"Henri, what's going on?"

Henri knew if he could trust anyone, it was Sam.

"I'm not sure. I haven't seen or heard from her in over a week. Usually by now—"

Sam held his hands up.

"Listen, my friend. Sophie's father just got a new appointment. He's a Nazi official now. And I think Gerd's joined in some capacity as well."

Henri was stunned by this bit of news. Even though he'd known something like this was a possibility, he'd been holding out that her family would come around.

"Anything else?" Henri wondered aloud.

"That's it."

Henri rose to his feet.

"I've got to talk to her."

"Henri, I don't think now's a good time—"

But before Sam could stop him, Henri bolted.

"She always said it wouldn't matter," Henri said aloud, to no one. Outside, he hurried past the beige café umbrellas across the way. A drizzle began to fall. She'd pointed out her father's jewelry store several times in the past; knowing how much her father depended on her Henri was sure that's where she'd be. He had no idea what he'd say when he got there but the rain urged him on.

5

As the weeks passed, Peilin made painful concessions to fit into the Kwan household. She'd become a married woman and widow simultaneously, but it was the role of daughter-in-law that proved the most difficult.

It was a venerable tradition for daughters-in-law to clean their mother-in-law's chamber pot. So, each morning Peilin dressed in one of her new cheongsam gowns and fetched the white enamel bowl from beneath her in-law's canopied bed. Peilin took great pains to steady the pot of stagnant urine. Back home, Peilin would've never worn such a fine dress to perform such a task. But her mother-in-law insisted that she don the outfit of a proper lady. Carrying the vessel outside, Peilin cautiously poured the liquid night soil into a designated pit. At the same time, she held her breath. Kwan Taitai's excretions emitted an especially caustic stench—most likely from the rich, oily foods she loved to eat. Once a day, Peilin wondered how such a fiery woman could consume so much grease and fat, yet still remain slim. Her yang energy clearly devoured more than the average person. No wonder Kwan Taitai often exuded such an unpleasant odor.

The Good Luck Lady had cautioned Peilin to carry out this duty with a joyful heart. According to the wise woman, it determined the future of a daughter-in-law's relationship with her mother-in-law.

Peilin wasn't sure she believed such superstition, but she hid her disdain beneath a faint smile, just in case.

More than once Peilin had had to change into another dress after this task. Once the chamber pot was cleaned, Peilin scattered pinewood sawdust along the bottom, in an attempt to mask the smell. She then returned the freshened container to its place under the bed. In the short time Peilin had been living with the Kwans, she quickly learned that it was far easier to adapt than to challenge. And the more she thought about it, the more she concluded that it was the price of survival. She sensed that just beneath the surface of a proper high-class lady, hostility and rage seeped through her body's pores and orifices. But Peilin had to admit that she, too, was hiding her own feelings below a respectful surface.

After breakfast, Peilin often went to the shack along Dragon Lake. There for the first time, she would prepare her mother-in-law's pearl powder. Seated at the table in the dark shed, Father Kwan would place a handful of pearls on a towel. Peilin could already see that they were various shades of white. Some even had a rose-tinted hue.

"First and foremost, only choose quality pearls," Father Kwan had instructed.

Peilin picked up one of the gems.

"You're going to use these beautiful specimens and grind them up? Why don't you use the broken and odd-shaped pieces?"

Father Kwan shook his head.

"No. Pearl powder must be made of the highest-quality specimens."

Peilin knew from her grandfather that the Kwan pearl powder was by far the best in the region. Grandpa Du had taught Peilin the pearl's medicinal functions, like lowering blood pressure. But because of its expense, she had rarely used it as a beauty tonic. Father Kwan watched over his oysters like children. Throughout the three years it took from inception to harvest, he cleaned barnacles and other parasites off the submerged shells to ensure the pearls their full nutrition as they grew inside. Peilin had come to see him as an unspoken ally. She'd been especially grateful for his understanding over her family's untimely deaths.

"Luster, nacre thickness, and outer appearance are most important," Father Kwan instructed. "First we'll pick out the best. Then I'll show you how to grind them down into a fine powder."

Using a magnifying glass and bright light, he picked up a bead and held it under the light. Peilin inched closer and peered through the lens as well. He turned the pearl in his fingers.

"Not just shiny, but look for a light reflected though the layers."

He picked up another pearl and held them side by side for comparison.

"The pearl has many layers beneath its surface—look and see."

As she studied, Peilin saw that coatings of nacre did indeed form tiers. Depending on the angle of the light, she could make out the shiny reflections reverberating through the gem. In a strange way, the pearl was like a chamber pot: both illuminated something much deeper than the surface, revealing the inner recesses of a central truth.

Father Kwan exuded a confidence working with the pearls that Peilin never saw when he was with Kwan Taitai. In the shed he beamed in a way that resonated with the pearls' pureness.

"Tell me more about your family. How did they come to work with the pearl?" she asked one day.

"Ah," he said rubbing his temple. "It was long ago. My family lived in a small village along the Pearl River. One winter, the rains were especially fierce. Not only was it impossible to tend to the pearls, but our homes, livestock, and people were being washed away by torrential floods."

"How horrible," Peilin replied, her eyes wide.

"Those left prayed to their ancestors' tablets; some even sacrificed their last morsel of food trying to appease the unhappy dead. Nothing seemed to work. Finally, it was my grandfather's great-great-grandfather who went to see the monk that lived in a cave high above the village. The wise man revealed that it was not an ancestor but the river dragon that was angry."

"Why?" she asked.

Father Kwan stared out the small window overlooking the lake. "Apparently the dragon felt someone had stolen one of his pearls."

"But with all the farms under water, how could you know which one?" Peilin wondered aloud.

"That was just it. With no time to lose, he gathered all the pearls in the village. When he found the largest and most brilliant, he took the pearl and bundled it in a rice sack along with a large rock. He hopped into the nearest boat he could find, sailed out against the river's current, and dumped the bag containing the pearl and the rock into the river's deep waters."

"Ah, he needed the pearl to sink," Peilin realized.

Father Kwan nodded. "Within hours the floods and rain disappeared. So it's my family's knowledge and protection of the pearl that I inherited."

Each night Peilin served her mother-in-law a silver spoonful of the pearl powder that had been prepared that morning. Kwan Taitai drank it down with a bowl of milk, a custom she insisted insured her youthful beauty.

Peilin then unwrapped her mother-in-law's bound feet. Holding her breath to keep from inhaling the foul-smelling odors, Peilin would gently encourage any new puss to ooze out of swollen cysts that had formed during the day.

"You're hurting me!" Kwan Taitai liked to cry out.

So Peilin slowed her pace. Kwan Taitai's feet were highly regarded as they measured exactly three inches in length. Not every female who suffered through foot binding could make that claim. Most ended up with feet closer to four inches.

Peilin cut the toenails back as far as possible; she then took a fine metal file and sloughed off dead skin cells. Peilin combined several herbs, including dried rhubarb and *fang feng* (siler root), into warm water and soaked each lily foot. As Peilin gently poured the water over the tiny feet, she was surprised that gangrene had not set in. Perhaps the nightly massages kept the blood circulating. When she finished drying her mother-in-law, Peilin dipped silk bandages into another herbal solution and carefully rewrapped each foot.

At the end of the day, Peilin retired to her own room. Here she could finally let go and be herself. It'd been nearly two months since she joined the household. With each day, she felt more exhausted, more hopeless. Although she tried to remain true to her words—*ren nai, zhong,* and *yong* (patience, loyalty, and courage)—Peilin's stamina was waning. She needed something—anything—to keep her hopes alive. As she prepared for bed, she gazed into the bronze mirror. The Good Luck Lady's voice floated into her mind.

"My *yin*-eyed bride—don't be sad."

"But my good woman," Peilin whispered. "I don't know what I'm doing here, other than fulfilling duty. Each day it's harder and harder to go on."

"Don't worry," the Good Luck Lady's voice continued. "Remember to look inside; see what is there that will carry you through these difficult days."

Peilin imagined the wizened woman brushing her hair as she had the night of her wedding.

"I wish to leave here," Peilin murmured. "I wish to leave Dragon Lake."

"Ah," replied the lady, "Then it's a feng-shui wheel you need."

65

At first Peilin didn't recall what the feng-shui wheel was. But as she thought about it, it came to her. Peilin went to her desk and pulled out a large piece of paper. After making her ink, she dipped her writing pen into the black liquid and wrote: "I wish to leave Dragon Lake." She scribbled this same sentence forty-nine times. Then she rolled up the paper. On the outside she decorated it with auspicious objects—pictures of dragons, phoenixes, and goldfish. Satisfied, she went to sleep.

At eight the next morning—the hour of the dragon—Peilin woke up and turned the cylinder wheel one complete revolution. She did this every morning for forty-nine days straight. Peilin wasn't sure it would work, but it gave her something to hope for.

In addition to her other duties, Peilin, as Yao's widow, climbed the hill to visit his gravesite. Each week she'd get down on her knees, pick the weeds, and brush away the dirt around his tombstone. Even though she never had the chance to talk to her husband or hold him in her arms, Peilin felt bound to him. She'd counted on life with Yao as her destiny. It vanished before she even had a chance to experience it.

She would sit by his grave for hours, sharing thoughts with the only person she felt could care. She told him how she missed her family and wondered about her brother Ping. Other times she'd convey her unhappiness with how his mother treated her. Sometimes she'd pound the ground, demanding that he take her with him.

"Surely the afterworld will treat me better than the life I'm living," she'd lament.

"Why did you have to die?" she'd cry, brushing away tears.

Forty-nine days passed. She waited days afterward, but nothing materialized. She was disappointed, but knew it just a way to keep her mood up. Realizing her hopes were futile, Peilin concentrated on her mother-in-law. The Kwan matriarch increasingly complained of headaches. Sometimes late at night Peilin would hear her scream out as if caught in a nightmare, but the next morning the old woman would deny it. Troubled by these symptoms, Peilin prepared several herbal remedies and teas, but none seemed to quell her mother-in-law's condition.

Then the anniversary of Yao's death arrived. Peilin prepared a special lunch basket filled with dumplings, rice, and dim sum. That afternoon Peilin and her in-laws made the hour-long journey to Yao's gravesite. Peilin spread a large blanket on the ground. The Kwans grieved in silence. Despite her dislike of the woman, Peilin could feel Kwan Taitai's heavy-hearted pain. And, Peilin's own mind churned with disappointment.

Peilin turned to see that her mother-in-law's skin had turned a pale white.

"Mother, are you feeling alright?" Father Kwan asked Kwan Taitai.

Peilin reached out and put her hand to her scalp. Her forehead burned.

"*Aiii!*" Peilin gasped.

"Take me home," Mother Kwan whispered, her hands trembling. "Quickly."

Father Kwan leapt to his feet and took one arm while Peilin grabbed the other. Due to Mother Kwan's unstable lily feet and feeble disposition, it took much more than an hour to reach the house. That night Kwan Taitai suffered high fevers. Peilin sat with her throughout the night, soaking a towel in cooling water and herbs. She massaged her temples. Delirium set in. Mother Kwan began hallucinating.

"No! Please, no," she'd scream. Other times she cried out, "Yao—come back! I'll do what you want."

Finally, after a fitful night, in which none of Peilin's herbal remedies helped, an exhausted Kwan Taitai regained enough consciousness to request a medium.

Later that afternoon, Peilin greeted the toothless woman who had sealed her fate years ago.

"Where is she?" demanded the Matchmaker, clearly upset with this sudden and unusual request.

"This way."

Peilin led the toothless woman to Kwan Taitai's bedside. Bamboo had just finished changing another cool cloth on her forehead. Father Kwan held his wife's hand. Shaking her mother-in-law gently on the shoulder, Peilin gained Kwan Taitai's lucid attention.

"The medium, she's here. Just as you asked."

Kwan Taitai opened her eyes and turned to Peilin.

"Go," she commanded in a wispy breath.

Peilin began to usher out Father Kwan and Bamboo.

"No, just you," Kwan Taitai insisted.

Peilin made her way out of the room. Distressed at being singled out, she left a slight crack in the door and quietly she pressed her ear closer so that she might hear.

"That's nonsense," she heard Kwan Taitai tell the Matchmaker.

"You ask me to mediate; that's what he's asking," the fortune-teller replied. "And he says he won't leave you alone until you do."

Peilin could not understand Father Kwan's muffled voice, but whatever he said didn't please Mother Kwan either.

"I'll treat her any way I see fit." Kwan Taitai grumbled.

After several more minutes, in which Peilin could not make out what was being said, the Matchmaker suddenly swung open the door and departed in a huff. Without knowing the specifics, Peilin surmised that the nightmares had something to do with her. A chill went down her spine. She was sure that Kwan Taitai would instill additional punishment the next day.

Father Kwan left early the next morning, before Peilin had

a chance to talk with him. Peilin would have to face Kwan Taitai's wrath alone. But to Peilin's surprise, Kwan Taitai ordered the servant Bamboo to clean her chamber pot that morning. Peilin could not believe she had been relieved of night soil duty. Without asking, Peilin continued her other chores, preparing the pearl powder and cleaning her mother-in-law's feet.

The next night, Kwan Taitai suffered her headaches again. Peilin asked if she wanted to see the medium, but her mother-in-law waved the suggestion away. Instead, she ordered Bamboo to wash and massage Peilin's feet. The third night, Mother Kwan slept much better.

Two weeks later, as Peilin and Kwan Taitai ate dinner, Father Kwan returned from the big city. He was wearing a Western suit. Bamboo trailed carrying his briefcase. He approached the dining table with a look that Peilin would have sworn had an edge of mischief. Had it not been for his somber attire, Peilin would have imagined good news.

"What is it?" Kwan Taitai demanded.

"Elderly uncle died," he told her.

Peilin sat still, not knowing how to react.

Kwan Taitai showed no emotion. Her eyes bored into her more delicate husband.

"Who will oversee the herb store now?" she asked.

"I believe we both know the answer," Father Kwan stated matter-of-factly.

He gave Kwan Taitai no room to make a counterargument.

"Peilin, you leave for Shanghai first thing tomorrow morning."

6

HENRI'S MIND RACED through the past year as he made his way away from the Jazzkeler and in the direction of the Kurfürstendamm shopping district. In March that year, Hitler had annexed Austria. In April, the Nazis had passed a law requiring all Jews to register their property, including furniture and jewelry. Violence had erupted throughout the country. This was only three months after their run-in with Dietrich, and Henri and Sophie had decided together that they would no longer talk after her sets at the jazz club; it would be better that way. Instead they increased the frequency of their visits to the bakery's secret basement. Thinking back, Henri realized the impact of only being able to spend time together in an underground hideaway. At first it had seemed exciting. The hidden medical room became a refuge for impassioned sex. Yet, at the same time, he and Sophie were talking less and less.

In June, Hitler had ordered all Jewish businesses to register with the government. That was when the sign designating Neumann's Bakery as "non-Aryan" went up. Soon afterward, storm troopers appeared in front of the family store. Each carried signs declaring *DEUTSCHE! WEHRT EUCH! KAUFT NICHT BEI JUDEN!*—GERMANS! DEFEND YOURSELVES! DO NOT BUY FROM JEWS! The SS Guards had smeared the store windows with crudely painted Star of Davids in thick yellow paint. Henri worried that he and Sophie would no longer be able to use the basement, but after a few days, the guards moved on.

As June turned to July, their clandestine trysts became less frequent, but they still clung to each other desperately whenever they were together. Sophie always told him that she loved him no matter what happened around them. They spoke in hushed tones about not being seen together in public. The more he thought about it now, the more he recognized they'd been trapped. There wasn't much either could do so long as the Nazis continued their openly hostile discrimination against the Jewish population.

As summer wound down and the high temperatures of August caused many to seek ways to escape the sweltering heat, Sophie cut back on her visits even more. She was now coming by one night a week, oftentimes less. Henri told himself it was better. She, too, clearly felt the strain of their furtive rendezvous. It gnawed at him that their time together was so unsatisfying. He blamed Hitler and resented the fact that their relationship had been reduced to an illicit affair. Henri had mustered up the courage to talk to Sophie about their predicament. But she gave him a pleading look, as if to say, *what's the point?*

The last time Henri saw her, Sophie had looked especially worn out. Once safely together in the basement, she turned to him.

"I need you, Henri. Now more than ever," she murmured.

Henri felt her hand inching up his thigh. She kissed his neck with a fervor he'd not experienced from her. He'd tried to come up for air, but her burning desires caused her to cling to him even more. She seemed desperate to have him, to take him into her. She gripped him with such compulsion.

"We can't know what the future brings," she whispered into his ear, her hot breath sending a sensation through his body that felt more intense than usual.

"We know what we want," Henri replied. "That's enough." He wanted to reassure her, calm her.

"I don't know about that anymore." She pulled away and looked at him, her large eyes glistening in the low light.

Henri had sensed that Sophie teetered on some unseen precipice. He couldn't begin to comprehend what she was saying.

At first she shook her head, trying to hold herself together.

"It's all right," Henri coaxed. "We have each other—an everlasting love—remember?" He stroked her hair.

Sophie gazed up at him, her eyes softening. "I just really need for us to be together—tonight. I don't want to talk."

"Of course," he'd said, but inside, Henri had felt a sense of panic. Flustered as they quickly undressed, he counted on the sex to ease the angst between them.

That was the last time they'd been together, and the last words they'd spoken.

Henri was so completely lost in his thoughts that he walked absent-mindedly, and so he was startled when he looked up and discovered that he'd already reached Saarlandstrasse. He hesitated, considering whether he ought to take another route. But he felt something stronger than himself forcing him to continue down the street toward Schweitzer's fine jewelry shop. For the past week, he had managed to hold himself back and stay away from her. Today he forged past the *JUDEN SIND HIER NICH ERWÜNSCHT*—JEWS NOT WELCOME—signs, staring ahead with resolve. But when he arrived at the shop, he froze. His heart pounded. He was desperate to see her again, to feel her gentle caress, to hear her easy laugh. She hadn't even bothered to break up with him; she'd done exactly the opposite. She'd engaged him in the most passionate sex of their lives, and then she'd simply stopped visiting.

Now, facing the boutique, he caught his breath as he gleaned her angelic blond hair and her bright blue eyes. How they sparkled.

Suddenly, as if she could sense him, she turned and looked out onto the street. They locked eyes. Henri searched for some sort of hopeful sign, but Sophie quickly turned away. Henri's body flooded with feelings of desire and remorse. He had thought their love was stronger than the politics that tore them apart. Sophie's rejection hit him hard.

He continued to stand in front of the store. Henri thought longingly back to a time when he'd felt that the whole future was theirs. They were young and in love—that's all that should matter. But that wasn't the case for them.

He now understood that she'd known it would be their last night together. She had planned it that way. But that's not how Henri intended for things to end.

Seeing her behind the jewelry counter, her face turned away, he realized that he needed her to admit that it was his being Jewish that had caused her to behave the way she had. Henri urgently needed to hear her speak the truth. He needed to know that he hadn't done anything wrong.

Henri waited until the store was free from customers before entering. He ignored the NO JEWS sign and walked in with his head held high. When Sophie looked up, she was visibly distraught.

"What are you doing here?" she asked, remaining stoic.

"I was worried. We need to talk."

"There's nothing to talk about—" she whispered.

Suddenly, her father, a hefty man, emerged from the back room. His eyes flashed with anger.

"Is this him? Is this that *Schweinehund* (swine) Henri?"

She bowed her head and nodded.

Henri felt every muscle in his body tighten as he held onto his clenched fists.

Sophie pleaded. "Go," she said.

Before Henri knew what was happening, her father kicked him hard in the shins.

74

"Get out!"

Henri turned to her.

"But Sophie, I love you—"

His declaration was met with a punch to the gut.

"I'm sorry—" Sophie called out.

Dazed, Henri tried to regain his balance. Looking again to Sophie, Henri thought he caught something in her eyes—*was there more to what she was saying?*

A sudden jerk of his hair caused Henri to twist in pain. Still, he managed to keep his eyes on Sophie. For all that he was suffering, she stood there, unmoving, a blank stare on her face.

"Sophie—Sophie—tell me why... "

Before he could finish, her father shoved him out the door. Henri looked back one more time.

"Sophie!" he pleaded.

But by then she'd already turned away.

Wiping the blood that oozed from his mouth, Henri dashed down the damp streets of Berlin. How could these people treat him as if he were some kind of animal? *I am a human being,* he told himself. *I'm just as good as they are.*

Once away from the store, he started to run. He had needed to convince Sophie that their love could prevail despite the Nazis, despite Hitler, despite her father, despite his being Jewish. But Sophie had succumbed to her father's will. Henri's mind was reeling. Still, he had to get back to the bakery. Patients were waiting.

By the time Henri finished up with his patients that evening it was past ten o'clock. He ate his dinner in the basement, comforted by the solitude and his supplies. Earlier, he had checked on Uncle Viktor, who seemed to be breathing better with the aid of Danziger's medicine.

Henri poured himself a tumbler of brandy and turned on his gramophone. With the volume low, he listened to one jazz record after another: Louis Armstrong, Bessie Smith, King Oliver. It was sometime after two in the morning when Henri was awakened by a loud clatter. The record player was still spinning. An empty brandy bottle sat on the counter. Another thunderous crash rang out from above. He sat up and turned off the light. Nazis. Heavy footsteps overhead marched up the second and third flights of stairs. Through the cracks in the floorboards, Henri could hear shouts of *Judenschwein!* (Jew pig!) echoing through the night air. Glass shattered and chairs tumbled. Muffled cries of protest emerged as his father and Otto were struck over and over. Henri heard his name, followed by more footsteps on the stairs. Uncle Viktor let out a scream.

"We know Henri has a medical practice set up here somewhere."

Henri's stomach clenched with the immediate recognition of Gerd's voice. *Gerd.* Henri realized that his attempt to see Sophie earlier that day had compromised him and his family. He cursed himself for having the audacity to try to talk to her. The voices were now coming from directly above. He held his breath.

"Sophie swore the room was here. He took her there himself."

His suspicions were confirmed. Henri had hoped against hope that it had been another informant. But it was Sophie. His heart raced with fear, anger, and betrayal. He wanted to check on his family, but he knew better than to move. The Nazis continued to ransack the bread shop overhead, toppling over ovens and breaking windows. Henri never flinched, crouching low in his hiding place, barely moving until he was sure the guards were gone. Then, he flew up the stairs faster than he ever had.

He heard the rumblings of Otto and his father, but he moved past them to his ailing uncle. "Uncle Viktor, are you hurt?" he whispered.

The old man emerged holding a bloody bandage to his forehead.

"I'll be all right, but you need to leave tonight, Henri."

"But what about father and Otto? I heard Otto being hit, and—"

"You—you must depart immediately."

Uncle Viktor pulled Henri in close. "They are looking for you. You must leave Germany."

"What—what about you? How can I leave?"

But his uncle was insistent. Henri took a look at the cut. It would heal.

"That was the Gestapo. They're after *you!*"

Uncle Viktor thrust a small sack into Henri's hand.

"Go! Go before they return!"

"But where?"

"Look in your bag!" Viktor uttered before urging him down the staircase.

Wide-eyed, Henri hugged his beloved uncle who pulled him close.

"*Überlebe* (may you survive)," Viktor whispered into his ear.

Henri felt a hot tear running down his cheek. Viktor turned and pushed him away. Henri dashed out into the darkness. He heard sirens roaring. Glancing back at the bakery, he saw that it had been ransacked—broken glass was all around him. He bolted. Looking up, he witnessed thick gray smoke billowing upward. Lofty flames leaped, engulfing the synagogue that he and his family had attended for years. Brownshirts rushed through the streets looting houses. As he hastened down a dark alley, Henri spotted another mob of storm troopers. He could hear more shattering glass nearby as mobs threw rocks and swung their axes at storefronts and apartment windows.

In the distance, Henri made out a large vehicle with SS soldiers aboard. As he strained to get a better look, he saw that the back of the truck was filled with people. Another Gestapo roundup. Henri turned and ran in another direction. Now realizing how dire his situation had really become, he opened the satchel and peered inside. An envelope. His uncle had the foresight to secure his one chance of escape: passage to Shanghai.

IT WAS PEILIN'S FIRST train ride, her first-ever trip to Shanghai. Father Kwan had stayed behind in Dragon Lake for the pearl harvest and Kwan Taitai wouldn't travel to the big city with her lily feet, so Peilin found herself alone. For the moment, she had no one to talk to or take care of. Solitude was new to her; yet she discovered she rather enjoyed it.

A male servant had awakened Peilin in the wee hours. He drove her forty miles to catch the train. At the station, he handed Peilin her ticket. She boarded the train and a conductor stowed her luggage overhead. She glanced around the narrow compartment filled with rows of seats and chose one next to a window. A snoring gentleman rested up front, a woman clasping a small wooden box sat to her left.

The train picked up speed, then roared through the countryside. Peilin pulled up the thick green window shade, which revealed a kaleidoscope of rivers, mountains, fertile farmland, and small villages. She had no idea how large China was; every turn exposed her to its varied and complex terrain. Children ran alongside, waving to anyone who glanced their way. Muscular men with harnessed water buffalo plowed the muddy fields south of Dragon Lake. Their reserved expressions reminded Peilin of Ping. Now that she was on her way to Shanghai, finding her younger brother would be one of her first priorities. His letter detailing their family's recent tragedy had sent her into a deep mourning and made her anxious to reunite with her only living kin. Ping was fifteen. Still she worried about him surviving in unfamiliar surroundings. Peilin rested her head against her seat. Lulled by the train's movements, she felt grateful to her grandfather for bestowing on her the herbal knowledge—that was her true passage to Shanghai.

Peilin knew it was rare for a girl to be taught this family education—it was a right generally reserved for male heirs. But Ping had never shown any interest—he had always been more interested in physical work. Grandpa Du had never made her feel like she wasn't wholly entitled to learn and work alongside him. Now that that experience had rescued her from a life of serving the whims of Kwan Taitai, she realized Grandpa Du was more shrewd than he even knew.

She emerged from the train onto the platform nearly four hours later. People pushed past her—some dressed in dark cotton, others wearing Western suits and dresses. A cacophony of car horns, clanging bells, and shouting vendors swirled around her. Peilin heard several dialects spoken simultaneously: Shanghainese, Cantonese, Mandarin. Peilin paused. Women her age were dressed in Western fashions and wandered freely. She, too, was a liberated woman now. Father Kwan had arranged for one of his drivers to meet her at the North Shanghai station. She peered at the crowd. How would she find him in all the commotion?

"Peilin!"

She spotted a small but energetic salt-and-pepper-haired man darting through the mob.

"I'm Ang, your driver."

He grabbed her luggage.

"You speak Mandarin," she breathed. "How'd you recognize me?"

"Father Kwan spoke of your far-reaching beauty—beauty as rare as a black pearl." The driver flashed a quick smile. "He was quite right. You easily outshine the rest."

Peilin blushed. Ang pointed to a shiny Buick. He came around and opened the rear door. Not quite sure of the proper protocol, she bowed and climbed into the back seat.

Peilin folded her white-gloved hands across her lap. Ang edged the glistening ebony-hued car onto the street; pedestrians, bicycles, rickshaws, and trolley buses competed for the same space.

Towering buildings crammed the streets. The dizzying array of electrical lines that crisscrossed the city sky mesmerized her. Fair-skinned people, some with golden hair, sauntered down the streets. She recognized their light features from Kwan Taitai's magazine pictures. At the busy intersection, turbaned men with bulky beards directed traffic. The Japanese military also had a strong presence. At the Garden Bridge, Peilin observed the khaki-uniformed soldiers push aside an elderly Chinese man to search his wooden cart. Peilin braced herself as the car drove over the bumpy overpass. Along with these foreigners, Peilin spotted Chinese mothers lugging babies and coolies balancing heavy bamboo poles across their backs. Peilin studied each face, hoping that she might spot Ping among the crowds.

"Your first time to Shanghai?" asked Ang.

Peilin focused her attention on the affable driver.

"*Hao*," she nodded.

"I remember my first time," he reminisced. "From Canton. I couldn't believe all the cars, trolleys, and people here."

When they reached the busy intersection of Wah King Street and Bubbling Well Road, Peilin stared at four enormous structures. "What are these?" she wondered aloud.

"Department stores." He glanced at her through the rearview mirror. "So many things to see inside: shoes, purses, scarves. You'll like the variety of pretty dresses, I'm sure."

She stared down at her silk dress. The fancy gown probably cost more than what her father and grandfather ever made in a year. It struck Peilin that Ang saw her as a wealthy woman, not the poor girl who grew up in circumstances similar to his own.

Turning, Peilin caught her reflection in the window and became more conscious of just how different her life had become. Her swept-up hair and ruby red lips revealed not even a shadow of her former self.

Suddenly, a rickshaw puller dashed across their path. Ang bore down on the horn, causing her to jump.

"Watch out—you nearly got yourself killed!" Ang shouted at the unfortunate driver.

They continued through the city, Ang eager to share his knowledge with her.

"Shanghai's divided into three areas: the International Settlement with its tall Western-styled buildings, the French Concession with its tiled Parisian roofs, and the *xiao xiang*—narrow alleyways off to the side of the main road."

Peilin looked around. "Where's the herbal store?"

"Almost there. It's just past the Bund."

"The Bund?"

Ang gazed at Peilin through the rearview mirror. "Yes ma'am— just look ahead. Many charming buildings—some say exotic—here along the riverbank."

Peilin stared out the window. It was indeed majestic and beautiful—clusters of tall pillared structures hugging the coastline.

"The Bund is business center—home of Eastern capitalism," he said proudly. "People from all over the world come to Shanghai's Bund. You'll see."

Peilin continued to stare at the impressive sights, excited that she'd soon be a part of it all, too.

Henri wore the same brown wool jacket he had on the night he fled Berlin, the only home he'd ever known. That evening, he'd made his way to the Anhalter Bahnhof station where he boarded an overnight train to Munich. There he found the steam engine headed to Genoa, Italy.

Viktor had packed an extra shirt, trousers, and razor. Underneath, Henri found a bundle of papers—his passport and medical credentials. Henri clutched the documents. Even under duress, his uncle had enough foresight to ensure Henri's ability to continue practicing medicine. Without these certificates, he would have had no way to verify his skills as a doctor. Then, a tattered picture slipped from between the pages and fell onto the train floor. Picking it up, Henri found a photo of himself with his uncle taken on the day Henri graduated from medical school. Viktor was so proud of him. Henri closed his eyes and leaned back in his seat. He didn't want to fathom the thought that he might never see his uncle again. And, he didn't even get a chance to say goodbye to his father or brother.

In Genoa, Henri walked several blocks to the loading dock. The seaport boasted a harbor full of boats large and small. Despite its charm, anti-Semitism brewed here as well. Henri took precautions not to draw attention to himself. He lit a cigarette and leaned against an empty pier post. He stared at the ocean. Out there somewhere was his future. But he couldn't imagine what that might even look like. He'd been fighting off a morass of hopelessness, trying to convince himself that he'd been given a new chance at life. Instead he wallowed in a mixed cocktail of anger, betrayal, and sorrow. He resented that Gerd led a band of Nazis to his apartment, beat his family, and vowed to arrest him—all because he was Jewish. And how could Sophie, the one person he loved, betray him like that? Would his heart ever beat without grief? If the life he knew was truly over, what was left?

Seven hours later, the *Conte Biancamano* steamship brought down the gangplank. Henri—lost and tired—climbed aboard for the two-month-long journey to Shanghai.

Other refugees, mostly Germans and Austrians, clung to their hats and coats to ward off the chilly winter winds. Henri still had no clear sense of what he would encounter when they arrived in Shanghai. *Where would he live? Were there other people besides the Chinese? Would he be able converse with them?* Although he had studied Chinese and was excited to try it out, he felt uneasy about his ability to speak the language. With only his uncle and the tutor to practice with, he knew his communication skills were sorely lacking. Henri worried about not having a visa despite the boat captain's assurance that Shanghai was open to Jewish refugees.

They sailed out to sea so that the shoreline was no longer visible. Henri found the absence of detectable land unsettling. But they were fed well on the trip, a stark difference to the way they'd been treated in their own countries. Twenty-one days in, Henri and others fought off seasickness during a turbulent storm. He shared what few medicines he had. His fellow travelers appreciated having a doctor aboard.

Once the storm passed, Henri escaped upstairs to the deck. The fresh air helped clear his mind of Sophie and everything that had transpired. The fact that Sophie had sent Gerd to root him out was still unbelievably painful. He gazed out into the vast sea. Miles of water now separated them. He no longer recognized Sophie and what she had become. He shoved his hand in his pocket and pulled out the silver timepiece she'd given him that Christmas. "My everlasting love—Sophie." The now offending words attacked his dignity. How could he have been so foolish to believe that she'd stand by him forever? His eyes welled but he knew what he had to do. He hurled the pocket watch over the ship's bow. The ocean swallowed the metallic timepiece whole; Henri's heart sank with it.

Nearly forty-two days at sea. He again turned his thoughts to his father and brother. Still, it was Uncle Viktor he missed the most. Henri pulled out the picture. "Überlebe—may you survive," was Viktor's last word. Just then, a large wave struck the ship's bow. The impact knocked Henri down. He sat up on the wooden deck to regain his equilibrium. Standing, he saw a glimmer of land in the distance—the coastline. After weeks of endless water—the future was in sight. Henri felt a shift—from victim to survivor.

Peilin stared out the Buick window. Ornate European-styled banks, hotels, and restaurants lined Shanghai's Bund. Ang veered off Bubbling Well Road. Drab, densely populated buildings marked the Chinese section. Ang pulled up in front of a small two-story store. Paper lanterns fluttered along the blue-tiled roof.

"The New Moon Herbal Shop," announced Ang.

Fear, apprehension, and excitement surged through her. Her wish had come true. He opened her door; she stepped out. He retrieved her luggage and handed Peilin the key.

"Anything else?"

Peilin shook her head.

He tipped his hat. "Good luck, Miss."

Ang climbed back into the black Buick. She wanted to shout, *Please don't leave me*, but the words caught in her throat. He drove away without looking back.

She inserted the key and pushed the door open. Overhead bells announced her arrival. The wooden floor creaked. Her nose detected familiar odors—pungent, salty, sweet. Peilin walked toward the mahogany counter. She touched the cool jar of ginseng root immersed in water. Canisters with labels like jasmine, reishi, and astragalus filled the shelves. Jars of Tiger Balm wrapped in colorful paper, bottles of analgesic White Flower lined another. Ointments, pills, packaged syrups—some familiar, others not— occupied the glass display case under the register. Behind the counter were hundreds of small wooden compartments. Peilin stepped forward, opened them one by one. Dried roots, flowers, and stems reminded her of her youth. Drawers of *chen pi* (orange peel), star anise, and sweet red *hong zao* filled her senses.

85

Grandpa Du would've relished the orderly boxes filled with such medicinal treasures. A petite stove was tucked in the corner. Her initial apprehensions disappeared; the store was more than she had imagined.

A narrow staircase led to a tiny apartment above. Peilin was used to the wide-open spaces of her childhood farm and then Dragon Lake, but here in the big city, Peilin relished the cozy private room that was now her own. A servant must have cleaned it up after the old man's passing. A clean bed prepared with simple white linens hugged one wall; a small wooden bathtub stood in a corner. A window over-looking the street showcased city life below. Her mind raced with excitement—so much to see and do. She'd never spent a night any-where truly alone. Peilin lay down on the bed. Her tired body drifted into a much-needed slumber. She was free.

The *Conte Biancamano* snaked its way up the Whangpoo River. Henri and other refugees rushed to the deck to get their first glimpse of Shanghai. Henri's emotions swirled—fear and excitement gripped him. Open sampans and fishing trawlers filled the crowded Whangpoo Harbor. Then they spotted drab gray warehouses along Putong—the flat southern shore.

"That's it?" voiced an older man.

Henri shook his head. He wasn't sure quite what he was expect-ing, but that certainly wasn't it. Then, a shout came from the starboard.

"Over here!"

Henri and several others rushed for a first glimpse of the north-ern shore. European-style buildings, much like those back home. This was the Shanghai cosmopolitan flair that Henri had heard so much about. He was particularly drawn to the tall green-steepled building that towered over the rest. It stood out—much like he would; yet it fit in, much like he hoped he could.

He was halfway around the world, far from his native homeland. He arrived with no job prospects or money, and he knew no one. For the first time, Henri was aware of just how uncertain his future was. His chest tightened. He was a homeless refugee.

The *Conte Biancamano* was too large to dock, so rowboats were sent out to the ocean liner. Henri, suitcase in hand, lined up with his fellow travelers. They loaded onto the watercraft six at a time. At the front of the procession, a white-uniformed volunteer, just a boy, held a pen and clipboard.

"How many members in your family?" asked the Jewish Relief Society boy.

"One," answered Henri.

The lad glanced up from his clipboard. "Could you step aside for a moment, please?"

Henri tensed. *Was he being rejected?* The boy signaled the couple behind him to board instead.

"Is there a problem?"

The boy turned. "I had two spots left. Just needed to fill this vessel to capacity. You'll be on the next one."

Henri stepped aside, relieved it wasn't due to his lack of a visa. He easily boarded the following boat for the quick ride to shore. They were ushered into the customs center where they would be checked in. The River Building was filled with more Jewish Relief Society volunteers. Henri's panic rose again. He held his passport, thanks to Viktor, but what if they asked for a visa? He reached the female caretaker, a Jewish immigrant like himself. He steadied his hand and held out the passport. She shoved it away.

"No need," she told him.

"*Danke*," he said breathing a sigh of relief. He must have looked as weary as he felt.

"Do you have a place to stay?"

He shook his head.

"Don't worry. We've a temporary shelter with food and cots." She extended her hand. "Welcome."

Henri and other refugees headed for the Embankment Building—a temporary emergency shelter—and lined up once again. In groups of forty, they were herded onto the back of an open truck, much like the ones Henri had seen the Nazis use to haul away prisoners. Again, he had to tell himself not to overreact. He was in China now, far from Hitler's reach. The driver revved the motor and the vehicle lurched forward.

The truck's raised loading area was an ideal sightseeing platform. The seaport bustled with cars, bikes, and trolleys. Raven-haired people crisscrossed the streets. The city's lively ambiance stood in stark contrast to Berlin's stern demeanor. Henri's ears picked up the high-pitched Chinese intonations. He could make out some of the words, but the rapid conversations reverberated like battling alley cats. Ponytailed men shoveled coal and hauled large bags of grain across the port. Others barked orders.

Farther up the road, Henri picked up scents of roasting pork, yams, and chestnuts along the outdoor stalls. He spied a pasta maker stretching dough through his fingers until noodles formed. The unusual sights made Henri feel like a curious child again.

The truck continued to inch its way north. Shanghai was a safety haven, but the war had not spared the Chinese. Japanese soldiers strutted through the streets, their imposing authority visible. Along the route Henri saw the poor, sick, and barely alive. Was it indifference or the unfortunate plight of so many that caused most to ignore the dying? Eventually officials with wheelbarrows hauled away those who died. It bothered him to see humans treated this way, even though he understood that the dead could not be saved. The dense population of those still alive took precedence.

Henri held onto the moving truck's side, peering ahead into the unknown.

Peilin awoke refreshed. She climbed down the stairs and opened the store's doors to let in the mid-morning air. It was almost noon. Across the narrow street, customers swarmed a small eatery. A sharp-tongued woman barked out orders from the busy counter. A nervous man wielded tongs for *chai sui* pork, roasted duck, braised chicken feet. Peilin decided to introduce herself to the neighbors later; maybe they'd know where she might start looking for Ping.

She returned inside. She dusted the counter; this is where she'd prepare herbal prescriptions. Nearby she found a measuring stick for herbs: a rod with metal weights on one end and a dish on the other. The bells rang overhead. Peilin looked up; her first customer—boils on his face—stepped inside.

She smiled. "Can I help you?"

The swollen-faced man looked confused. "Where's Chang?"

Although he spoke in Shanghainese, she knew what he was asking.

"Chang passed away. I'm the new herbalist. Sit here and I'll fix—"

The door slammed shut. It wasn't the reception she was expecting.

Hours later, a pregnant woman entered.

"*Hao*," greeted Peilin.

"Chang?" inquired the expectant mother.

"He's gone. But I can help."

"A woman herbalist?"

"*Hao*. My grandfather taught me."

"Never mind."

Peilin stared at the door. She knew she was capable, but what would happen to her if the locals weren't willing to give her a chance?

The Jewish refugee center was a multistoried building near the Garden Bridge. Sitting along Suzhou Creek, the Embankment Building bordered the International Settlement and the poor Hongkew district. He might have considered his new temporary *Heim* (home) primitive back in Germany, but Henri tried to make the best of the situation. The alternative—remaining in Berlin to face Nazi persecution—would surely have been a death sentence. He worried about those left behind; they were worse off. Henri needed to be strong and face the unknown with a sense of hope and possibility. After all, he had escaped the Nazi's terror thanks to caring people back home. He needed to survive for them.

Henri and the group entered the reception hall inside the embankment building. Shouting children played soccer with a ball constructed out of wadded paper. Men gathered around tables to concentrate on their chess games; at others, women chatted. The converted area held a large influx of refugees with nowhere else to live. Most had arrived with no means of making an income.

Henri was issued a tin dish, a blanket, and a sheet. He followed the others up to the floor furnished with cots. He stowed his belongings near a corner bed. His stomach growled; he hadn't eaten since early morning.

The downstairs kitchen served a simple *Eintopfgericht* (hotchpotch) meal. At least the thin watery soup would satiate his empty stomach. It was quite a shift from the plentiful food served on the ship. The crowded mess hall was packed with displaced people, young and old. Henri picked up sounds of German and Austro-Bavarian, as well as some Italian and French. All were Jewish. All had been uprooted by Hitler. Henri wondered what would eventually become of them. He found a spot at a benched table and sat. He'd been lost in thought for some time; the sound of someone speaking to him startled him.

"May we join you?"

Henri looked up. A bone-thin young man and woman stood with their metal food trays.

"Please," Henri responded. He motioned for them to sit.

"*Danke*," replied the slim woman as she climbed over the bench to sit.

"Have you just arrived from Germany?" asked the fellow who sported a heavy beard.

"I have." The couple shared a concerned look between them.

"Were you there the night of Kristallnacht?" the woman asked, her voice trailing off.

"I was."

Now the young man spoke. "We heard how horrible it was—synagogues ablaze, stores destroyed, broken glass everywhere."

"*Ja*." Henri felt his eyes mist up. "My father's bakery was demolished; the neighborhood on fire. Men and women struck with clubs; blood everywhere. Others were rounded up and taken away. Screams and gunshots echoed in the darkness. Storm troopers beat my father, brother, and uncle. They were after me—I barely escaped with my life."

Henri noticed that the frail woman was visibly shaking.

"Excuse me," she blurted and walked away.

Henri turned to the man.

"I'm sorry for upsetting her. I shouldn't have depicted it in such graphic detail."

The man shook his head. "She wanted to know. Only—" He hesitated. "Inga's upset because her cousin was taken during that riot." He paused. "We think he's in Buchenwald."

Henri shivered. "I'd be there, too, had I not escaped."

The bearded man clasped Henri's hand. "You're quite lucky my friend. May God continue to look over you."

That evening Henri retired to the crowded sleeping quarters. He felt vulnerable in the chilly, open space. Henri kept his jacket on and pulled the sparse blanket on top. Others tossed restlessly, he, too, lay there awake. Mothers sang lullabies to crying babies; some talked in whispered tones. Tethered ropes and hung sheets created interim veils of privacy. Behind one, Henri detected the low moaning of love-making. He closed his eyes; eventually he fell into a fitful sleep.

That afternoon, Peilin ventured out. The day failed to produce more customers and she was eager to start her search for Ping. She locked up the herbal shop and headed to the eatery. The sizzling wok sent up a blast of steam as she entered.

"*Ni hao*," greeted the gray-haired man.

"Hello," replied Peilin. It seemed enough people also spoke Mandarin, easing her concern.

The woman with the narrow-spaced eyes soon appeared from the back room, retying her soiled apron.

"You must be the Kwan daughter-in-law," acknowledged the woman, her mouth pressed tightly. "We noticed you earlier across the way."

"*Hao*," answered Peilin.

Peilin pulled a tattered picture from her purse and held it.

"My brother," she said pointing to the photo. "By any chance, have you seen him? He arrived here from Jiangsu about six months ago."

The wife shook her head. "If he's from the North, you might ask around the creek. Many find work there."

Peilin sensed the woman's growing impatience, but wasn't sure why.

She placed the picture back in her purse. "Thank you."

Peilin was not used to maneuvering through the dense crowds of Shanghai. She'd been protected by Ang's car the day before, but now she fought her way like all the rest. Beggars huddled around improvised fires created with broken furniture and paper scraps. She jumped at the sight of a dead body lying in the gutter. Peilin did not know what to make of such a vast and numbing disregard for others. She bent down and touched the body, but could find no pulse. There was nothing she could do. She pressed on; her energy was spent tending to the living.

The old wooden pier swarmed with people, including a group of European passengers. Peilin spotted the large steamship out in the water and guessed that the well-dressed travelers had just disembarked. Most looked uncomfortable in their heavy, wool coats; many clutched small suitcases. Some were being helped onto the back of an open truck.

Along the Whangpoo River, shirtless coolies loaded and unloaded heavy cargo. Ditchdiggers plugged away, their rhythmic shoveling keeping pace with the overseer's bellows. Peilin presented Ping's photo to person after person, but no one recognized him. She scoured steamy kitchens and dank warehouses searching for any information that might lead to her brother.

But luck was not with her. Evening approached; Peilin trudged back toward the store. She knew the city was large, but she had no idea how intricate and complex the metropolis really was. It would probably take days for her to canvas the area for Ping. For now, she'd regain her strength until morning.

She forged through packed sidewalk stalls selling fresh fruits, vegetables, meats, and grains. Peilin chose a leafy head of bok choy. She paid the vendor. A limping figure caught her attention. *Ping!* She grabbed her purchase and ran. Her heart beat. Finally close enough, she reached out. He turned. She took a step back. It wasn't her brother after all.

Peilin continued on to her herbal store. She'd allowed herself to believe that he'd be easy to locate. She'd been in Shanghai for only a short time. There were so many people. *How was she ever going to find him?*

Unlike the wide perimeters of the metropolis, her tiny apartment safeguarded Peilin like a protective cocoon—alone in the big city.

8

Henri woke startled. It took him a few moments to remember that he now lived at the *Heim*, a refugee dormitory. His ears picked up the chatter of the other Germans and Austrians. More must have arrived overnight. He rose from bed and dressed. Kids raced through the aisles, probably more freely than they could back home. He enjoyed their rambunctiousness. If only he could let go of his own angst and adapt as easily to his new surroundings. The society volunteers had told him of a nearby organization that had been set up to help refugees find employment. It would be his first order of business.

Henri exited the dorm. It was a cool, overcast day. He focused ahead toward the bustling Shanghai streets. The job search both excited and worried him. He found immense fulfillment as a physician. Helping people kept him connected emotionally to his uncle, as well as to his late mother. But here Henri had no family or friends. He was entirely dependent on the Relief Society.

He made his way down Bubbling Well Road and admired the European-style buildings of the Bund up close. His favorites included the green-roofed Cathay Hotel, and a pair of bronzed lions gracing the entrance to the bank. English, American, and French who had made their way to Shanghai years ago populated the International Settlement and French Concession with reminders of home. Imported Buicks, Volvos, and Packards clogged the congested roadways.

Well-heeled Westerners in long fur coats and hats also crammed the streets. Just off the main path, Henri noticed narrow alleyways. Signs filled with brushstroke characters hung over building doorways. He recognized some familiar symbols: "restaurant" and "store."

Then his ears picked up recognizable words shouted by vendors hustling vegetables, fruits, and baked yams. The language was far faster and more frenzied than anything he'd attempted to speak during his lessons back home. Bicycles and rickshaw drivers weaved their way through the crowds. Jade statues and colorful fans adorned store windows. His mouth gaped; his wide eyes stared. He felt the acute sense of having been transported to another world, not just another country. Before China was but a far-off place he had studied in books. Now the people, their language, and everyday life stood before him.

He wanted to wander around, but reminded himself of his morning mission. He would save his exploration for another day. He turned south onto Kiuking Road. A few blocks ahead stood the International Committee for European Immigrates' office. He stopped at the door. *What if they didn't accept his medical papers?* He really had no other experience. What would he do? How would he survive? He gathered himself and took a deep breath. He would just have to deal with things as they presented themselves.

Tall metal cabinets lined the walls. A messy, dilapidated desk stood in the room's center. Henri stood waiting for what seemed like a long time. Finally, he was met by a stout, heavy-set man.

"Welcome," the man said in uneven German. "Can I help you?"

Henri tried to hide his grin. The middle-aged Hungarian's triangular face reminded Henri of *Mohntaschen,* the three-cornered, poppyseed pastry his mother used to make. Then, realizing the man was waiting for a response, Henri cleared his throat.

"I'm looking for work," Henri announced, trying to inject some confidence. "I've just arrived from Berlin."

"Yes, of course. So tell me, what skills do you have? Typing? Locksmithing? We just received word of an opening for a welder."

Henri wasn't sure how to respond. He'd heard that other immigrants with professional expertise needed more practical skills to survive in a foreign country. Henri had never taken the time to learn skills other than those needed to practice medicine.

"I'm a doctor."

The man's brows knit in consternation. He stepped closer to Henri. Henri's worries escalated. This man wouldn't be able to help him. The recent influx of refugees arriving in such large numbers was dimming the job prospects for new arrivals. It reminded Henri of times at the hospital when an epidemic of flu broke out and there weren't enough beds to accommodate all his patients.

"You look awfully young for a doctor."

Henri straightened his shoulders. He gazed at the man with clarity and directness he hadn't quite harnessed since he'd arrived in Shanghai. He reached in his pocket and pulled out his papers. "I trained in my uncle's medical clinic. He's also a doctor." Henri handed the Hungarian his credentials, thankful once again for Uncle Viktor's foresight. "Medicine's in my blood."

Henri stood strong. The man studied the paperwork. He pulled down his reading glasses that sat atop his head. He reached for a notebook and examined each page. Henri grew apprehensive.

"Ah," he finally blurted. "The new Jewish refugee hospital. It's just opened. They're in need of help."

"I'll take it," said Henri, breathing a sigh of relief.

"It doesn't pay much," the man warned.

But Henri didn't care, so long as it was something. And he'd be working in medicine. At this point he didn't even care if he worked as a doctor or an orderly.

"It's a start." Henri felt a new sense of optimism.

The Hungarian nodded. "It is. You're lucky to have such skills." He wrote down the address. "Good doctors are very valuable."

Henri stared down at the paper. He had a job.

"Report to Dr. Rosen. Tell him I sent you."

Along Chusan Road, Henri let out a gleeful whistle, then turned up Washing Street. He was thinking about what to say to the medical director when a rickshaw—attached to the front end of a bicycle—pulled up alongside.

"Ride?" shouted the Chinese driver, who couldn't have been more than fifteen. Henri was surprised to hear this boy speak English.

Henri shook his head. "*Wo mei dai ling qian*—I have no coins, no money." Henri said eager to test his Mandarin and pleased that he remembered the word for coins. He pulled out his empty pockets for emphasis.

The boy jumped off his bike and started walking next to Henri.

"Later?" inquired the persistent driver.

Henri observed the boy's disfigured face and pronounced limp. Yet, the driver had a strong backbone, etched muscles formed by years of laborious work.

Henri shrugged. "Probably not."

The boy smiled and rode off.

Henri watched the driver pedal down the street. *What had happened to that kid?*

Peilin opened the door to her herbal store and breathed in the crisp morning air. She ignored strange looks from passersby—those still wary of her because she was a woman. Father Kwan had warned her of the possibility and had supplied her with a small monthly salary until business picked up. Peilin worried that she might not be able to establish herself with such a scrupulous crowd. *How long would he support her if she was unable to generate an income?* She resolved not to return to Dragon Lake and Kwan Taitai. That would be the worst fate of all. And Ping was here somewhere in the vast boughs of Shanghai; she was determined to find him.

Another two weeks passed before a woman dusted in soot and covered in rags entered the store. She carried a young child about five years old in her arms.

"Please miss," pleaded the poor woman. "My son..."

"Bring him here," Peilin motioned toward a bamboo chair. She took his wrist and felt for a pulse: weak and thready. Peilin bundled the boy in blankets.

"He suffers from stiffness and lethargy," she told his mother. It was evident to Peilin that they had no place to live and braved the outdoor cold.

"His constitution's damp and weak."

"Will he be all right?"

"Yes, but we must dispel the cold energy."

Peilin took a cooking pan and heated a handful of raw rice with slices of ginger root. She poured the grains into a pillowcase and handed it to the mother.

"This will warm him," she instructed.

The mother gave a weak smile and did as she was told. Peilin opened the herbal drawers; she measured out equal portions of dried *du huo* bark and slivers of *sang ji sheng* twigs. Both plants expelled wind, dampness, and cold. Peilin added more—seeds, stalks, and leaves—just as Grandpa Du had taught her, until she had all the necessary ingredients.

Peilin filled the glass pan with the herbs and water. She boiled, then strained the decoction several times over the next hour.

The mother's own strength was nearly as weak as her son's. When the tea was ready, she poured two cups—one for the woman as well.

"Drink this," said Peilin. "It'll warm you."

The thankful woman did as she was told. Peilin removed the

covers and coaxed the boy to drink. After a sip, he pushed away the bitter concoction.

"It's for your own good," Peilin insisted.

"Drink," his mother urged and held out her own empty cup for him to see.

Finally, he gulped it down.

Peilin covered the boy again; he soon settled into a fitful sleep. The mother, too. Peilin speculated they had little money; she was again reminded of Ping and prayed that he was not suffering from the cold. How many had come to the big city in hopes of a better life? Seeing the sick and dying on the streets, Peilin knew that the transition was not easy. Most, herself included, had nothing to return to. Others had been born here, already poor and hungry.

A few hours later, her patients woke. Peilin could see that both had benefited from the warming tea. Peilin prepared several more herbal packets; she handed them to the woman.

"Thank you," said the grateful woman, "but I've only a *yuan* for payment."

Peilin pushed the coin back into the mother's hands. "No payment necessary. These are for you."

The woman bowed. "We'll remember your kindness."

Just before the boy's mother closed the door behind her, she turned to Peilin one last time. "I know you are new and a woman. No one has come to your store. Give it time. This will change."

The two then disappeared into the street, leaving Peilin pondering their prediction.

The new Jewish refugee hospital was a russet-colored building with rooms on two floors. The smell of disinfectant brought back memories of the teaching facility where Henri learned to thrive on little sleep. He continued down the corridor—he estimated about sixty beds.

A petite young woman donning a tight uniform and thick, auburn hair counted inventory. She looked no more than twenty. She glanced up; her piercing dark eyes scanned over him.

"Pauli? Pauli, is that really you?"

The woman leapt to her feet as she took him in her arms.

"I never thought I'd see you again," she said.

Henri flinched. He had never seen this woman before in his life.

"Actually, my name's Henri Neumann. The IC sent me. I'm here to see Dr. Rosen."

Henri had expected the sprightly lass to turn with embarrassment, but instead she gave him a quick hug.

"I'm so sorry. You look so much like my boyfriend from Austria. I'm afraid…" her voice trailed off. She dabbed her eyes.

For a moment Henri felt the pain of her sadness; he chided himself for being skeptical about her. He'd heard that Austrian women were more open with their emotions, but this felt a bit excessive. Still he was the new guy and wanted to make a good impression.

"I'm deeply sorry," Henri replied. "I hope you'll be reunited soon."

She tucked the tissue into her pocket. "Brigitta Wiesner, head nurse. Welcome. Dr. Rosen's in his office. Let me take you to him."

Henri followed her through the hallway. Her openness shifted to caginess at the sight of Dr. Rosen. Henri silently wondered what that was all about.

"A new doctor's been sent from the IC. This is Dr. Henri Neumann."

Rosen looked up. The doctor had an athletic build, and Henri estimated he was in his midforties. Henri handed Rosen his credentials.

"I really need someone with more experience, but I suppose you'll do."

Henri felt his own mix of tension and ease.

"We've received an influx of dysentery patients—can you start tomorrow morning?"

Henri nearly forgot to speak. Brigitta gently poked him in the side.

"Yes. Of course. Thank you, sir."

"No need for thanks. Just be here 7:00 AM sharp."

Henri exited the hospital and whistled even louder. *He had a job.* He headed up Nanjing Street toward the refugee camp when a familiar voice called out.

"Ride?" The limping rickshaw driver scurried to catch up. Henri scratched his head. *How did the rickshaw driver find him? Had he been following?* No matter. Henri was in a good mood. He figured the boy's badly scarred face scared many away. The marks were old, probably something that happened when the boy was very young.

"Jin tian bu xu yao la—not today," answered Henri, proud to recall his Chinese lessons more and more, although his conversational skills were still lacking. He pulled out his pockets again to show that they were still empty.

The pedicab driver nodded. Henri was surprised when the teen continued walking alongside him.

The youth pointed to himself and then to Henri.

"I lookee for you," he said in broken English.

"Me?" said Henri pointing at himself. "What for?"

The boy struggled to find the words. He continued to gesticulate, pointing to his head and his mouth.

"You teach. I learn English. Make mon-ee."

He took off with his carriage for a short distance to illustrate. He had a simple yet enterprising way about him. Henri found himself entertained by the boy's earnest intent to communicate.

"I'll tell you what," Henri offered, "I teach you English." He pointed to himself and then to the driver and then back to himself. "You teach me Chinese."

The boy's face wrinkled. "You talk Chinese."

"Need to speak better," Henri replied.

The young driver's head bobbed his head up and down. "Okay. Deal."

There was an eagerness that reminded Henri of Gerd. The company of someone younger buoyed Henri's spirits. "Henri," he said, pointing to himself. "Happy to meet you."

"Happy to meet you," imitated the boy. The rickshaw driver then pointed to himself. "Call me Ping."

It had been several days since Peilin had tended to her first patients. She prayed they were drinking the warming herbs and staying out of the cold. Peilin hoped to run into them while searching for Ping, but the city seemed too vast to just happen upon people that way. Was her brother in a similar situation? Worse? She had searched for him along the river and through the *xiao xiang* until her feet could walk no more. Yet she was determined not to give up.

One morning a genial-looking man entered her store.

"Excuse me," said the middle-aged man. He removed his hat. "Are you the doctor who helped the homeless Shen boy?"

"I helped a young child suffering from the cold. Is that him? How's he doing?"

"He's quite well. A miracle, actually."

Peilin blushed. "I only did what I knew best."

"That's why I'm here," the man replied. "I haven't been able to find someone who could assist me. Would you be willing to try?"

"Of course," she said and offered him a seat.

She checked his tongue and pulse. His condition was too much wind—rheumatism. She prepared herbal packets and sent him on his way. Later another customer came in complaining of stomach pains. Over the following days Peilin received more and more patients. Each had heard of the young boy Peilin had cured; each looked to Peilin as a special healer. Ailing customers consulted her for fevers, dizziness, and gout. Some had also heard about her search for Ping. Peilin felt a new sense of community developing around her. Her confidence grew. With the added security that others were also keeping an eye out for her brother, it would be only a matter of time before she would find him. Peilin had just finished with a young woman suffering from cramps when the door opened again.

"I'll be right with you," she said looking up. They were not new customers at all. They were her neighbors, Jing-Li and Zhao.

"We've noticed quite a number of patients here lately," chirped Jing-Li.

Peilin forced a smile. She wasn't sure why, but something caused Peilin to feel a tinge of apprehension.

"A few," she replied. She kept the conversation light and was relieved when their brief visit was over. It had been a long day.

Peilin locked up the store and made her way to the outdoor market. She needed some bean curd, watercress, and bitter melon. On her way back, Peilin then stopped in the grocery store for some salty plums. There was a long line in front of the cashier. Peilin stood patiently when she heard rumblings and became aware of an increasing commotion at the counter.

"Thief! Stop him!" cried out the cashier.

Peilin caught a side glimpse of a ragged teen. A whole chicken was tucked in his jacket. He dashed toward the door. Peilin ducked as the rushing kid weaved through the crowd. The shoplifter bumped into her. Peilin fell. For a moment they locked eyes—it was Ping!

Both froze in recognition of one another. "Police!" shouted the storeowner. "He's over there!"

Before Peilin could say a word, Ping dashed off—even with his pronounced limp—into the dark, congested street.

9

HENRI HAD SUGGESTED to Ping that they meet in Shanghai's Chinese section later that afternoon. It'd be their first language lesson. Ping had offered to pick Henri up with his rickshaw, but Henri had declined, preferring to walk. He had arrived only a day ago. Already he had a new job and a new friend. Between these starts and the cool mid-January air, Henri felt invigorated. The walk was a perfect opportunity to explore his surroundings. The *xiao xiang* were a stark contrast to the Bund's flamboyant style.

He studied the crude map Ping had drawn. Henri crossed the Garden Bridge that separated the European section from the Chinese area. Japanese soldiers scrutinized the Chinese; Henri passed without being stopped. A crumbling stone gate marked the entrance to the native borough. From there, he journeyed deeper and deeper through the twisted alleys. Henri had heard that most Europeans preferred to limit themselves to the International Settlement and French Concession. Henri had now traveled farther into the city's interior than most of his peers. Small garden areas housed coal stacks and rusted bicycles. Above, drying clothes flapped in the breeze.

Inside one of the open doors, Henri spotted children dressed in outfits fashioned from old rice sacks. The mother cracked a smile; several of her teeth missing. What an oddity it must be, he thought, for the Chinese to see him in this section of town. Others tipped their heads as he passed. He felt no fear, though. They seemed curious, yet accepting of him—a welcome relief given the prejudice he'd so recently experienced in his own country.

Henri noted how the Chinese transitioned easily from the domestic to business arenas, which were often connected. Alley dwellings included shops facing the main street. There was an outdoor stall selling hot water to those who didn't have indoor plumbing. Nearby was a long line of shoppers waiting for rice. Henri continued on. Cigarettes and toilet paper were also popular commodities. Mixed among the merchants were outdoor barbers, ear cleaners, and dentists.

Henri was not sure if it was the cool afternoon or the dense dwellings that brought so many of the Chinese outdoors. A crowd surrounded several card tables along the sidewalk. Shouts and laughter mixed with loud clacking sounds dominated the table focal points. Cigarette smoke hovered above. Henri peered over a player's shoulder. The foursome shuffled small green and white tiles, then tossed and scooped them. Henri wanted to stay longer, but he needed to meet Ping.

As he continued, the dwellings became more desperate. Huts pieced together with wood, bamboo, and discarded sheets of metal for roofs—broken chairs and soot-covered sofas were scattered among the crude dwellings.

He neared the riverbank; his nose caught a strong stench. There was evidently no plumbing. Farther up, chattering women rubbed soiled garments along wooden washboards. Kids ran along the shoreline; some toting handmade fishing poles. Henri could have spent the whole day observing life here, but he was feeling pressed for time. No doubt he was going to be late. Worse, he wasn't exactly sure where he was—there were no clearly marked addresses or streets this far back into the *xiao xiang*.

Henri was about to head in another direction when his ears picked up on that familiar voice.

"Hen-ree!" He turned to see Ping waving his arms. The teen

clamored out of a hut built over the creek itself. Ping motioned for Henri to clamber over the muddy sludge via planks leading to his dwelling.

"You find me good," he said in broken English.

"*Hao*," Henri replied, pleased by the opportunity to speak Chinese again.

Henri entered the tiny *shui ge lou* (water loft)—a hovel barely large enough to hold one. His eyes widened; he had never seen such poverty. The refugee dorms were a luxury compared to this. Shanghai was decisively divided between the haves and the have-nots.

"I make tea," Ping announced. "Have cook-ees." The boy held a few in his hands.

Henri took the plain biscuit and bit into it. As poor as he was, Ping was pleased to display his hospitality. He placed the teapot between them. Henri observed how easily the teen adapted to his environment. He didn't seem to need much or to take notice of the surrounding hardship. Even the stench enveloping the habitat did little to deter him. Yet, Ping seemed unusually quiet. Seeing the boy's pitiful surroundings, Henri wondered if he should have come—perhaps Ping didn't really think Henri would show up.

"*Nin yao wo jiao nin ma?* (You want me to teach you?)" Henri inquired in slow, broken Chinese as he pointed to himself and then to Ping.

"Yes," the young boy answered. Yet he stared off into the distance. Henri even heard a gentle sigh.

"*Ye xu wo bu ying gai lai ?* (Maybe I shouldn't have come?)" Henri stood; motioning toward the door in a gesture he hoped would let Ping know that he would leave if that was what the young boy wanted.

"No, no," Ping said, jumping to his feet. "Not you. My heart is," he paused, looking for the right word in his limited vocabulary, "hea-vee."

Henri nodded. Although English was a second language, he'd studied it in grade school since he was six years old and it came easily to him. He sat back down. He waited while Ping gathered his thoughts.

"Sister," the teen said.

"*Zhe li, zia Shanghai?* (Here, in Shanghai)?" Henri asked.

"Yes."

The anguish in his new friend's voice was clear. Ping then broke out in rapid Chinese, but it was too much for Henri to understand. He put up his hands.

"*Wo bu dong* (I don't understand)," Henri admitted.

Ping then gestured with his hands. Henri could see he was frustrated. Finally, his friend pointed to his ring finger.

"Married," Henri concluded.

Ping clasped Henri on the shoulder and smiled. Henri felt the relief, too. Still he longed for the day when he would be able to speak without so many gestures to help him along.

Henri knew that once a Chinese woman married she was considered a part of her husband's family—and no longer a member of her natal kin. Henri couldn't imagine what that must feel like.

"But me—happy," Ping continued, pointing at his face and forcing a smile.

Henri grinned, too. He was glad there was someone to brighten Ping's meager existence, but he still wasn't clear about the situation. If they hadn't seen each other for months, why the sadness?

"I miss her," Ping said. Henri took the boy's hand in his own and patted it sympathetically.

Henri struggled to find words that Ping could comprehend. "Why not talk to sister?"

The teen pretended to blow a whistle. "Pole-leese," he heaved. Henri couldn't understand how the police came between brother and sister. It was obvious from Ping's expressions that it pained the young man. The teen buried his deformed face in his hands, unable to convey his dilemma any further.

"Go now plees," Ping whispered, unable to look at his friend.

"You okay?"

The boy nodded. Henri didn't like leaving his friend. Yet, he knew the boy wanted to be alone now. Henri was not exactly clear on the situation. For the moment, he'd have to wait.

Peilin swept shattered glass onto a piece of cardboard and dumped it all into the trash. She'd accidentally bumped the display case, causing several analgesic bottles to tumble onto the floor. She'd been unable to sleep the last few nights—ever since she had come face-to-face with Ping. The moment of recognition passed too quickly and with the blink of an eye, he was gone. She tried chasing after him, but with all the frenzied commotion—police, angry shopkeepers, and confused onlookers—she lost track. He dashed into the crowded street and disappeared.

Now each night when she closed her eyes, Ping's hollow image appeared—hungry, cold, and alone. Resorting to stealing meant he was barely surviving. She'd arrived in Shanghai with a place to live and money to sustain her. Her brother, by contrast, had nothing. She had returned to the area more than a few times, hoping to run into him again. But each time she failed to find him her anxiety grew.

Peilin couldn't stop fretting, even when loyal customers entered the herbal shop.

"I saw him—my brother!" she told one after another. At first they seemed happy for her, but voiced their concerns when they saw how visibly upset she was.

One man pointed out that at least she knew Ping was alive. Seeing her weary condition, he also urged her to get some sleep. But each night, she tossed and turned, anxious to find her only brother.

It disturbed her to see him reduced to such desperate actions just to stay alive. Both had suffered so many losses in the last year—a year that was supposed to fulfill a destiny Grandpa Du had so carefully tried to shape for her. How was it that no one foresaw that she would become widow and bride on her wedding day, marrying a dead man she barely knew? Or that Japanese soldiers would storm her small village and ignite a raging fire that would sweep away the lives of her beloved Grandpa Du and her parents—robbing her of any chance to bid them a proper farewell? Now fate had played her another cruel twist—a momentary but thwarted encounter with her only living relation.

Thoughts of Ping jabbed her heart. Since arriving in Shanghai Peilin longed for a family connection. But would that now elude her, too? Past events were decided for her—by others. Now she had the opportunity to determine what would happen—she'd search the city until she found him.

The next morning—his first official day at work—Henri arrived early. He'd been so excited to have a job that it was only now that he took in just how bleak the refugee hospital really was. Cots crammed into every nook and cranny of the open ward made it hard for nurses to maneuver. Thin tattered curtains were the only privacy between patients, if they were lucky. If he'd taken more time to survey his surroundings the day before, Henri wouldn't have been so surprised when Brigitta handed him a pair of dingy, moss-colored scrubs instead of a crisp white doctor's coat. Henri had to remind himself that this was a refugee hospital—there was a war going on.

Henri reported for duty.

"There you are Neumann," as Rosen liked to refer to Henri. He checked his watch. "Not a moment too soon."

Henri tugged at his scratchy, ill-fitting garb. Even though the head doctor had been there nearly half the night, Rosen still appeared full of energy. He was clearly a man devoted to his job. A family photo on the desk corner caught Henri's eye. It was hard to imagine the stern doctor as a caring husband and father of two young sons. Then again, Henri's own father had little emotion to share. Thank goodness Uncle Viktor was around while he was growing up.

Dr. Rosen tossed the manila folder he'd been reading across his desk.

"Get started on this right away. Let me know what you decide."

Henri studied the file as he headed down to the ward. The patient, Valda Eilser, suffered from campylobacteriosis, an infection caused by ingesting contaminated food and water. Henri had seen a few cases in Berlin. He suspected many recent refugees here caught the disease.

He found Valda in the far corner, occupying cot number forty-six. The harsh years of discrimination had taken its toll; her chart listed her as thirty-five, but she looked more like fifty. Henri noted the raised purple veins on her wrinkled hands. Valda also suffered from dehydration.

She tried to reach up, but she recoiled with abdominal pain. Henri gently patted Valda, trying to give her some reassurance.

"How long have you been like this?"

"A week," she whispered.

Henri took her temperature. He pressed down on her abdomen and felt her distention.

"Diarrhea?"

"Yes."

She'd endured so much—traveling a long distance to a strange country. He related to the rapid adjustments in a short period of time.

"Do you boil your water before drinking?" he inquired.

She closed her eyes. "When I can. The stove broke. I was thirsty. Now I can't hold anything in."

"So you know it was probably the drinking water."

She nodded. "I never thought it could be this bad."

Henri turned to the attending nurse. "Let's start saline injections."

He squeezed her hand. "Don't worry, Mrs. Eilser. I'll be back to check on you shortly."

He noticed a distinct look of relief spread across her face. He wished he could do more to ease the pain. Medical supplies were in high demand and often not readily available.

The Shanghai strain of campylobacteriosis was more severe than those he'd treated back home. He'd monitor her progress more closely, make sure her body responded well to the saline.

Henri continued to make his rounds in the large open sea of bed-ridden patients when Brigitta appeared.

"Good morning, Doctor."

"Brigitta," he said, recalling her name. "Any news about Pauli?"

She shook her head. "I'm afraid not."

"Have faith," he said placing a reassuring hand on her shoulder. "Do you have family here?"

"My parents died in a car accident when I was a teen."

"I'm sorry," Henri acknowledged. "My mother passed away when I was young, too."

She seemed to appreciate this bit of knowledge.

"By the way, there's something you should know about Rosen."

She leaned in.

"His family—you saw the picture in his office?"

Henri nodded, recalling the photo on Rosen's desk. "A wife and two kids."

"Before he came to Shanghai, they were taken by the SS. Rosen managed to escape, but the rest of them—"

"Does he know what happened?"

"No, there's never been any news, but I figure it explains his behavior."

Henri could see how the doctor's stern demeanor concealed such an enormous loss.

"I appreciate your letting me know."

"I wouldn't bring it up with him," she replied.

"Of course."

Brigitta reminded him of the lonely neighborwoman back home who was constantly gossiping. Perhaps it was her lack of family that made her so needy.

"So, how was it that you ended up here in Shanghai?" Henri asked.

"My parents left me some money," she revealed. "An aunt helped me find a ticket and here I am."

An attendant approached the desk.

"Nurse Weisner, you're needed down the hall."

"I'll be right there," she told him.

Henri watched as she hurried down the corridor. If nothing else, he definitely had to be mindful of his actions around her. The last thing he needed was to become fodder for her gossip.

Henri was about to continue on his rounds when Dr. Rosen appeared.

"I understand you just ordered saline injections for the Eilser patient."

"That's right; she's severely dehydrated."

"You neglected to check with me first."

"It's a straightforward procedure."

"I approve all courses of medical action. I expect you to follow this protocol from now on."

Dr. Rosen stormed off without another word. Brigitta's warnings about him proved true. Maneuvering between the head physician's iron-fisted management and Brigitta's gossiping would be one of his most difficult tasks at his new job. He even suspected that Brigitta had feigned her reaction to him when they first met. He had a hard time believing that she actually thought him to be her boyfriend, which made him even more cautious about her intentions.

That evening, Henri found Ping waiting for him after work. Henri smiled. He hoped whatever had taken place between the teen and his sister had resolved itself. Ping waved and approached him as usual.

Henri gestured back and pointed to the young boy.

"*Ni hao,*" Ping nodded. He motioned for Henri to climb onto the rickshaw, but Henri declined. They walked side by side.

"Talk to your sister?" Henri inquired, using his hands to form a talking mouth.

Ping shook his head. Henri took in that his friend had not said a word yet.

"*Yi qi qu zhao ni de jie jie* (Let's go find sister)." Henri pointed at the two of them and then to the streets ahead.

"No." Ping said adamantly. He then indicated himself. "Ping bad."

Henri could not imagine what Ping had done that was so awful, but he decided not to probe him further. Perhaps in time, Henri would learn what had happened to separate them.

"You teach-ee," Ping continued.

Seeing how adamant his friend was, Henri agreed. Together they headed back to the *xiao xiang.*

It had been nearly a week since Peilin had seen her brother. There was no time to waste in her quest to find Ping. She decided to close her shop early that afternoon. She suspected that his situation must be dire if he had to steal food and evade police in order to survive in the big city.

Patients and neighbors had pointed Peilin toward the narrow alleyways as the most probable place to find her brother. The alleys' commonness had caused her to overlook them. In contrast to the large buildings of the Bund, the unobtrusive thoroughfares blended easily into the backdrop. Peilin recalled an old Chinese proverb Grandpa Du liked to repeat—*She shi wu da* (One often turns a blind eye to a familiar sight). "Where others saw weeds," he'd point out, "the herbalist saw medicine."

She searched that day and the next without luck. Rather than succumbing to defeat, her resolve to locate him intensified. After two months, the guarding Japanese recognized and allowed her to pass. Once out of their sight, Peilin made her way toward the *xiao xiang.* The narrow alleys continued to open up new areas of exploration, and Peilin soon came to understand that she had only searched around the perimeter of Shanghai's deep belly. It wasn't until late March that she'd finally entered the heart of the district. This, she discovered, was where those who had migrated from the rural countryside found shelter in the large city. For many of the Chinese, Shanghai was a wartime safety zone. And like Grandpa Du's herbs, the faceless population subsisted out of sight of the general public.

Unlike the larger thoroughfares, these alleys snaked their way through low-rise apartments. These *hu tongs*, some with a small courtyard, housed teachers, artists, shop clerks, office workers, and priests. Thick soot languished on the brick dwellings casting an uneasy shadow over the crammed settlements. Auspicious street names inscribed above the arches encouraged Peilin—*Fukang Li* (Alley of Fortune and Good Health), *Yongxing Li* (Neighborhood of Perpetual Prosperity).

Despite the inviting alley names, residents seemed to take little notice of Peilin unless she stopped to have them glance at Ping's picture. Most shrugged their shoulders or shook their heads. Peilin continued showing Ping's picture to anyone who would stop long enough to engage her. More than not, they stared back with hungry gazes. Gone were the open fields. Like Ping, many struggled to survive from day to day, meal to meal. They'd come to Shanghai for a better life, but the city had its own rules of existence.

Each visit took Peilin deeper into the alleys and she detected a distinct shift in the housing construction. Instead of two-story brick buildings, the area gave way to *xinshi gongyu* (single-story apartments) and *shikumen* (old-style housing). Gone were the small courtyards. Here the pathways became even more constricted. Each time Peilin returned, she noticed more and more. Alley names were now handwritten in lime wash or chalk—*Lao shao ping an* (All Is Well) or *Siji Taiping* (Four Seasons in Peace). Peilin sensed the wishful blessings offered protection for those who lived there. Peilin recognized hard work and thrift—families, including children, swept floors, worked in mills, and gathered fire chips.

Peilin learned that lucky women worked in cotton or flour factories; their husbands ran rickshaws or small businesses. Those not so fortunate became street peddlers. These workers hauled bamboo baskets across their backs. Some sold soy milk or fried dough sticks, others green onions and ginger roots.

During other trips, Peilin observed beggars—too poor to sustain their own wares—selling trash. Discarded cabbage and rotted carrots became prized finds. Peilin imagined Ping too proud to beg, which is why he resorted to stealing.

But even with the hard existence, Peilin saw moments of levity. One day in April, she came upon an alley filled with entertainers. Peilin watched a magician pull a ball out of a child's ear; a monkey danced to music. Others played music or performed puppet shows. The carnival-like atmosphere buoyed the spirits of all around, including herself. She hoped that wherever Ping was, he, too, had a moment to stop and enjoy something like this.

Then, just as the flowers began to bloom in May, Peilin came upon an alley named *Lian le Li* (Alley of Joint Pleasure). Red lights and lanterns with names such as "Orchid" and "Lilac" adorned the street. Peilin blushed as she recognized that it marked the prostitutes' district. Nearby, she caught sight of dazed men with their lips sucking on a long skinny tube connected to a flask. She had heard of opium dens, but she had never actually seen one. She peered into the squalid lairs and observed dozing men sleeping off the effects of the drug.

As spring turned to summer, Peilin continued to search for her only brother with increasing desperation. The more she searched, the more vast and crowded the city seemed. Chinese from all over the country had migrated to Shanghai--several spoke dialects she had never knew existed. Some were friendly, others not.

She thought she'd seen the worst of it when she stumbled upon a cluster of straw shacks. Made of bamboo, straw, and mud, the single rooms were divided into a few compartments by wooden boards. But even more squalid were the shantytowns along the Whangpoo River and the outskirts of Shanghai—shacks that could barely be called homes. These *gundilongs* (rolling earth dragons) were crude dilapidated huts built by tilting together thin bamboo strips to form a triangle. Not even tall enough for a person to stand upright inside, these straw shacks sheltered thousands.

Chickens, pigs, dogs, and ducks roamed the area. Odors of decaying garbage, pig dung, and dampness filled Peilin's nostrils. Many were lured by tales of a better life in the city, but to Peilin this was actually worse. And like Ping, these poor had nothing to go back to. Peilin realized that had she not been married, she, too, would be living in these slums.

It was here, after nearly six months of searching, that someone finally recognized Ping's photo. Several pointed to a small hut hovering over the creek.

"Ping!" she called out. But no one answered.

"He's not here right now," a bearded man offhandedly mentioned.

"Do you know him? How is he?" she asked.

The man shrugged and walked on.

Determined, Peilin waded through the water to take a look inside.

She could not believe her eyes. A handful of bamboo poles were driven into the smelly sludge. Broken boards placed on top of the mud served as an improvised floor. But large gaping holes exposed the putrid slime beneath. Peilin gasped at the stench. She swatted away mosquitoes and water flies, horrified at his wretched living conditions.

The sun began to set. She wanted to wait for Ping to return, but with night falling she needed to leave now—the herbal shop was four hours away. As close as she was, she'd have to wait at least one more day until she could reunite with her brother.

Over the next six months—January to June—Henri had coaxed Ping away from his muddy hut many times. Each instance they took the opportunity to stroll the crowded streets filled with vendors hawking everything from sesame cakes to roasted walnuts. One peddler carried a movable kitchen on a bamboo shoulder pole. Henri learned to use his growing Chinese vocabulary to order bowls of fresh noodle soup and baked yams.

Henri enjoyed engrossing himself in the culture. He could see that Ping had a stubborn streak about saving face and it was important to the boy that he earn his keep. Henri often challenged his young friend to a game of pointing and naming items in their respective languages. Henri learned that noodles were *mian-tiao,* chickens *ji,* and tangerines *mi ji.* He had Ping count money in English—one, two, three—knowledge that would attract foreign customers to trust the enterprising rickshaw driver as a businessman. As they continued through the *xiao xiang,* it was hard not to notice Ping's distinct gait or ignore the purple scars that tore down his nose and across his left cheek. People dismissed him as ignorant because of his disfigurements, but Henri knew otherwise. Ping had had no occasion for any formal schooling, yet he had a hunger for knowledge. The city held opportunities, and the teen embraced whatever he could.

Late one hot June afternoon, Henri remembered that he needed to return to the dorms sooner than usual. He was working an early shift in the morning and wanted to be alert in his dealings with Dr. Rosen.

"I drive you," Ping offered.

Henri resisted. He did not feel comfortable having another human—a friend—pedal him home.

But Ping insisted. "I drive you."

Henri could see that it was a sense of pride for Ping as well. The boy wanted to reciprocate.

"All right. It'll give us more time to practice our languages."

Henri climbed aboard Ping's homemade pedicab. He marveled at the teen's ability to adapt the rickshaw and bicycle to create his own vehicle. As the two headed through the crowded alleyways, Henri noticed summer rain clouds forming overhead and although it was warm, he pulled his jacket around him to keep dry. Soon he'd be back at the *Heim*.

Peilin felt the light summer rain sprinkle on her face as she headed back into town. Although it was June, evening fell quickly. She became aware of the peddlers, entertainers, and shop owners packing their wares and rapidly disappearing for the night. The *xiao xiang* were now deserted; people had scurried inside whatever shelter they could to avoid the wet rain. A strong breeze kicked up. Vulnerable, she clutched her hat and bowed her head as she struggled to remember the way back to the city.

Peilin caught sight of a lone moving object in the distance. At first she thought it was a bicycle, but it seemed to have a cart attached.

Her heart pounded; the bicycle-cart headed toward her. She glanced around but there seemed nowhere for her to duck out of sight. The figure pedaled faster, still gravitating toward her. Peilin broke into a run; the traveling shape chased after her. Just as Peilin was about to let out a scream, she looked up to find herself staring face-to-face with Ping.

10

THE WARM JUNE DRIZZLE continued to fall. Peilin had nearly fainted from the anxious nerves coursing through her body. It'd taken her a moment to realize the *xiao xiang* stranger was no stranger at all but her own brother. Ping, on the other hand, remained calm. Peilin recalled that he'd always had a composed demeanor. She took him by both hands, grabbing him by the shoulders. He was real.

Flooded with emotion, Peilin no longer held back her feelings.

"Ping—It's really you! You don't know how long I've been looking… searching—" she touched his face and then broke down sobbing with relief and happiness.

"I told myself I wouldn't give up," she said choking back more tears. "But there were days when I thought I'd never find you."

"Sister," he said gently.

She moved to embrace him. But her brother suddenly turned and looked away. She sensed his downcast eyes clouded with pain.

"Don't look at me. I've lost face." Ping buried his head in his hands; then collapsed to the ground. "You caught me stealing chicken."

Peilin saw that behind his quiet presence, he was a guilt-ridden reservoir of shame.

Others concentrated on his outer flaws; Peilin knew that her brother's scars ran deeper than most. She recalled the young boy who clung to life after the raging water buffalo nearly trampled Ping to death. Her nose twitched as she remembered the oily scent of the bone-setting liquid that she massaged into his broken ribs and crushed foot. Grandpa Du worked quickly to sew up the bleeding face wound. He instructed her to boil healing herbs; she then coaxed Ping to drink even though his lips were badly swollen. Other healers had thought Grandpa Du's relentless attempt to bring such a broken body back to life a fool's obsession. But Peilin had joined Grandpa Du's fervor to save her only brother.

She turned to him now wishing she could heal the disgrace that bound him. She placed her hand on his shoulder.

"Remember what Grandpa Du always said: *eating is as important as the sky*."

Ping looked up. Peilin helped him rise back to his feet.

"There's no dishonor in being hungry. An appetite for living is what's most essential."

Brother and sister stood taking in each other's presence.

Finally Peilin spoke up. "This alley's so dark. How did you know it was me?" she asked, brushing away the steady downpour of droplets that had grazed her cheeks.

Ping's crooked smile melted her fears. "I didn't know. I saw a lost woman. I came to see if I could help."

"I almost ran," Peilin admitted. She mopped up beads of rain and tears on her face.

"Good thing you didn't," he replied. "Then we would have missed each other again."

He paused for a moment. "What are you doing in Shanghai? What happened in Dragon Lake? Did things go badly with the Kwans?"

Peilin smiled to reassure him. "No, everything's fine. Father Kwan sent me to run the family's herbal store. I've been here, alone, for nearly six months."

"Ahh," admired Ping. "You always did have a way with Grandpa Du's healing knowledge."

Peilin spied the makeshift rickshaw that Ping had hitched to a bicycle. It was an inventive device to overcome his handicap. A cloudburst erupted.

"Hurry sister, it's starting to rain!" He pulled out a cardboard scrap he'd tucked away and held it over her head. He signaled for Peilin to climb aboard his rickshaw. "Let me take you home," he insisted.

Peilin nodded, grateful for his protection.

His strong legs pumped the rickshaw against the wind. Peilin couldn't bring herself to ask Ping about her parents, their grandfather, or the details of their final fate. She'd read the letter; she knew a fire had killed them, but somehow over these months she'd allowed herself to engage in some denial. She preferred to remember them at the farmhouse, as if they were alive and well, as if she were simply away in Shanghai, living apart from them.

And now here was Ping at last.

"I want you to come back and live with me," Peilin shouted through the thundershower. "We're family. You and me."

Henri was glad he'd left the *xiao xiang* early the previous afternoon; a heavy rain had started the moment Ping had dropped him off at the dorms. This morning, Rosen had him on a full schedule. Henri had made his rounds on both floors when Brigitta ushered him toward one of the emergency treatment areas. She was all business.

"What is it?" he asked.

Brigitta dropped a chart into his hands.

"This patient's complaining of pain in the upper right portion of her abdomen. And there's blood in her stool sample. Rosen said you should handle it."

She pointed to a cot half-hidden behind a curtain. Six-year-old Kaethe Lowen wore a tattered green dress. Probably one of the few things she was able to bring with her he deduced, knowing too well that the refugees escaped with very little. She clutched her stomach.

"Hello Kaethe," Henri greeted.

The young girl regarded him.

"Am I going to die?" she blurted.

Henri grasped how frightened the young girl was. He took her hand in his.

"Sweetie, you're not going to die."

"Then why did I have to come to the hospital?"

Henri gently pressed her upper right abdomen. The girl winced.

"So you can feel better."

For a moment, his patient looked relieved.

Then another wave of pain attacked.

"You've got a tummy ache, don't you?"

She nodded. "It hurts a lot."

He stroked her hair. "Don't worry. After a few days here you'll be feeling much better."

Kaethe smiled for the first time. "That's good. I don't want to get behind in my schoolwork. We're learning how to add and subtract in math class."

Henri admired her eagerness. "Don't worry. I'll make sure you're back in no time. I'm going to get your medicine."

Henri emerged from behind the curtain. Over the last six months, he'd made it a point to jog down the hall for Rosen's approval. Once the head physician gave his authorization, Henri rushed back to the nurses' station. Today Brigitta was stocking the saline supply.

"We need to start emetine injections on our young patient right away," Henri told her. "Amoebic dysentery. If we can stabilize her fluids quickly, she'll have a faster recovery time."

"But we're out of emetine," Brigitta said dryly.

"Again? How do they expect us to run this hospital?"

"We're anticipating a shipment later today." She paused. "But we've been expecting that same shipment for the last two weeks."

"Of course it is—it's wartime," Henri said, echoing what he had heard so many times before. "Supplies are in high demand all over the place."

With more patients than medicine to handle each case, he felt aggravated he couldn't do anything for them; a few had even died. It was painful knowing they'd be quickly treated and on their way to recovery if they only had the supplies they needed.

"What about the Chinese?" Henri asked a little too loudly. "They've been battling this disease for centuries. Surely they must have a local medicine to treat it."

Brigitta shook her head. "Dr. Rosen's absolutely against administering Eastern medicine."

"Has he tried it?" asked Henri, frustrated. Now several nurses and attendants started to gather around; Henri felt self-conscious of his outburst.

Brigitta took Henri aside. "He's voiced his opinion against it several times. You know how he is."

Henri did know. He recalled such ignorance before. Henri was certain that his mother would be alive today had there been doctors who were more open and familiar with Eastern medicine. Henri knew that Brigitta was only trying to save him from Rosen's wrath. Henri relented for the time being.

"I see," said Henri. "Let's start Kaethe on some saline in the meantime—until the emetine arrives."

"I'll take care of it."

"Thank you," responded Henri, grateful for her assistance.

"You must feel alone here sometimes without your uncle for support."

Henri nodded.

"I'm still learning my way around."

There was a moment of silence between them. Henri was about to check on patients upstairs when Brigitta lightly touched him on the arm.

125

"Say, do you like American movies? *It Happened One Night* is playing at the Lyceum Theater. It'll take our minds off of things. ..."

He was tired from the long day and he knew better than to decline since she'd just helped him through his frustration.

"Sounds like fun."

Ping and Peilin had traveled for hours from the *xiao xiang*, delayed by flooded streets. Luckily Ping knew detours so that when he pulled the rickshaw up to the herbal shop, Peilin was happy to escape the wet weather and show him inside. He carefully walked over to the large chest of drawers and ran his hand along the brass knobs.

"Go ahead," she encouraged. "Open it."

Ping pulled on the handle. He peered inside the different herb-filled compartments.

"This is all yours?"

She nodded.

Her brother broke out in a wide grin. "Nice."

She then took him up the narrow stairs to her small but private quarters. Peilin studied her young brother's expressions; he marveled over the feather bed piled with silk blankets; he was awed by the kitchen area with its own small indoor stove.

"If I didn't know better, I'd think that we both died and our relatives are burning paper money for us to enjoy in the afterlife!" exclaimed Ping.

Peilin smiled. "There is just you and me now. We must take care of each other in this lifetime."

Ping took his time wandering up and down the stairs. Peilin heard the rain outside now tapping on the window. The steady drops reminded her of another time when water came to their rescue. It was a warm summer day on the farm. She was twelve, Ping eight. The two were hoeing Grandpa Du's herbal garden. A lone bandit jumped out of the brush and grabbed Peilin. She struggled but couldn't break free.

"Help!" she cried out.

Ping turned and ran to her.

"Let her go," he demanded.

But the robber held on tight.

"I need food. Feed me or she dies," the gruff man told Ping.

Ping scurried from the field, limping as he hurried into the house. He returned with a bowlful of pork dumplings.

"Give it to me," the bandit roared.

Even then, Ping had an enterprising mind.

"Let her go first."

Ping held onto the bowl. He refused to bring it closer until the bandit released Peilin. Finally, the man gave in. He let Peilin go. Ping left the bowl on the ground. Brother and sister bolted for the river. The bandit stopped to eat.

At the river, they jumped into the stream's deep waters. Tall bamboo hid their whereabouts. The water protected their submerged bodies like a mother's womb. The cool stream nourished Peilin. The bandit came looking for them. Peilin peered through the tall reeds. The water continued to shield them and the thief eventually disappeared.

That first night together, Peilin prepared Ping a celebration dinner. It'd been a while since she had the pleasure of cooking for someone besides herself. Steaming noodle soup, tangy Chinese broccoli, and salted shrimp filled their ravenous stomachs. The meal was more elaborate than usual because she wanted to commemorate their reunion. Ping slurped the noodles and plopped the shrimp one by one into his mouth. He ate heartily, and she was more than happy to serve him seconds and thirds. For dessert, she served red bean soup with lily bulbs, a treat from their childhood. Both savored the warm, sweet-tasting indulgence that they had enjoyed on holidays.

Peilin insisted that her brother rest while she cleared the dishes away. When she returned, Ping had already fallen asleep. She found a blanket and wrapped it around him. She then headed to her own bed.

Brigitta found two seats near the front. Henri sat on the aisle. It had been a long time since he'd been inside a movie theater. He'd been on his feet most of the day. The plush burgundy fold-down seat was a pleasing relief.

"I'm so looking forward to this," Brigitta said.

"Me, too," he replied halfheartedly.

Sounds of the flickering film gearing up could be heard in the background. The lights dimmed. Brigitta offered Henri some of the popcorn he'd bought her; he declined.

Henri expected the movie to start right away. Instead they were shown a war newsreel. Both sat in silence and viewed Nazi troops taking control of Czechoslovakia. Henri had read about the takeover back in March, when it had happened. Now nearly three months old, the film clip was obviously dated. Still, it was a sobering reminder of the ongoing battles in Europe. He realized that he had not heard from his family in six months, even though he'd sent at least a half-dozen letters. Henri had a hard time keeping up hope that his family members, especially Uncle Viktor, were holding up against Hitler's terror.

Once the reel ended, the movie began. Though he'd tried to relax, Henri instead found his mind wandering back to the hospital and his young patient.

The more Henri thought about it, the more he grew uneasy about Kaethe's illness and the lack of medicine available to cure it. Rosen's rules were being upheld at the expense of his patient. Henri could understand how the application of Western medicine first applied since that's how they were trained. But they were in China now. After six months of service, Henri had already encountered several tropical diseases he'd only read about in textbooks. If the disease was native to the area, then surely the Chinese must have an available cure.

Henri continued to ponder the situation. Brigitta nudged him and offered a sip of her soda, but he shook his head. He then snapped out of his internal dialogue and became conscious that he had not paid any attention to the movie they'd come to see.

Henri now heard the laughter around him. Brigitta chuckled out loud. Onscreen, Henri watched Gable's frustration at hitchhiking upstaged by Colbert's flirty skirt lifting. He had to admit it was funny.

The movie ended with Colbert finally realizing that Gable was her true love. Despite the happy ending, Brigitta had tears in her eyes. He pulled out a tissue he'd tucked in his pocket. She nodded.

"Are you okay?" he asked.

"Oh Henri, wasn't this simply romantic?" Brigitta placed her hand on his arm and leaned in. "Colbert's character thought she was in love with one man, when really her true love turned out to be the other." He gently removed his arm from hers.

"Did I do something wrong?"

"What about Pauli?"

"Pauli's miles and miles away. I don't know if I'll ever see or hear from him again

"I'm sorry," he replied.

"But Henri—who knows what'll happen tomorrow? We could all be dead from the dreadful war!"

"Besides, maybe he's not my true love either.…"

She let her words linger in the air. He knew what she was getting at. But Brigitta tugged at a part of Henri he no longer felt.

"Please don't take it personally. I'm just not interested in *any* relationship," he explained.

He sensed Brigitta's feelings give way to a nasty pout. With the movie over, they rose to exit. She pulled away. Her eyes stared straight ahead. He trailed after her.

Then he remembered.

He'd forgotten to meet Ping after work.

The next day at the hospital, Henri greeted Brigitta with his usual morning hello. She tossed her head and turned away. Henri didn't want to spend the day ensnared in her cat-and-mouse game.

"I'm sorry if you felt hurt after last night," Henri offered, "I only meant to be honest."

He held out his hand. "Still friends?"

Brigitta drew in a deep breath. "I suppose. You'll let me know if you change your mind?"

"Of course."

They shook. It wasn't perfect, but at least he'd soothed things over enough so that they could work together.

He now had a more pressing issue. He climbed the stairs and found Kaethe Lowen.

"How're you today?" Henri asked and felt the girl's forehead.

"About the same," she told him. "Maybe a little worse."

Just as he'd feared, her condition was deteriorating without the emetine. "Your fever's still high. Let's see what we can do about fixing that today."

Henri ran back downstairs to the nurse's station. Brigitta was still there.

"Did we receive any new medical supplies today?" he asked.

"A shipment arrived, but there was no emetine… again."

Her lingering coolness was palpable.

"There has to be something we can do. Waiting for medicine we haven't seen in weeks isn't helping my patient."

"Dr. Rosen's at another hospital today. He won't be back until tomorrow."

"I can't wait that long."

"You're going to have to."

Henri didn't like what he was hearing. The rest of the day he monitored Kaethe's worsening condition. He'd promised the young girl that she wouldn't die and he meant it. For some reason he felt manic, almost obsessed with her case. He worried that hospital rules were overshadowing their true mission—to save lives. After all, wasn't that what being a doctor was all about?

That night after work, Henri waited eagerly for Ping's arrival. Soon the familiar sight of the cycling rickshaw with its affable owner appeared. Henri waved.

"Ping! I'm so sorry about yesterday!" Henri blurted out before the teen even had a chance to come to a complete stop. "I met a colleague after work. I—forgot."

Henri expected Ping to be somewhat miffed. Instead his friend wore a big grin.

"I forget, too," admitted Ping. "I fall asleep. Sister okay."

"You were with your sister?"

Ping nodded.

"She found me... I found her... we found each other."

Henri gave his friend a warm pat on the back.

"I'm happy," he told Ping. "Very happy."

The two commenced their ongoing lesson. Ping rode his rickshaw while Henri walked alongside.

"Henri okay?" asked his Chinese companion.

Henri looked over at Ping. Although the two were cultures apart, Henri often felt that he and the boy connected in a way that went beyond the spoken language. Henri shook his head.

"I've got a sick patient. She needs medicine." He threw up his hands. "We don't have the medicine. I don't know what to do."

"You need medicine?"

Henri nodded.

"I know," Ping said. "Come. I'll show you."

131

Henri had no idea what Ping knew, but he was curious. He followed the boy to the Chinese section just beyond the Bund. There, his friend directed Henri to a small herbal shop.

"Follow me," Ping insisted.

Henri took his first step inside. He heard the tinkling of a bell overhead, announcing their arrival. Looking around, he was mesmerized by the wooden boxes and jars filled with mysterious roots and stems. He'd always wanted to meet a Chinese medicine man.

Ping ran up the stairs. Henri was lost in reverie when Ping descended with a young lady at his side. With her upturned hair and golden high-collared dress, she smiled at him. Henri was immediately struck by the demure woman and her exotic attractiveness. The beauty mark on her upper lip reminded Henri of a rare black pearl. Her dark eyes met his with a serene intensity. It was as if she could see deep into his soul. For a moment, he felt a strange sensation. The beautiful girl bowed slightly.

"Chinese doctor help Henri," Ping told him. "This my sister. This is Peilin."

11

HENRI STOOD GAZING at the exquisite woman before him. Since arriving in Shanghai, he found Chinese ladies beautiful, but this young woman took his breath away. Her tranquil face illuminated an innate wisdom, yet there was clearly an innocence about her. As she glided toward him; Henri was reminded of a gazelle he once spotted along the Rhine—graceful and resilient.

"*Ni hao.*"

Her smooth melodic voice beckoned him closer.

"*Ni hao,*" he stuttered.

She stared at him somewhat stunned. Henri noticed her inquisitive glance toward her younger brother.

Ping grinned and spoke in rapid Chinese, some of which Henri was able to catch.

"Sister, this is Henri."

Peilin repeated his name. "Heen-ri." It was as if a new soul had just uttered its first words.

Henri nodded in her efforts to communicate.

"*Hen gao xing ren shi ni* (Nice to meet you)," he said taking pride in how much his Chinese had improved over the last months.

Bewildered, she turned to Ping again.

"He speaks Chinese?"

But before Ping could answer, Henri jumped in again. "*Hao. Nin de xiao didi yi jing jiaogou wo* (Yes. Your brother's been teaching me)."

"He knew some," Ping beamed, "but he's getting much better."

Peilin glanced between the two of them. Henri sensed her trying to figure out how their odd pairing could overcome their outward differences. Henri watched her sincere confusion turn to pleasant bemusement. He wondered if Peilin believed that Ping taught him all that he knew in such a short time.

"Your Chinese is quite good," she confessed. "Quite good." She smiled at her brother. "Ping, you're an excellent teacher."

"Yes, he is," Henri agreed. "I've learned more recently than all my years studying back home." As he thought about it, Henri wished his uncle could see how learning the language had now paid off.

Ping interjected, "Your Chinese is better today than it was yesterday." He signaled to Henri with a thumbs-up. Henri once again admired this young man with the infectious grin.

"Each day my vocabulary," Henri continued in Mandarin, "improves with his help."

"You two are friends," she deduced.

Ping readily bobbed his head up and down.

"Friends," he repeated.

Henri noticed the satisfaction on Ping's face. It struck him for the first time that perhaps Ping didn't have many fellow companions.

"I have to say," Henri agreed. "Your brother—" he struggled to find the right word in Chinese. "Your brother is most persistent."

"Lucky for me," Ping insisted.

Henri patted a beaming Ping on the shoulder, "Me, too."

"I've been here for about six months, but I still feel new to this city," she admitted. "Until I found Ping," she confessed, "I really knew no one here."

"I've only been here since January as well, so I understand how it feels."

Until this moment, it hadn't occurred to him that she could be an outsider to Shanghai as well. No matter if someone had just arrived or had lived in the same place their whole life, people everywhere are easily isolated. After all, he and his family had been abandoned and persecuted in their own country.

She turned toward him and it seemed to Henri that she was about to say something when her younger brother piped up.

"Henri arrived on a large boat. He's from Germany," said Ping as the unfamiliar word rolled off his tongue.

Peilin glanced at both Ping and Henri.

"Is that a European country?"

"Yes," Henri responded. "It is. You probably know it better as *De Guo.*"

"Ahh, yes," Peilin said, nodding.

Ping interjected again, "He needs your help, sister."

Peilin turned and now listened carefully to her brother.

"Of course," she offered, her hands open as she focused on her guest.

Henri wasn't sure why, but her deep-pooled eyes seemed to grow larger with genuine concern.

"Not for me," Henri was quick to establish. "I'm a physician. My patients—"

For a moment Henri caught himself, unsure if he should continue knowing Rosen's policy against deviating from Western medicine.

"My sister's a very good doctor," Ping insisted. "Please. She wants to help."

"Where's the patient?" she asked.

"Back at the infirmary," Henri told her.

He looked around the herbal shop. There before him, he saw years of research and medicine that his uncle had longed to understand. Now was Henri's chance. Policy or no policy, as a doctor, he was committed to saving lives. He couldn't sit idly by when there was help available. "Our hospital is short on medicine due to the war."

"Go on," she encouraged. "Tell me about more about this case."

"She's six years old, originally from Europe. She suffers from a high fever, abdominal and rectal pain, and pus and blood in the diarrhea," he continued.

Peilin did not respond with words. Instead, she seemed to mentally hold a conversation within herself. Henri turned to Ping. Maybe his Chinese was not clear enough. Perhaps she couldn't help him. Or worse, she didn't want to. But before either he or Ping could speak up, Peilin finally addressed him.

"What about her tongue?"

Henri recalled his diagnosis. "Yes, I checked her tongue. It was—" he struggled again for the words, "dry and parched, consistent with the dehydration she's experiencing."

But his answer only seemed to confuse her more. Her head tilted slightly. "I meant what kind of coating on her tongue?" Peilin asked further.

Now it was his turn to be puzzled.

"Tongue coating?" he repeated.

"In Chinese medicine," she explained, opening her mouth and pointing, "the tongue's the window to the body. If the tongue's unusually red, then the body suffers from excessive heat. A thin, white coating indicates a spleen deficiency."

He shook his head.

"I don't know."

"Usually I cannot treat unless I have tongue and pulse diagnosis," she told him. "But since you're a doctor, too, will you check for me? Then come back and let me know."

Henri pulled out a pen and small notebook and began jotting down what she said. "All I can tell you is that in Western medicine, her condition is called—" he reverted to English, "amoebic dysentery."

He turned helplessly to Ping, but the boy only shrugged his shoulders. It frustrated Henri that he could not communicate better, but Peilin seemed to be forming her own conclusions. "I suspect her pulse will be thin and sinewy," she surmised. "Her tongue may have a yellow coating."

Henri had never heard a patient's symptoms described in that way.

"I don't understand," he confessed.

She motioned for Henri to roll up his sleeve. Cradling his arm, she gently pressed two fingers into his wrist area.

Henri's body trembled as she placed her warm fingers on him.

"Feel this?" she asked.

Henri nodded. The pressure from her contact accented his quickening heartbeat.

"Your pulse has a strong, even rhythm."

Henri closed his eyes. He could feel his heart's steady beat.

"Yes," he agreed.

"If it was thin, the beat would be faint," she told him. "If sinewy, it'd feel more drawn out."

She tapped her finger on the table with a thump and glided it across to demonstrate what she meant.

Peilin then moved her fingers up his wrist slightly and applied pressure again.

"Good spirit," she announced.

Henri wasn't sure what she meant, but he decided to stay quiet and absorb what was going on.

She moved her fingers up his arm a third time.

"Not hard or collapsing," she told him. She looked up. "Now you check my pulse."

Henri didn't know why, but the thought of touching her suddenly made him anxious. He brushed the feeling aside; after all, he was a doctor and handled patients all the time. He pressed down on her wrist; she continued to explain.

"In Chinese medicine we combine several herbs to restore balance to the body. I'll prepare formula to clear the damp heat in her lower *du zi* (abdomen). This is causing the dysentery. We must also cool the blood and relieve the toxicity."

Henri took it all in as fast as he could, but his Mandarin was still lacking so he missed a word here and there. He didn't want to stop her train of thought, so he did the best he could to write down as much as possible.

She led Henri to the large wall full of drawers that he had admired earlier. Each compartment was engraved with Chinese writing. From one drawer she pulled out a tangled web of dried, tan-colored roots. He watched as her delicate fingers instinctively measured each herb. It was as if the balance of the medicinal cure rested in her touch.

"*Bai tou weng*," she pronounced slowly. "Chinese anemone root. Relieves toxicity, clears damp heat in the stomach," she told him. "The root properties are *ku* and *han*—bitter and cold—*yin* assets."

He scribbled more notes. She laid out portions of the root on several sheets of white paper. From another drawer she pulled out pieces of thin, pallid wood shavings.

"*Huang bai*," she told him, "Cork tree bark. This'll drain the damp heat in the lower *du zi*—extinguish the kidney fire."

Henri watched with fascination as she portioned out equal amounts of the bark onto the paper. She reached for a third drawer. This time it looked like some sort of red fruit leather.

"*Shi liu pi*," she announced. "Pomegranate husk to stabilize the kidney and help her retain her essence. Its properties are sour and astringent, warm and toxic."

Henri perked up hearing the name of a fruit familiar to him.

"In my culture, the pomegranate represents fertility and long life," he exclaimed. He was excited to share his knowledge as well.

Ping piped up. "Chinese like long life, too."

Peilin smiled at them both as she continued to work. He watched Peilin stop and offer her brother some rice cakes. Even though this was the first time he'd seen them together, Henri recognized how she doted on Ping. Looking around the tiny but cozy store, Henri was relieved to see that his friend was now living in the herbal shop and no longer in the slums. Over the last six months, he'd grown to really care about Ping. Henri sensed just how much he shared with her, their mutual affection for the young, disfigured boy.

She returned to her medicine. From a fourth drawer she pulled out another barklike herb.

"*Qin pi*—ash bark," she told him, "This is from a tree that grows back in our village. It'll clear away liver heat."

Some of the herbs sounded familiar from his early herbal readings back in Germany. With each new bit of information, Henri felt both confused and excited. Finally Peilin reached her last drawer.

"*Huang lian*—Chinese golden thread. Relieves diarrhea caused by bacterial infection, high fever, and restlessness. Restores liver and stomach harmony."

Notably proud of his sister, Ping grinned. "My sister learned from our grandfather. They saved my life when I was young."

Peilin blushed but was quick to return his praise. "I'm lucky to have Ping as my brother."

Henri's ears perked up; he wanted to hear more about Ping's young life. He made a mental note to ask later. At the moment, he continued to study Peilin who took the mixture of herbs from one sheet and poured them into a pot of hot water.

"I'll show you how to make the first batch of tea," she continued. "Then you'll know how to prepare." Peilin took at least a dozen herb bundles and wrapped them up. She handed them to Henri.

"*Xie Xie*," he said, thanking her.

"Each herb bundle will provide a day's dosage," she said.

As it began to boil, Henri detected the pungent odor. His nostrils flared and he caught Ping grinning at him.

"You like?" Ping teased, reverting to English.

"If it works—I like," Henri shot back at him, retaining the English so as not to embarrass Peilin.

Peilin had become quiet. Yet whenever her keen eyes looked up at him, Henri felt as if she saw beyond his skin, to his very core. Henri wondered what she thought of this strange white doctor who came seeking herbs.

After she had boiled the concoction down twice, she drained the herbs and poured the brown liquid into a jar.

"Have her drink one cup three times a day," she told him.

He stared at the murky fluid that reminded him of muddy water.

"*Xie Xie*," he said, thanking her again.

She dipped her head slightly and then gazed up into his eyes. Something about the way her eyes lingered on him made Henri blush. He turned toward the door, trying to hide his embarrassment. She stirred up sensations inside him that left him feeling a little lightheaded.

"It's late. I should leave," he said. "I'll be sure to come back and let you know about the patient's condition."

Peilin nodded. "I look forward to seeing you again."

Henri thought he detected a slight smile on her face when Ping suddenly grabbed him by the arm.

"I'll show you the way," his friend offered and the two exited.

Although she'd passed Europeans on Shanghai's main streets, Henri was the first one Peilin had ever spoken to. It felt exotic and strange. She was intrigued by his angular nose and alabaster skin, the curly hair that seemed to dance atop his head. Peilin was even more surprised by how well Henri spoke Chinese. She found his interest in her work invigorating, especially to talk with someone who also understood medicine. She hungered to share her love of herbs with someone as curious as Henri, and to learn more about his practice.

She swept the floor once they departed. Ping returned about a half hour later. He seemed happy. Peilin thought she detected a bemused grin.

"How did you meet him?" she asked, trying to seem casual.

"He's a regular rickshaw customer," he said almost matter-of-factly.

Peilin nodded. Her brother had always been inventive in his ways of maneuvering through the world. The unusual friendship proved yet another example of Ping's ability to adapt and survive.

"And his family?" she continued. "Have you met them?"

"He has no wife or children. He's a refugee. Henri lives in a dorm."

Peilin dusted shelves near the front of the window. Ping regaled her with stories about his nightly language lessons with his new friend. As she listened, Peilin felt a warmth in her heart. She pictured Ping over the last six months exploring Shanghai's streets with a Westerner. The odd friendship sustained her brother through his otherwise bleak existence in the big city.

Even she found herself curiously drawn to the foreign man who'd shown up so unexpectedly. He defied her expectations of Westerners. Her previous encounters had not been as positive. She'd bumped into a European man who spit on her just a week ago; another had rudely asked her to get off the trolley. Today, Peilin enjoyed her conversation with Henri. He was a novelty to her, and she welcomed the openness he exuded.

She sensed his unflagging dedication to his patients. He'd clearly gone out of his way to seek out complementary medicine not familiar to him or his colleagues. His concentrated gaze studied every move she made, as if he, too, were trying to feel the coarse herbs measured through his own touch. She watched his nose wrinkle when the aromatic plants emitted their pungent odors. When she offered him a taste of the tea, she observed his throat tighten over the cooling medicine's sensation.

Yet, on more than one occasion in their brief visit, Peilin had detected a small flicker of guardedness in Henri's eyes. And once, when their hands accidentally touched, he quickly pulled away, as if he'd been burned long ago. She wondered how this unhealed wound could still be so painful.

It was Ping's giant belch that brought her back to the present.

"Sister, where did you go?"

"I'm right here, Ping."

"In body, yes, but your mind was far away."

Peilin felt her cheeks warm. She gathered her dusting rag and turned away. "I was not."

But despite her objection, Ping continued to smile, even as she readied to retire up the stairs.

That night Peilin couldn't fall asleep. Instead her thoughts floated back to her encounter with the German doctor.

Henri clasped the jar filled with the medicinal tea with both hands. It was late. He hurried down the darkened streets illuminated by the full moon's bright light. He'd have to tiptoe into the dorm to avoid waking his bunkmates. He glanced at the jar once again. He found himself smiling—he couldn't stop thinking about the beautiful herbal doctor. Henri thought all Chinese women shared the duty to bear their husband's sons. If a Chinese woman had to work, they were usually employed as amahs and servants, or, if they were lucky, at the cotton mills or silk factories. Henri thought that Ping had told him that his sister was married, yet he saw no indication of a spouse. It seemed rare for a Chinese woman to be alone without a husband.

Even more surprising to him was the fact that Peilin was Ping's sister. Henri silently scolded himself for assuming that Ping's relative would be ordinary looking at best. Ping himself might have been quite handsome had it not been for his unfortunate accident. Henri wondered how two siblings could have traveled such different life paths. He thought about his own life—who would've ever thought Henri would be living in Shanghai?

Damp heat; kidney fire; restoring balance—Peilin's whole method of thinking about medicine differed from anything Henri had ever encountered. For Peilin, healing was tied to nature, balance, harmony. Henri grew up seeing medicine as a science with diseases and cures. Henri felt himself drawn toward the Chinese and their culture. He then recalled a moment when Peilin's hand lightly brushed over his as she measured out the herbs; he had unconsciously pulled away. In hindsight, he realized it had been a while since he felt the soothing touch of a woman.

But just as he found himself about to savor the moment, he wondered what his fellow refugees would think if he were ever to get involved with a Chinese woman.

The next morning Henri dashed up the hospital stairs and bolted down the hall to see his young patient.

"How're you feeling?" he asked Kaethe.

"Hot."

He brushed her tangled hair away from her face and felt her forehead. "Burning up, I'd say. Let me see your tongue again."

Mustering up her strength, she stuck her tongue out. He again noted the deep lines of dehydration, but the tongue's coating was indeed yellow.

Henri wondered about Chinese medicine's method of analysis. It went beyond science itself and used the body's own signals. Rather than extricating the illness, restoring balance was a key component in Eastern healing.

He took his young patient's wrist and felt for the three pulse areas Peilin had shown him. Kaethe's pulse was rapid, to be expected since her body was fighting the infection. He then pressed the tips of his fingers deeper into her wrist. Yes! There it was—the thin, sinewy beat Peilin had predicted.

Henri nearly leapt to his feet.

"I'll be back," he promised.

Henri retrieved the tea jar from his locker. Glancing around, he returned to Kaethe's bedside and pulled the threadbare curtain around them. He opened the container and poured some of the liquid into a cup.

"What is it?" Kaethe asked.

"Medicine," Henri replied.

Kaethe took a whiff. "It smells awful."

Henri held his finger up to his lips. "This is a special medicine, for little girls like you," he whispered.

"You mean like magic?" she asked.

Henri nodded. "That's right. We need to keep it a secret for now—so the magic can work."

He held it out for her to drink. "Here."

Kaethe pinched her nose while she drank. "Yuck!" she said, nearly choking.

"Tell you what, for being such a good girl, I'll bring you some candy to help take away the taste. Will that help?"

She nodded. "I love peppermint."

"Peppermint it is. Now remember what we talked about," he said, putting his finger up to his lips again.

Henri pulled back the curtain and discovered Brigitta approaching.

"What were you two whispering about?"

Henri wondered for a moment if Brigitta had been eavesdropping.

"Magic tricks. Right Kaethe?"

"That's right."

Henri had to think quickly. He needed to redirect Brigitta's curiosity.

"Dinner?" he offered.

Brigitta swung around. She stared at him.

"But I thought—"

"Two friends can have dinner together, can't they?"

It took a beat before she warmed to the idea. "I've had a craving for *Wiener schnitzel* lately. How about the Little Viennese Cafe?"

Henri felt a moment of relief.

That night after dinner, Henri and Brigitta sauntered through the section of Shanghai where German and Austrian refugees had set up small businesses.

"A little slice of home," Brigitta exclaimed.

"Yes," Henri agreed. It was as if a piece of Europe had landed halfway across the world.

Henri was happy to take Brigitta's mind off things. She'd even forgotten about Kaethe. Electric trams hustled down the street. Along the way, they spotted a clothing store displaying fine European coats.

"You'd look good in the navy jacket," she told him.

"That and a decent haircut."

Henri peered through the large barbershop window next door. Men slathered in menthol-scented shaving cream reclined in adjustable leather seats. Henri could see that the shop served as a gathering place for many expatriates who shared stories and exchanged news from back home.

Further down, familiar sounds of Mozart wafted from an outdoor café. Henri even sensed the familiar smells of fresh *weßbrot*—white bread—much like his father's and brother's—escaping from the bakery. He picked up the sweet smell of recently brewed coffee and recognized the freshly made donuts topped with powdered sugar and filled with plum jam. The tiny area brimmed with the customs, civility, and traditions of the old country.

"Did you hear the announcement on the radio? Sounds like Hitler's taking over *all* of Europe," Brigitta commented.

He nodded, but he was barely paying attention. For Henri, Germany seemed far away. He still hadn't heard from his family, despite continuing to send a weekly letter. Perhaps his notes were being intercepted. Or his family had been forced to move. Whatever the circumstances, Henri silently prayed that they were somehow safe.

A young Chinese beggar rushed by. Clutching a package of meat, he brushed Brigitta's sweater.

"My silk cardigan!"

She examined the damage.

"Blood spots."

Henri took a look. The stains weren't as bad as she made them out to be. Why was she making such a scene? As a nurse, Brigitta had seen plenty of blood. Henri wondered if she was being overly dramatic to draw more attention to herself.

"They'll come out with some club soda and a little scrubbing," Henri assured her.

She peered ahead, searching for the boy through the crowd.

"Filthy Chink," she yelled after him.

"Brigitta!"

"Well he is—they all are. Don't tell me you didn't detect that nasty smell?"

"He's hungry and he's broke."

"I don't care. They need to stay in their area. We don't venture into theirs," Brigitta shouted.

"But this is *their* country—they live here. They opened their doors to us when nearly every other country turned us away."

"You sound as if you like them, Henri Neumann."

Henri considered Brigitta. He knew that some people didn't fare well outside their comfort zone. Still under the wartime circumstances they found themselves in, Brigitta's outburst was nasty and self-centered.

"Why not?" asked Henri.

Brigitta couldn't seem to come up with a better response except to pout. Such a tactic probably worked when she was a child, but it was unbecoming on a grown woman.

Henri looked around and spotted a street vendor holding out an array of candied mango. Henri held up his hand and waved the Chinese peddler toward them.

"*Ma fan ni, gei wo liang ge* (Please, I need two)," Henri shouted in fluent Chinese.

Now Brigitta stared at Henri.

The seller handed him two of his honey-laced slices on a stick.

"*Ji qian* (How much)?"

"*Liang kuai qian* (Two yuans)," replied the merchant.

Henri handed him several coins and thanked the gentleman.

He turned and offered the fruit to Brigitta.

"Henri, have they brainwashed you? Remember who you are and where you're from." She waved her arms. "Don't forget. This is all temporary--the humidity, the bugs. It's so—so uncivilized."

Her latest outburst irritated him even more. Still he wanted to calm her.

"Why don't we just enjoy what's here, rather than continue to point out how it doesn't meet your standards."

Brigitta put her hands on her hips. "How dare you talk to me that way," she sulked. "I'm entitled to my feelings."

Henri couldn't take her tantrums any longer. He walked ahead. Brigitta ran to catch up. She seemed more conciliatory, as if she knew she had gone too far.

"All right, all right. I can appreciate your curiosity," she said catching up to him. "I'm just glad we have each other to remind ourselves who we are and where we're from."

He wanted to leave her behind, but he knew if he did, she'd most likely start another protest; he was tired of arguing with her.

He was beginning to see how crafty she was at mixing sincerity with manipulation.

"It's just that I can't wait to leave this place," she persisted. "I'm sure you can understand that."

Henri looked at her but said nothing. They continued down the street in silence. It dawned on Henri how much he felt disconnected from her. The more Brigitta lamented how much she wanted to leave, the more Henri knew he wanted to stay.

Peilin decided to prepare some wilted greens with a spicy garlic dressing. With watercress's cool nature, the vegetable would help them sleep through the summer's warm, humid nights. The oil in the wok started to smoke. Peilin tossed in the greens, soy sauce, minced garlic, and rice wine. As soon as the leaves were slightly wilted, she scooped the watercress into a serving bowl. Along with steamed rice, their meal was ready.

"Ping!"

Her brother, who'd been outside smoking, entered and grabbed a bowl. Using chopsticks, he gulped down the vegetables. Peilin sat beside him; in contrast, she delicately lifted small portions to her lips. She wasn't really hungry, but she knew she needed to stay nourished. Earlier she'd placed burning incense near the window. Ping now gazed at it.

"Is this the anniversary of Yao's death?" Ping finally asked.

Peilin shook her head. "His birthday. Yao would've been twenty-two today."

She stared off into the distance. "I still can't believe he was killed fighting the Japanese." She winced. "His head was severed, propped up on a fence post like a decoration." She paused. "Although I barely knew him—still he's my husband."

"Those barbarians!" Ping exclaimed a little too vehemently.

Peilin was confused by Ping's enthusiasm. He was more outspoken than she'd remembered. Then again, she'd been alone for the last six months; perhaps she'd just become used to the silence.

She rose from the table and began clearing the dishes. Ping made some excuse about work and slipped out the door. Although it was late, she was relieved to have some time to herself.

Her thoughts returned to her husband. She'd built an altar near the front store window. Once the dishes were cleaned, she pulled up a seat opposite the white-lit candle and picture of Yao. His frozen face in the photo forever stared back at her, unable to show her longing, happiness, or affection. She'd never feel the warmth of his skin or the tender touch of his hand. She mourned for the possibilities that would never arrive—the love of a man, the joy of children. And because she was without these, her fate was uncertain.

She turned away from the altar and peered out the window. Her mind drifted beyond the *xiao xiang* and across the bridge, toward Henri who was living somewhere amid displaced refugees. There was something about his energy, his being, which made her heart beat a little faster. Still grieving, she felt confused. Sadness, fear, anger, flickers of joy swirled within her. Could thoughts of Henri cause her dead husband to become angry with her?

The turmoil reminded Peilin of a story Grandpa Du once told her about a village along the Yellow River. Although its walls were as tall as seven men, constant rains caused the river to overflow. The water churned and broke down the barrier protecting the city. Men, women, and children drowned as the angry flood tore down their huts and flooded their farmland. Then an old man spotted a carp flopping helplessly along the shore. He picked it up and put it back in the river. Suddenly the waters receded—the village was saved. By putting the fish back in the water, the old man had restored nature's balance. If only Peilin could find a way to steady her own precarious feelings.

12

H ENRI ARRIVED at the hospital early the next morning. He darted straight to Kaethe's bedside.

"How're you feeling?" he asked.

Kaethe yawned, still waking.

"I'm not sure. About the same. Maybe a little worse."

He felt her forehead. Still hot.

He pulled out a small brown bag hidden in his coat and handed it to his young patient.

"*Mmmm,*" she said popping a mint into her mouth.

Henri studied his patient. Perhaps he didn't understand as much as he thought. Perhaps he had been expecting too much. Then he felt a presence behind him.

"How's our girl doing this morning?" asked Brigitta.

"Not so good," Henri admitted.

At Brigitta's prompting, Kaethe spit the candy out into a tissue. The nurse then stuck a thermometer into the girl's mouth. Brigitta smiled at Henri as if nothing had ever happened the night before. He marveled at how her personality could vary so dramatically from day to day. She pulled out the thermometer and read Kaethe's results.

"You're right, it's still high."

"Did the emetine arrive yet?" he asked.

"I'm afraid not."

He was expecting as much, but he needed to weigh the options. The fact that Kaethe's condition had not improved with the Chinese medicine was a personal setback for Henri. But he'd come this far, and at the moment there was no other alternative.

He returned to Kaethe's bedside. "Don't worry," he said, laying a reassuring hand on her shoulder. "Keep drinking the medicine," he whispered. "The peppermints will help. You'll be feeling better soon."

Kaethe looked up and gave him a weak smile.

Over the next week, Henri monitored Kaethe's condition every day. He held onto the optimism that something would change for the better.

Then on the seventh day, her fever broke.

Henri was cautiously hopeful. He knew more evidence of Eastern medicine's effects was needed. What if Kaethe relapsed? He glanced at Brigitta, who was unaware of Henri's clandestine treatment.

Then he felt an added strain. Rosen appeared.

"What do we have here?" the head doctor boomed.

Henri piped up. "The amoebic dysentery's dissipating. Kaethe's improving despite the lack of proper medication."

Rosen glanced from Brigitta to Henri and then to the patient.

"Really?" said the head doctor.

"Her fluids have stabilized as well," Brigitta announced. She handed Rosen the chart.

Henri scrutinized Brigitta and Rosen; he wondered if either suspected anything.

"See, Neumann," the chief snapped. "Sometimes the body, especially a young body, will fight the infection off itself. No need to panic about supplies."

Henri paused and then carefully chose his words. "Perhaps. But there can be a lot of factors. Maybe it was something we haven't considered yet."

Rosen's eyes narrowed.

"I've been practicing medicine since before you were even born. I'll have you know I not only graduated first in my surgical class but I've also published over thirty-five medical studies," he barked. "You question my authority?"

They were still standing near Kaethe's bedside.

"We need to take this conversation somewhere else," Henri coaxed his colleagues.

Kaethe had covered her head with the blanket. Henri gently patted her shoulders and then joined the others.

But Rosen stormed out of the room.

Perhaps the chief felt threatened by him. After all, Henri was younger, quicker, and more up-to-date on the latest medical advances. Rosen's unprofessional outburst in front of patients had been grossly inappropriate. All the more reason, Henri thought, to keep the Eastern medicine a secret for now.

A week had passed since Peilin had seen the German doctor. She wondered if Henri would return to report on the progress of his patient as he had promised, or if he'd disappear into the vast sea of people that made up Shanghai. By the eighth day, she'd convinced herself that Henri had probably been feigning interest in her herbs so as not to affront her or Ping.

So when she returned downstairs to her shop later that evening she was surprised to find Henri, his back to her. He peered into a jar. His focus was so intent on the herb that he didn't detect her arrival.

Peilin took the moment to study his physique. She hadn't noticed the firm muscles of his forearms or his large, brawny hands the first time she'd met him.

"That's ginseng," she said. "Its Chinese name means man-root."

Henri twisted around, looking almost guilty. He regained his composure. She wondered what thoughts she might have interrupted but didn't dare ask.

"The two roots that split off from the main body look like they form a pair of legs," she explained.

Henri examined the root more closely.

"Yes, I see that now," he said. "Must be a very important herb to be displayed so magnificently."

Peilin nodded.

"This herb's good for male virility."

"Do you use the same root for women?"

Peilin shook her head. "Different root—*dong quai*—nourishes the blood and the heart. Actually *dong quai* is good for both male and female sexual hormones."

Peilin suddenly stopped.

"I'm afraid I've said too much," she apologized.

Henri walked over to her.

"Not at all. We're both doctors."

Henri brushed the dust off his knees.

"The patient, Kaethe, is recovering well. It took a while but her fever and dysentery are now gone."

"I've heard our remedies do take longer to work than Western medicine," Peilin confirmed. "I'm pleased to learn of her progress."

"Do you have time for a cup of tea?" she offered.

"I'd like that," he said and took a seat.

She felt his steady gaze. She selected a combination of ginseng, schizandra fruit, lycium, and dried astragalus—a longevity tonic.

"Will you teach me? About the herbs?"

She felt her cheeks redden.

"I've no idea where to start," she stammered.

"It doesn't matter," he encouraged.

She breathed in. How to condense so many years of training into a conversation?

"Well," she began, "too much yang results in fever."

Henri took out his small notepad and began writing.

"What's yang?" Henri asked.

Peilin paused. At first she was surprised that the German doctor didn't know something so basic. Then she realized that the concept was not part of Western thinking. "Yang is like positive energy, warm. But body also needs yin, like passive energy, cool, for balance."

"Yin and yang," he repeated. "Interesting. Please tell me more."

He continued to scribble his notes, much like a young scholar.

"Every herb has its own unique properties or energy—cold, cool, warm, or hot. Most cool or cold herbs treat fever, sore throat, thirst, and other heat-related diseases."

Peilin wondered what he must be thinking. While she talked, Peilin felt his tender gaze. Although she realized his interest was in the herbs, she found his rapt attention invigorating.

Then, as if he could not get the words out fast enough, Henri blurted, "Then warm and hot energy herbs must treat cold diseases—chills, cool limbs—those sorts of symptoms."

"That's right," Peilin responded. "Besides energy, there's taste—sweet, sour, salty, pungent, and bitter."

Peilin then went to her drawers and pulled out two herbs for him to taste. The first one looked like fine golden strands.

"This one's *huang lian*. *Huang* means yellow. *Lian* means thread."

He held the delicate herb between his fingers. "I can see why."

"It's a plant root from the Sichuan region," she continued.

"What's it used for?"

She dropped the yellow threads into boiling water.

"It's one of the most effective herbs for stomach ulcers."

She wondered what he thought of such a simple herb and its ability to aid with such a persistent ailment. She glanced up. He smiled at her. She shyly turned. She hoped her eyes hadn't given away the lighthearted feelings she was experiencing inside. She'd never quite felt this way before. Her heart raced with the speed of a humming-bird's wings. The sensation energized her. Soon the tea was ready. She got up to pour a cup.

"*Gan bai* (Drink up)," she told him.

He took a sip. His face scrunched up immediately.

"Tart. It's worse than vinegar."

He wiped the corners of his mouth.

"*Hao*, it's one of the most bitter herbs we have," she told him. "Not very popular with patients, I'm afraid, but it's effective for infections."

"It better be. A gulp of that stuff would send a dragon running for the hills," he concluded.

He cleared his palate with some water. She opened another drawer and pulled out several slivers of bark. She came back and placed them in his hand.

"*Gan cao*," she told him. "Sweet herb."

"Anything has to taste better than the first one."

He held it up to his nose. "Smells familiar."

"You may know this as lic-o-rice," she said, stumbling to pronounce the foreign word. She wondered what Grandpa Du would think of her, teaching a Western doctor about their herbal tradition. She imagined he'd be proud.

"Ah, yes," Henri said. "Licorice. It's used in candy back in Germany."

Once she had boiled the licorice into a tea, he took a sip. This time, he savored the taste.

"This one, I could drink all day," he smiled.

"It has all sweet properties—it tonifies, strengthens, moistens, and nourishes the body. It relieves pain and harmonizes other herbs. That's why it's in many formulas."

She poured him another cup.

"So now you know two more herbs."

Henri looked to her with a satisfied grin.

"Yes, with opposite tastes. Like yin and yang."

"That's it," she said, happy to see that he was catching on.

"Fascinating." He took a moment. "Can an herb have more than one flavor?"

Peilin nodded. "Each herb has at least one taste, but yes, they can have more than one. And there are a few with no taste. We categorize them as neutral."

She continued to explain the Chinese principles behind the herbs. At the same time, an inner liveliness flourished. Her heart ached with both excitement and fear. Could opposite feelings exist inside a person, too? She found herself wondering about that longing between male and female—yang and yin again. A budding energy rose up from her being's core. She longed to smell his musky scent, drink in his essence, touch his face. But an inner voice reminded her of her status as a married woman and her obligations to the Kwans. It kept her secret yearning at bay.

Still, they continued their conversation well into the unfolding summer night, staying up much longer than either of them had intended.

When they finally said good evening, it was after 1:00 AM. Henri reached his hand out. Peilin—her hands clasped—bowed in return. He stood for a moment, then nodded. Peilin closed the door; then her lights. In the dark she gazed ahead as he disappeared down the street.

As June turned to July, a new influx of refugees arrived at the dorm. For Henri, the increasing population accentuated the intensifying summer heat. Crammed into the tight quarters, Henri bristled at the acrid odors of sweat surrounding him. Despite the stifling humidity, his fellow expatriates clung to their thick European wools.

Henri had observed the locals and adjusted to the escalating heat by trading in his heavy garments for thin, cotton clothing. The breathable fabric allowed his body to cool quickly. He'd suggested the lighter garments to his peers, but with little money and the undying hope that they would soon return home, most kept to their heavy suits and dresses.

Even at the hospital, Rosen ran the staff as if they were back in Germany. The strict protocol and unquestionable power reminded Henri of his early days as an intern. No matter if Henri had treated the situation many times before, the chief's eyes darted distrustfully over Henri's every move. Henri could see that the man was brilliant, but as someone who took delight in finding faults in others, he was woefully closed-minded and filled with suspicion. It was a constant uphill struggle with Rosen; Henri had to choose his battles carefully.

Despite the chief's overbearing authority, Henri was grateful for the work. Jobs were hard to come by for most refugees. Although he didn't earn more than a few yuans a week, it provided some spending money. More important, his ability to help others made him feel useful. Kaethe's progress had been encouraging, but there was still a lot of learning that lay ahead. Until then, he'd abide by the rules, however restrictive.

As much as everyone else wished and pretended otherwise, they were in China. For his peers, it was due to unlucky circumstances. But for Henri, it was as if China spoke to something deep inside him. In fact, he found this aspect of their predicament energizing. Perhaps it was the trace of Chinese blood hidden somewhere within his DNA. Whatever it was, Henri felt his luck turn since arriving in Shanghai.

Ping encouraged Henri to accompany him home for dinners. Most nights he was able to leave work and enjoy tasty dishes of stir-fried long beans, savory rice dumplings, or green turnip soup.

The engaging herbalist had taught him to eat foods with cooling properties—such as lettuce and watermelon—to help the body cope with the hot summer nights. Her tonics harmonized with nature, just as she flowed with life. Each time she prepared an herbal remedy, he became more and more mesmerized by her intuitive assessment of the body and its needs. Henri marveled over her skills. She opened drawer after drawer and carefully measured out each herb. Every formula formed a distinctive combination suited for that individual patient. Her womanly grace only heightened Henri's sense of awakening.

Peilin had welcomed him into her tiny home and freely shared her knowledge. His uncle had yearned for this information years ago. Since Sophie, Henri had hardened his feelings to all but that which would help his patients. Not even Brigitta could break through his callused heart. So how could this unassuming Chinese woman awaken a sensation that he had long thought extinguished?

Water chestnuts sizzled in the wok. Peilin enjoyed the routine of cooking a midday meal for herself and her brother. Since they'd reunited, Peilin felt more secure in Shanghai, like a jigsaw puzzle that had finally been completed. Peilin wondered how Ping had survived the past year alone. It hadn't been easy for her, but she had the herbal store and the financial support of the Kwans. Ping had arrived with nothing. Yet here he was—repairing a broken wheel spoke.

"How did you get here from our village?" she asked him. "Did you have money for the train? Did you ride the bus? How did you know the way?"

She wondered why she hadn't asked earlier, for now her questions poured out of her mouth like rising water spilling over a dam.

"Not to worry, sister," he said laying down his repair work.

"At first I didn't know. Then I joined others who'd lost their farms and families to the enemy." His voice trailed off.

Peilin sensed her brother's mind clouding over.

"Are you okay?"

Ping shook himself as if to be rid of a bad dream. His eyes narrowed.

"Those damn Japanese soldiers—they deserve to die!"

There it was again. Peilin reeled back, unaccustomed to the raw anger that spewed from his mouth. It felt like some unseen apparition had just entered the room.

"Ping!"

Her brother just as quickly became withdrawn.

"Forgive me sister. To answer your question, sometimes we walked; other times we hitched a ride."

He grabbed his chopsticks and began to eat. At first Peilin was flabbergasted by his outburst. Now she wondered if something was wrong. Ping wasn't an unhappy or angry person.

"Is there something you want to talk about?"

Ping stared at his noodles. She thought his mind had ventured away to some far-off place.

"No," he replied.

Whatever it was, he instead retreated within.

She liked taking care of him, but sometimes she wondered who was really taking care of whom.

She knew Ping depended solely on himself. Even when the water buffalo had trampled him as a young boy, Ping drew on his own inner resources, his will to live, to pull himself through. Ping had always been one to survive tragedy and turn it into strength. He didn't let things hold him back. He had hope despite dire circumstances. Without knowing the outcome, he continued on. Such fortitude was worth more than all the gold in a rich man's treasure.

Ping cracked a wry smile at Peilin. She smiled back, but inside she had a nagging feeling that she could not shake.

"Once I came to Shanghai, I started my own business, to make my own money," Ping said, opening the conversation again.

"How did you meet Henri?" Peilin asked.

"I saw him walking. He offered coins to a beggar, even though he too was poor," Ping reminisced.

Peilin nodded. "If you want happiness for a lifetime, help someone else," she recalled. It was a favorite saying of their grandpa's.

Ping nodded. "That's how I knew he would be a good friend," he revealed.

He turned to his sister.

"What about you?" he asked. "Tell me about your life during the time we were apart."

There was a genuine interest in Ping's face. Peilin realized that neither of them had shared much about what had transpired during all their months apart. They'd instead chosen to talk about the present, to be in the day-to-day. It now struck her as odd, and she wondered how much she didn't know about Ping.

"The Kwans took me in as their daughter-in-law even though Yao had already died. At first, it was hard to adjust to life at Dragon Lake. Kwan Taitai could be quite strict. Father Kwan taught me how to string and harvest pearls."

"But you're here now."

"Yes," Peilin replied. "It's my responsibility to run the family store since an uncle died."

"Is this what you want?" he queried.

Peilin wasn't sure she understood the question.

"What do I want?" she repeated.

Ping nodded. "I mean, since Yao is gone, you're alone."

"What else is there?" she wondered aloud.

Ping pounded the table and stood.

"Sister, your life shouldn't always be about what others want," Ping declared.

"I'm a married woman. That's more than I could've hoped for."

"Hope has to continue and grow," Ping told her. "Not grieve for the past, but look out into the future—live life."

Ping soon left for work. Peilin cleared the dishes and pondered their conversation. *What did Ping mean?* Peilin hadn't considered her life beyond being with the Kwans. It wasn't up to her—or was it?

A few nights later, in the July heat, Henri and Ping met after work. On this day, it seemed that something weighed heavily on his friend's mind.

"Something bothering you?" Henri finally asked.

"The Japanese Army has been dropping bombs from the air onto Chongqing. Many innocent people have died." Ping hesitated for a moment. "It bothers me to know that such pain still goes on."

Henri studied the teen, astonished at his intensity and knowledge. Although Ping couldn't read or write, he somehow managed to stay informed. Chongqing was nearly nine hundred miles away.

"How do you know all this?" Henri asked.

Ping looked surprised at the question.

"I hear on the street," the young boy told him. "Other rickshaw pullers—their families, like mine—die at the hands of the Imperial Army."

They continued toward the herbal shop. Henri noticed Ping's forehead scrunch up, as if he wrestled with something in his mind.

"For me, I'd fight for my family," Ping suddenly announced.

Henri felt a sense of alarm. He knew how much it would upset Peilin if Ping left to fight.

"Your government needs to fight this war with the Japanese."

Ping considered Henri's words for a moment.

"In China, there are two armies. Both fight the Japanese. But the two armies also fight each other."

Now it was Henri's turn to shake his head.

"I don't understand."

Ping tried to explain.

"My own country cannot agree. One side believes in communism—everybody the same. No one rich, no one poor."

Henri nodded. "Russians live this way."

"Then there are my countrymen, who follow Chiang Kai-shek. His vision is democracy—people to make their own destiny."

Henri nodded again. "Most of the Western world lives by this creed, or at least tries to."

Ping became quiet.

"There's so much suffering. Too many families destroyed." He paused. "I want to join the army."

Henri felt his own heart stop.

"But Peilin's your family. You don't want to leave her now, do you?" he asked.

Henri noticed Ping hesitate with his decision. Then he shook off the confusion; he appeared more determined.

"My sister doesn't understand. Family honor must be avenged. As the only son, it's my duty. My destiny."

"You could be killed fighting. Do you understand that?"

Ping stood firm.

"If that's my fate, so be it."

Henri felt frustrated. Ping was as stubborn as the water buffalo that maimed him.

"You're from another country," Ping reasoned. "In China, the Japanese kill good, innocent people. Take what does not belong to them. We must defeat them."

Henri closed his eyes. The words were all too familiar and painful. He turned back to Ping. "Because of war, a lot of people from my homeland are dead. A man named Hitler is responsible."

Ping cocked his head. Henri felt that Ping was seeing a side of Henri's past he'd never considered.

"You left and let the enemy take over?" Ping gasped.

Henri's shoulders fell.

"I had no choice," Henri replied.

The two walked in silence. Henri wondered if Ping had lost respect for him. After all, he'd fled his country.

Ping stopped for a moment.

"Maybe for you that was best," he nodded. "For me, that's not possible." Ping gazed off—as if he'd mentally wandered back in time and place.

"I never told anyone. Not even my sister," Ping started to confess. "The night the Japanese burned down our house and killed my family—I was there."

Ping shivered even though the night was warm.

"I can still hear my mother's screams," Ping revealed.

He covered his ears, closed his eyes.

"They made me watch. I tried to turn away, but they forced me. I closed my eyes. They shoved knives into my eyelids and pried them open."

Then Ping's eyes flew open.

"They raped her." The look on Ping's face was unlike anything Henri had ever seen.

"Your mother?" Henri asked.

Ping nodded.

"They tore her clothes off. I'd never seen my mother naked. She shrieked for the soldiers to kill her, to spare her the indignity. Instead, they laughed."

Ping shuttered.

"Soldier after soldier pulled down their pants and forced their way between my mother's legs. Each time, she screamed until there was no life left in her."

Ping turned away.

"Her cries will haunt me forever."

Ping spit into the night air.

"I'm sorry," Henri whispered. But even those few words felt small in comparison to the nightmare Ping lived.

"Please don't say anything to my sister," Ping said as they continued to walk.

"Of course not," Henri agreed. "It's just between us."

They arrived at the herbal store just as Peilin was locking up. Henri had almost forgotten—the three had planned to spend the evening exploring the Qixi festival.

Peilin greeted Henri.

"There'll be beautiful weaving and carved melons on display."

"Tell me again, what are we celebrating?" Henri asked.

Ping piped up. "The Night of Sevens celebrates love between a mortal and a fairy. Because the two lovers are from different worlds, they're separated. But once a year, the magpies form a bridge so that they can meet up."

They walked toward the village square. A quiver ran through Henri's spine. People were staring at him. They must think his accompanying Peilin odd. He chose to ignore their gawking. He barely knew Peilin. Their lives had come together due to circumstances larger than either of them could have foreseen.

Peilin seemed unusually quiet. Ping ran ahead and pointed out handwoven baskets. Dexterous young girls weaved the soft bamboo. Farther ahead were displays of intricate melon carving—horses galloping, turtles swimming, young maidens playing flutes. A stunning chrysanthemum etched into pink watermelon flesh caught his eye. Henri turned to Ping, but the young teen had disappeared. Maybe he ran into his rickshaw buddies.

"He's listening to the pan flute," Peilin said, catching Henri's look of concern. "Don't worry. He'll catch up."

Henri squeezed through the crowd to keep up with Peilin. They viewed white gourds carved into swans and silk spun from cocoons. He followed as she made her way to the riverbank. There, actors in bright costumes prepared to reenact the fairytale. With so many crowded around, Henri had to lean in closer toward Peilin in order to see the stage. He smelled the fresh scent of jasmine in her hair; her deep-red lips reminded him of summer cherries. Most amazing were her eyes—large, brown pools that seemed to hold deep secrets within.

The play began. Seven fairy sisters pretended to swim in the lake. When the sisters discovered that a cowherd had stolen their clothes, they chose the youngest to retrieve their garments. Henri's mind floated into a timeless dreamlike state; he imagined Peilin as a fairy from another world.

Back on the stage, the pixie found the cowherd and their clothes. In order to get them back, she agreed to his marriage proposal. They lived happily together. Henri felt his spirits buoyed as well. But when the Goddess discovered that the fairy had married a mere mortal, she forced the fairy back to heaven.

Henri surprised himself—he sympathized with the broken-hearted man. The determined cowherd dropped everything and followed his wife to the heavens. Henri wondered if he would ever feel such an overwhelming draw. But the Goddess threw the cowherd out and scratched a wide river through the sky—the Milky Way—separating the lovers forever. Henri glanced at Peilin. He wondered if the story affected her, too—or did she see it as mere fantasy? Her serene features gave no indication either way. Henri thought the play was over, yet the actors regrouped for one more scene. Taking pity on the couple, the magpies form a bridge once a year—the seventh night of the seventh moon—and the lovers reunite.

When the play was over, Henri felt an unusual warmth in his chest. Peilin smiled at him ever so slightly. Again he pondered what she was thinking. Had Peilin wished for a good husband like the girl in the story? In China, the choice was out of the women's hands—they were passive bystanders to their own destiny. Henri then thought about his own journey—*was he in charge of his destiny? Or was he subject to fate?*

Before Peilin knew it, the sweltering heat of August was upon them. The three had become a small family of sorts. Henri was regularly joining Ping and her for dinner, and she looked forward to their nights. In fact, they'd be arriving soon. She chopped the broccoli and checked on the simmering rice. Considering all that her brother had been through in his life, he still found hope and moved forward. *What did he say to her a month ago—to live life?* That seemed to be the opposite of fate—or was it? Was fate what brought her here or was it a series of unfortunate accidents?

What if chance and choice collided together, making it possible to create a new determination? Then it occurred to Peilin that perhaps that was what Grandpa Du had intended all along. Maybe Ping, too, was guiding her toward the path of—dare she say—happiness?

Her mind wandered back to the night of the Qixi festival. That evening Ping had disappeared, leaving her alone with Henri. Since then he'd made a point now and then to get up and retire early. Peilin suspected how intentional these small acts actually were—and she was secretly pleased.

She allowed her mind to linger back to that night, reviewing the small exchanges, moments she'd savored ever since. The doorbell chimed overhead; Ping and Henri entered. She quickly returned to her senses.

"*Ni hao,*" she greeted.

Henri breathed in the hearty aroma of the oyster mushrooms sizzling in the wok.

"Can't wait to dig into that," he said, smacking his lips.

"So far, I don't think there's anything you haven't liked."

"That's because you're such a great cook."

She noticed that he often praised her; it secretly made her heart sing. She detected, though, that Ping was unusually quiet this evening.

"Are you okay?" she asked, concerned that he might be coming down with a summer cold.

Ping nodded.

"We had a stimulating conversation on our way over here," Henri said. "I'm afraid I've worn him out."

Peilin glanced between the two. She sensed something was lurking in the air. She decided to let him be. Along with the sizzling mushrooms, she dished out the Chinese radish, cuttlefish soup, and boiled bird's nest. Whatever it was, she was sure Ping would talk when he was ready.

"Sister," Ping blurted, "I want to join the army."

Peilin caught herself, grabbing onto one of the wooden stools. The room whirled around her. She stared at Ping as if he had just stabbed her. She couldn't hold herself back.

"No—I won't lose you, too!" she cried out.

Peilin reached for him, but Ping quickly stood and backed away.

"It's not for you to decide!" he shouted back.

Peilin trembled; she fumbled for her balance. Henri stood between them.

"It's a lot to take in," Henri interceded. "Why don't we all sit down and discuss this?"

Peilin's whole body was now shaking.

"He simply cannot go."

Ping threw up his hands. "I'm leaving."

Rarely had she seen him so angry. But before she could protest, Ping bolted out the door.

That night, Peilin was inconsolable. "I don't want him to go." She choked back tears.

Henri sat down next to her.

"Young boys are drawn in by the uniform," Henri consoled, "lured by talk of defending their motherland."

Peilin turned toward her friend. But for a moment, Henri seemed to gaze off to some faraway place before shaking himself. His tender eyes refocused on her.

"Give him some time," he continued. "It's just a passing interest. Something will come along and change his heart."

Henri tried to calm her with his words; but the truth was they were empty expressions, a futile attempt to ease her pain.

13

SEPTEMBER 1939: Henri had been in Shanghai for nearly nine months. He wasn't up for socializing tonight, but Rosen insisted he attend the lavish party hosted by the Kadoories—a wealthy Sephardic Jewish family whose generous donations supported the hospital.

Henri had heard of the sprawling two-story Colonial-style mansion on Bubbling Well Road. Outside, tall white-marbled columns and French doors lined the ground level. Inside was just as impressive—in fact more extravagant than he'd expected. Black-and-white parquet floors adorned the lengthy hallways. Alabaster marble was everywhere, including the staircase leading to the second floor. Swirling wrought-iron banisters topped with rich teak handrails enveloped the main foyer. Henri imagined they'd been transported back to Berlin.

"Wow," said Brigitta under her breath. She was clad in a flowing pink dress with laced shoulders. Rosen had cleaned up his beard. In his tux, he exhibited a refined demeanor Henri had never experienced before. The guests—all European ex-patriots—were dressed in elegant suits and long dresses. Henri shifted uncomfortably, hoping no one would notice the moth holes at the bottom of his coat. While most had arrived in Shanghai recently, some had lived there for decades.

"We're here to show our appreciation," Rosen instructed. "The

Kadoorie donations as well as those of other wealthy supporters are what keep the hospital running."

"Steady employment," he said pointedly to Henri.

A servant ushered Henri, Rosen, and Brigitta toward the ballroom. Their host, Sir Elly Kadoorie, was an avid tango dancer. The vast room displayed a dozen glittering chandeliers suspended from fifty-foot-high ceilings. A string quartet, including two violins, a cello, and a bass, provided soothing melodies. Tinted lights overhead changed the ballroom setting from pink to red to blue. Black marble fireplaces crowned with elaborate mirrors governed each end of the eighty-by-fifty-foot room. Butlers held out trays flowing with mini beef wellington, chicken skewers, and bruschetta.

Brigitta grabbed Rosen and locked arms as they entered. Henri wandered off on his own, strolling toward the sizeable crystal punch bowl near the large bay window. A servant offered him a goblet. Another appeared with a tray full of mushroom hors d' oeuvres. Henri took one out of politeness.

The music started up again—this time a waltz. Dancers glided across the marble floor, their bodies flowing across the room. A jovial Rosen sipped brandy with a man sporting a monocle. Although different, the cheery atmosphere reminded Henri of the Jazzkeler. Funny—he hadn't thought about that place since escaping Berlin. In his rush to flee, he'd left his entire record collection behind. Maybe when he had time, he could find some of his old favorites here in the International Settlement.

Brigitta twirled past him on the dance floor, her flowing pink dress nearly brushing Henri aside. Her partner was a distinguished gentleman dressed in a crisp white uniform with colorful pocket stripes. Probably a wealthy benefactor.

Within the opulent setting, Henri overheard conversations of home—be it Germany, Austria, Russia, or elsewhere—the war was on everyone's mind. Many were still rattled by Hitler's Reichstag speech—an open threat to the Jewish population. In June, a thousand Jewish refugees were turned away by Cuba and the United States—forcing the ship back to Europe. Rumors filled the dance hall, including unwanted passengers sent to concentration camps. Everyone here either knew or knew of someone adversely affected by the war.

Yes, everyone, he thought. Henri sauntered over to the long bay window. Though it was dark, he could make out the well-manicured east lawn. Henri gazed beyond the Marble Palace's wrought-iron fence in the general direction of Peilin's store.

Peilin had been somber and subdued since Ping announced that he wanted to join the army. Ping returned each night to sleep, but according to Peilin, her brother avoided her, slipping out before dawn. Henri hadn't seen Ping since the night of his distressing confession.

The quartet engaged in a lively foxtrot. Henri's attention returned to the party. Their host, Elly Kadoorie, now sat a few tables away. A tall balding man with a portly demeanor, Elly modeled a wispy mustache. Back at the hospital, his picture, as well as portraits of his sons Lawrence and Horace, hung prominently on the wall. According to Rosen, the Kadoorie family hailed from Bombay; they immigrated to Shanghai nearly a hundred years earlier—around 1880. Elly and his brother, Ellis, earned their success through banking, real estate, electricity, and rubber plantations. Their success blossomed in the East, and they gave charitably to the community. The elder statesman glanced in Henri's direction. Appreciative of the family's generosity, Henri tipped his head in gratification.

Then Henri noticed Rosen beckoning him from across the room. He wound his way through the crowd. Rosen put his arm around him; Henri presumed the liquor had loosened the stiff doctor's rigidity.

"Henri Neumann, meet Ezra Hershberg and his wife, Arabelle," Rosen announced. "They're generous donors to the hospital." Then without another word, Rosen took off. Henri stood nearly speechless in front of his new acquaintances.

"A pleasure to meet you," Henri stuttered.

"And you as well," Arabelle replied.

Arabelle had a Rubenesque figure. At first Henri thought she might be sickly due to her sallow skin, but changed his mind.

"How are things at the hospital, doctor?" Ezra asked.

"Not bad," Henri began.

Beneath the dark beard, Ezra looked about Henri's age. And when he spoke, Henri immediately recognized the accent.

Just then another well-dressed lady tapped Arabelle on the shoulder. She whispered something into her ear. The two women chuckled. Arabelle turned.

"Excuse me," she interrupted. "I'll be back in a moment."

The women took off in the direction of the bar. Henri turned back to his new associate. "I'm from Berlin, too. Are you by chance related to Jakob Hershberg?"

"Yes," he replied. "He's my brother. Do you know him?"

"He was a year ahead of me in school. Soccer player, very friendly. Is he here in Shanghai?"

Ezra's eyes clouded over.

"No. Jakob's still in Germany. I'd been receiving letters from him steadily—every two weeks."

Ezra pulled out a worn envelope from his coat pocket and showed it to Henri.

"Here's his last letter dated March 10, 1939—nearly seven months ago. I fear he's been arrested or worse—killed."

Henri hadn't heard from his own family in nearly as long. But—unlike Ezra—Henri held onto hope. He had to.

Ezra pulled out a clean handkerchief and blew his nose.

"I'm very sorry," Henri consoled.

Ezra shook Henri's hand; he excused himself to the restroom.

With both the Hershbergs gone, Henri stood alone in the large crowd.

A moment later, Brigitta swept him onto the dance floor. She flashed a confident smile.

Henri quickly gained his footing.

"Having fun?" Brigitta laughed.

"Of course," replied Henri.

"Wallflower!" Brigitta teased. "I saw you standing there."

"Guilty as charged," he countered.

The music's tempo quickened. Henri kept up, impressing even himself. It'd been a long time since he'd danced. But just as he was getting the hang of it, the melody abruptly ended.

"Ladies and gentlemen," bellowed the stoic announcer. "Sir Kadoorie has an announcement."

Guests, including Henri and Brigitta, cleared the floor. The elder statesman took center stage.

"What's going on?" Brigitta whispered and huddled closer.

"I'm not sure," Henri replied, not wanting her to sense his own concern.

The muffled chatter died down. Elly Kadoorie cleared his throat.

"Thank you all for coming tonight," he said with a steady tenor voice. "I was hoping to bring a bit of temporary merriment during these trying times, but I've just been informed of news that unfortunately affects us all."

Henri felt the muscles of his chest tighten.

"Hitler, you may have heard, invaded Poland several days ago," Kadoorie began. "Now, we've learned that because of these actions, England and France have declared war."

Gasps and a few cries echoed through the large hall. Brigitta grabbed Henri and buried her head into his chest.

"Hold me."

Henri felt his arms wrap themselves around her. She rested her head against his chest. He felt uncomfortable. Still, he didn't want to be the cause of a scene by refusing to acquiesce. Instead, he stood motionless.

The crowd's nervous chatter continued to build. Many people's thoughts returned to their European roots. Some wept. Others decried Hitler's name. Henri worried what this meant for his father, brother, and especially his uncle. Viktor knew a lot of people, and Georg was resourceful. Henri prayed they'd find safety.

Brigitta lifted her head. Her intent gaze caught Henri off guard.

"I've been thinking. We don't live in Austria or Germany anymore. We're here in Shanghai."

Henri nodded.

"Now with this dreadful war, we can't really count on returning home... or even having a future. All we have is now."

Henri felt a rising sense of urgency in Brigitta's voice. Her eyes glistened.

"Is everything okay?" Henri asked.

"More than okay," she said dabbing the corner of her eye. "All this thinking has helped me realize," she whispered, "that I just need to listen to my heart."

Before Henri realized what was happening, Brigitta leaned into his ear.

"I'm in love with you, Henri," she whispered.

Henri wondered if it was the champagne they'd been drinking that prompted Brigitta. He fumbled for something to say.

"Brigitta, that's so... so flattering," he heard himself say. "You're beautiful and smart and any man would be lucky to win your heart."

He stepped away.

"But I've explained to you that I'm not interested in a relationship. I don't... I don't have the same feelings for you."

The words had barely escaped Henri's lips before Brigitta burst into tears.

"No—you don't really mean it!"

"Lying about how I truly feel would be worse. I'm sorry."

Brigitta let go. She ran straight to Rosen. Henri couldn't control what would happen next. He only knew that he had to speak his truth. Henri left the party. Outside he breathed in the night air, searching once again for the Shanghai that infused his soul. He recalled his recent conversation with Peilin. She'd revealed—after confiding her fears about Ping's desire to join the army—that she was a widow. Her husband-to-be had been killed in China's battle against Japan. Her revelation answered a lot of questions. Henri had wondered how a young and beautiful woman like Peilin came to live alone in the city.

It also shed light on Peilin's vehement reaction to Ping's announcement. After suffering such a major loss, she couldn't possibly lose her only brother. Perhaps her kindness toward him was only because he was Ping's friend. Was she still in love with her dead husband? Despite these unanswered questions, he wondered if there wasn't some invisible connection between Peilin and himself. In Peilin's presence, he'd felt his body melting, like ice into water. The more they talked, the more Henri felt something he hadn't felt in a long time. He gazed out into the night. What was she doing? Had she thought of him since their last visit?

Peilin hadn't slept in nearly two weeks. Since Ping proclaimed his desire to join the army, he avoided her; slipping in after she'd retire to bed and taking off before she woke. She heard him enter and leave but decided to give him some space. She trusted he'd come to his senses and change his mind. Henri had tried to console her after Ping's abrupt departure that night. Henri, too, was at a loss. Henri promised to talk with Ping the next time he saw him. Perhaps coming from a male friend, Ping would realize that staying with her in Shanghai was best. There was hope.

Peilin thought back to the first time she met Henri. Even though they'd come from two very different worlds, she felt they spoke the same language. He, too, came from a family of doctors. She was surprised by how quickly time had passed since she began to share her herbal knowledge. He was a quick learner. She was saddened to hear of his uncle's unsuccessful quest for Chinese herbs to aid Henri's mother. Great pain had shaded Henri's early life. While she never wished heartache on anyone, it was a feeling she understood well.

When Peilin was about seven, she spotted a baby turtle near the riverbank. She went to pet it; the creature snapped and bit her. It didn't occur to Peilin that such a small wound would cause problems, but when she returned to the house, she noticed that her now aching finger was as large as a radish bulb. She ran to Grandpa Du. He applied a medicinal salve that included raw and steamed ginseng. It cooled the inflamed wound. With his treatment, he offered a lesson: "To feel your own pain gives you the pathway to understand another's. Without this knowledge, your actions remain on the surface. Shallow. Without great pain, there can be no true feeling."

From that time on, Peilin tried to welcome her pain as a lesson in empathy. With the recent loss of her parents, Grandpa Du, and husband Yao, her understanding was especially keen.

Talking with Henri the last three months, Peilin felt even more confident about her fate and her reasons for being sent to Shanghai. Her destiny to protect her younger brother was clear. She was now more determined than ever to stop him from going to war.

Peilin heard the door chimes. She turned to greet the customer. Instead, a familiar-looking servant held the door open. Peilin squinted from the bright afternoon sunlight. Father Kwan entered.

Peilin was shocked. She hadn't thought about the Kwans for some time, even though she was married to their dead son.

"Daughter-in-law," Father Kwan greeted. "I hear business is going well."

At first Peilin didn't know what to say. She feared any news of her prosperity would send Kwan Taitai into a jealous rage. Worse, she didn't want him to take the store away from her. Peilin bowed her head.

"I make enough to earn my keep, Father," Peilin responded.

Somehow he looked different—more tense than she had recalled.

"*Hmm.* I think you're too modest. The Chens across the street have reported a constant flow of customers. Even a *hai-gow* (white man)."

Peilin's eyes darted from the floor to Father Kwan and back to the floor. She understood now why she never quite fully trusted them—the Chens were Father Kwan's spies!

"So you have come to collect my earnings," she surmised. She avoided his comment about Henri.

"No. I have tried to protect you as much as I could," he told her, "but Kwan Taitai insists on an heir to carry on the Kwan name since Yao's death."

As Father Kwan spoke, Peilin's stomach began to churn.

"But how—I mean—"

Her father-in-law raised his hand.

"Not to worry. We have a surrogate. The baby's due this spring—April."

"That's about seven months," Peilin quickly calculated. "What do I need to do?"

"You'll adopt the baby and raise it as your own. When it's time, you'll return to Dragon Lake."

A few days later Henri again dressed in his only suit. It was the start of the High Holy Days. The last place he'd thought he'd find a synagogue would be China—but Sir Jacob Sassoon, a Baghdadi Jew and contemporary of Sir Elly Kadoorie, had established the Ohel Rachel Synagogue. Wearing a borrowed *kippah* (rounded skullcap), Henri entered the plain-looking building. The sparse gathering hall housed neatly lined rows of wooden benches—at least a dozen. Rosh Hashanah, the Jewish New Year, was normally a festive celebration. This year, however, the war took center stage. Many from the small Jewish community were in attendance—even Rosen and Brigitta. It shouldn't have surprised him to see them together, but something was uneasy within him.

"Shalom (peace)," Henri greeted them both.

Brigitta smiled but said nothing. Henri continued ahead and took a seat near the front. He felt their gaze burning into the back of his head. Even though they'd danced together, Henri and Brigitta hadn't addressed the night her sweater was soiled by the Chinese beggar. Henri knew her alliance with Rosen put him in a vulnerable situation; still had she no regard for this country's natives? Henri had never been overly religious. Yet he took the opportunity to pray for life.

Ten days passed. Henri returned to the synagogue for the holiest day of the year, Yom Kippur—the Day of Atonement. Henri joined the rabbi and pounded his fist to his chest. They recited traditional prayers asking for forgiveness and peace. Henri added his own tacit entreaty for an agreeable work environment—navigating successfully between Rosen and Brigitta while he healed patients. The somber day of penance included a twenty-four-hour fast. Luckily for Henri and others at the dorm, their stomachs had shrunk quite a bit since arriving.

Once the fast broke, Henri returned to his regular routine. Henri hadn't seen Ping for some time, so he was especially excited when the limping rickshaw driver appeared one night.

"Ping!" Henri shouted.

He ran down the street to catch up. Ping turned but didn't stop. Ping's eyes were red and he ambled more slowly than usual.

"I've missed you."

"I've been busy," Ping replied.

The two walked in silence.

"Your sister's concerned about you."

Henri let the words linger in the air. Ping exhaled with a sigh.

"I didn't mean to upset her."

Ping continued to look straight ahead. "And I haven't changed my mind."

"I didn't think you would," Henri responded.

Ping turned and studied Henri for a moment.

"Here, I had been avoiding you because I kept thinking you would try to make me stay, for my sister's sake."

They approached the Bund. Henri stared out at the steamship entering the bay—its lights blazed through the darkness.

"I'm sure you're torn," Henri said. He felt more like a big brother than he ever had in the past.

"It's what I'm meant to do."

Henri detected a hint of whiskers growing on his young friend's chin. He recalled his own brink of manhood, when his mother fell ill and passed away. That uncertain and impressionable time had been a turning point in his own life. He and his uncle bonded more closely than Henri ever had to his own father. It was Uncle Viktor who insisted his nephew save himself and escape to Shanghai. Henri missed his conversations with Viktor. He recalled a time when he had asked his bachelor uncle about finding his *beshert*—his true love.

"Ah," he recalled Viktor sighing. "You use the word to mean a wife," he said tousling young Henri's hair.

"Of course," Henri had responded. "Mutti is Papa's *beshert*, she's told me so many times."

Viktor bent down on his knees so that he could face his nephew.

"Well I don't have a wife, but I have a *beshert*."

"How could that be?" Henri wondered at the time.

Viktor smiled. "*Beshert* has another meaning—destiny."

"What's your destiny, Uncle?"

"To help people."

As Henri reminisced, he realized his own fate had introduced him to Peilin. He turned and saw Ping staring at the river water just beyond the Bund.

"Just as my destiny brought me here," Henri responded.

Ping turned.

"Then you understand," the young boy replied solemnly.

Now it was Henri's turn to gaze at the vast body of water.

"I do."

The two stood there in the darkness, each contemplating their fate. Henri's brows furrowed. Even if Peilin was his beshert, would he ever be able to touch her? Hold her? In her culture she was still considered a married woman. Besides, a relationship with those outside your race was considered taboo. He had heard of one couple that had been ostracized by both sides of their families. He sighed. Even if he could be with her, his true love was forever beyond his reach.

Peilin lit the sweet ylang-ylang incense and bowed to her dead husband's tablet. The altar was filled with offerings of oranges and pomelos, peanuts, and a candle—all presented as humble gifts from a dutiful wife. It had been almost a week since Father Kwan's surprise visit. To be married to a ghost husband carried extra responsibility. The dead could see their living spouse's every action; enact their displeasure in ways more powerful than if they had still been alive.

Ever since Father Kwan's appearance, Peilin could not stop thinking that her dead husband was somehow displeased with her. She worried that—as a ghost—her husband could read her thoughts, thoughts that no married woman should entertain.

So it was her punishment, in the form of Kwan Taitai that

intervened. Peilin was to adopt a baby they'd found for her. After all, the second most important duty of a married woman was to bear children, especially sons. But how could she carry out such an obligation when she had never shared a bed with her husband?

Peilin continued to sit in front of the altar. Her thoughts dwelled on Father Kwan's unexpected announcement. Most men had concubines, but Kwan Taitai had forbidden her husband any. Peilin knew that her mother-in-law had felt confident that the family line was assured heirs through their son. Now Peilin realized why the Kwans insisted on going forth with the wedding even though Yao had perished in the war.

Since arriving in Shanghai nine months ago, Peilin had reunited with the only person she really considered family, Ping. While brother and sister were barely speaking, Henri had promised her that he would talk to Ping. She felt better knowing that Henri felt as she did about the war. Peilin hoped Henri's words would put an end to Ping's desire to fight.

Her feelings lingered on the German doctor. Peilin felt strange stirrings in her body—the kind that caused man and woman to come together. She should push such thoughts away. Instead she kneeled before her husband's altar torn between duty and desire. She knew what was expected of her, but inside she yearned for something else. The more Peilin mulled over Henri's deep eyes and the musky scent of his skin, the more she hungered to feel his body next to hers.

14

HENRI ARRANGED to pick Peilin up on a mid-October morning in 1939. Ping was still not talking much to her, but he'd agreed to pass along Henri's message that their doctor friend had been working long hours at the hospital due to an outbreak of malaria. Peilin, too, had been unusually busy with patients. It eased her mind to learn that he wasn't avoiding her.

It was an extra treat that their reunion fell on the Chinese holiday of *Zongyang jie*—the Day of the Double Sun. It wasn't one of the major celebrations, but Peilin was fond of the day that focused on attracting long life and escaping danger.

He greeted her in a white long-sleeved cotton shirt and jacket that accented his broad shoulders. She was dressed in a slender, silky cherry-blossom-colored cheongsam dress that reached down to her toes. She carried a matching parasol to shield her delicate skin from the sun as it gathered strength during the day.

"You could be a model for *Life* magazine," he quipped.

Peilin smiled. "I'm looking forward to our picnic."

When she'd realized they'd be meeting on such an auspicious day, she had suggested a picnic and hike, customs to honor the legendary *Huan Jing* who saved his family from a plague. When she was young, she and Grandpa Du used to enjoy gorging on the juicy dogwood fruit. After their picnic, they'd take red silk cloth, fill it with the plant's leaves, and tie it to their arms as an omen to prevent misfortune.

Henri led the way through the crowd of people gathered on the street. The narrow lane was bursting with yellow, crimson, orange, and deep purple chrysanthemums. Peilin loved the bold pom-pom–like blossoms that adorned many of the storefronts as street vendors hawked a special tea known for its ability to fortify the body's immune system and promote long life. Peilin noticed a white-haired man leaning against a brick wall. His squinting eyes darted from Henri to her and back to Henri again. She ignored the old man's disapproval. She instead ran to catch up to Henri who had rushed ahead.

Zongyang jie was also a time for families to visit the gravesites of their ancestors. Since Yao's grave was up at Dragon Lake, Peilin instead made an offering at her home altar. She felt conflicted about not making the journey back, but she would be returning to the Kwan household soon enough. Father Kwan's surprise visit a few weeks ago still haunted her. She wished it'd been a dream. She couldn't help feeling resentful of Father Kwan's new plans. After all, wasn't it he who sent her to Shanghai? She'd carved out a life for herself here. She wanted to close her eyes and make the whole situation disappear.

All she could do now was enjoy what little time she had left in Shanghai. They arrived at Whangpoo Park just east of Shanghai's bustling metropolis. Many families had already spread out blankets under the willow trees. Henri found a spot near the river. He laid out the frayed coverlet he'd borrowed from the refugee dorms.

Peilin surveyed their surroundings. A young Chinese girl stood with her mouth gaping. Her older brother pointed in their direction. Henri noticed them, too.

"Maybe we should go somewhere else," Peilin said, ever more conscious of the unsettling stir their presence caused.

"Nonsense," Henri replied. "We're just two people here to enjoy the outdoors like everyone else."

Peilin stood on the blanket. A pair of kite-flying kids rushed by and bumped her from behind. Peilin lost her balance and landed in the soggy riverbank below. She fell hard but was more embarrassed than hurt. Henri was immediately at her side; he pulled her up to drier ground.

"Are you okay?"

"I think so. It happened so fast. One minute I was on land; the next minute, I'm soaking wet!"

She tried to laugh off her embarrassment. If he suspected her discomfort, he didn't show it. He took off his jacket and wrapped it around her. His scent embraced her shivering body. Then her eyes met his. Henri gazed at her with such care that it took her breath away. She felt warmed—like a bit of sunshine flickered her way—as if only *she* mattered.

The hospital overflowed with cases of cholera. Henri had increased fluid and electrolyte intake. He wanted to make sure those infected avoided shock complications. A female patient smiled when he stopped by. It reminded Henri of Peilin's surprised look during their picnic a few days ago. He grinned.

"Henri," said a voice, instantly familiar with its guttural ring.

Henri turned. At first it took him a moment to place the stout German with the heavy beard.

"Remember me? We met at the Kadoorie party last month?"

Then he remembered. Henri greeted his compatriot with a hearty handshake.

"Ezra. How good to see you again."

"I'm sorry to bother you here at the hospital."

"Nonsense," Henri replied. "You're always welcome here. Can I help you with something?"

Ezra glanced down both sides of the hallway. A nurse wheeled a patient into the x-ray room.

"Is there somewhere more private that we could talk?" Ezra whispered.

Henri could tell from Ezra's tone that discretion was paramount. "Follow me."

Henri led Ezra down a narrow staircase near the back of the hospital. When they reached the bottom, Henri opened a door to the boiler room. Although the tiny area was humid, it was secluded.

"Now," Henri continued, "how can I help you?"

Ezra cast his eyes downward.

"I'm afraid I've come down with a case of the clap."

"Symptoms?"

"There's stinging when I urinate," Ezra winced. "A painful burning sensation. I can't take much more of this agony."

Henri remained motionless, not wanting to show any sort of reaction. "You must bring your wife in for treatment, too."

Ezra shook his head. "My wife doesn't have it."

Henri understood. "Whoever she is, she needs to be treated."

Erza nodded.

"This probably looks bad," Ezra confessed, "but I do care for Arabelle. It's not what you think."

"You have your reasons," Henri reassured him. "I'll prepare some silver injections."

Ezra shook his head. "I hear there's a new treatment for gonorrhea now—penicillin."

Henri was astonished by Ezra's medical knowledge.

"That's true," Henri nodded, "but antibotics are difficult to obtain—in fact, nearly impossible at the moment."

Ezra's shoulders fell.

"Is there an alternative?"

The silver injections were painful, but Henri sensed that Ezra would be able to handle the sting. It was his mistress that made him so persistent.

"There may be another treatment," Henri said. "Let me see what I can do. Come back tomorrow at this time."

"*Danke.*"

Ezra stepped out of the boiler room and disappeared up the staircase without another word. Henri waited until Ezra was gone before emerging.

Like her rooster birth sign, Peilin rose with the sun. She looked forward to mornings and her meditative tai chi exercises. Others gathered in parks to practice the slow, invigorating movements. Peilin preferred to perform the ancient art alone. Standing in the middle of her second-floor bedroom, Peilin's arms floated up with a gentle roll. Her body undulated, ascending and descending with the flow. Peaceful energy circulated through her body.

She had just completed the eight essential poses when she heard a knock coming from the front door below. Peilin ran downstairs; she opened the door. It was Henri. His cheeks were flushed.

"I need your help," he rushed to tell her. "I've a patient suffering from a venereal disease—gonorrhea."

Peilin shook her head—he'd said the last few words in German.

"Symptoms like a burning sensation when urinating—"

Henri fumbled for the right expression—pantomiming pain in the groin area so that she might understand. Finally Peilin grasped his meaning.

"Don't worry," Peilin assured him. "The red lantern ladies consult me all the time for this sort of thing."

Peilin smiled to herself, realizing that Henri must be embarrassed. He'd become so good at speaking the language that she often forgot he was a foreigner. Peilin wasted no time getting to work.

"I'm making what's called the Lotus Seed Formula."

She opened the first drawer and pulled out a handful of round, off-white seeds. She sprinkled a few into Henri's cupped hand. He rolled them around in his palm.

"Is this the lotus seed?"

Peilin nodded.

"It tonifies the spleen and arrests seminal emissions. It's bitter in taste, but we'll add other herbs to mollify this." From another drawer, Peilin pulled out light brown discs. She handed them to him.

"*Fu ling* (poria)," she told him. "It's a fungus that grows on pine trees. It tonifies the spleen."

"They're spongy," he acknowledged.

Henri's intrigue spurred her on. She presented him with another herb. He pressed his finger into the pliable dried plant.

"Taste it," she urged.

Henri placed it in his mouth.

"It's sweet."

Peilin agreed. "It's also a mild sedative."

"The other main ingredients are astragalus root and *ren shen*—you remember the man root?"

Henri smiled.

"Ginseng."

He picked up the gnarled pieces.

"Ginseng balances the excess heat and stimulates the immune system," she explained. "It also benefits the heart. Now smell this one."

She gave him thin tan slices of bark—astragalus.

"It's also sweet," he said.

She smiled.

"It protects the liver."

Peilin measured each of the herbs with her measuring stick and poured the contents into several packets. She handed the bundles to him.

"Make sure they boil down the herbs twice," she instructed.

"*Xie Xie*," Henri thanked her.

She felt a pang of sadness knowing that he was about to leave.

"Will you be seeing these patients soon?" Peilin asked.

He shook his head.

"Not until tomorrow morning."

Then, he surprised her.

"Can you get away for a while? There's someplace I'd like to show you."

Peilin sensed his eagerness. Lately she'd felt confined to the store. An outing appealed to her.

"I'd like that," she said, flashing him a smile.

Henri stood outside. Peilin locked up her store. Across the way, he noticed an older man staring. The man must have said something to his wife, because she, too, fixed her eyes on Henri. He ignored their glowering. He wasn't going to let some strangers' curiosity ruin his afternoon with Peilin.

The Western-styled buildings along the Bund reminded Henri of his long journey. It excited him to share a bit of European charm with Peilin. Henri's immediate reaction was to quicken his pace, but when he realized that Peilin was nearly running to match his stride, he slowed down. He caught sight of a young Caucasian couple enjoying the river's view. The young woman took a bite of her sandwich; she then offered it to her partner. He took a bite. Henri felt himself drawn into the connection shared between the couple. It was hard for Henri to admit that after all the hurt he'd endured, he longed for such a bond. Brigitta was not the answer—there was something about her that made Henri bristle. And although he enjoyed Peilin's company, he had to remind himself that not only was she Chinese, she was a married woman.

They continued east to Avenue Joffre. The sycamore tree–lined street amazed Peilin. She'd heard that the shopping district here was the most expensive in Shanghai.

"Even back home the French were known for their upscale tastes," explained Henri.

The long avenue stretched in an east–west direction. To one side, she recognized the Jin Jian Hotel with its distinctive Shanghai Deco architecture. Gazing in the other direction, she witnessed the tall, tapered pillars of the Russian Orthodox Church.

They rounded the corner to Bubbling Well Road. Henri covered her eyes. He guided her a few paces forward and then let her go.

She'd never seen anything like it before. The wide residential lane featured large, expensive houses. One in particular—with its many windows, tall white columns, and spacious gardens reminded her of an emperor's palace.

"Does someone live here?" she wondered aloud.

Henri smiled.

"The Kadoories—a wealthy family that emigrated from India a long time ago. They own rubber plantations, electrical plants, and real estate. Many of the buildings along the Bund belong to them."

Peilin continued to stare at the house. She estimated that the dwelling itself covered more land than a dozen farms from her village back home.

"They're Jewish," Henri explained. "They're generous donors to the hospital and refugee dorms. It's a *mitzvah* for them."

"*Mitzvah?*"

"It's a good deed," he told her.

"Like the Chinese proverb," Peilin recognized. "'A person's future will change when he does good for others.' Obviously this family's helped many."

Henri nodded. "Inside, there's white marble everywhere. We partied in the ballroom that nearly took up the entire upper floor.

Huge crystal chandeliers hang overhead and the ceilings are as tall as the sky. Music filled the air."

Peilin took several steps closer to the tall, wrought-iron fence. She closed her eyes and imagined what it might look like inside.

"So much luck," Peilin acknowledged.

She gazed through the railing long enough to spot a bald Chinese servant running toward them. Smiling, he waved at them rather frantically.

"Dr. Neumann? Is that you?" he hollered.

"We didn't mean to disturb the household. I only wanted to show her the house," Henri shouted back, pointing to Peilin.

Peilin couldn't help but notice how the rotund man's bald head glistened under the afternoon sun.

"Not at all, Dr. Neumann," the servant said, catching his breath. His cherubic face flashed another friendly grin. "The Kadoories are away on a short holiday. I'd be happy to show you and your lady friend inside."

Peilin looked to Henri. He responded without hesitation.

"We'd love that."

The amiable man unlocked the gate. "Good afternoon, miss. Please come in."

He led them up the long path toward the front of the house. Up close, the tall white columns flanked with moss created an even more romantic setting. Gold leafed lionheads crowned the entrance. Inside the black-and-white-checkerboard tile further intrigued her. She turned back to make sure Henri was not far behind. He nodded and urged her forward. Upstairs she entered into what she understood must be the ballroom. Inside it was larger and more opulent than she had envisioned. The ceiling stood at least three stories high. French glass doors framed with elevated archways surrounded the entire room. More windows appeared above. Sheer white curtains added an ethereal mood.

Peilin wandered toward the middle of the room. Overhead the entire ceiling was hand-painted—just as Henri had described. Magnificent crystal chandeliers glistened from above. Henri finished conferring with the servant and joined her. She sensed his delight in her awe. Music began to play over loudspeakers and infused the room with a sultry melody.

"It's Louis Armstrong's 'I'm in the Mood for Love,'" Henri commented. "This is one of my favorite jazz pieces. Would you like to dance?" Henri asked her.

"I'm afraid I don't know how," she said, turning her head slightly with embarrassment.

Henri reached for her and gently pulled her back toward him. They were now face-to-face. He smiled and held out his right palm.

"Just follow my lead."

She put her hand in his. With Henri's gentle guiding, Peilin felt herself gliding across the floor, nearly swimming across the room like a water lily swept up in the current's flow. Peilin looked up and Henri gazed back at her.

"What do you think?" he whispered.

Peilin gazed into his eyes. "It's like I'm floating."

They sashayed across the dance floor. His eyes seemed to wander off to a time and place of long ago.

Moving instinctively to Henri's gentle touch, she let the music infuse her body. Peilin had never felt so in sync to another human as in this very moment.

It was nearly dark by the time they left the Marble Palace. Neither one said a word as they made their way back through the streets of Shanghai. Peilin could hear the smooth jazz playing in her head; still feel herself gliding across the floor in Henri's arms. She walked beside him, wondering if the invisible red string of fate had brought them together.

They reached the herbal shop door. She slipped the key into the lock, Henri close behind her. His hot breath warmed her neck. She turned; her lips quivered. She wanted it, too. She closed her eyes. Just as she was about to give in she pondered—*what if the meddling Chens were spying?* She lurched back. Henri's eyes flew open. He reached for her, but she pulled away.

"Is everything okay?" he asked.

Peilin unlocked the door.

"The neighbors," she whispered, "they may be watching."

"You think so?"

"I know so," she sighed. "They've made comments."

"It was a lovely day." Her hand lingering on the doorknob. "Good night."

Henri looked at her pleadingly, but said nothing.

"Good night," he finally echoed. He continued to stand at her front entry. Against her private yearnings, Peilin slowly closed the door.

She purposely kept the lights off. Peering out the front window corner, she could see Henri still standing there. He reminded her of a train that had come to a sudden halt. His eyes drifted ahead, still searching for its destination. After a few moments, he left.

Inside, she'd hoped to find Ping waiting for her or, at the very least, fast asleep after a long day's work. But the store was empty. Her shoulders fell as she realized he had not been home at all. They'd barely spoken to one another these last couple of months, and now she didn't even know where he was. Henri had spoken to him on her behalf, but this seemed only to create more distance between brother and sister. Lately, when their paths had crossed, Peilin's comments and questions went unanswered. The silence was growing unbearable.

Peilin headed upstairs. She had to admit that she, too, was stubborn. After all, beyond the fact that the war killed her husband, her mother, father, and Grandpa Du, it disrupted the balance of life. With chaos came destruction. It had altered her destiny. She didn't want it to change Ping's fate any more than it already had.

Henri didn't utter a sound. Peilin shut the door, closing him out. He'd hoped she might invite him in, but once he realized she was being cautious of her neighbors' scrutinizing eyes, he felt stung by the awkward end to the evening. Recognizing that he must look foolish standing alone at her front door, Henri took off for his dorm.

He'd walked nearly twenty minutes when he remembered Ezra's herbs—they were still with Peilin. With no time to waste, he rushed back, retracing his steps with double the speed he'd just traveled only moments earlier.

Henri wasn't sure what to do once he reached the store, knowing that he could hardly knock on the door again given Peilin's concern over the prying neighbors. He decided to slip around back with the hope he'd get her attention another way.

He tiptoed through the narrow side alley. Henri was careful not to make noise and call attention to himself. He emerged out back. It was hard to manage anything in the dark, so he took a few steps back for a broader outlook of the landscape. A light from an upper window prompted Henri to look up. Through the tiny glass panes, Henri spotted Peilin. But he was too low for her to see him. Eager to catch her eye, he scrambled for something to stand on. It took him a few moments to find an empty trash can. He placed it as close to the house as possible and hoisted himself up. He was at the level of her feet, but he had a clear view of her apartment. Her back turned toward him—bathing. She sat on the edge of the wooden tub—nude.

He felt shocked and embarrassed—he was now the spy. This was her private moment; yet he couldn't pull himself away. His gaze lingered over her beauty. She lifted a sponge and squeezed the water around her bare shoulders. Then, she rotated, bestowing him a full frontal view of her nakedness. The long curves of her torso and the full roundness of her chest mesmerized him. Henri was captivated by the splendor of her body. He'd never quite seen a physique like hers, so graceful and sensuous. Her porcelain skin reminded him of freshly fallen snow, delicate and soft. She dipped the sponge into the basin of water again and let it trickle over her arms and across her breasts.

Henri perceived her nipples constrict, the tips darkening as the water's cooling took effect. Again, she submerged the sponge into the tub. This time she dribbled its wetness across the curves of her waist. Her naked belly rose and fell as water cascaded down her body.

A sudden noise echoed from the front of the store. He ducked, terrified of what her reaction might be if she were to catch him staring at her. He was also aware that he was compromising her safety. He hopped off the metal can and slipped through the alley and back to the main road. He wouldn't take back that moment for anything, but he wasn't sure how to feel about witnessing Peilin's exquisite beauty. He did long for her now—more than he ever had. He plunged into the night's dark shadows, resolved to return first thing in the morning.

Peilin reached for her towel on the chair and dried herself. She gazed out the window into the dark night. She'd seen Henri rustling around in the back looking for a way to get her attention, but she'd decided to let it play out and see what he was up to rather than opening a window and arousing more suspicion. She'd felt his eyes on her back. She'd consciously continued bathing, partly out of routine and partly because she wanted Henri to see her. She'd never appeared before a man unclothed; she wanted to experience what it would feel like to be seen for the woman that she was. She was surprised at her own actions, but the more she soaked in his gaze, the closer she felt to him. Her time in Shanghai was coming to an end soon. In a few months, this instance would be no more than a sweet memory.

15

HENRI JUMPED to an early 8:00 AM start the next morning, knowing that Ezra would be by the hospital soon. He'd forgotten Ezra's herbs after walking Peilin back from the Marble Palace the night before. When he tried to retrieve them, he found himself instead viewing Peilin as she bathed. A lifelong student of the human body, Henri marveled at her beauty. Numbed feelings he thought had long died reawakened. The unusual stirring both excited and scared him. His body shuddered; he felt himself wanting.

He inhaled the cool air in an effort to compose himself. Henri expected to find Peilin alone, perhaps just waking. But when he arrived the door was open. He stepped inside; Peilin was already conversing with a couple.

The visiting woman turned in his direction and Henri recognized her beady eyes. They were the neighbors from across the street—the scrutinizing eyes that Peilin was concerned about. If this couple was that vigilant, Henri feared that they saw him peering into Peilin's window as well. The trio's conversation came to an abrupt halt and turned in his direction. It was too late to turn back now.

"*Ni hao,*" Peilin greeted him.

She was more formal than usual, which confirmed Henri's suspicions.

"I forgot my herbs yesterday," he said, catching his breath. He, too, maintained an air of decorum. Peilin nodded toward the string-wrapped paper packets still sitting behind the counter.

Without a word, she retrieved the herbs and handed them to him. Henri perceived a growing awkwardness in Peilin's manners. He then wondered if she was upset about last night. Had she seen him peering into the window while she bathed? His heart raced; mortifying embarrassment came over him.

"*Xie Xie,*" he thanked her.

He then made a hasty exit.

It wasn't until he arrived back at the hospital that Henri felt a sense of relief. Indoors among the familiar rows of cots, white netting, and IV poles, Henri busied himself. There'd been another outbreak of dysentery. With limited supplies and medication, Henri did the best he could. He'd been encouraged by Kaethe's recovery, but Henri hadn't tried herbal remedies on any other patients. It was only Ezra's request for an alternative that had prompted Henri to seek out another Eastern remedy from Peilin.

Ezra arrived later that morning. Dressed in a dapper navy coat, he held a steady arm around a young Russian woman. Her dark brown hair cascaded around her face. She wore a saffron-hued scarf. Henri made note of her strong bone structure. Despite any negative connotations their relationship would receive under the public microscope, Henri recognized that Ezra cared deeply for this woman.

Henri had heard from people at the hospital that Ezra had married very young. His wife Arabelle was the daughter of his father's business partner. Although it was in no way an arranged marriage, Henri was sure there were unspoken pressures. They were an affable couple, probably with similar social upbringings. Ezra and Arabelle fit into the community well. Arabelle had a strong network of friends.

But seeing Ezra with this other woman now, Henri sensed another side of Ezra—an independent Ezra who was with this woman because he alone wanted her—despite what others might think. She wasn't pretty by society standards; her uneven teeth revealed a different class of people. Still there was something real and earthy, a genuine warmth about her.

"This is Rita," Ezra introduced her.

"Nice to meet you," Henri said in an effort to help her feel more comfortable.

They shook hands. Henri noticed Rita's clammy palm—she was clearly nervous. Not wanting hospital staff to see him with the herbs, Henri pointed toward a side door.

"Why don't we step outside for a moment? I could use the fresh air."

"Certainly," Ezra replied.

Although it was a short distance, Henri sensed Ezra's careful concentration; he guided the weakened woman and assured her of his rock-strong presence.

"Don't worry; I've got you."

Once outside, Henri found a bench for Rita to rest. He then handed the herbal packets to his friend. Ezra discreetly tucked the packages in his coat pocket.

"Empty the contents into a pot. Fill it with enough water to cover the formula and boil for thirty minutes."

Henri perceived Erza's focus.

"Then, drain off the tea, leaving the herbs in the pot. Refill the pot with water and repeat a second time. Each of you drink one cup three times a day."

"And this will cure us both?" Ezra asked.

Henri nodded.

"They're powerful herbs."

Ezra grabbed Henri's hand in his and shook it. Henri felt his friend's earnest appreciation.

"I can't thank you enough."

Erza helped Rita to her feet. She wrapped the scarf around her neck and took his arm. Ezra hailed a taxi.

"Come back and let me know how you're doing," Henri called out.

He watched the couple huddle together in the back seat and felt a tinge of envy.

Peilin was not expecting the Chens this morning; their pretentious friendliness irritated her all the more. She couldn't believe it when they presented breakfast dumplings to feign their delight about the upcoming Kwan baby. She wondered if they were that oblivious to time or if they were playing some sort of game.

"As soon as we heard, we clapped with excitement for you," Chen Jing-Li told Peilin. "What good fortune for you and the Kwans, a baby to be born in spring!"

Peilin wanted to ignore their fake sincerity and order them out the door. But she'd come to suspect that Father Kwan paid them money to keep an eye on her, so she fell into the role of dutiful daughter.

"*Hao*," exclaimed Peilin. She knew she had to play with equal pretense if she wanted to protect herself from their intrusive prying. "It is most fortunate."

"You'll be leaving to return to Dragon Lake then," the husband said, as if searching for confirmation.

Peilin didn't respond. They already knew Father Kwan's plans for her.

"What'll happen to the store?" Jing-Li asked.

"I don't know," Peilin responded. "You need to ask Father Kwan."

It was at that moment that Henri entered. Peilin was just as shocked as the Chens by his presence. When he mentioned the herbs, she realized he'd forgotten to take them the night before. Peilin was glad that Henri didn't linger. Did he realize that the Chens were her neighbors or was he upset with how the night ended? Peilin also worried that the Chens would say something about the baby in front of Henri. Luckily they did not. But as soon as Henri left, the Chens resumed their questioning.

"Who was that?" Zhao asked, interrupting Peilin's thoughts.

"A friend of my brother's," Peilin offered.

"He speaks Chinese?"

Peilin witnessed Jing-Li's crinkling nose.

"My brother taught him."

"Ping's friend seems to spend an awful lot of time with *you*," Jing-Li continued, emphasizing the last word.

"He's a doctor," Peilin explained. "He consults me on cases at his hospital."

Peilin noticed the Chens share a conspiratorial glance between them.

"But isn't he a *Western* doctor?" Zhao probed.

She felt them circling in.

"What could a *Western* physician possibly want with Chinese herbs?" asked the wife. She then turned to her husband. "Unless that's not the real reason."

Peilin's eyes darted from Zhao to Jing-Li. She hated the game they were playing but Peilin was determined not to let them get the best of her.

"Let me assure you, nothing is going on between us," Peilin countered. "I'd never dishonor my husband or his family."

"We're sure that you wouldn't intentionally disgrace the Kwans. They're a powerful family—practically a dynasty."

The words lingered in the air.

203

He headed back to the dorms. It was well past midnight when Henri was finally able to leave the hospital. It'd been a long day, starting with his morning dash to Peilin's herbal shop. Because he was so tired, it took him more than a few moments to realize that someone had emerged beside him.

The limping figure fell into step with Henri. The two walked in silence. It'd been several weeks since Henri had seen Ping. The boy's body looked thinner.

"Good to see you," Henri said.

"I've not been myself lately," Ping confessed.

Henri sensed some guilt in the tone of the teen's voice. It was obvious that Ping was worried about hurting his sister by joining the army. Yet the memory of his mother's death at the hands of Japanese soldiers still deeply affected him.

Henri knew Ping to be a physical person. He worked things out through sweat—mostly while peddling the cumbersome rickshaw. But this time bodily exhaustion failed to dissipate Ping's problems. The inner calm Ping sought was more complicated now. The simple answers that probably sufficed in the past were no longer effective. The not-quite-boy, not-quite-man inwardly battled the chaos without success.

Henri fumbled for something to say.

"I've missed you."

Ping stared at Henri as if he wanted to say something, but instead grew agitated—like an injured animal ready to cry out.

"What is it?" Henri asked. "You can tell me."

"I ne—ed," Ping stuttered. His eyes opened wide.

Had Ping had gotten into some sort of trouble since they last spoke? If he had, Henri worried that the young boy feared reproach.

"It's okay, whatever it is."

Ping seemed at last ready to talk.

"I need you to sign paper," Ping confessed.

He pulled out the crumpled page. Henri seized it. It was written in Chinese. Henri shook his head.

"I don't understand," Henri told him. "What is this?"

Ping took the paper back.

"It's a medical release."

"To join the army?" Henri blurted.

Ping nodded.

Now Henri felt conflicted. He knew that no other doctor was likely to sign off, given Ping's deformity. And how could he betray Peilin by agreeing to support Ping in this endeavor? Ping needed to avenge his mother's brutal death. He needed to defend his family's honor. War was savage and barbarous. But it gave Ping a way to express his life's purpose, the destiny he was now fated to fulfill.

There was no escaping it. He pulled out his pen and signed. Fighting back tears, he handed it back to his young friend.

"*Überlebe,*" Henri whispered. "May you survive."

"*Xie Xie,*" Ping murmured back. "Please tell my sister that I do this for the love of our family."

"Aren't you going to say goodbye to her yourself?"

Ping shook his head. "Too painful."

Henri quavered. Then he recalled his own anguish the night he parted from his uncle. He placed his hand on the teen's shoulder.

"I understand."

Ping disappeared into the black night. Henri had made a choice. At the moment, he had no idea how he would explain this to Peilin. He would deal with that later.

After a busy morning of patients, Peilin carried the pot of boiling water from the stove and made her favorite *hong zao* herb tea. Her chest felt heavy and the red date soothed her heart. She'd been in Shanghai ten months now. Since it was fall, she added *pei lan,* the orchid smelling plant that she'd been named after. Grandpa Du had suggested her name. The dried leaves were known for inhibiting influenza. More important, the herb—also known as boneset—demonstrated devotion.

The tale told of two women, sisters-in-law. When Pei Lan fell ill from sunstroke, her sister-in-law Huo Xiang journeyed to the mountains in search of a cure. The next morning Hou Xiang returned, bitten by a poisonous snake. Pei Lan sucked the poison from the wound. But both women's efforts to save each other's lives ended in their deaths. A neighbor discovered their bodies. Nearby were two mountain herbs that were never prepared for Pei Lan. As legend has it, the village named the herbs after the women—Pei Lan and Hou Xiang.

Peilin remembered how she asked Grandpa Du to tell her the story over and over again. Each time, young Peilin marveled over the faithfulness the two women shared.

Because Peilin had been named in the spirit of loyalty, her devotion to her family flowed without a doubt. She'd never considered that life could be otherwise. But since arriving in Shanghai, Peilin felt her dedication wavering from the Kwans. She'd followed through with the wedding and joined her husband's family. She dutifully suffered through her mother-in-law's unreasonable tirades, even when Peilin suspected Kwan Taitai feigned illnesses just to test her daughter-in-law's devotion. When Father Kwan finally sent Peilin to Shanghai to run the family store left by a late uncle, Peilin felt she had been spared from an abusive situation.

Shanghai was a turning point. For the first time in her life, Peilin was on her own. Her journey led her to Ping. But it was the unforeseen friendship with Henri that had helped her grow the most. At first she was intrigued with his interest in Chinese medicine. A Western doctor, Henri opened her eyes, too. Peilin took delight in his use of the herbs and the positive results he'd received so far.

Their mutual interest grew. Peilin found that she couldn't stop thinking about spending more time with him. It was as if they connected on a deeper level, beyond their work. She was often surprised to find her body wanting him, responding to him. A part of her knew she should feel ashamed for such thoughts, yet the stirring desire continued to beckon her.

Peilin shook herself from her reverie. She cleared away her teacup. The reality was, she couldn't be with Henri. And the Kwans were calling her back to Dragon Lake. She'd have a baby to raise soon.

Peilin sighed. Her duty remained with her ghost husband and in-laws.

Over the next week, Henri immersed himself in work. Brigitta had stopped talking to him, at least on a personal level. Of course, there were work conversations, which could be awkward, but it was a relief to not have to deal with her drama.

Henri felt a lingering guilt—not only about signing Ping's papers, but also about the discomfort on the night he'd gazed at Peilin through her window. At the time, he couldn't take his eyes away. Her beauty took his breath away. But in hindsight, he should've turned away.

Both of these actions took risk and courage—and both caused him angst. How could this be? Perhaps these opposing forces were interconnected—like the *yin-yang* symbol. According to Peilin, the circle of black and white formed an emblem of complementary opposites. Yet they supported one another—they formed a greater whole.

"There can't be light without dark," she once told him. "There can't be happiness without sadness. There can't be love without hate."

Her voice echoed in his head. The Chinese belief of balance permeated not only their medicine but their life choices.

When he thought about sister and brother, it was as if they, too, were complementary opposites. While both held steadfast to family loyalty, they carried out their devotions in different ways. Ping's was a grittier allegiance—like a lion defending his family without hesitation or fear, even if it cost him his life. It was a natural gender role.

On the other hand, Peilin would rather hold on, build some sort of shield. Both grew up on a farm, yet her way of dealing with the world was more cultured. Some people find refuge in the harsh side of life while others, given the chance, turn into pearls. Perhaps she'd been groomed this way in preparation for her marriage. She'd hardly lived a life of fortune, yet she seemed to move through the world with an uncanny grace, resilient despite the struggles life presented.

So it is no wonder that he could not take his gaze off her that night. It was natural for such a rare beauty to be admired. Peilin gleamed with a luster he had never seen before. It was as if Shanghai was her oyster and Peilin the pearl—growing ever more brilliant in its surroundings.

Past midnight, Henri made his last rounds through the hospital. He was about to sign out from his night shift when Ezra appeared. It'd been a week. Ezra's skin had returned to a more youthful appearance since starting the herbal remedy.

"How're you feeling?"

"Much better, thanks to you," Ezra nodded.

Henri could see that something still weighed on Ezra.

"What is it?" Henri asked.

Ezra removed his hat.

"It's Rita. I gave her the herbal tea and she drank it—just as I did."

Henri studied Ezra who choked back tears.

"But I'm afraid she's not recovering. In fact, Rita's getting worse."

Henri cupped Ezra's shoulders. He felt his friend's genuine concern and anguish.

"Where is she?"

"Outside in a taxi. She was too weak to come inside."

Henri followed his friend to the alley. Ezra opened the rear door. There, flushed with fever, Rita rested her head against the window.

Henri took his fingers and lightly pushed them into her wrist. Recalling Peilin's instructions, he distinguished her pulse as rapid and wiry.

"Can you open your mouth?" he continued.

She complied. Henri discerned a greasy, yellow coating covering her red tongue. He felt her forehead—she burned with fever.

"What do you think?" asked Ezra.

Henri gently pressed on Rita's abdomen. She winced.

Although he was troubled by Rita's worsening condition, this was just the excuse he'd been waiting for. He now had good reason to visit Peilin again.

"It's serious but don't worry. I'll find another cure."

16

PEILIN TOOK ONE MORE look at Ping's empty bed before retiring to her own. It'd been a week now. Still no Ping. It was late October and since their reunion nearly five months ago, he'd never stayed away for so long.

She worried that he'd retreated to his old shantytown. Peilin retraced her steps and returned to the *hu tong*. But he was not there; those she questioned said they hadn't seen him. *Did Ping have a secret he wasn't sharing? Maybe he'd met a woman or taken up gambling or opium.* Before their confrontation, Peilin hadn't considered such clandestine behavior. But lately even she'd been keeping information about herself from the two people closest to her—Ping and Henri. It was more out of her own fear, yet she was just as guilty.

This reminded her of Henri. She was concerned that she hadn't seen or heard from him the last week either. Her visits with him were regulated by his schedule and desire to see her, and not the other way around. Yet it would be unthinkable for her to seek him out at the hospital, a situation that struck her as unfair in this moment, as she was feeling quite lonely and increasingly worried about Ping's whereabouts.

She suspected the reason for Henri's absence—he knew she was aware of him watching through the window that night and she'd gone on anyway. Maybe he found her actions unbecoming. What must he think of her now?

Before, Peilin fretted that if she told him about the baby and her impending return to Dragon Lake, things would change between them. He could withdraw, seek out another herbalist, or worse, go away all together. With five months left in Shanghai, Peilin didn't want anything to change between them. When the time came, she could leave Shanghai knowing she had experienced all that she could before relinquishing herself to her fate on Dragon Lake. Now she worried that her spontaneous decision to continue bathing that night had ruined it all.

Feeling lost about the situation, she pulled out a piece of paper. Jotting down a few of the characters she knew helped her clear her mind, or at least helped to soothe her thoughts. She found her brush still neatly tucked in the tiny desk drawer. After grinding the ink stick into the stone, she began to write. Her first brushstrokes intuitively formed the symbol for "happiness." The character reminded Peilin of a drummer happily dancing through the streets. She dipped her brush in the ink again and drew the character again—"Double Happiness." It was the symbol used at marriages. The union of two loving people doubled one's joy. Peilin felt happy whenever she was with Henri. But they were not married.

Peilin absently scribbled the two characters across the page. She pondered over her inability to tell Henri about her return to Dragon Lake. For Peilin, their mutual love for herbal remedies had provided them a way to get to know and experience each other. Peilin often thought of their outings and the conversations they'd shared. Yet she was bound to the Kwans. She could've ended up like her brother—poor, homeless, and alone. Marrying Yao had given Peilin a place to live, food to eat, and a place at the family altar upon her passing. Peilin had known other girls in her village were envious of Peilin's good fortunes and betrothal into such a prominent and wealthy family. She knew that should be enough—she'd been awarded a better life than the one her parents had lived. But what confused Peilin was the undercurrent that stirred within her whenever she was with Henri. When she was with him, she sensed herself as well.

Her apprehension about the recent weeks made her fear the worst—that she'd never see him again. Perhaps her in-laws' summons back to Dragon Lake to raise an adopted child was best after all.

Still, even if she wanted to, she didn't know how to tell Henri about her situation. She wasn't sure he'd understand. Europeans didn't have arranged marriages. Or marry ghosts. How could he comprehend the Eastern intricacies of cause and effect—especially pleasing gods and ghosts of the afterworld? Or—suffer their repercussions of famine, poverty, and even death? Peilin knew that in the Jewish tradition people prayed to one God, that humans were responsible for themselves and their own actions. They remembered the dead but didn't burn paper money to assure their ancestors' comfort in the afterlife.

Peilin had stopped scribbling. She folded up the paper and cleaned up the ink. If she did see Henri again, she didn't have to tell him about her future right away. There was time.

Henri jogged the now familiar route to Peilin's herbal store. He worried about Rita and her deteriorating situation. Luckily, he had the day off. He'd yearned to see Peilin sooner, but his decision to sign Ping's medical paper still weighed on his mind. He neared the herbal store, realizing he'd no words to explain his long absence.

It was about nine o'clock in the morning when he turned the doorknob and found it unlocked. The bell tinkled overhead, and his eyes adjusted to the interior. Then he realized that Peilin was observing him. At first Henri thought he saw consternation in her face. He wondered if she knew what he'd done.

"*Ni hao*," was all Henri could muster.

At first Peilin said nothing. He worried that she was upset. Her pleading eyes revealed that his absence had caused her some anxiety.

"I'm sorry I haven't come by sooner. I've been busy at work," he heard himself replying.

Another beat. Henri's heart began to pound. Then, finally she spoke.

"I've been hoping you'd come by again," she replied. "Has something been bothering you?"

Henri wasn't quite sure how to answer. The silence grew once more.

"My time has also been occupied," she at last continued. "There's been a lot on my mind lately."

Henri was relieved that she didn't require any further explanation from him. Then he caught her staring out the window.

"Ping hasn't been home for a week now."

She avoided looking at him. Standing, Peilin returned to her task of refilling the herbal drawers.

Henri flinched; his guilt rose.

"He's young," Henri blurted. "Perhaps he's with friends?" He didn't understand his need to protect himself from Peilin's reaction, but the notion that she might never speak to him again pressed him to weave a deeper web of lies.

Peilin shook her head. "I've looked everywhere for him."

She cupped her hand over her mouth. Henri saw that she was holding back tears. She needed answers, to know what had happened. He wavered on the verge of divulging his misdeed. But he couldn't bring himself to tell her the truth.

"I'm sure he's all right," Henri assured her. "He'll return. You'll see."

Peilin nodded.

"I suppose. There are many things that attract a young boy in a big city."

Henri wanted to take her into his arms. He feared that any display of physical affection might make her uncomfortable, cause her to push him away. That was the last thing he wanted. Then he remembered the herbs.

"The clap remedy—" he said.

"How are they?" she interrupted.

It was obvious she was eager to change the subject, too. And, as before, Henri recognized her prompt concern for others, even in the face of her own worries.

"Ezra—he's better," Henri explained. "But the woman—I'm afraid her symptoms have worsened."

"What signs does she have now?"

"I checked her pulse—rapid and wiry," Henri replied. "Her tongue's bright red with a greasy yellow coating. She's burning with fever."

Peilin paced the room, her clutched hand to her lips.

"Too much yang energy."

Peilin persisted in hushed contemplation. Her caring concern for others attracted him to her even more, but he, too, was growing nervous.

"Is there something else we can try?" he said, interrupting her silence.

Henri expected her to design a new medicinal mixture. Instead, she grabbed her coat.

"We need something stronger than what I have," she explained. "Master Hwang—the doctor that tutored my grandfather—he'll know what to do."

"Is he here in Shanghai?" Henri asked.

Peilin shook her head. "He lives near my village. If I hurry and leave now I can catch the ten o'clock train and arrive in Tongsan by two this afternoon. I'll return on the four o'clock and be back here before the day's over."

"But you'll have to close your store. I don't want you to do that," Henri insisted.

"But she needs help."

Peilin couldn't be dissuaded. Once she made up her mind, there was no arguing.

Henri had to think quickly. Peilin locked up the store. He worried about her safety; his instincts compelled him to protect her. He did have the day off. Henri pulled his coat on.

"Wait. I'm going with you."

Peilin was silently thankful that Henri insisted on accompanying her. It was only the second time in her life that she'd traveled on the train. She ignored the stares of others; she noticed Henri did, too.

The locomotive roared toward Tongsan. Memories of a much different lifestyle flooded Peilin's thoughts. Most existed off the land—a life of unwavering physical labor. Some men married and then often moved to the city to earn income. These husbands sent money to their families; they returned only for holidays. No matter how long or how far the men traveled, they still belonged to the village. But when a woman married and left the village, she no longer belonged; she became part of her husband's community. Even when she died, her ancestral tablet remained. Knowing this, Peilin recognized her freedom to return today was all the more special.

When she glanced at Henri, he, too, seemed to be lost in thought. The train wound its way across the countryside. Peilin recognized the familiar sugarcane, sorghum, and terraced rice fields along the hillsides. Women waded through the mud, bent over as they planted seedlings one by one. Some hauled babies on their backs. Peilin often wondered how her own mother worked while balancing the wiggling bundle at the same time.

The fertile land was often the family's sole means of support. Her father deposited baby fish in the muddy waters and the growing rice. Come fall when the rice was harvested, he'd snatch them back and dry them. The fish—now several inches long—fed the family through the winter.

Out the train window, Peilin spotted a young boy wearing a wide-brimmed straw hat; he directed a water buffalo along the murky banks. Peilin's thoughts turned back to Ping. *Where was he? Was he with friends? Could he have run off to join the army? Wherever he was, she prayed that he was safe.*

Henri had fallen asleep. Peilin watched him shift unconsciously on the wooden bench. He seemed oblivious to noises on the train—cackling hens, people chatting, the clatter of mahjong tiles. She wondered if he was counting down the days until he could return to his homeland.

After a while, Henri stirred. His eyes opened; he adjusted to the unfamiliar surroundings. He smiled at her. She smiled back. But her heartache must've been evident on her face.

"Are you okay?" he asked, sitting up.

Peilin gazed back out the window. She tried to hide her anxiety about Ping; she knew it upset Henri, too. And Peilin thought if it hadn't been for Ping, she would've never met Henri. Ping brought them together.

"Do you think Ping joined the army?" she asked.

He shifted again on the hard seat.

"Is that what you believe?"

"I don't really know what to think anymore. He was adamant that night."

Peilin felt a sudden chilly wind pass between her and Henri. She wrapped her coat tighter around herself; she worried that Henri was still upset with her. Perhaps she should've hidden herself the night he gazed through her window.

"I don't know anything for certain," he said and looked the other way.

Henri didn't like to lie, especially to Peilin. It was hard enough knowing that he wasn't being honest with her; worse that she was obviously worried sick about her brother. He felt selfish now, as Peilin journeyed to help him cure one of his patients. Henri just knew that if he told her, she would be grief stricken. She'd be angry knowing Henri helped to make Ping's entry into the army possible. He told himself he was sparing Peilin from the initial pain. Perhaps Ping would quickly avenge his family honor, or turn around on his own. Anything, Henri thought, to spare himself the agony of telling Peilin the truth.

Through the window, Henri caught sight of a village in the distance. Two large auburn-colored birds swooped down overhead. The train slowed. Anxious travelers gathered their belongings and forced their way to the exits. Henri and Peilin, too, pressed their way toward the doors. Henri wasn't used to the tightly packed mobs, but to the Chinese, close proximity to one another was normal. Strong and acerbic smells enveloped him. Henri wrinkled his nose.

They disembarked from the train; the crowd scattered. Peilin was right. The open countryside was an intense contrast to dense Shanghai. He felt as if he'd been transported back to a simpler time and place. He followed Peilin to a small courtyard.

Henri scanned their surroundings. Shops encircled the area. Candles, cigarettes, pickles, firecrackers, soy sauce, straw hats, and paper fans were all prominently displayed. Past the dirt road, he spotted pig sties, brick latrines, and large spherical grain bins. The center of the courtyard was reserved for an ornate, gold-tiled temple. Odd animal-like sculptures perched atop the roof and each face contorted with some angry expression.

"*Wenzhou* (protective animals)," Peilin pointed out. "They guard the village."

She gestured toward the largest figurine—a fierce-looking creature, part dragon with a giant set of wings and a long fish tail.

"That's *tunjishou*—a ridge-devouring beast. According to Chinese legend, he's the Dragon King's son; they rule the seas. These gods stir up ocean waves for rain."

"Water for crops?"

Peilin nodded. "We honor the same legend in my village."

Peilin pointed toward the small cluster of rudimentary buildings just beyond the river.

"Do you miss your old home?"

"No. Better to live with my memories. It'd be too painful to see it now; especially after the fire."

He nodded sympathetically and recalled the horror of Berlin burning the night he fled Germany.

He followed Peilin through the courtyard. Henri observed birdcages hanging beneath several large willow trees. Colorful warblers with tresses of red, blue, and yellow chirped happily amongst themselves. Several of the cages hung close enough so that the birds sang to one another.

Peilin also stopped to admire the feathered animals. "Birds bring good luck."

Henri recalled the russet-colored birds he spied when they'd first arrived; perhaps they, too, were a sign of good fortune.

The two continued along the dusty road. Henri pointed to a group of people moving slowly in unison.

"*Qi-gong*," Peilin explained. "Exercises that help circulate body energy."

Henri watched in fascination. It was as if they were swimming through air in slow motion.

"How does it work?"

He wanted to find out more about this ancient art with healing properties, but Peilin grabbed Henri's hand.

219

"If we're going to catch the four o'clock train back to Shanghai, we've got to hurry."

From the outside, Master Hwang's shop was a plain, unassuming building, much like the other one-story mud-brick structures surrounding it. Distinctive smells of pungent snake wines brought back memories of Peilin's visits as a young girl. Grandpa Du had taken her to see Master Hwang on several occasions, particularly when he needed help with a difficult medical case.

Unlike Peilin, Master Hwang carried large jars of the restorative elixirs. She remembered when the astute man first gave her a sip of one of his tonics. At first, the bitter taste nearly caused her to spit it out, but Grandpa Du gently patted her back to help soothe the potent brew down her throat.

Peilin wondered if the doctor would remember her. She hadn't seen him since she was a little girl and she'd accompanied Grandpa Du. When the old man appeared, it was as if the years had not come between them. Peilin noticed the speckles of gray on Master Hwang's long thin beard. Still his slender face beamed with compassion and genuine warmth.

"*Mei mei* (little sister)," the old physician said with a wry smile. "It's an honor to have you visit again."

Peilin bowed in deference to Grandpa Du's revered teacher. "The honor is mine."

The herbal store had been in the Hwang family for generations, since the Ming Dynasty. According to Grandpa Du, legend told of the practitioner's distant ancestor who came to the aid of an ill, visiting monk. Healed by the Hwang relative, the grateful monk in turn presented an ancient formula used at his temple. The medicinal remedy cleared the lungs of pneumonia. Even to this day, Master Hwang dispenses this treatment to the needy for free.

The wise man had trained his only son Zhangzi to carry on the tradition, but the boy died during a terrible flood, leaving no successor. That's when Master Hwang took on Grandpa Du. Now, with Grandpa Du's recent passing, Peilin saw for the first time that Master Hwang had a new apprentice. The quiet lad looked no more than eight.

"I adopted him," the old man explained. "He was the fifth son in another family. He's a slow learner, but once he gets it, he never forgets."

Master Hwang took Peilin's hand in his own.

"I'm sorry to hear about your family's misfortune," he said, offering his condolences. "Your grandfather's passing was especially sad news."

Peilin bowed her head.

"I appreciate your kind words," she replied. "I know he thought very highly of you."

"As I did of him," the percipient man echoed.

Henri's presence had not gone unnoticed by the Chinese doctor. Despite Master Hwang's wariness of strangers, Peilin knew that he would open his arms to a fellow physician and more important, a trusted friend of Peilin's. She could see that the old healer was intrigued by Henri, whose fair skin and angular looks caused many in the village to stop and stare.

"Master Hwang, this is my Western doctor friend," Peilin introduced.

"It's an honor to meet you," Henri said in Chinese.

The penetrating man smiled at Henri's mastery of the language and greeted him with a respectful bow.

"Your journey from so far away humbles me. What brings you here to Tongsan?"

"My patient—" Henri seemed at a loss about how to begin, "her pulse's wiry and rapid, her tongue coated a greasy yellow—"

"Ah," Master Hwang said. "An astute pupil."

"The woman has—" he paused for a moment.

"*Lin bing* (gonorrhea)," Peilin interjected. "I prepared the Lotus Seed Formula, but her condition persists. And she now has a chronic fever and abdominal pains."

The herbal master tugged on his long beard.

"She's in need of stronger medicine," Peilin concluded.

"The intense heat condition concerns me," he replied. "This *yin* illness is a fierce one."

Peilin turned to Henri.

"*Yin* illnesses expand. Her high temperature has spread through her body."

Henri nodded.

"So we need to extinguish the flame."

Master Hwang grinned.

"You've been taught well."

Peilin blushed. Although Henri accompanied her for treatment purposes, she was secretly pleased to see her training efforts validated by the elder tutor.

Master Hwang collected a number of dried herbs from drawers similar to Peilin's. She recognized many—Chinese azalea fruit, peony bark, and wild chrysanthemum flower among them. Placing them in a pot full of water, the old man began to brew his medicinal tea.

The liquid boiled. Master Hwang stepped over to a glass case and extracted a petite white snake.

"What's it for?"

"*Fanshe*—this snake's one of the best remedies to dispel wind syndrome," the bearded physician explained.

Master Hwang laid the reptile down lengthwise and slit the creature open. Peilin thought she saw Henri flinch.

He squeezed the reptile releasing a green fluid that oozed into the boiling tea. The dying snake quivered and went limp. After some time, he poured his decoction into a glass jar. Peilin wondered if Henri would turn down the unusual medicine.

"A poisonous snake?" Henri asked.

The doctor nodded.

"Right again. Its toxicity's reduced in this remedy, yet it will fight the seriousness of your patient's condition."

"I realize this may be a bit different than what you're used to," Peilin whispered, "but his snake wines are highly regarded."

"Western medicines can also be toxic," Henri conceded.

"If it helps, I've drunk several of Master Hwang's tonics." She pointed to a bottled snake that had been drowned in yellow rice wine. "We eat the organs of chickens and cows—why not snake bile, especially if it can cure?"

Master Hwang concurred. "Snakes are revered for their flexibility, speed, and ability to shed skin. Because of their elasticity, they aid in the treatment of stiff joints and what you in Western medicine call arthritis," he explained to Henri. "Their swiftness combats wind syndrome—much like your patient's condition."

Peilin recognized the look of intrigue on Henri's face. It was the same look that drew her to him the first night she spent introducing him to her herbs.

Peilin was silently pleased that Master Hwang had taken such a liking to her Western friend. It gave her reassurance that Grandpa Du would've liked Henri, too.

Henri glanced up at the clock.

"We're going to miss our train," he interrupted.

Peilin turned, her heart beating. "What was I thinking? We must hurry."

The old physician tried to be helpful. "The train doesn't always leave on time. Maybe it's running late and you'll be lucky. Be well, *mei mei.*"

Peilin and Henri hurried out the door. She realized that they had

223

been unrealistic about how much time they'd needed for the journey. They reached the train station within minutes, but it was too late. The last locomotive headed for Shanghai had already pulled out. The next train didn't depart until seven the following morning.

"I'm supposed to be back at the hospital by noon tomorrow," Henri said concerned.

"The seven o'clock train should make it back to Shanghai before then," Peilin consoled. "I'm so sorry."

"Please, no. Thank you for all your help. If it goes as scheduled, I can just make it," Henri stressed.

Although he was feeling pressed for time, Henri also realized that Peilin had gone out of her way to help him. He worried that she was feeling responsible for what happened and his subsequent tardiness to work.

"It's going to be okay," Henri said. "I'm glad we're here."

"Really?"

"Yes. Since we have some time, why don't you show me around?"

Henri could see Peilin's distress subside. He hoped the distraction would also ease her worries about Ping. They walked across the village courtyard toward the riverbank. The sun dipped behind the evening horizon. Several wooden rafts floated downstream; fishermen tied cords around the long necks of gray birds. Henri pointed.

"What are they doing?"

"Those birds are cormorants. The fishermen send them out to trawl."

"You mean to fish?"

Peilin nodded.

"But won't the birds just swallow their catch?"

Now she smiled. "Watch and see."

The fishermen tossed the yellow-beaked ducks into the water.

Swimming in front of the raft, each cormorant bobbed their heads—appearing and disappearing beneath the water's surface. After several attempts a bird emerged, his throat swollen. The owner—waving a long netted bamboo pole—scooped their duck onto the boat. They squeezed the cormorant's throat pouch and a fish jumped out and flopped helplessly along the deck. The fisherman grasped the slippery catch and threw it into his basket. Then he'd send the duck out again.

"Amazing," Henri said.

"The rope tied around the bird's neck prevented the cormorant from swallowing his catch," Peilin explained.

Henri continued to watch, mesmerized by the working relationship between fisherman and bird. He would've sat by the river's edge all night had Peilin not pulled him away.

"They're setting up for the night market," she told him. "Come, let me show you."

Numerous hawkers with their wares congregated in the square. Some sold handmade straw hats; others bamboo-carved flutes. A child, probably the vendor's son, serenaded the crowd with an ethereal melody. Henri spotted a beautiful porcelain teapot.

"When I was growing up, Ping and I would share a bag of roasted peanuts and a cup of ginger ice here," she continued excitedly.

The carnival-like atmosphere enveloped them. Music played, jugglers tossed batons, and a man entertained children with a monkey who performed tricks. The smell of baked yams, steaming won tons, and barbecued meats filled the air. People pushed and pulled their way through the crowd like swarming bees. Henri strived to keep up with Peilin. As he caught up to her once again, he witnessed her scan the market for more favorite treats. But it was Henri's eyes that flew open when he spotted an exotic skewer of deep-fried scorpions.

"People eat that?" he whispered, not wanting to offend those around them.

"Scorpion's a *yin* food," she explained. "It relieves wind-damp conditions like boils. Grandpa Du had a mouth ulcer once. It made it difficult for him to speak."

Peilin handed the vendor two yuan, insisting that he keep the extra coin.

"*Xie Xie*," she said appreciatively as he handed her a stick.

Henri scrutinized the toasted insect. "Do you eat the stinger, too?"

"Of course." Peilin bit into its crackling outer shell.

"Mmmm, very good," she said, smiling at the vendor.

She held the food out to Henri. He hesitated; he lifted his hands. "I'm not sure I'm up for it."

"Try it," she urged. "After eating five of them, his sore went away," she continued happily. "The next day Grandpa Du could talk again."

Henri bit into the delicacy. He expected it to be dry, but the crispy outside gave way to a soft, fleshy center.

"Well?" Peilin asked.

"Not bad."

He held out the skewer for Peilin to take another bite; their hands touched. Neither pulled away. She met his eyes. He knew how strongly the Chinese valued family ties, especially wife to husband, child to parent. But for a moment it seemed as if her filial piety had faded away. Peilin stood before him, independent and strong.

Loud, clapping cymbals diverted their attention. Henri looked up to see a toothless man accompanying a hunched gray-haired woman.

The enigmatic woman hobbled toward them. Henri observed the old woman's flared nostrils sniffing the air. She held up her hand and motioned for her partner to stop.

The obliging man grabbed the wooden pail hanging from his arm and turned it over. Placing it on the ground, it became a stool for the matron to sit on.

"Come closer," the old lady motioned to Peilin.

Henri was surprised that Peilin acquiesced, but he sensed a connection between them.

The woman reached out; her hands discovering Peilin's face.

"The bride with inward eyes; I never forget you."

Henri looked to Peilin for an explanation. She faced Henri, her eyes bright.

"My Good Luck Lady," Peilin whispered with a pleased grin.

The astute woman smiled.

"I've prepared many brides," she went on, "but never as special as the one before me now."

Henri noticed Peilin bow her head.

"Do not have doubts," the old woman said soothingly.

"But Good Lady—" as Peilin spoke, Henri heard her choking up.

The old woman put up her hand again. Turning, she scanned the stall until she found a large yellow citrus. The vendor, an obvious friend, handed it to her.

The matron peeled the membrane and loosened a segment of the grapefruit-like citrus and placed the pink fruit into Peilin's mouth. Its sweet aromatic smell piqued Henri's senses as well.

"Remember when you bathed in the hot bath of the pomelo-infused waters?"

"I do."

"The waters still guide you now."

"But—" Peilin stuttered.

The old woman quieted her bride once again.

"Sometimes the waters overtake us, like drowning."

Peilin nodded.

"Let waters carry you," the Good Luck Lady counseled. She handed Peilin another pomelo to take with her. Peilin bowed in appreciation.

Henri watched as the pauper woman signaled to her son that it was time to move on.

The young man banged the cymbals once again; the wise woman seized Peilin's hands into her own.

"In time, flow brings us to the place that we are meant to be."

The clamoring cadence faded. With the open-air market now closing, Henri and Peilin continued in silence. Searching for a place to wait the night out, Peilin pointed toward a large willow tree.

"I could use the rest," Henri acknowledged.

But just as they neared its trunk, Henri tripped and fell to the ground.

"Are you okay?" Peilin said rushing to his side.

He clutched his ankle. The stabbing pain was intense.

"I'm not sure."

Peilin pulled up his pant leg and examined his swollen joint.

"Lucky for you, it's not broken."

Henri inspected it for himself.

"Do you think we can find some ice?"

"I know something better." Peilin took his ankle and gently placed it between her hands. "Let me help circulate the *qi*," she told him. "It'll heal faster."

"*Qi*?"

"Energy."

Henri was too tired to resist. It was late. Everyone had gone home. They were alone. Peilin circled her hands around his ankle. He felt her gentle movements create a soothing warmth. He felt himself drawn to her. He wasn't sure if it was appreciation or exhaustion or both, but as the two sat under the twinkling stars, Henri leaned in and kissed her. Her lips greeted his with longing that matched his own. Their bodies drew closer; his hands caressed her silky skin—he felt electrified. Her body responded with unfolding desire, a yearning that he, too, had kept in abeyance.

Then, as quickly as they had begun, they stopped. For a moment the two held onto each other, neither moving. Henri wondered if he had gone too far. But as if to answer him, she rose again. This time, her hungry lips met his with an unleashed fervor. Henri kissed her back with equal passion. In that moment, it was as if a wall had finally been torn down, as if some invisible armor surrounding his heart had finally dissolved. He held her in his arms and breathed.

17

THE MORNING LOCOMOTIVE raced back to Shanghai. Peilin's mind whirled. She'd been up all night. Seeing Master Hwang would have been enough on its own, but then there was Henri's lingering kiss. She glanced over at him sleeping by her side. The steady rise and fall of his breath calmed her. Last night stirred up passions she'd wondered about since her wedding night. Her body had yearned for physical connection, but she had kept those feelings submerged—until now. Under the tree and night sky, Peilin's emotions swept over her—opening her heart to a love she never thought possible. This morning, she realized it was unacceptable behavior for a properly married Chinese woman.

The more Peilin thought about it, the more the other startling encounter in Tongsan weighed on her mind—a chance meeting with the Good Luck Lady. Yet it was almost as if the luminary expected they'd meet again. And still she was going on about the inward eyes? Peilin had forgotten about that observation until the gray-haired woman brought it up. Peilin thought back on the last year since her marriage. Could it be her inward eyes that had helped her to find Ping? And Henri? Peilin always felt that her herbal knowledge relied on an intimate connection with a visceral awareness. Now she wondered if this internal direction was perhaps guiding her in other ways. Was this what the Good Luck Lady meant by inward eyes?

Grandpa Du had been aware of such inner vision. She recalled a blind and deaf man in their village. As a child, Peilin was afraid of the unkempt man who often begged for food and slept with stray cats. Some of the villagers threw stones, but Grandpa Du taught Peilin to respect him.

"Despite his disheveled appearance and bad smell, the man knows when the winds come before there's even a rustle of a single tree branch; he knows when the rain's to arrive before the wisp of a cloud appears."

"How could this be?" she remembered asking.

"The blind man sees beyond sight; he hears beyond hearing. Be open with your heart and you, too, can see and hear those in-between spaces."

For Peilin, the train ride seemed to take much longer than the actual four hours. By the time they returned to Shanghai, she was anxious to be on her way home. She was also cognizant of Henri's schedule and his need to get to work—he may be late.

She touched his shoulder and shook him awake.

"We're here," she whispered.

Henri appeared a little disoriented but regained his composure. He grabbed Master Hwang's jar of medicinal tea.

"If you run, you'll probably make it to the hospital just in time," Peilin figured.

Henri shook his head. "First I'm taking you back to your store."

"But you'll be late for work."

"My boss isn't due in until later today. You went out of your way to help me. The least I can do is to make sure you arrive back safely."

They darted through the streets. Neither mentioned the kiss under the tree, yet Peilin felt his continued company was a lingering effect of their connection. Peilin smiled to herself, but as they neared the shop, her fears rose. Had the Chens or other neighbors noticed that she'd been away for the entire night? But surveying the people walking and conducting business along the street, she was relieved that the Chens were nowhere to be seen.

When she arrived at the store, she discovered a slip of paper tucked into the crease of her door.

"A note?" Henri asked, his look adding to Peilin's distress.

"Perhaps one of my patients is in need of medicine."

Henri stood by her side as she unfolded the paper. She didn't recognize the writing, so she quickly scanned down to the bottom for a signature. It was dated nearly four days ago.

"What does it say?" Henri asked.

Peilin could not speak. As she read the letter, her hands began to tremble. She looked up at Henri, her eyes tearing up from what she had just read.

"It's Ping." It took her a moment before she could continue. "He's joined the Kuomintang army."

Henri stiffened.

"Really?" she heard him ask. But Peilin's eyes had already started to mist over.

"I can't tell you where I am, dear sister, but my troop grows with new recruits. We are now twenty-seven. I was given a knapsack and quilt. On a good night, we have millet or peanuts. Even if it's only flatbread, I'm satisfied."

Peilin looked up at Henri.

"Is there more?" he asked.

Peilin nodded.

"To avoid air attacks, we march at night and rest by day in caves or thick brush. During training, one soldier shot himself in the hand. He thought a small bullet wound would keep him behind, away from combat. Unfortunately the bullet exploded in his hand and the whole limb needed to be amputated."

Peilin glanced at Henri, who continued to listen.

"Unlike the injured boy, I'm not afraid. In fact—" she could barely finish saying the words out loud, "I've found my destiny."

Peilin then read the next line without emotion. She was neither anxious nor attached to how Henri might react. She felt as if the world had stopped altogether.

"Don't be mad at Henri. This is what I wanted. He was only trying to help."

Henri stood. She couldn't fathom what kind of reaction she was hoping for.

"You knew. All this time, you knew," she whispered.

Henri bowed his head.

"Why? When you knew how worried I'd been? How could you not tell me?"

"I wanted to. I really did," Henri stuttered. "I was trying to find the right time, the right moment… " his words trailed off. "I didn't want to hurt you."

But all Peilin could take in was that he'd betrayed her—and all this time, she'd been so worried. She'd confided her concern for her only living relative and Henri had lied to her face. She threw the letter at him, bolted into the store, and slammed the door, leaving Henri outside.

Henri stood staring at the closed door. He'd hurt her. Worse, she felt deceived. He asked himself over and over again. *Why? Why did I hold back from telling her?* He pounded the wall. Then he glanced at his watch. With no time to waste, Henri broke out into a run. It was nearly one o'clock—he was already an hour late. He raced through the city, telling himself the reason he withheld his knowledge was to protect her, but deep down he knew the real answer. He was afraid.

Yet he hadn't been afraid to kiss her last night. They hadn't spoken about that either, he reasoned. Henri wondered if some things were better left unsaid. But immediately he sensed the rationalization for what it was—he didn't want to confess to Peilin that he'd specifically done something he knew she was opposed to. He hurried along the Whangpoo River bank. It was low tide; two fishermen grappled to free their dilapidated sampan from the river's muddy bottom. It seemed the more they pulled, the worse the situation became; the boat's hull settled deeper into the sticky sludge. Like the watercraft, Henri felt the weight of his own decisions pulling him downward.

It took close to a half hour before Henri arrived at the hospital. He sprinted down the long corridor; it seemed abnormally quiet. At first, Henri wondered if something was wrong, and he was surprised by his sense of relief when he saw Brigitta's familiar face as she turned the corner.

"You're late," Brigitta said unsympathetically.

Henri was taken aback by her antagonistic tone, but then he remembered. She'd wanted him. He'd made it clear that he had no romantic interests. And now they had to continue to be civil to each other.

"I have to warn you," she said staring down. "Rosen's not been in a good mood this morning."

Henri stopped. "I thought he wasn't due in until later today," he replied, catching the tone of shock in his voice.

"Change of schedule."

Henri sensed her restrained delight at the fact that he was late, and probably going to get into trouble. She walked by without looking at him, then disappeared out of sight. He supposed she enjoyed seeing him squirm.

Henri went to his locker and pulled out his tattered coat. He tucked the jar of tea into an oversized pocket. He raised the sleeve over his right shoulder; his arm became tangled. Henri was struggling to free himself when he felt a presence. He looked up—Rosen stood at the door. Rosen's imposing figure seemed to fill the hallway, his arms crossed tightly over his inflated chest.

"Nice of you to finally show up."

"I apologize. First time—I swear. It won't happen again."

"I don't care if it was your first. Tardiness is grounds for dismissal."

Henri knew Rosen despised anyone who was late for work, but he sensed an increased agitation in Rosen's tone. Not wanting to make the situation worse, Henri offered a solution.

"You're absolutely right. I'll make up the time at the end of my shift."

But no sooner had he taken a step when Rosen's hand bore down on his shoulders.

"Where do you think you're going, Neumann?"

"Nowhere, sir," Henri responded, feeling the tension in the room rise again.

"I understand you've been treating my patients with Chinese herbs.

How could he know?

"Only one," Henri stuttered. "And that was because we couldn't get the medicine needed."

Rosen waved his finger in Henri's face. Henri tried not to flinch, but his boss's intimidating gestures crossed into Henri's personal space.

"That's not what I've been told. There've been several. Right here in this hospital."

Henri caught his breath.

"Who told you that?"

"It doesn't matter."

But Henri already knew the answer. Brigitta. He just didn't know *how* she knew.

"It was *one* patient," Henri repeated. "And she recovered," Henri said, trying to redeem himself.

"You disobeyed my orders. You broke the rules."

Henri felt his heart quickening. No matter what he said or what progress he made, Rosen discounted it, preferring to stick to his rigid policies. Henri surmised that the man needed to assert his authority to mask his insecurity.

Rosen began sniffing the air around him.

"Whad'ya do, sleep in a barn full of smelly hogs?"

Rosen's comment caught Henri off guard. He surveyed his rumpled clothes, trying to figure out what Rosen's senses might be reacting to. Then he remembered Master Hwang's pungent medicinal tea. Rosen's eyes focused on Henri's bulging coat pocket.

"What's in there?"

"My lunch."

"Hand it to me. Now."

Henri knew it was useless to argue with Rosen. Someone had it out for Henri and he knew exactly who it was. Henri handed it over.

Rosen opened the jar up and smelled its murky contents.

"This is it!" Rosen gagged. Holding the open jar away from his nose, he took another look at the murky brown tea.

"Not treating with Chinese medicine, huh? What do you call this?"

Henri's knees weakened. "Please sir. Okay, I admit, it's an herbal tea, but it's mine—it's not for hospital patients."

Rosen screwed the lid back on the jar and thrust the glass container back at him. Henri clutched the medicine that he and Peilin had traveled so far to retrieve. Thoughts of fear, anger, and retreat raced through his mind.

"Get this out of my sight," Rosen seethed. "You're fired, Neumann."

Peilin stood in her room clutching the heavy pomelo from the Good Luck Lady. The fragrant citrus reminded Peilin of her wedding day.

Now nearly a year later, Peilin took the new fruit and squeezed its juices once again into a small tub of water. Peilin needed to wash away the pain of Henri's betrayal. As the steam rose, the Good Luck Lady's words washed over Peilin again.

"Remember Lao Tzu's proverb," the Good Lady had told the young bride. "Water is fluid, soft, and yielding."

"*Na, na, na,*" she'd repeated in her methodic tone. "Water wears away the rock, which is rigid and cannot yield."

Peilin recalled how the Good Luck Lady rubbed the hardened pumice stone along the bottom of her feet to encourage new skin.

"Ah, whatever is fluid and yielding can overcome that which is rigid and hard."

The Good Luck Lady had then held Peilin's face up to the hand mirror.

"Another paradox," the wise woman continued.

Peilin gazed at her own reflection.

"What is soft is strong," the Good Luck Lady had said, the words now echoing in Peilin's mind.

At the time, Peilin wasn't exactly sure what the old woman meant, but now as she dried herself off, she realized that perhaps the Good Luck Lady sensed strength in Peilin that even she hadn't yet deciphered.

Exhausted from the events of the past twenty-four hours, Peilin went to bed early. Somewhere in the night she was awakened by a loud and persistent knock at the door. It took her a few moments to realize what was happening. She tiptoed downstairs toward the unrelenting pounding. If it was Henri, she'd already decided that she'd refuse to let him in. But when she peered through the window to see who it was, she was astonished by the unexpected sight: Father Kwan.

Peilin unlocked the door.

"Father-in-law," she greeted him.

She observed his stern countenance and his Western clothes—a sign of serious business.

"Pack your belongings," he said without greeting her. "The driver will bundle your herbal supplies."

His command alarmed Peilin. It was all happening so fast.

"I don't understand," she replied. "Why pack now? The baby can't be this early—it's only November. There are still nearly five months."

He lit a cigarette and shook his head.

"Kwan Taitai's ill. She's requested your assistance. You're to return to Dragon Lake immediately."

Father Kwan remained at the doorway. Peilin ran upstairs to pack her things. At first, she wondered if the Chens had alerted her father-in-law about yesterday's overnight trip. But how could they've told him so quickly? Was Kwan Taitai really sick? Or was Father Kwan just saying that to get her away from Henri as swiftly as possible?

She heard the driver packing her herbs from the shop below. There was no time to find Henri and tell him that she was leaving. By holding onto her news about the baby, she'd missed her opportunity to at least prepare Henri for her departure. Now it was too late.

Yet as she filled her suitcase, Henri's betrayal reemerged strong in her mind. *How could he have kept such a secret from her? How could he have lied?* Henri had actually signed Ping's medical papers. It was still too much to take in.

Early the next morning, Peilin stood outside as Father Kwan locked the herbal store for the last time. Shivering from the cool air, she wiped away tears running down her cheeks. She was sure her father-in-law must have thought that she was sad to depart, but in that moment Peilin was actually relieved to be leaving Shanghai, and Henri, behind.

Henri wanted to at least say goodbye to his patients and let them know what was happening, but Rosen would hear none of it. The head doctor instead directed two burly orderlies to escort Henri out of the medical center. Henri struggled against their grips as they led him out the infirmary door.

He wasn't allowed back inside; still Henri had unfinished business. He remained near the hospital entrance. Hours later, Brigitta emerged. She wrapped her scarf tightly around herself to stave off the November cold, then stridently took off. Henri waited until she was some distance from the infirmary before approaching her.

"You succeeded in punishing me," Henri announced as he strode up next to her.

"It was your own undoing," Brigitta replied, unruffled by his sudden appearance. "I was only doing my job."

"How did you know?" he asked coolly. "Were you spying on me?"

Brigitta's lips curled up, exposing her teeth. "Oh don't be so naive, Henri. Six-year-olds don't keep secrets very well."

Little Kaethe? He could hardly be mad at the young girl. Yet the more he thought about it, the more he was sure Brigitta conned it out of the child.

"But you lied," Henri snapped. "You know I only treated one patient when we had no other medication available. And you saw how she improved. We saved her life."

"I know you intended to treat others. I know you love the Chinese ways," she said with a disdainful twist of her lips.

She continued on her way. But Henri wasn't satisfied with the conversation ending on her personal analysis. He caught up to her as she passed the Hong Kong Bank, its imposing lion statues standing guard.

"Why did you tell Rosen I'd treated *several* patients with Chinese herbs?"

Brigitta stopped.

"I did what I thought was right. You crossed the line—whether it was one, ten, or forty people, you jeopardized their safety. You do what you want, regardless of other people's feelings."

Henri felt confused. "You find me that insensitive?"

Brigitta's eyes welled up. Then it dawned on him.

"You're getting back at me... because I don't love you." Realizing this, he searched for something more to say. "It's not something that you can will. It's either there or it isn't."

But instead of soothing the situation, Henri struck the wrong chord.

"That's what you told me. At first I believed you. I believed that you weren't open to love—anyone. That would have been okay—"

Then Brigitta lashed out at him more strongly than even he could have anticipated.

"But then I discovered that wasn't true!"

Henri threw up his hands.

"What are you talking about?"

"The Chinese woman. What about your feelings for her? I heard about the Marble Palace."

Henri was caught. But he was entitled to his life away from the hospital. This time Brigitta had pried too far.

"Did a six-year-old tell you that, too?" Henri scoffed.

Brigitta stood firm. "This is a small community. People talk, Henri. If you must know, the Kadoorie servant mentioned it to his boss. Sir Kadoorie mentioned it to Rosen. The news trickled back to me."

Henri was taken aback by the intricate network by which Brigitta had gathered her information.

"So who's calling whom a liar here, Henri? You tell me you can't love, but the truth is your heart had already been taken. I opened my heart to you and you run off with some foreigner. You never gave me a chance."

He wished he could be bigger and apologize, but her finger pointing was too raw.

As they reached the Bund, Henri grabbed Brigitta by the arm but she pulled away.

"Will you just stop all this drama?" he exploded.

But before he had a chance to say another word, she forged ahead, holding her head high. He was tired of chasing her, tired of her games. He fumed as her clicking heels melted into the distance, leaving Henri alone by the river's edge.

The morning sun cast a glare on the Buick windows. The same driver who had met her at the train station nearly a year ago now drove silently along Bubbling Well Road. Peilin remembered the wiry and energetic Ang, who'd proudly told her about the city. Now he was taking her back. Father Kwan sat next to her in the back seat. She smelled the familiar scent of his cigarettes.

"This isn't what I wanted," her father-in-law said, breaking the silence.

Peilin didn't know what to say.

He went on.

"She insisted. She's been asking for you. I put her off many times… " he paused. "Finally I had to come. It's my duty."

Peilin didn't know whether to believe him or not. The last time he saw her, he'd promised her five more months in Shanghai. Yet he arrived much sooner and, without giving her a choice, packed up her things and now whisked her back to Dragon Lake. She still suspected her neighbors but had no way to prove it.

Father Kwan reached into his coat pocket and pulled out a string of pearls. He handed them to her.

"For you."

Peilin held them between her fingers. The cool pearls soothed her. She knew how strong-willed Kwan Taitai could be. Perhaps he was telling the truth. Perhaps he did care about her. She nodded toward her father-in-law in appreciation.

Her duty was, after all, to be loyal to her husband's family. At the moment though she felt as if her world had just been turned upside down; she wasn't sure what to think. After she had arrived in Shanghai, she thought things began to look up. She'd found Ping. She'd befriended Henri. Now Ping was somewhere fighting with the army. She shuttered thinking how they were torn apart again. Yet her sudden departure was a welcome escape. After the other night, she was actually relieved to be away from Henri.

Dawn continued to break over the Whangpoo's eastern shore. Peilin peered through the window as she crossed the Garden Bridge for the last time. Just beyond the steel structure she craned her neck for a glimpse of the Bund. Reflections of the imposing European-style buildings and the tree-lined street became etched in her mind. She felt herself being ripped away from her freedom. Being on her own had verified her strength and her ability to help others and, most important, provided a brief glimpse of who she was without the obligations of wife and daughter-in-law. Rarely was a woman allowed such independence. She realized now how different her life would be as she returned to tradition and all that was Dragon Lake.

Would she have been better off if she'd never experienced Shanghai? No matter. She was leaving the same way she arrived— property of her husband's family.

She continued to stare straight ahead, yet she viewed her father-in-law out of the corner of her eye. His eyes cast a weary gaze. His hand trembled even though he was sitting still. He'd changed drastically, even since she'd last seen him. She turned toward him, but he looked away as if he, too, was lost in private thought.

Peilin felt her insides whirling; she couldn't think clearly. A part of her wanted to scream out, yet she sat stoically. The car surged ahead. She hid the depth of her feelings, like the lake's pearls underneath. Her face—like the water's surface—the water's calm.

The city receded in the distance; one last thought emerged—if she'd never experienced Shanghai, she never would've left with a broken heart.

Henri spent a restless night. Not only was he fired, but he'd been unduly dismissed due to Brigitta's venomous lies. She was a crafty, jealous woman. He was still shocked that she knew of his Marble Palace trip with Peilin. The recent disclosures confirmed his suspicions about the extent to which she disliked the Chinese. Henri recalled her response to the pauper boy who accidentally bumped into her that night. Brigitta lashed out at any Chinese who crossed her path.

Morning arrived. Henri dressed and raced through the city streets. He knew Peilin was probably still upset about Ping, but he needed to be with her. He needed her support more than ever. Peilin understood him. Whenever he was with her, it was as if he felt calmer… and more alive.

He knocked on the door several times but Peilin refused to answer. The shades were drawn. Desperate, he peered through the window blinds. The shelves were empty.

Henri stood inert, unable to comprehend what he was seeing.

Then he noticed the couple from across the street walking toward him.

"You're Peilin's *qing ren* (lover), aren't you?" the husband inquired.

"*Péngyou* (Friend)," Henri corrected. "Have you seen her?"

The woman smiled. Henri sensed that she might actually like seeing him in pain.

"Her father-in-law arrived last night," she replied. "He took her back to Dragon Lake."

"For the baby," her husband added.

Henri's eyebrows rose.

"Baby? What baby?"

"Didn't she tell you?" the woman asked. "Her baby."

Feeling lightheaded, Henri lowered himself down to the sidewalk. As he sat, he folded his arms across his knees and he buried his head.

"I didn't know."

"Oh yes," continued the woman. "We're hoping she's honored with a son."

The husband pointed down the empty road.

"Peilin is gone."

18

A HEAVY FOG SHROUDED the jagged limestone mountains surrounding Dragon Lake. Peilin pulled her coat tighter around herself on the cool and eerie November afternoon. It'd been a long journey during which neither Father Kwan, Peilin, nor the driver uttered more than a few words. The silence continued as they emerged from the car. Peilin stepped onto the dirt path; her legs buckled from fatigue. Father Kwan went inside. She stood as the driver removed her suitcase from the sedan's trunk.

Peilin surveyed the familiar house and its surroundings—nothing had changed from nearly a year ago. The same tall cypress and pine trees lined the narrow dirt path. The same wooden boat sat on the lake near the shed. The same servant, Bamboo, she recalled, appeared to help her inside. Peilin's mind flooded with memories of her ineptitude. This was the girl who'd helplessly flailed about when Kwan Taitai was choking the morning after Peilin's wedding. But when she took the whole of Bamboo in, Peilin noticed one change— the servant's belly was notably swollen. Bamboo haughtily grabbed Peilin's bag and dragged it into the house. Feeling a sudden moment of empathy for the pregnant girl, Peilin moved to take the luggage herself, but Bamboo grudgingly snapped it away.

"Kwan Taitai's instructions," the servant girl grumbled.

Peilin followed Bamboo who wobbled across the hard tiled floor. Peilin guessed that she was about five months pregnant. Then it dawned on her—the infant growing in Bamboo's belly was to be Peilin's child, the Kwan's grandson and heir. Peilin wondered who the father might be—did he work here at Dragon Lake? Perhaps the baby's father was a poor peasant. If that were the case, he couldn't come close to giving his child a prosperous life like the one it would have as part of the Kwan family. Down the hall, the young girl dropped Peilin's luggage with a thud. With an insolent turn, Bamboo disappeared, leaving Peilin alone once again in the same room where she'd spent her first night with the straw mannequin. Peilin shivered. It'd been a long time since she'd felt so alone.

Peilin was relieved to see the desk that had brought her solace back then. She found comfort in its presence. She sat down and opened the first drawer. Inside she rediscovered her writing tools: brush, ink stick, paper, and ink stone. She opened a second drawer and pulled out the bronze mirror. Peilin rubbed her hand across the back. Carved with the figures of the dragon and phoenix, it symbolized nature's *yin-yang* balance. She gazed at her aching reflection. There was no denying it now. She was reminded of a poem—two separated lovers and the broken mirror they shared between them. With her brush in hand, Peilin began to write:

You left me with the broken mirror,
But absent are you.
I gaze in its reflection; I seek your face,
But I see not a trace.

When she was done, she set her writing brush down and went over to the bed. Tired from the long journey, she rested her head and soon fell asleep. She woke nearly an hour later and finished unpacking her things. Father Kwan soon appeared at her bedroom door. He seemed less tense than he'd been on the ride back from Shanghai, but the weariness was still there.

"Kwan Taitai requests your presence," he said.

Peilin started to brush her hair, but Father Kwan pulled her away.

"Not to keep her waiting."

She trailed him down the hall.

"The doctor who traveled here a few days ago told me that she suffers from inflamed bowels."

Peilin refrained from replying, as she couldn't think of anything encouraging to say in response.

Before they'd reached the last door, Peilin detected the heavy camphor odor. Mother Kwan had requested that the drapes be drawn, even during the day. Peilin entered the darkened room. Bamboo was at her side, dabbing cool water on Kwan Taitai's forehead. Peilin could hear her mother-in-law's labored breathing. Peilin felt the woman's cheek. She was burning up from internal heat—a fire condition. The old woman's domineering personality was like a flame, constantly leaping forward to consume more fuel. But now her driving demeanor had turned inward, causing the old woman's body to be consumed by fever. Although she had few tender feelings for her mother-in-law, Peilin took the ailing woman's hand into her own. Its leathery texture reminded Peilin of *chen pi*—dried orange peel.

"Kwan Taitai," Peilin said softly. "I have returned."

The old woman's eyes fluttered just enough to take in her daughter-in-law.

"Finally. I've begged my husband to get you."

Peilin now realized that her Shanghai neighbors hadn't been responsible for Father Kwan's sudden arrival. Mother Kwan was truly sick and had summoned Peilin herself.

Mother-in-law snapped her hand out of Peilin's grasp; she waved her wrinkled hand toward the servant girl.

"Leave us immediately," Kwan Taitai ordered. "Now!"

Bamboo scrambled to find her balance. Father Kwan quickly moved in to help the pregnant girl to a standing position. In that brief moment, Peilin caught a glimpse between the young maid and her father-in-law—a tender glance that could only indicate one thing:

Father Kwan was the baby's father. He couldn't suppress a look of pride. The girl's growing belly was a testament of his virility. The girl turned, but Peilin still made out the corners of her grin. Kwan Taitai stirred. Father Kwan instinctively flinched and struggled out the door, urging the servant girl forward.

Peilin poured a glass of water and held it to the old woman's parched lips.

"Drink," she coaxed.

Kwan Taitai sipped a few drops and swallowed hard.

"We've been waiting for you," the old woman whispered. "Now that you are here, Yao will calm down and I can sleep."

Mother Kwan closed her eyes. Peilin sat by her side. Was Yao visiting his mother from the world beyond? Or was Kwan Taitai hallucinating? Either way, Peilin perceived that the old woman's breathing soon found a steady rhythm. Peilin glanced out the window to the placid lake. It struck Peilin how different they were—Kwan Taitai so linked to fire, while Peilin found solace in water.

Henri flailed about the streets of Shanghai, unsure of where to go or what to do. Everything that linked him to Shanghai—his job, his connection to Ping and Peilin—had been yanked from his grasp. The only matter he could concentrate on now was delivering Rita's herbs.

Henri studied the address on Ezra's business card. His office wasn't far from Little Vienna and Henri's *Heim* (dorm). This section of the Hongkew District consisted of the brick structures that had been partially destroyed by Japanese bombs in 1937. Henri recalled seeing the buildings from the deck of the Italian steamship when he had arrived nearly a year ago. With thin walls and leaky plumbing, the ghetto area provided minimal shelter for a dense population. But because of their dilapidated condition and affordable pricing, a number of refugees took up housing in the area north of Soochow

Creek, along with Chinese, Russian, Indian, and Japanese civilians. The two- and three-story brick buildings were tightly huddled together, rows of attached houses linked by narrow alleys. Fastened across cord lines that stretched between windows, laundered shirts, trousers, and undergarments flapped in the wind.

Henri dodged past rambunctious children playing soccer in the alley. Locating Ezra's downstairs flat, he knocked on the door. A moment later it swung open.

"Henri! Come in, come in!" shouted Ezra.

Henri noticed the *mezuzah* angled on the doorpost. Instinctively he kissed his fingers and then touched the small metal box, a reminder of his faith. While many of the refugees displayed simple *menorahs* and handmade *dreidels*, Henri found the *mezuzah* in this unlikely spot a welcome sight. Ezra's apartment was divided between living quarters and office space by a thin bamboo screen; yet paperwork piles were spread equally between the separated areas. Tattered photographs of Berlin and Russia, some framed, some not, adorned the otherwise dull white walls. Henri recognized Tiergarten Park in one of the photos.

Ezra moved several piles of paper from the burgundy couch.

"Please, sit."

Henri pulled out the jar of tea and handed it to Ezra.

"Make sure she drinks a cup three times a day."

"*Danke,*" Ezra replied. "Will you excuse me for a moment while I take it to her? She's been asking about it."

"Of course."

Ezra ducked down the hall. Henri could make out a conversation, but not the words themselves. A moment later, Rita appeared. She'd lost a significant amount of weight since he'd seen her; circles darkened her eyes.

"Thank you," she whispered and disappeared back down the hall.

A few minutes later Ezra reappeared.

"She drank a cup and is lying down again," he reported.

"Hopefully she'll be able to sleep and recover soon," Henri encouraged.

Ezra nodded. "I've no doubt."

Henri felt his friend's deep concern. Yet their connection was still a mystery.

"Do you know each other from Berlin?"

Ezra shook his head. "I met Rita here in Shanghai," he explained. "She was a taxi dancer."

"A taxi dancer?"

"It's not what you think. She wasn't a prostitute; she was a professional dance partner—better than Ginger Rogers. We met during a foxtrot."

Henri was reminded of his Marble Palace dance with Peilin.

"I can imagine," Henri replied. "When you're with someone special, it's like dancing on air."

Ezra nodded. "Her family was originally from Russia. They're stateless like we are. They were exiled and relocated to Shanghai after the Russian Civil War in 1923. It was difficult for Rita's father to obtain work. Luckily her dance money provided for the family."

"That is fortunate," Henri agreed. He knew how challenging it'd been for many of the dorm refugees to find employment.

"Rita speaks several languages, including English and Chinese. Her skills have been invaluable for my business."

"Is that why you're together?"

"It's how it started. I enjoy Rita's down-to-earth ways. There isn't the pretense that goes along with endless parties and social engagements. With Rita I can be myself."

"I'm jealous of the love you two share."

"There are a lot of things I find refreshing in the Russian culture. Although they are a stoic society, they know how to have a good laugh." Ezra sighed before continuing. "My marriage to Arabelle was set up by my parents. We were both sixteen. What did we know about love? She's a good woman, but, alas, the love between us is purely platonic."

Ezra padded around the room in his stocking feet, clearing off more paper stacks from a wooden chair. While he was very good in social situations, it was obvious to Henri that Ezra wasn't used to visitors.

"So how are you?" Ezra asked, finally able to focus again.

Now Henri shifted with discomfort.

"I—I, I've been fired from the hospital."

Henri's head drooped, the full weight of all that had happened hitting him hard. He recalled a similar feeling back in Berlin—the loss of his medical license, his mother, and Sophie.

"Rosen and Brigitta. They—"

Henri sensed Ezra's hand on his shoulder. The warmth felt gentle and kind.

"Don't worry. Whatever it was," Ezra whispered as if it were a prayer, "*Yihyeh beseder*—it'll all work out."

"I don't know what I'm going to do," Henri continued, too ashamed to look his friend in the eye.

"You've an excellent reputation in the community. Why don't you open your own practice?" Ezra suggested.

It took a moment for Ezra's words to sink in. His supportive proposal reminded Henri of Uncle Viktor, who liked to utter, "*Hamatzil nefesh achat, k'ealu hitzil olam vemlo'o*—Whoever saves a life saves the world." His uncle recalled those words whenever he needed to renew his purpose in life. Now the phrase echoed in Henri's mind, spurring him in a new direction.

"That's a great idea," Henri responded. "But where? And how? I'll need equipment."

Ezra stood and walked to the other side of the room. He opened a door that Henri hadn't noticed previously.

"Here."

Henri joined his friend and inspected the back room. It had enough space for two. There was even a side door that led out to the street.

"Why do you keep this space empty?"

"We've been meaning to rent it out," Ezra explained. "But we haven't found anyone that we felt comfortable with—until now."

He reached into his pocket and handed Henri some money. Henri didn't know what to do—it was a chance at a new beginning.

"For equipment," Ezra continued. "You'll open your clinic here."

Peilin sat with Mother Kwan through the night. It was a fitful sleep marked by tossing and muttering. At first Peilin couldn't make out what the old woman was saying, but as the night wore on, it became clear that she was dreaming.

"No!" Kwan Taitai often screamed out.

Peilin tried to calm the woman down, but her erratic shouts persisted.

At one point, Kwan Taitai's eyes flew open—yet her vacant stare failed to notice Peilin.

"Why do you continue to roam the earth a hungry ghost?" Mother Kwan pleaded. "I've left offerings of your favorite foods. I've burned incense and cleaned your gravesite." She trembled, "I've brought your wife safely back into this house."

Peilin now knew the real reason for her return. She sat still, hoping to hear more.

"Yao," the old woman muttered, "you'll soon have an heir."

Kwan Taitai smiled proudly to herself. "An heir who will honor you… and honor me," she whispered.

After a while, Mother Kwan fell back asleep. She seemed more at ease. Peilin felt her cheeks—they were still burning. Peilin dipped a cotton cloth into cool water and dabbed her mother-in-law.

Kwan Taitai stirred.

"Daughter-in-law," Kwan Taitai said, recognizing Peilin. "You must remain chaste to your husband, never remarry. Otherwise your ghost husband will haunt you and you'll never have peace."

The more Peilin thought about it the more she rationalized: *Perhaps this was meant to be*. It was her duty to be loyal to the Kwans—to follow what was socially expected. Maybe this is what the Good Luck Lady meant when she talked about the inward eyes—a ghost marriage that bound her to the dark and unseen.

Henri stared into the empty room after accepting the money Ezra had offered. Henri felt dazed but was already beginning to calculate what he'd need to get started.

"Thank you," Henri said and graciously shook Ezra's hand. "You're more than generous. How will I ever repay you?"

"You went out of your way to help us. It's an honor to return the kindness. As Rita often likes to say, 'As the call, so is the echo.' It's an old Russian proverb that reminds me of the *mitzvah*."

Ezra opened a bottle of wine; he offered Henri a glass. The two returned to the couch and sat.

"So tell me, how long have you and the herbal woman been together?"

Henri was taken aback. "You know, too?"

Ezra smiled. "This is a small community. Everyone talks."

Henri lowered his head into his hands.

"Is everything okay?" Ezra asked.

Henri could see that Ezra was sincere. And it was nice to finally have a friend again.

"The herbal woman," Henri began, "is married."

Henri could see Ezra's eyes widen with interest.

"I suppose I feel the same way about her as you do about Rita,"

Henri continued. He heaved another deep breath. "But something has happened—she's left town. She didn't even say goodbye."

"What? Without saying a word?"

It took Henri a few minutes to compose himself before he could speak again.

"Her neighbors told me that she's returned to her in-laws," Henri continued. "And there's a baby."

"Is it—?"

Henri shook his head. "No. We've never—but the fact is she never told me. Now she's gone and it's probably my fault."

"How could that be?"

"I kept a secret from her. I never told her that I helped her brother join the army. She found out the day before she departed."

Henri waited for Ezra to say something, but he provided only his silent reassurance.

Henri slumped over onto the couch.

"I fear I've lost her forever."

A sliver of morning sunlight sliced through a gap in the drapes. Peilin woke with a start. She'd drifted off in a chair near her ailing mother-in-law's bedside. But now Bamboo had returned. With chopsticks in hand, the maid was feeding the old woman hot peppery pork and noodles, one of the matriarch's favorite dishes.

"*Aiii!*" gasped Peilin. "Dear mother, spicy foods are not good for your condition," she advised. "Your body already suffers from an inner furnace. Feeding the fire will only inflame the internal heat and continue to cause you pain."

Peilin sprang to her feet and grabbed the bowl; Kwan Taitai waved her off with a dismissive hand.

"Nonsense," the elder woman chided. "It's what'll make me strong."

Peilin felt a bit of shock. Although she knew that the woman was dying, her strong will and determination fueled up her vigor. Peilin had seen many stubborn people outlive their time. Peilin rose and exited the oppressive room. She knew from Grandpa Du's teachings that fire demanded more fuel. And as the internal flames grew, they would consume a person's rational thoughts. Peilin shook her head, knowing that Kwan Taitai's unruly behavior would only become worse.

Peilin wandered outside toward the lake. Her father-in-law emerged from his work shed. He wore khaki trousers tucked into a pair of tall black rubber boots. He seemed more at ease this morning. Since Peilin had spent the dark hours watching over Kwan Taitai, she guessed that it had freed the servant girl up to spend the night with him. He walked toward her and wiped away the sweat from his brow.

"Ah, Peilin," he addressed. "I've not had a moment's rest since yesterday. I know it's not ideal, but it's good that you're here now. I hope you understand."

Not waiting for a reply, he headed into the house. Peilin hid her disappointment. Since her arrival, she'd had little time to process all that that happened to her. Only a few days ago she was with Henri waiting for the morning train back to the big city. Now she stood before the vast lake, far removed from her Shanghai life.

The empty boat moored at the dock rocked idly. Without thinking, Peilin climbed aboard. She used a rod to shove the vessel out into the water and toward the neatly lined rows of long bamboo poles that marked the freshwater pearl cages suspended below the lake's surface. She found solace away from the house and the Kwans.

She arrived at the first row of oysters and hoisted up the leading cage. Carefully maneuvering the rusted chicken wire overrun with a stringy yellow growth, she pried open the barred enclosure and removed the oyster. It felt slippery and cool. With a sharp knife she scraped away slimy barnacles attached to the shell. Without such cleaning, the oyster could die from these leeching organisms.

With each scrape, the hard shell returned to its smooth, dark surface. Peilin marveled at how such a simple exterior of a seashell could be nurturing a beautiful object such as a pearl inside. She recalled how pearl powder was one of Grandpa Du's most treasured herbs. Through its own protein-rich and iridescent complexion, the nacre renewed skin cells, even those that had been badly damaged by the sun.

Peilin stared out over the lake's still waters. Peering through its depths, she searched for her own reflection. But the murky waters only offered back a vacant shadow. Although she'd convinced herself that her life on Dragon Lake was meant to be, she still felt conflicted inside. Peilin could not shake the lingering thoughts of a different life—sharing her passion for herbal medicine with someone who made her feel alive. She finished the set of oysters and returned the cage back to the lake's cold waters. Perhaps her time in Shanghai was no more than a fleeting phase—an empty illusion.

The guilt of not revealing Ping's whereabouts and the pain of Peilin's sudden departure had caused Henri several sleepless nights. He needed a temporary reprieve to numb the anguish inside. Boosted by Ezra's generosity, Henri plunged into his mission of setting up the new clinic. In a systematic and orderly approach, Henri drew up office diagrams. Initially, it was strange working alongside Ezra and Rita. Henri felt like an intruder in their private space. But as time went on, he felt their acceptance and warmth. Rita's condition steadily improved, giving Henri fresh hope for his practice and plan to combine Eastern and Western medicines. She set a regular dinner plate for Henri and he joined them for dinner. While Ezra and Rita credited Henri for their improvement, Henri felt that he was the person who'd gained the most from their connection.

Ezra kept two homes, one with his wife, and another with Rita in the office. Henri felt it best to give his friend a couple of nights alone with Rita. On those nights, Henri would excuse himself for a walk along the Bund. The warm spring evenings along the river also provided Henri time to himself, time to think. He tried to forget about recent events, but each Asian face reminded him of Peilin. He couldn't help but wind his way down the Chinese *xiao xiang*. There along the familiar street, Henri stopped in front of the herbal shop. With each visit, Henri hoped to see the lights on, the door open, and Peilin's alluring smile. But each visit found him staring into the store's vacant window, and his own empty heart.

19

S HE'D SLIT HER HAND cleaning an oyster. She applied pressure with
the opposite hand, but the blood oozed through the cloth rag.
Peilin struggled; with one hand she paddled the boat to shore. Just as
she dragged the vessel onto the beach, a voice called out.

"I've been waiting for you."

Peilin couldn't believe it. She recognized the wispy sing-song
intonation and glanced ahead. There she was—the Good Luck Lady.
It felt so long since she encountered the wizened woman in Tongsan;
yet it had only been a few days.

"Good Luck Lady," Peilin whispered. "For what fortune do I owe
the pleasure of seeing you here?"

"The world is full of messages... all the time... all the time," the
matron answered. "Everybody draw to them what they need," she
continued. "So I come."

Peilin still wasn't quite sure how the Good Luck Lady came to be
by her side. She wanted to ask more questions, but she was already
feeling faint from the blood loss. That was when the old woman
noticed Peilin's injured hand.

"*Aiii!*" exclaimed the Good Luck Lady. "Must be fix—no time to
waste."

Peilin was too tired to insist that she could manage on her own;
instead she allowed the Good Luck Lady to guide her into the house.

In the kitchen, she sat Peilin down and worked swiftly to wash the cut. Once it was cleansed, the Good Luck Lady applied a poultice made from the *gui jiu* (mandrake) herb. The numbing agent took effect quickly, granting the elder woman time to stitch up the wound. After the cut had been sewn, sleepiness began to overtake Peilin. Peilin laid down and nodded off to sleep, but not before she realized how happy she was to see the kind woman again.

December 1939: It was just over a year since Henri was forced to flee Berlin. The Shanghai Jewish community buzzed ever more intently now with wartime news from abroad. Hitler had announced a formal proclamation to isolate Jews. The ex-pats also heard reports that all European Jews were required to wear a yellow badge with the Star of David. A smuggled Nazi newspaper, *Der Stürmer,* found its way to Shanghai. In it, they read, "The Jewish people ought to be exterminated root and branch. Then the plague of pests would have disappeared in Poland at one stroke." Rumors about death camps were flying. Henri worried about those he had left behind—especially Viktor, Georg, and Otto. Recently, Ezra learned of his brother's official internment; now Henri feared the worst.

So when Henri finally received a letter from Uncle Viktor, he was more than anxious. It'd arrived for him at the dorm. Since he'd moved out last month, it took a while for Henri to learn of its existence.

Henri stood before Ezra holding the open pages. "It was written a couple of months ago in October," Henri told him.

"That's not uncommon. What does it say?"

Henri's voice trembled:

My dearest nephew,

I hope this letter finds you safe and well in your adopted land. Know that you are in our thoughts daily. I've tried to write many times before, but we've vacated the apartment and have been constantly on the move, especially since Hitler invaded Poland. France and England declared war on Germany, but it seems nothing can stop that madman. We're currently living with others. The situation is not ideal, but we're thankful to be alive. Listening to foreign radio has become punishable with a prison term and we're no longer allowed to own radios. Georg and I take care of one another now since Otto's departure for Brazil. South America was not his first choice; he wanted to wait until he had papers for all of us, but we encouraged him to escape while he still had the chance.

Do you remember our neighbors the Steins? Herr Stein was dragged away by the SS late one night nearly two months ago. His wife pleaded with the Gestapo for his release. She was finally told that he had been sent to Buchenwald. Although we're told it's a labor camp, we've heard stories of human experimentation and even extermination. We pray for Herr Stein's health and safe return.

We've been at least spared this tragedy. There are rumors that we'll be forced to move into designated areas, but so far this has not come to pass.

Your former acquaintance Sophie has been in the news. Her family's quite prominent since her brother Gerd's appointment as one of Hitler's key advisors. Sophie's father Roland also serves the Führer. We hear Mr. Schweitzer's knowledge of precious metals and stones have helped the Third Reich attack using funds raised from the jewelry confiscated from Jewish homes.

You may have also heard of another Hitler confidant, Armin Frick. It's rumored that he helped mastermind the Austrian invasion that left thousands of us homeless. This sparked the horrible riots of Kristallnacht—and your need to escape. Frick's engagement to Sophie was just announced. They'll wed this summer.

Henri, I can hardly believe what's happening. In all my life, I never imagined a government that could be so heinous. The nightmare continues to grow darker with each passing day.

Take care and be well, my nephew.

Henri put the letter down.
"What's going to happen to them? To all of us?"

It took a day before her wound stopped hurting and Peilin felt strong enough to return to her duties of tending to Kwan Taitai. Peilin entered the kitchen where the Good Luck Lady was preparing tea.

"*Wah!*" The old woman gasped and ran to Peilin's side. "You not to do much yet. Better you heal."

"But what about Kwan Taitai?" Peilin asked.

"I take care until baby comes," the Good Luck Lady said.

In that moment, it dawned on Peilin that the Good Luck Lady was here to assist the baby's prenatal care and birth. Still, Peilin benefited from the astute woman's presence.

"How's the baby?" Peilin finally asked.

The old lady took her time before she responded.

"The baby grows," she said. "But Bamboo need be more careful, not make bed play like before."

Peilin wondered about the mother, still a girl at fourteen, who didn't have the sense to know that too much sexual activity so late in a pregnancy was foolish and risky.

"Good Luck Lady," Peilin murmured. "So many things have happened. I'm feeling confused."

"When winds blow, churn water," she imparted and escorted Peilin back to her room.

The Good Luck Lady sat Peilin on the bed. She pulled out a hair brush and began to stroke Peilin's hair.

"It's like I'm being pulled under," Peilin explained.

"Ahh, yes. When air gusts create waves, form undertow. Great disturbance. Must still inner turmoil. Calm mind."

The Good Luck Lady finished brushing Peilin's long trusses. Peilin had not worn her hair down since the day of her marriage.

"Use your inward eyes," the old woman encouraged.

There it was again, Peilin thought.

"I don't understand," Peilin admitted. "I don't see ghosts."

"No, not ghost seeing. Inward eyes not literal seeing things," said the Good Luck Lady. "Inward eyes recognize that which cannot be seen. It is seeing with the heart."

Peilin cocked her head, feeling very much at a loss.

"Let me show you," the percipient matron offered.

The old lady searched through the drawer until she found the bronze hand mirror. She held up it up in front of Peilin.

"What you see?"

Peilin shook her head. "I see me."

"No, look again. Look with your heart."

Peilin stared again at her reflection. At first, she didn't see anything distinguishable. But the more she stared, the more she began to notice that she did look different. Not the innocent and married woman from a year ago. As she observed herself beyond her nose, her teeth, and her skin, Peilin detected strength of mind. She turned to the Good Luck Lady, who nodded.

"You see to core of your spirit," the old woman smiled. "Must never forget this."

Peilin looked back into the mirror. This time she saw only her face as she would any other day of the week. The strength she'd tapped into was gone.

"It's not there now," Peilin confessed.

"Don't worry," the Good Luck Lady said soothingly. "It will return. It is getting stronger every day."

The white-haired woman placed the mirror back in the drawer.

Peilin sighed. She wondered if she would ever be able to live in a way that reflected who she felt herself to be inside. Peilin gradually realized that the world was bigger than the physical one before her. Looking inward opened her up to a universe of meanings beyond the physical, beyond the words. It went beyond messages from ancestors and ghosts. It was an unseen feeling. Grandpa Du's words echoed in Peilin's mind—she realized that only with the heart can one see the truth. Truth often dwells beyond what is visible to the naked eye. This was what the Good Luck Lady meant when she talked about seeing the world through inward eyes.

Henri sat alone in his room. Dim lights escaped beneath the door to Ezra and Rita's quarters. Henri still held the letter from Uncle Viktor in his hand. He worried about his family's safety but felt helpless—they were so far apart. While Sophie had been long gone in his mind since arriving in Shanghai, the letter brought back memories and pain—pain that he thought he'd forgotten.

What disappointed him the most was how deeply she'd betrayed him. Now she was marrying a Nazi. Everything that she'd become was despicable to him. He'd let go of yesterday. He'd embraced Shanghai. But it seemed no matter how hard he tried, he was still being tossed by the far-reaching winds of the past. Should he have left Berlin? Perhaps he should've waited for papers to South America, like his brother. So much had been weighing on him lately: choices made, decisions postponed. Either way, they had consequences. Even procrastination created its own chaos. He'd waited too long to tell Peilin the truth, and now he'd lost her. Even with good intentions, Henri had failed again at love.

Four months had passed since Peilin had returned to Dragon Lake. It was now March 1940. Budding green leaves and birds building nests—early signs of spring—emerged around Dragon Lake. Luckily Peilin's hand had healed completely within weeks. She was glad Father Kwan had hired the Good Luck Lady to deliver the baby. Peilin suspected that he wanted to do everything possible to ensure the child's health. As for Kwan Taitai, in addition to her irritable bowels, she now suffered from arthritic pain—making it difficult for her to walk.

Bamboo's belly continued to grow, but the baby wasn't due for another six weeks. So it was a shock to everyone the night the servant came running from her quarters, soaked by fluids that had gushed uncontrollably between her legs.

"Help me," Bamboo pleaded to the old woman.

The Good Luck Lady woke Peilin.

"Her water has broken," the learned woman reported.

Peilin rose quickly from her bed and came to the Good Luck Lady's aid.

"I lay her down, help keep calm," the matron informed. She gazed back to Bamboo. "Are you having contractions?"

The servant shook her head.

"Then we must bide our time," Peilin remarked.

They waited several hours. Daylight broke, but Bamboo failed to go into labor. When it was nearing night again, Peilin and the Good Luck Lady agreed it was time to take action.

"I'll prepare an herbal remedy," Peilin offered, "to help induce the contractions."

"*Aii*… yes," the Good Luck Lady nodded.

Peilin grabbed her herbal bag and headed into the kitchen. The Good Luck Lady gathered as many towels and wash rags as she could find, along with blankets, bowls, cotton, a couple of stools, and rubbing alcohol. Once she had what she needed, the old woman led Bamboo down the hall.

Peilin readied an herbal combination that included *hei sheng ma* (black cohosh), blue cohosh, and red raspberry leaf. Cohosh regulated and strengthened contractions. Red raspberry leaf reinforced the muscles needed to give birth.

Peilin gently poured boiling water over the tea and let it steep. She then placed the cup on a tray and carried the tea down the hall.

A room in the middle of the house was designated for the birth. Kwan Taitai had consulted a feng-shui master many months earlier to ensure the best possible environment for her new grandchild. She'd been told that the center room represented the "bosom" of the house, a space that provided a feeling of security. Per the feng-shui master's instructions, the room had been painted a soft tea green to promote serenity. The birthing bed was positioned against the farthest wall, facing away from the door to avoid *chi* (energy) from escaping. A jade *chi lin* amulet in the shape of a dragon horse was tied to the bedpost with red string to provide protective energy once the new life emerged into the world.

Peilin poured a cup of tea and urged Bamboo to drink. The Good Luck Lady was already applying acupressure to a point halfway between the indentation in the buttocks and the spine. Peilin recognized the spot as a point known to help induce labor. Peilin was surprised to find the room with spectators. Despite her weakness, Kwan Taitai had already made her way into the birthing room with the help of her cane. Father Kwan propped up several chair pillows to ease his wife's discomfort. It seemed odd to have the family gathered around the pregnant girl as if it were a festive banquet. Yet

Peilin sensed that the servant enjoyed being the center of attention. Still giving birth in front of Kwan Taitai had to add uneasiness to Bamboo's already awkward position.

Mother Kwan hovered, hawklike. Father Kwan held his wife's feeble hand. Peilin scrutinized his vigilance for the young woman.

About an hour after Bamboo drank the tea, she felt her first contractions. The Good Luck Lady positioned the pregnant girl at the edge of the bed, her feet propped up on either side by stools.

"Push," the wizened woman coached.

"It hurts," Bamboo wailed.

She cried out in pain as the baby's head tried to force its way into the world. Peilin hurried to Bamboo's side and held her hand. Finding the point between Bamboo's thumb and forefinger, she began to rub the point to further stimulate contractions and encourage the baby's birth. Peilin observed Kwan Taitai squeezing her husband's hand with anticipation. Father Kwan twitched with every scream. Bamboo reached out for him, but Kwan Taitai tugged him toward her.

"Breathe!" continued the Good Luck Lady. "Push down!"

Now shrieking, Bamboo bore down. Harder and harder, faster and faster, they continued to urge the pregnant girl on until the baby's head emerged.

"Again!" said Peilin, who was breathing just as rapidly as Bamboo by this point.

With a final shout, Bamboo gave it all she had. The Good Luck Lady deftly steered the baby from the birth canal and quickly cut the cord.

"It's a boy!" the wise woman announced.

Bamboo sighed with relief; Peilin wiped the sweat from the young woman's forehead. Kwan Taitai faced her husband and clapped with delight.

"A grandson!" she rejoiced.

The baby was premature; Peilin wasn't surprised that he weighed only five pounds. She held her ear close to his mouth to be sure that he was breathing. The Good Luck Lady laid her hand on his chest. He cried out.

"His lungs strong," the matron exclaimed.

Peilin agreed. "He's very lucky."

"Of course my grandchild is lucky," piped up Kwan Taitai.

A sigh of relief escaped Peilin. Had the child been a girl, her mother-in-law would've blamed the Good Luck Lady and possibly even thrown the new mother out on the street. Fortunately, this was not the case.

The caretaker bathed the newborn and placed it in the young servant's arms. Peilin witnessed Bamboo smiling—first at the baby and then toward Father Kwan. Kwan Taitai must have seen it, too, for she rose from her seat and snatched the baby from Bamboo.

"Enough!" Kwan Taitai shouted.

She hobbled a few steps and placed the baby in Peilin's arms.

"Baby belongs with its mother," she retorted. "Not with servant girl."

Peilin was as stunned as the others. The baby cried. Before she realized what was happening, Bamboo lurched and grabbed for the infant. Peilin instinctively retreated.

"The baby belongs to me!" Bamboo wailed. "Father Kwan, you promised. Do something!"

Despite her fragility, Kwan Taitai swung her brass cane and whacked the servant's hands. Bamboo recoiled.

"You silly girl. The driver's packed your things. You're to leave immediately."

"No!" howled Bamboo. "I will not leave Dragon Lake. I will not leave my baby!"

But before she had a chance to reclaim her son, a couple of strong laborers entered and ushered Bamboo out.

Peilin held onto the bawling baby, shielding him from the animosity that filled the air. Bamboo continued to call out to Father Kwan, begging him to fight for her. Although they weren't close, Peilin felt for Bamboo. She knew as a doctor that a woman who's just given birth needed her rest. She also understood how difficult it was to deal with Mother Kwan. Peilin watched as her father-in-law stood motionless, unable to take a stand. Even the Good Luck Lady seemed to turn a deaf ear as the tension mounted. Then, remembering the sage woman's words, Peilin concentrated on seeing with her heart, her inward eyes.

"Husband, come to me," Mother Kwan summoned.

He took his place beside her. Outside, a car motor revved. Peilin could only imagine Bamboo's pain as the car rushed away. Peilin held the baby in her arms. His skin was soft and had a sweet scent. Peilin touched his tiny hands, wiggled his tiny feet. He cooed; his toothless grin made her smile. Although she wasn't his biological mother, she felt an immediate connection to her new son.

The last months had gone by quicker than Henri realized. Rita's health returned with Master Hwang's remedy. Henri had felt nervous when he first accepted Ezra's offer to move in, but over time he and Ezra had become close friends. Because of the war and dwindling supplies, it took a few months to obtain the equipment and provisions he needed to set up his private clinic. Henri reviewed the operation of each apparatus and arranged his supplies so that they were easy to locate. His new clinic was so organized that Henri could maneuver through it with his eyes shut. Luckily, once he was set, he had no trouble drawing steady patients to his practice. And even though he was excited to be venturing out on his own—much like Uncle Viktor had back in Berlin—Henri still sensed a part of himself lost since Peilin and Ping had departed from the city. Without them, Henri felt disconnected from his surroundings.

The warm March day had turned into a pleasant but cool night as

Henri walked briskly through the familiar paths of Shanghai. Except for these nightly strolls, he tended to stay among the Jewish refugees within the Little European area in the Hongkew district.

Henri felt lost without his companions—especially Peilin. He'd formed a deep connection with her, yet he let fear rule him. Instead of telling her where Ping had gone, Henri avoided the truth. She trusted him unconditionally. By keeping the knowledge to himself, he lied to her. He would take it all back in a moment if he could, but it was too late. The guilt weighed heavily. He regretted it all. He was reprehensible, unworthy of her.

He didn't know why, but each night he returned to the *hu tong* and Peilin's vacant store with the vague hope that she'd one day be there again. If she did return, he could at least tell her how sorry he felt. Each visit he'd search for any signs—something to indicate that Peilin might be back. But despite his hopes, he saw nothing change at the store. The door remained locked, the windows boarded. At the very least, seeing the store helped Henri hold a connection to the woman he loved, even if only in his mind.

On this night, however, Henri couldn't believe it when he spied a small slip of paper tucked into a crack in the door. As Henri edged closer to take a better look, thoughts of Peilin raced through his mind. Perhaps it was a letter from her to let him know that she was all right. Without hesitation, Henri plucked the note from the door and unfolded it.

Luckily for Henri, his Chinese was good enough to make out the crude writing. He began to read and realized it was not *from* Peilin, but rather *to* her. His heart quickened.

To sister of Soldier Ping,

I write you to fulfill a promise to my dear friend and fellow soldier. It's with much regret that I must inform you of your brother's untimely death. Only two nights ago, we were ambushed by the Japanese in a ground raid. Know that Ping fought bravely before they robbed him of his life. Be at peace knowing that he died a brave and unselfish soldier in the battle to protect our homeland. Your ancestors will surely welcome him for a battle well-fought to honor the Du family.

By the time Henri had finished reading the letter, tears blinded him. He felt horrified and weak, which was why he did not see the nosy neighbors making their way from across the street.

"Why you come here every night?" Jing-Li asked point-blank. "Peilin is not coming back."

Henri was in no mood for the couple.

"Please," he told them, "leave me alone."

But the prying couple pressed on.

"Note not for you," the man Zhao scolded.

Suddenly Henri's anger flashed.

"How do you know? Did you already read it? The note's certainly not for either of you."

The meddling couple stood their ground.

"You not belong here," the woman scowled. "Give note to us. Now."

Jing-Li attempted to snatch the note. Henri retracted.

"How dare you interfere! This is none of *your* business. You've been snooping around since the day Peilin arrived—prying into our affairs. You must be the ones who prompted the Kwans to come and take Peilin away!"

Jing-Li and Zhao backed away. But Henri continued to shout. Nearly everyone along the narrow alley stopped and watched the ranting foreigner.

But no matter how loud he yelled, Henri's pain continued to swell—his heart tormented by a mixture of anger and sorrow.

20

HENRI SHIFTED IN a creaky wooden seat as the train sped toward Tongsan. The journey felt different this time. Not only was he alone in the crowd, he was changed. How events had shifted since he and Peilin traveled this same route only four months ago. Immediately after finding the note of Ping's untimely death, Henri sought out Ezra's advice.

You must find her—Ezra's words now echoed in Henri's thoughts.

"But how? I don't know where Dragon Lake is," Henri told his friend.

"Then do what's necessary to find it," Ezra counseled. "There're moments in life where you must search farther than you think you can."

Henri had thought about going to see Master Hwang many times, but he didn't have a good reason. Now he did.

Ezra agreed. "Surely the old herbal doctor will know where to find her."

Henri prepared to leave; his good friend quietly handed him some money.

"What's this for?"

"Just in case," Ezra replied. "It's a long journey."

Henri had gratefully put it in his pocket. Although his business was growing, he wasn't sure what to expect; the extra cash might come in handy.

Henri's thoughts then drifted to the faces of the Chens--the nosy neighbors and how they'd stared at him. He felt out of control, defensive, swinging at anything that came his way. Now that he'd had a moment to reflect, he felt the burden of what was really weighing on him—his own guilt.

Could he have stopped Ping from joining the army? He certainly could've refused to sign his medical release. He could've told Peilin about Ping's departure. Instead, he'd signed the papers willingly; he stood as Ping ran off. Now Henri was responsible for Ping's death.

Peilin's biggest fear had come true. She was alone. Her entire natal family—mother, father, Grandpa Du, and her only sibling—were all dead.

Would she ever forgive him? He'd be the last person she'd want to see; he knew it. Still, it was his responsibility to deliver this final news to her. It'd be painful, but better than not knowing, better than being left to forever wonder about her brother's fate. He knew that telling wouldn't erase his guilt, but he owed it to her. Even if Peilin screamed, even if her anger erupted, he needed to accept responsibility for his actions. Hiding from it would only confirm his cowardliness to her.

Sitting on the train, Henri at last admitted to himself—he loved Peilin. Not only had she been a part of his experience of Shanghai, she'd become a part of his life. Since their first meeting, she'd opened herself up to him, shared her herbal knowledge, her home, and her food. When he needed a stronger remedy for Rita, Peilin didn't hesitate—traveling overnight to help Henri get what he needed. She taught him a different way of thinking about medicine. Before China, he'd only had an inkling of what was possible from Uncle Viktor's curiosity about Eastern medicine, but Peilin showed him how nature and balance were key elements for health. She was an integral part of his new growth—introducing him to fresh surroundings, encouraging him to try new foods, taking him to strange places he never knew existed. Then there was the kiss. When Henri thought back to his last days in Berlin and the hurt he felt from Sophie's betrayal, he realized that Peilin had reopened his heart.

How could he have let her down? He'd ignored the balance of yin and yang. He'd avoided the difficult conversation that needed to be had. Henri had overlooked her needs in favor of his own. In the crowded train cabin, Henri touched the vacant seat beside him—its cold emptiness a chastising reminder of his blunders.

Peilin cuddled the sleeping baby, his tiny hands and feet tucked into a blanket to ensure his body's warmth. Although she hadn't given birth to him, Peilin loved her son more and more each day. His body flinched; he began to wake. His large dark eyes fluttered open. She smiled. Born in the year of the Dragon and at Dragon Lake, the baby's lucky double link to the powerful creature was acknowledged in his milk name (nickname): Little Dragon. Informally naming the baby after an animal was an ancient practice; it was believed to scare away evil spirits from harming the child.

It'd been nearly a month since the baby's birth and the Kwan household bustled with activity. Cooks had prepared a multitude of colorful dishes, including a distinctive ginger chicken soup with special tree-eared mushrooms. Banners announcing the new family arrival embellished the walls. Now that the baby was four weeks old, he'd be given an official name at the red egg and ginger celebration. Peilin held Little Dragon while Kwan Taitai, in a bright crimson dress embroidered in gold, passed out scarlet-dyed hard-boiled eggs. Father Kwan made sure their guests had enough wine and tea. There was even *Hong zao* cake, a favorite of Peilin's. The Chinese date continued to fortify her heart. Presents of new clothing and *li shi* (money wrapped in red envelopes) poured in as the visitors welcomed the new Kwan boy into their fold.

Peilin gazed at the baby—her son—in her arms. Earlier she and the Good Luck Lady had dressed him in a tiger hat, tiger shoes, and a tiger bib. The animal was deemed to protect children, especially newborns. The Good Luck Lady had sewn gold, silver, and jade charms onto the hat for good luck. Peilin embroidered large open eyes onto the tiny slippers. They reminded Peilin of Little Dragon's large dark eyes, which gazed at her between naps. By focusing in on her heart's vision, she found her own troubles fading.

On this day, the boy's horoscope was to be cast and his head shaved. Peilin watched as the Good Luck Lady laid out a razor and red fabric on a table set up in the main living room. Kwan Taitai hobbled into the room for the auspicious occasion. The frail woman gripped Father Kwan's arm.

Peilin's mother-in-law coughed to clear her throat. "Just as my son," she whispered to the Good Luck Lady, "you must do for my grandson."

The discerning woman nodded. Peilin knew that as a diviner, the Good Luck Lady's impending declaration of Little Dragon's future was important to the Kwans.

Peilin looked on as the Good Luck Lady pulled out the character signs that formed Little Dragon's official name. There appeared a slight frown on the old woman's face. The Good Luck Lady quickly scribbled another character into Little Dragon's name.

Kwan Taitai noticed the addition, too. "What's that?" she demanded to know.

"Of five elements that form baby's constitution, wood was lacking." The old woman explained. "But no more."

The Good Luck Lady held up Little Dragon's official name, which now included the character for wood. Kwan Taitai leaned in and studied the scroll. After a few moments, she sat back. A satisfied smile spread across her face. Peilin knew that by adding the wood character to Little Dragon's name, the young boy's foundation was now balanced.

"Like his father before him, Little Dragon bears the fortune of a prosperous life full of good health," the Good Luck Lady pronounced.

The time came. The wise woman nodded. Peilin laid Little Dragon's head across the red cloth. She steadied the squirming lad. With gentle and quick movements, the Good Luck Lady picked up the shaver and snipped a swath of the soft dark hair from his scalp. She then wrapped the locks in the red fabric.

The Good Luck Lady held up the hair sachet. "When Little Dragon reach one hundred days, Peilin must take this hair packet and toss into lake. This will make the young Kwan baby courageous throughout life."

Little Dragon screamed out. Peilin cradled him in her arms. In that moment, she made peace with her future in Dragon Lake.

The following afternoon, Kwan Taitai fell ill—a fever consumed her body. Peilin prepared a special lotus root cooler. She cut the fresh, pale vegetable into one-inch lengths. Its cooling energy detoxified the liver and balanced the excess fire energy. She then dropped the lotus root sections in a pot covered with water and added raw barley sugar. After ten minutes, she strained the liquid.

Peilin carried the tea tray into Kwan Taitai's darkened room. Seeing the woman who was known for her blazing strength now lying nearly lifeless on the bed caused Peilin to soften toward her once again.

Peilin poured the tea and held it up to the dying woman's lips.

"Drink," Peilin said softly. "This'll soothe your blood."

The old woman's eyes flashed with a fiery glare. Peilin reared back in shock—causing the tea to spill.

"The ancestors call to me," her mother-in-law murmured. "I'm being pulled to the other side."

She coughed violently; her body shook. Though these were surely her last breaths, she was determined to speak to Peilin.

Kwan Taitai squeezed out a couple of breaths.

"Don't—" she gasped, "forget Yao."

She collapsed. Peilin rushed to her side trying to revive her, but the old woman was gone.

Peilin called in the Good Luck Lady, whose divining duties were needed once again. With her reference books and abacus, she declared the day and hour of Kwan Taitai's passing. As was also time-honored, the wizened woman consulted her books and chose a fortuitous day for the funeral ceremonies—a week from the day of Mother Kwan's death.

Kwan Taitai's body was moved to the ancestral hall for burial preparation. Peilin recalled the first time she had stepped foot into the single twelve-by-twenty-foot room. It'd been her wedding night. That evening she bowed in front of the large carved-wood altar and worshipped the Kwan family ancestors for the first time. Here she took her vows of duty and fidelity to her ghost husband. It was in this room where Kwan Taitai first knocked the ceremonial tea out of Peilin's hands.

Now Peilin bathed the front of Kwan Taitai's body seven times and the back eight times—fifteen times in all during the week—an odd number to ward off evil spirits. She then wrapped her head, limbs, and body in silk. Peilin's eyes teared up. She never had a chance to honor her own mother, father, and grandfather this way. Her only hope was that they'd found peace in the afterworld.

On the day of the funeral, she dressed Kwan Taitai in a gold embroidered dress with the traditional high-collar that the matriarch favored. Peilin took a hemp cord and bound her mother-in-law's feet together. This tradition, Peilin reminded herself, prevented the body from jumping should the recently deceased find herself rebuked by evil spirits in the afterworld. Finally, Peilin wrapped a pearl in red paper and placed it between Kwan Taitai's lips.

And so life to death—the body was placed in a black lacquered coffin that had been purchased from the best local woodworker. All of Kwan Taitai's expensive silk dresses were tucked into the box, along with her jewels. Eight pallbearers, including Father Kwan, placed the heavy coffin on a cart decorated with flowers and a satin canopy. The somber parade of mourners followed the body as it was pulled by horse to the family burial grounds a few miles away. It was a calm, woodsy area, a place for quiet reflection.

Peilin observed Father Kwan's stoic demeanor throughout the funeral. She wondered if he was still in shock or if this was his way of handling grief. He seemed anxious, as if he was nearing the end of a long and enduring wait.

Kwan Taitai was laid to rest next to her son. A spot had been saved next to the old woman for Father Kwan's eventual resting place. As Peilin watched Kwan Taitai's coffin lowered into the ground, she realized that there was another empty space—on the other side of her husband, Kwan Yao. It dawned on Peilin that it was being saved for her, to take her permanent place in the Kwan family cemetery. She shuddered to think that her life had already been planned out right down to her final resting spot.

Lychee candy was given to each guest. The sweet confection was to be consumed by each individual before leaving to prevent evil spirits from following them home. Peilin put the candy in her mouth and sucked on it until it dissolved. With the funeral completed, Peilin resumed her role as Little Dragon's mother. She was fortunate to have the Good Luck Lady's continued help with the baby. Peilin enjoyed his calm and happy demeanor.

Less than a week had gone by since Kwan Taitai's burial when Father Kwan returned home with Bamboo at his side. Peilin caught a glimpse from her room window. Holding the infant, Peilin saw that the servant girl was no longer dressed in thin course cotton. Instead she stepped out of the car outfitted in a bright tangerine-hued cheongsam dress and fur coat. Her hair was now swept up in the fashion of a married woman. Father Kwan held out his hand for Bamboo. The driver removed a large suitcase and followed the couple inside.

Peilin clutched Little Dragon as they entered the living room. No sooner had Bamboo entered than she threw her coat down. She looked to Peilin and Little Dragon.

"My child!"

Before Peilin knew what was happening, Bamboo lunged for the boy and grabbed him out of Peilin's arms. The baby wailed.

Shocked, Peilin turned to Father Kwan. Her father-in-law removed his hat and flashed a rueful smile. "Bamboo is now your new mother-in-law."

Peilin tried to hide the disappointment on her face. Her father-in-law must have sensed it anyway.

"Don't worry. You'll still be the boy's caretaker."

Peilin looked up. "What about the Good Luck Lady?"

"She'll be leaving soon."

Peilin felt a mixture of sadness and contentment. She was not happy about Bamboo's return, but at least she would continue to spend time with the baby.

Henri stepped off the train. He ignored the stares from the Tongsan villagers and he sprinted to Master Hwang's herbal shop.

Master Hwang was sleeping outside when Henri arrived. Henri listened to the old man's gentle snoring before he awoke with a start.

"I've been waiting for you."

Henri was confused. "But how could you've known I was on my way?"

Master Hwang waved his hand in the air; he rose to his feet.

"I felt your energy," the herbalist told Henri. "Like a strong wind blowing up from the south."

Henri shook his head. "I've never heard such a thing. It doesn't seem possible."

"Many things don't seem possible at first glance. It's not until you truly sit with yourself that life's possibilities start to unfold."

The herbal master headed into his shop. Henri followed, not knowing quite what to say.

"You're quite nimble for your age," Henri commented.

The old master stopped. He turned. "How old do you think I am?" he asked.

Henri took a moment to study the herbal master. Henri had observed the bodies of all ages.

"Somewhere around sixty," Henri decided aloud.

Master Hwang smiled. "I'm over one hundred years old."

Henri was again shocked by this man and allowed his expression to show it.

Master Hwang only smiled.

"Tell me now—why have you come today?"

Henri cast his eyes down, feeling the weight of his guilt.

"I need directions to Dragon Lake."

Master Hwang rubbed one hand along his long white beard. Henri felt the herbal master's keen eyes studying him.

"I cannot share that information with you," he replied.

Hearing Master Hwang's words, Henri shrank with defeat.

"You don't understand. I must see Peilin. I need to make amends. I need to—" Henri's words fell short.

Master Hwang held up his hand.

"The Kwans are very private. They're not open to uninvited visitors."

Henri had traveled all that way for nothing. His face must have registered his deep disappointment.

"It's just—" Henri was at a loss for words. "It's just that she trusted me. We'd become very close."

He didn't know what else to say. Silence fell between the two men. Henri couldn't make out the herbal master's frame of mind. He decided to risk sharing the news.

"I've unfortunate news about her brother. There was a note left at her shop back in Shanghai—"

"I see," Master Hwang responded.

Henri felt the comprehending man softening.

"You're in love with her, aren't you?" Master Hwang finally said.

Henri nodded. "More than she'll ever know."

Silence filled the room again. Henri felt exposed. He wanted to flee. Just as he compelled his legs to march toward the door, Master Hwang spoke.

"I understand the great despair that weighs you down." Master Hwang walked over to a desk where he pulled out a sheet of paper. "I'll draw you a map... for love."

Henri's heart quickened with Master Hwang's change of heart. The old man sketched out directions to Dragon Lake. The diagram revealed that the Kwan residence was farther north, near some secluded mountains. The wise man informed Henri he would have to travel by bus until he reached the top. The rest of the way he'd walk. Once Master Hwang was finished, he rolled up the map and handed it to Henri. Henri bowed gratefully. Flashes of anticipation over seeing Peilin again rose inside him. He then felt another concern.

"Master Hwang," Henri stammered. "Is it ever possible for a Chinese woman to remarry?"

The herbal master took a moment to contemplate.

"It's possible but it's not easy. One must first satisfy the ghost husband so that he'll release her."

These were the first encouraging words Henri had heard in a long time.

"How?"

"On your way back through the village, you'll see a store that sells joss sticks and *ming qian*—paper currency for the dead. Ask for lotus sticks. The scent promotes the departed to seek its highest level of spirit."

Henri took notes as Master Hwang continued to describe the items he needed. He wasn't sure if he understood the process, but he had come to trust the old man.

"Also purchase basil scent to improve sympathy between people."

"How much *ming qian* should I buy?" Henri asked.

"As much as possible. Make sure the paper funds bear the red ink seal. The paper cutouts representing money, clothing, and servants are to be burned at Kwan Yao's grave. These offerings are for his use in the heavenly world."

Fruits and nuts were added to the list. Master Hwang then instructed Henri on the proper way to bow and chant.

"Make sure you always face the grave. If you turn your back, you'll anger the spirit."

When he was done, the learned man paused for a moment. "Even though you present the proper ritual, remember this: Peilin has the final choice. The decision to stay or go lies solely within her."

Henri nodded.

"I understand."

After putting Little Dragon to sleep and making sure her new mother-in-law didn't require any teas or other necessities, Peilin was finally able to retire to her room. Since Kwan Taitai's death and Bamboo's return to usurp her role as the new head of the household, Peilin had been relegated to the servant role. Peilin wanted to cry but couldn't let go. If she did, she might feel the full burden of how far she'd fallen. Fortunately the baby gave her comfort, a reason to go on. The unrelenting requests of the others had taken precedence over her own needs; she'd been justifying it all for months. Peilin found the bronze hand mirror and gazed at herself—the first time she'd done so since her conversation with the Good Luck Lady about inward eyes. She almost didn't recognize the person she'd become.

Her small room had grown into a refuge from the chaotic whirlwind of Bamboo's demands. Instead of simple dinners, Bamboo insisted on four-course banquets, even if it was only shared between her and Father Kwan. Previously, Peilin had enjoyed making Little Dragon laugh with silly looks and simple hand games, but Bamboo now required structured readings or full-scale puppet plays, even though he was still an infant. Peilin found it easier to comply than to point out the excess frivolity of it all.

One night, after she had retired to her room, Peilin found a large ceramic ginger vase near her bed. It was decorated with an elaborate array of painted blues depicting a bright full moon shining over the ocean. Peilin lifted the jar and studied the soothing image.

"You like?"

Peilin jumped. She was not expecting anyone. But she recognized the voice of the Good Luck Lady. Although it'd only been a few days, Peilin felt like she hadn't seen the kind woman for some time. The respected matron had gone to help another family with the birth of their child. Now she returned wearing a broad smile. Peilin was happy to see her again.

"Is this your vase?"

The Good Luck Lady nodded.

"For you," she urged. "Take a lookee, see?"

The old woman traced her finger along the water's edge.

"Dreams like the ocean, fluid and deep." She then pointed to the large moon glistening above the water. "When you sleep, nighttime thoughts emerge—visions of your hopes and desires."

The Good Luck Lady turned on a light.

"In light, nocturnal thoughts disappear, mind forgets."

The wise woman sat next to Peilin. Taking the large jar, the Good Luck Lady put her hand inside.

"When you wake up, remember to place your nighttime thoughts inside this vase so as not to forget. This jar help you capture your dreams, remember who you are."

Peilin felt a deep sense of connection to her mentor.

"Once Little Dragon gain enough weight, I leave for good," the woman continued.

"I know. I'll miss you."

"Do not worry. I will be with you still." The Good Luck Lady pointed toward Peilin's temple.

"Inward eyes, remember?"

Peilin smiled. "Yes inward eyes. I know now."

That night, the heavy rains outside induced Peilin into a deep sleep. Thoughts of Bamboo, Little Dragon, and Father Kwan floated away. Instead, memories of Henri flooded her being—sensations she thought long gone reemerged.

After purchasing incense, paper money, and a few provisions, Henri was ready for his journey to Dragon Lake. Per Master Hwang's instructions, Henri boarded the bus headed north. He politely took a seat, now used to the strangers staring. The vehicle climbed the steep dirt roads, Henri closed his eyes. Soon he'd see Peilin again.

The bus stopped several times along the way. Each time, a handful of people would depart and a few more would join the traveling crowd. Henri would nod as they passed by. Then a steady downpour of rain delayed the journey; the bus fought its way through limited visibility and muddy roads. It was not until the next morning when the vehicle finally arrived at his destination. Henri grabbed his belongings. It took a moment for his feet to find their strength on the rain-soaked ground. He looked skyward. Although it was cloudy, there was no precipitation. The bus doors slammed shut; the vehicle roared back down the hill, leaving behind deep trail marks in the waterlogged path. He was the only departing passenger. It wasn't even a village, but merely a point of reference marked by a cluster of willow trees. Henri pulled out the map Master Hwang had drawn and studied the landmarks. The rest of the foot journey to Dragon Lake took him up a windy road.

He headed east. Henri wondered what Peilin's reaction would be when she saw him. Would she see him? Henri erased the thought from his mind. His intention was to make amends.

Master Hwang's diagram marked the Kwan cemetery ahead. Henri could see now see the lake in the distance. His heart beat a little faster, knowing he was nearby.

Deep in a wooded area surrounded by pine trees, the gravesite was a protected by a horseshoe-shaped wall. Henri removed a stick of incense and lit it. Holding the stick in both hands, he stood before the gravesite and bowed deeply. Henri felt a bit ridiculous, but Master Hwang had convinced him of its symbolic significance. More important than what Henri thought was how he could help Peilin. Once he completed the greeting, Henri presented the paper money, before Yao's grave. The *ming qian* felt coarse in Henri's fingers; he folded them into small bundles. Henri lit the incense and spirit money on fire so that it could travel to the afterworld. According to Master Hwang, the burning of the spirit money helped ancestors to purchase necessities and luxuries in the afterlife. He had used up a good portion of Ezra's funds, thankful again for his friend's foresight.

"For your comfort," Henri whispered. "And the humble request for a special favor to release Peilin's fate back to the living."

He then approached the grave with offerings of tangerines and almonds. Closer up, Henri noticed not one but two headstones. He leaned in closer. Henri could read enough Chinese to recognize Kwan Yao's name etched in the stone marker. The other marker however was made of wood. It bore no name. A recent death. Henri's mind flashed with concern—*what if something happened to Peilin?*

Henri was on the verge of panic. Then he heard the crunch of footsteps treading across nearby fallen pine needles. He hid himself behind a large tree trunk. Henri worried that the Kwans or one of their servants had spied him on the hill.

A figure appeared carrying a baby. He quieted his breathing, not wanting to make any sound that would draw attention to his hiding place.

A woman neared the gravesite and Henri's recent offerings. *Could it be? Was it a ghost?* From behind the tree Henri recognized Peilin.

21

PEILIN WALKED ALONG the wooded path near the lake's edge. After the heavy spring rain, the brisk air invigorated her lungs. Little Dragon sat on her hip, a familiar and comfortable position for both these days. His luminous, brown eyes were still too fogged over to enjoy the scenery, but nevertheless, Peilin took delight in his presence. She'd left the house without finding Bamboo to let her know they were headed out, but Peilin planned a quick turnaround and decided to let it go. She wound her way toward the Kwan family cemetery. She'd not forgotten Kwan Taitai's dying words to remember Yao. Peilin carried gifts of apples and walnuts in a small sack. Now that her first mother-in-law was dead, it was up to Peilin to watch over the gravesite and ensure that neither her husband nor Mother Kwan were lacking in offerings to keep them comfortable in the afterworld. With Father Kwan attending to the extravagant whims of his new wife and their growing family, Peilin alone cared for their ancestors.

When Peilin arrived at the family cemetery, she was stunned to smell the recent scent of musk. As Peilin glanced around she found several red joss sticks still burning. Next to the incense were tangerines and almonds. There was also black soot—evidence of burnt paper offerings. These offerings were recent—but they weren't hers. *Where did they come from? Had Father Kwan made a surprise visit?*

Peilin hugged Little Dragon tighter; she glanced around. At first, she didn't see the figure in the shaded area between the tall pine trees, but as her eyes adjusted to the dimness she recognized him. It was Henri.

She gasped. So many emotions ran through her simultaneously—excitement, anger, and fear.

"Is that really you?" Peilin asked.

Henri emerged from the shadows.

"It is."

For a moment, Peilin was at a loss for words. Silence filled the air between them. Then Henri took a step forward.

"Is this your baby?"

"The servant girl was pregnant. The baby was to be mine—but circumstances have changed." Peilin sensed Henri's anxious confusion abate somewhat. Still, she, too, had questions.

"How did you get here—why—" Peilin didn't know where to start.

"Master Hwang—" Henri began. "I went to him. At first, he wouldn't tell me the way. But when he realized how much I cared for you—" Henri's voice trailed off.

Peilin recalled their last time together—the kiss in Tongsan, their return to Shanghai, the note from Ping.

"How can you say you care about me," Peilin wondered aloud, "after helping Ping join the army when you knew I was against it?"

She noticed Henri's hand trembling.

"You're right about that," Henri admitted. "That's why I had to find you. I'm so sorry for everything that's happened."

Henri pulled out a crumpled note and handed it to her.

"I came to try and make amends. I understand that you're still upset with me, but I needed to give this to you."

"What is it?" Peilin asked, not sure if she should be wary or relieved.

"It was tucked in your doorjamb back in Shanghai," Henri explained. "It's about Ping."

Hearing her brother's name, Peilin unfolded the note and began reading. She clutched the baby at her side. But as the news of Ping's death penetrated her heart, Peilin felt herself crumble.

"No!" she heard herself scream. "Not Ping—not him, too!"

Peilin couldn't stop shaking. She felt Henri take a hold of her in that moment. She was too devastated to resist. He held on tight as Peilin wailed in her sorrow. Little Dragon started to cry, too.

"I'm so sorry," she heard him whisper. "I know how alone you must feel right now," he murmured. "While I can't bring Ping back, I was hoping... "

Henri stopped midsentence. Concerned, Peilin looked up at him through her bleary eyes.

"I spoke to Master Hwang—he told me what to do," Henri said rapidly. "I've been praying and sending offerings, see?"

Henri pointed to the ground where Peilin had previously noticed presents of fruits and nuts, as well as the burnt paper money and incense. Peilin realized it was Henri who'd bestowed the gifts to her ancestors.

"You can be free... to make a choice," he continued in his hurried speech.

Peilin was confused. She wasn't quite sure what Henri was talking about. She stared at him, unable to take it all in.

"I don't understand," she whispered.

Henri hesitated a moment, as if gathering courage. He faced her.

"Peilin, will you marry me?" he blurted.

It took Peilin a moment to realize what he had asked.

"What are you saying?" Peilin heard herself murmur. She stepped back.

"First you bring me a note about Ping's death. Now you're asking me to marry you?"

"I know this all must seem sudden, but I've been doing a lot of thinking," Henri said trying to reassure her. "Peilin, I—I love you."

Peilin didn't know how to respond. Little Dragon let out a squeal. "I must get the baby home," she stammered.

"But what about us?"

Peilin's mind was spinning.

"I can't—I can't—" she said and stumbled back down the dirt path.

All Peilin could think about was getting away. She hurried toward the Kwan residence and heard Henri call out again.

"I'll wait for you right here."

Henri watched Peilin's figure disappear down the muddy path. He realized too late that he'd frightened her with all the information. He hoped that allowing her some space would help her process it all. He had time. After all, according to Master Hwang, Henri needed to perform more rituals to honor and appease Peilin's ghost husband.

Realizing that he'd be spending the night in the woods, Henri searched the nearby area until he found a small alcove for temporary shelter. Henri wasn't sure if it'd rain again, and the dampness from the earlier showers already added a chill to the air. Wisely, Master Hwang had insisted that Henri pack a blanket, tarp, and some provisions for the journey. Henri found a dry area in the cave and laid out his belongings.

He wasn't sure how long it'd take for his prayers and offerings to be accepted by those in the afterworld, so he was actually calmed to have additional time by the gravesite. He didn't believe in ghosts, but if the rituals helped to release Peilin from her obligation to the Kwan family, he'd pray and burn incense as long as it took.

Henri's thoughts drifted back to Peilin. Perhaps his talk about freedom and marriage were too much and too soon. After all, Henri had had time to process Ping's death. She had not. A large mossy rock provided Henri with a resting spot. He sat. He'd been in China now for nearly a year and a half. Before Shanghai, Berlin was the only other place he'd ever known. Henri had grown to embrace his temporary Asian home. But what would happen when the war ended? Would he be able to return to Germany? It'd been a long time since Henri had seen Uncle Viktor. He worried that the hardships of the last few years had taken a toll on his uncle's health. Not only had Viktor been more of a father to Henri than Georg, but he'd been the first to introduce Henri to the Chinese herbal medicine. It occurred to Henri that Uncle Viktor would like meeting Peilin. But would Peilin agree to leave China? There were still so many unanswered questions. What Henri most yearned for was roots—a family and a place he could finally call home.

Peilin took several shortcuts through the wooded terrain as she hurried back home. At one point, she had to double back when a downed tree trunk, probably hit by lightning the night before, blocked her path. Little Dragon was now hungry, which added to his discomfort. Peilin felt her own distress over Henri's appearance, marriage proposal, and news of Ping's death. Her mixed emotions filled her with anxiety. It was hard for her to feel excitement at seeing Henri once again. She was still very angry at him. Because of Henri's actions, her only brother was now dead.

Even Peilin's cooing could not soothe Little Dragon's wailing. By the time they reached the Kwan house, he was exhausted. Peilin had planned to dash inside where she knew she could find a bottle of milk. But they were met outside by a very stern-looking Bamboo, who snatched Little Dragon away.

"Where've you been?" Bamboo demanded. "I've been worried sick. How dare you take Little Dragon without telling me!"

Peilin bowed her head. "I took him for a walk. I'm sorry if I worried you."

Bamboo held a bottle of milk and immediately fed the hungry child.

"You're *not* Little Dragon's mother," Bamboo reminded Peilin.

Peilin knew that was the reality, but emotionally she felt that bond to the boy.

"I know," Peilin replied. "It's just that—I thought you wouldn't mind."

As soon as she had spoken the words, Peilin realized it was the wrong thing to say.

"Thought I wouldn't mind? My son must always know that *I'm* his mother."

Peilin didn't know what to say. Of course, she knew this, but still, if she had to live out the rest of her life here at Dragon Lake, raising the child was one of her sole pleasures. While Bamboo embraced Little Dragon, Peilin walked back toward the house. Bamboo called out to her.

"As punishment for my worry, you're confined indoors until further notice."

Peilin turned and stared at the young girl who'd gone from servant to wife in a few short weeks.

"That's right, you heard me," Bamboo continued, "you're forbidden to leave."

Henri continued to wait for Peilin's return, determined not to depart until he had an answer. Because he had no idea how long he would be staying, Henri had already eaten the extra tangerines he had brought with him by the afternoon. By the end of the day, he was hungry. He dared not touch the nuts and fruit he'd already offered to Peilin's dead husband. He forged out into the wooded area, hopeful that he could find some berries with the new growth of spring. He was careful to make a mental note of the path he took, so as to be sure to find his way back. When no berries surfaced, he headed down to the lake for a drink of water.

Henri guessed that Dragon Lake was about fifty square miles across its smooth placid surface. Relatively small, the fresh waters were surrounded by tall limestone hillsides that jutted toward the sky. A layer of fog had begun to settle in, giving the panoramic view an almost mystical appearance. Master Hwang had mentioned that the Kwans owned not only the lake but all the land surrounding it for as far as the eye could see. Henri looked around and spotted a rocky islet shaped like a dragon's head—probably the inspiration behind the lake's name.

He peered into the water. Thirsty, he cupped his hands and dipped them into the cool liquid, spotting some small fish beneath the surface as he did so. Food—but how could he catch them? He then remembered the small piece of dried meat Master Hwang had insisted he take with him. Henri dug into his pocket and ripped off a leathery chunk. He then took off one of his shoes. Removing the lace, he tied it around the dried meat. He lowered the bait into the water. As the meat softened, fish began to nibble. Henri carefully immersed his empty shoe behind the fish but they quickly swam away. After nearly an hour he still hadn't caught a single one. Frustrated, he nearly quit, but after many more attempts, he finally caught five. He then gathered tinder and started a small fire and the roasted fish satisfied his hunger.

He returned to the gravesite at the top of the hill. It was the first time he noticed that the private cemetery sat on a slope facing the lake. At the foot of the large granite headstones etched with Chinese characters, he placed more paper money in both stone altars, not wanting to offend either of the deceased. He lit the offerings and incense again, noticing as he did so that his anxiety over Peilin decreased. When night came, he huddled in the alcove. Gray clouds had gathered overhead and Henri worried that it might rain again. A chill from the damp ground underneath seeped through the tarp; he pulled the thin blanket around him.

The early morning outburst of rain caused Henri to huddle in the rocky recess as he tried to keep dry. Once it stopped, Henri spent the second day much like the first. Whenever he heard a sound, he turned, expecting to see Peilin. But he was only disappointed time after time. When the second night approached with no sign of her, he collected brown pine needles and laid his tarp and blanket on top. The gathered needles formed a layer of insulation. Curled up with his blanket wrapped tightly around him, Henri blew warm air through his clenched fist and fell into a fitful sleep.

When Peilin failed to appear by midafternoon the third day, Henri felt nearly panicked. He repeated the rituals once again, hopeful that each cycle would help bring Peilin back to him. Henri didn't want to admit it, but he was starting to despair. He'd spent the last seventy-two hours hungry and cold and braving the outdoors, in close proximity to the woman he loved, yet farther away from her heart than ever.

He thought more about their recent exchange. He'd definitely come on too strong, too fast. She wasn't expecting him. And then within moments of seeing her, Henri had unveiled his deep feelings of love and news about Ping in practically the same breath. No wonder she took off so suddenly. Hadn't he signed Ping's papers knowing it would upset her? Hadn't he withheld information about her brother's departure knowing she was against it? She wasn't in love with him. She was angry. She fled Shanghai, didn't she? She'd returned here to live with her in-laws. And she was caring for a baby she obviously loved. What more did Henri need to finally understand that she was done with him? Henri hung his head in the knowledge that his long trip to Dragon Lake and his foolishness in assuming she would want to be with him were all in vain.

The awareness sank in; Henri buried his face in his hands. He had his answer long before he'd started this journey. She wasn't coming back.

Still restricted to the house, Peilin worried that Henri was going to starve and freeze to death in the rugged outdoors. Each night she went to bed but couldn't sleep, feeling guilty that she was warm and dry while he was out in the cold waiting for her return. It'd been three days. What if Father Kwan discovered him hiding there? The Kwans weren't used to visitors. Worse, Henri had arrived uninvited. Without her there to explain, Peilin feared Father Kwan might order his servants to inflict harm on him. Yet she dared not say a word to anyone. For the moment, all she could do was sit out her confinement until she could figure out what to do. She didn't know how to handle his arrival. She was still reeling from her conflicting emotions—particularly surrounding the news of Ping's death. Peilin couldn't take in Henri's proposal after such devastating news. In a way, Peilin welcomed her internment to the house. It gave her an excuse not to address Henri immediately. However, as the days continued, she knew, as stubborn as he was, Henri wouldn't wait forever.

Peilin sat out her confinement inside her small bedroom. She felt stuck, trapped in her confusion. So far Bamboo hadn't lifted her ban and Peilin hadn't seen Little Dragon.

Since Henri appeared, Peilin hadn't eaten. She wasn't hungry. So when the Good Luck Lady brought in a steaming bowl of won ton soup, Peilin feebly sipped its broth.

"Why you not eat?" the old woman gently scolded.

Peilin knew that the Good Luck Lady was only looking out for her health.

"I haven't been feeling well."

The compassionate woman felt Peilin's forehead, studied Peilin's tongue.

"Not physical."

"I've a lot on my mind," Peilin admitted.

The Good Luck Lady took another glimpse at Peilin. She peered deep into her eyes.

"You lovesick."

Peilin felt the shiver of being exposed run through her core, yet she continued to hold onto her self-denial.

"I'm confused," Peilin insisted.

The Good Luck Lady sat silently by her side. After a while, Peilin felt the need to share her heavy burden.

"Henri's here," Peilin confessed.

Peilin wasn't sure how the old woman would react to such information, but she only nodded knowingly.

"Ah, yes. Man from Tongsan. Where is he?" the Good Luck Lady replied, glancing around the room.

"Not here," Peilin corrected, "at the cemetery. He was making offerings to Yao."

The Good Luck Lady said nothing.

Peilin felt her lips tremble, her heart pound.

"My brother—Ping—"

She swallowed hard.

"He was killed—fighting for the Kuomintang."

Tears cascaded down her cheeks as she heard herself say the words for the first time.

The Good Luck Lady took the weeping Peilin into her arms.

"*Nah, nah, nah,*" the kind woman cooed. "A life eclipsed too soon."

Peilin dissolved into the Good Luck Lady's embrace. After a few moments of silence, Peilin caught her breath.

"That's not all," Peilin whispered.

The Good Luck Lady gently stroked Peilin's hair.

"It's okay," the old woman replied. "Take time."

Peilin nodded. It helped to share her dilemma.

"He asked me to marry him," Peilin blurted. "He's making offerings—he wants Yao to release me." Peilin drew in another deep breath. "Wasteful energy, don't you think? Not to mention how angry I am at him for helping Ping join the army."

Peilin lifted her head and looked to the Good Luck Lady. The matron remained quiet for what seemed like a long time.

"Hen-ree force Ping to join army?" the old woman asked.

Peilin shook her head. "No. Ping wanted to fight. Henri signed his medical release."

The Good Luck Lady nodded. "Why did he sign Ping's papers?"

"No one else would," Peilin answered. "Ping suffered from injuries as a young boy."

Peilin noticed the Good Luck Lady rub two fingers along her chin.

"So Ping follow his need to honor family," she concluded.

Peilin nodded. After a short time, the Good Luck Lady took Peilin's hand in her own.

"Sadness, yes," the soft-spoken but astute woman agreed. "But anger, no." The Good Luck Lady smiled. "Hen-ree friend to your brother, help Ping to follow his path."

For the first time in days, Peilin felt her stagnant thoughts start to break up.

"Whatever is to happen," the Good Luck Lady continued, "your forgiveness must first clear the way. Look with your inward eyes— don't you see?"

It took a few moments for Peilin to realize what the Good Luck Lady was saying. She searched inside herself for an answer.

"Even if I can forgive him, I cannot leave this house," Peilin told her. "He is waiting for an answer."

"Write to him," the wise woman nodded. "I will deliver your message."

22

THE GOOD LUCK LADY left so Peilin could compose her note to Henri. For a long time, Peilin stared at her ink pad, brush, and paper, unsure of how to begin or what to say. It took several starts, which were promptly discarded, before she finally found a way to begin.

Dear Henri,

Because I'm currently confined to the house, this letter comes to you by way of a trusted ally. To answer you, I must first provide some background information. Last fall, Father Kwan made a surprise visit to me in Shanghai. My in-laws had growing concerns about heirs—grandchildren to carry on the Kwan family name and to continue to honor the ancestor graves. He informed me of Kwan Taitai's plan for a baby to become mine. I was to leave Shanghai and return in seven months. At that time, I'd known you for about six months. I enjoyed our time together and feared if I told you of my in-laws' plan for me, you'd disappear from my life. So instead I selfishly continued our friendship, without telling you of my impending departure. I believed I had time and that as the date grew closer I'd tell you.

But the day we returned from Tongsan, Father Kwan appeared—unannounced and five months early. Kwan Taitai was very ill. All my things, including my herbs, were packed that night. I had no opportunity to tell you goodbye.

Peilin wanted to stop writing, but she knew she needed to press on until she'd addressed all his concerns. She dipped her brush into the ink once again. Peilin fought back her tears, but she found the resolve to continue. She wiped away strands of hair that swept over her eyes.

Regarding my brother, I was angry. I felt betrayed by you. But now that I've had some time, I finally understand your reasons. You were a friend to my brother when he had no one else. You were only trying to help him fulfill his wishes. Please accept my forgiveness.

Peilin drew in a deep breath. She placed her brush on the table. Her hand was starting to tire. Yet she had to continue. She picked the brush up again, even though she could feel more tears welling up.

I do not understand Master Hwang's instructions to you regarding your offerings at the gravesite. I'm bound by my natal family's promise to the Kwans. It was my Grandpa Du who arranged for my betrothal to Yao. Even though my husband is dead, I'm still obligated to the Kwan family— father-in-law, his new wife, and their baby.

Peilin was now openly crying. She could barely see as she composed her final thoughts.

Regretfully I must turn down your marriage proposal.
—Peilin

The Good Luck Lady returned several hours later. By that time, Peilin had cried her eyes dry. She handed over the note and told the Good Luck Lady where to find Henri.

"Please give him my best," Peilin whispered.

The Good Luck Lady nodded and proceeded out the door. Just as she was headed up the wooded path toward the cemetery, she was intercepted by Father Kwan.

"What's that in your hand?" he inquired.

"Note," the Good Luck Lady answered. "Make delivery for Peilin."

"Deliver it where?"

"To grave," she told him. "Man waits for Peilin's answer."

Father Kwan beckoned the Good Luck Lady closer.

"Let me see it."

The old woman did as she was told. Father Kwan opened the letter and read. He folded it back up.

"Go back to the house," he told her. "I'll deliver the letter to this Henri myself."

Henri returned from the lake again with several more fish to cook. Glad that there'd been no further rain, he was huddled near his campsite when he heard the crackle of footsteps nearing. Anxious, he jumped to his feet and headed toward the path. Expecting Peilin, Henri was surprised instead by an older man wearing Western clothes. Henri assumed it was Peilin's father-in-law. After a few moments, the two men stood face-to-face. Henri wondered if he was going to be asked to leave. The elderly man said nothing but instead bowed. Henri bowed back. Father Kwan then held out a slip of paper. He nodded for Henri to take it.

Henri unfolded the thin paper, curious to find out what it said. It was from Peilin. At first Henri was surprised to learn that she had been confined to the house. Since she didn't explain why, Henri wondered if she was sick. He wanted to ask the old man, but seeing Father Kwan kneeling before the two graves made him turn back to the letter. He continued to read; his heart sank. Despite all his efforts to appease Peilin's deceased husband, she still belonged to the Kwans.

Henri felt his eyes well up. The loss was crushing. He turned away, not wanting Father Kwan to see him weep. Not since his mother's death had Henri felt such pain. He wanted to shout, but his anguish stuck in his throat. Henri felt his body shudder in grief.

He folded up the note and slipped it in his pocket. He surveyed the woods that had been his home for the last three days, unsure of what to do next. Father Kwan was in a deep meditation in front of his first wife and his son's grave. Standing with his hands folded, Father Kwan began a series of bows. The steady rhythm and simplicity mesmerized Henri. Father Kwan's movements were somewhat reminiscent of his own attempt to honor the dead, but the older man's gestures seemed to embody a deeper sense of reverence, reminding Henri of his own connection to those he had lost. Without saying a word, Henri joined Father Kwan.

The two men bowed in unison. After a while, Father Kwan stopped. Kneeling down, he cleared away the weeds, leaves, and mud that had accumulated around the family cemetery. Henri followed, brushing away the debris as well. Once the area was clean, Father Kwan took out a long red string and tied it around Yao's gravestone. Henri looked on as the old man laid the string down in a straight line. He wondered if this was some sort of father-son bonding ritual. Henri continued to watch while Father Kwan pulled out several sheets of mock paper money, similar to the ones Henri had offered at the gravesite earlier. The elder man folded one in half and handed it to Henri. Taking another and folding it for himself, Peilin's father-in-law then slipped the red string through the fold. He motioned for Henri to do the same. Henri wasn't quite sure what was going on, but he continued to follow Father Kwan's lead. In Henri's other hand, the man placed an incense stick. Henri wanted to ask questions, but worried that speaking aloud might disrupt whatever Father Kwan was trying to accomplish. As Henri stood in front of Yao's marker, Father Kwan pulled out two large cleavers from a tool belt strapped around his waist. Henri lurched back at the sight of the sharp knives; Father Kwan lifted them into the air and banged the two blades together. The loud clanging broke the peaceful silence. Peilin's father-in-law started reciting an incantation of some sort. Henri strained to make out the words, but their meaning was lost on him. Then, with a swift whack, Father Kwan swung the cleavers, cutting the red string inches in front of Henri's fingers. He swung again, this time cutting the string in front of himself.

Henri wondered at the significance of Father Kwan's actions. But based on his calm demeanor, he knew it wasn't an attempt to chase him away.

Father Kwan then pulled out a black, ceramic bowl. He dropped the string, paper money, and incense inside; he motioned for Henri to do the same. Henri watched as the elder man walked a few feet away and lit the bowl's contents on fire. Henri was surprised at how quickly it dwindled. He stood silently by Father Kwan's side listening to the snapping sounds of what remained in the bowl. The sweet aroma of the sandalwood incense filled the air. Smoke rose upward. Henri trembled over his own transitory connections as he witnessed the bowl's contents transform to ash.

Peilin could not stop thinking about Henri and the Good Luck Lady. Even without being there in person, Peilin could sense his disappointment when he read the letter. She hoped the Good Luck Lady would find a way to ease his pain, just as she'd done so many times for Peilin. Forgiving Henri helped Peilin release her anger and renew her affection for him. She bit her lip to keep herself from crying out.

Knowing she'd never see him again was bittersweet. Although their time together had been brief, it felt like a lifetime.

Peilin recalled how Ping had first introduced her to Henri. Ping—now gone forever. A wistful sadness swept over her. Without his body, she had no way to give her brother a proper burial. His spirit roamed the earth a hungry ghost—lost and uncared for. Peilin needed to find a way to help his soul find peace.

It wasn't long before Peilin heard the door open. The Good Luck Lady had returned. The old woman removed the scarf from around her head and laid it on a nearby chair. Peilin wondered how she could've made it all the way to the cemetery and back in such a short time. She anxiously greeted her messenger.

"Was he there? How is he?" Peilin asked nervously.

"Not know," the old woman told her. "Not go."

"But I thought—what happened? Where's the note?"

The Good Luck Lady sat. Peilin studied her face for clues.

"I go," the woman began to explain. "Then Kwan Father stop me. Read letter."

Hearing the turn of events, Peilin sat down, too. Her mind took her thoughts in many directions at once, each with a dreadful outcome.

"He read my letter?"

The Good Luck Lady nodded.

Peilin felt shattered knowing that Father Kwan had read her private communication to the man she loved. Yet she didn't know what to do, too exhausted to be upset.

"What happen now," the Good Luck Lady whispered, "is up to fate."

Once the ashes had cooled, Henri watched as Father Kwan tossed them into the air. A gentle wind scattered the remains over the ground. Henri was reminded of the cycle of life—"*Asche zu Asche, Staub zu Staub* (Ashes to ashes, dust to dust)."

Henri still wasn't sure about Father Kwan's intention, but he sensed something larger than either of them was taking place. Although neither had said a word to one another, Henri felt Father Kwan's actions spoke a language that went beyond everyday conversation. And aiding Peilin's father-in-law in what felt like a time-honored tradition gave Henri a sense of connection not only to Father Kwan but to the universe beyond. Henri felt oddly at peace.

With the ceremony apparently over, Father Kwan gathered his coat, knives, and ceramic bowl. Peilin's father-in-law then wandered back down the path. Unsure of his own next move, Henri stood watching. He'd spent so much time waiting that it was hard to believe it was now time to go. He hadn't prepared himself for the possibility that he'd leave Dragon Lake without Peilin.

Unexpectedly, Father Kwan motioned for him to follow. Perhaps the elder man was guiding him out of the woods so that he could find his way back to the city. Henri decided to abandon his sleeping gear and hurried to catch up.

They maintained their silence. After a brisk walk, they arrived at a large dwelling along the lake's edge. Henri assumed he was to continue down the path along the side of the house. He was about to part ways when Father Kwan turned and held up his hand.

"Stop. Wait here," he instructed Henri.

Henri stood motionless by the wooden gate. It was the first time Father Kwan had said a word to him, so Henri was careful to remain in the spot designated by this enigmatic man. Henri still had no idea what Father Kwan was up to, but he'd grown to have faith in the unknown.

Peilin heard Father Kwan's heavy footsteps as he entered the house. He called out to the Good Luck Lady. Peilin kept herself hidden in her room, but she eavesdropped, hoping to hear something about Henri.

"Find Peilin and escort her outside," her father-in-law commanded. "She's to leave for good."

Peilin couldn't believe what she was hearing. She opened her bedroom door and surreptitiously observed Father Kwan disappear down the hall. A few moments later, the Good Luck Lady appeared.

"Peilin," the kind woman said. "Pack most precious things. Then follow me."

It was all happening so fast that Peilin found herself too startled to ask questions; she did what she was told. Surveying her sparse belongings, Peilin grabbed a few articles of clothing and stuffed them into her suitcase. She found her herbal bag and hastily searched for the bronze mirror. Glancing at her reflection, she perceived the fear and sadness swirling inside her. Just as she was about to dash out, she remembered the pearls Father Kwan had given her. She scooped them out of her dresser drawer.

With her suitcase packed once more, Peilin trailed behind the wise woman. Without looking up, Peilin knew that they were headed for the wooden gate—the entrance to Dragon Lake. Knowing that her father-in-law had read her letter and discovered her feelings for Henri, Peilin believed she was being banished. She guessed that Father Kwan was so angry that he refused to see her out; he'd enlisted the Good Luck Lady to do his dirty work instead. But as they neared the gate, Peilin looked up to find Henri standing there.

"Henri—" she heard herself utter. "What're you doing here?"

Her heart pounded. She wasn't sure if she should be happy or sad. Henri took her into his arms.

"Your father-in-law brought me here. I had no idea—after he handed me your letter, he performed some sort of ritual cutting a long red string that he'd attached to Yao's gravestone."

Peilin looked into Henri's eyes. She could see he was holding back tears.

"He recited some sort of chant," Henri continued. "He needed help, so I held the string for him—but I could only touch the paper money surrounding it."

Peilin gasped.

"What?" Henri asked.

"My father-in-law was performing a ritual usually held in the ancestors' hall. But in this case he performed it at the gravesite."

"Why would he do that?"

Peilin's eyes grew with recognition.

"Father Kwan has released me from my ghost marriage."

"But that's what I was trying to do."

Peilin nodded. "But only a father-in-law has the true authority."

She smiled at him and turned around, searching for the Good Luck Lady. But she must've known and returned inside the house.

"Stay right here," Peilin told Henri. "I'll be right back."

Peilin rushed inside, but the Good Luck Lady was nowhere to be found. Peilin continued down the hall. As she entered her room, Peilin found the old woman.

"You forget vase," the Good Luck Lady said, holding up the blue pottery.

"Yes," Peilin nodded, gently taking the dream jar out of the kind woman's hands.

"How could I? I can't leave without this," Peilin said, rubbing the smooth ceramic. "It means so much to me… just like you."

The Good Luck Lady took Peilin by the hand. "I not forget."

Peilin smiled at her mentor and confidante.

"When I heard my father-in-law tell you that I was to leave, I thought he was turning his back and punishing me," Peilin murmured, "but that's not the case, is it?"

The Good Luck Lady shook her head. "Only want you happy."

Tears began to cascade down Peilin's cheeks.

"But why?"

The Good Luck Lady stroked Peilin's shiny hair.

"Suppose you born—told you were weed," she began. "You learn bending—not take up much sun. You eat not much so to not take from flowers nearby. But each time flowers bloom—hard for you to be weed."

Peilin nodded in recognition as the wise woman continued.

"When breeze arrive, you feel stirring. One day someone walk in field. He sees you. He shout, 'What lovely flower!' First, you not believe him. But more you look at self, more you see, too—you not weed—you flower."

Peilin nodded as she wiped away her tears.

"Whenever I'm with Henri," she revealed, "I feel that stirring... I feel my heart opening."

The Good Luck Lady was now beaming.

"And he see you... see true essence."

Peilin smiled. "Yes," she murmured.

"But know," the gentle mentor continued, "whether or not Henri is with you, you've always been that flower."

23

Peilin was still in shock. At first she thought her father-in-law was turning his back on her. She never imagined he'd release her from the Kwan family. He'd bestowed a rare gift. In the secluded hills of Dragon Lake, her role as wife and daughter-in-law bound her to duties, customs, and ascribed family rankings. She was obliged to devote her energies to others. Now, she was free to pursue her herbal medicine—and her own happiness.

She turned back. Her father-in-law was nowhere to be seen. She entered the house once more and called out, but no one answered. Not even Bamboo or Little Dragon. The living quarters were completely empty. Peilin sensed that Father Kwan was too proud to say goodbye. Bamboo was probably glad. She purposely prevented Peilin from saying farewell to the baby she had loved and cared for.

For a moment, Peilin felt an overwhelming sadness. Once again, she wasn't able to say goodbye to her family. But as she walked back outside, Peilin realized that when she arrived at Dragon Lake, Yao was already dead. She was obligated to the Kwan family, but they weren't really her kin.

Even though she loved Henri, she was on her own now. She stood tall and felt her own strength. The Good Luck Lady had been right—she was that flower.

It'd been a long and emotional day. She and Henri barely made it down the hill in time to catch the overnight bus for the one-hundred-and-eighty-mile trip back to the nearest village. By daybreak, they reached the Tongsan train station and found two seats in the crowded locomotive cabin. In four hours, they'd be back in Shanghai. She glanced out the window. As the morning sun rose, she could see that they were still winding their way through outlying farms and villages. She'd been confined to Dragon Lake for nearly six months; she was now anxious to be among the enormous buildings, bustling streets, and hawking vendors once again. It comforted Peilin to hear the cacophony of noise onboard the train. She could already feel herself reawakening to the freedom of the big city.

Peilin gazed at Henri by her side. He smiled and took her hand in his. She dipped her head shyly as he moved closer. Before she realized what was happening, he gently lifted her chin. He bent down and kissed her. She gave into his open affection, realizing they no longer had to conceal their feelings.

"I'm sorry," he whispered. "I'm sorry for not telling you about Ping sooner."

Hearing Henri, Peilin gave into her own sadness.

"I'm sorry, too. I should've told you about the Kwans' plans to take me back to Dragon Lake to raise Bamboo's baby as my own. I grew to love Little Dragon—" she felt herself choke up. "But I know he'll be well attended to by his mother."

Peilin felt Henri's finger on her lips as he attempted to comfort her.

"Of course," he murmured, "he'll be more than fine."

Henri put his arm around her.

"The important thing is we're together now."

It dawned on Peilin that this was the first time they were in public as a real couple. Their relationship was no longer forbidden. She glanced and noticed a toothless woman nudging her sleeping husband. Peilin detected a slight nod in her direction as the man awakened. He cast a disapproving glance. Peilin turned away. No matter what people thought of them as a couple, Peilin knew she could survive with Henri at her side.

Henri must have also caught sight of the wary man and his wife. "Once we marry, what would you say to living in Germany?"

"Germany?" Peilin repeated. "But I thought there was a war, that it was unsafe for you—"

"After—when it's over. I'd like my uncle to meet you. I know he'd love you, too."

Peilin didn't know what to say. She liked that family was important to Henri, yet the thought of living somewhere unfamiliar was daunting. But with the ongoing war, they had some time before they could even consider traveling to his homeland.

For now, they had Shanghai. As she thought about her journey, Peilin recognized that the city had helped her reach within herself and find her inner strength. Despite the sadness she'd endured, she knew few Chinese women were given the opportunity to be on their own as she was.

She revisited Henri's question in her mind. *What did it matter where they lived so long as they were together?*

Peilin nodded. "I'd like to meet your family. But before we do anything, I need to tend to my brother Ping—to ensure that his spirit's at rest."

It worried Peilin that her brother's ghost wandered the earth.

"Of course," Henri agreed. "But what'll we do without a body?"

Peilin had been thinking about this, too. She knew that her brother's remains had been left behind, probably in some shallow ditch, as the Kuomintang continued on with their fight.

"We'll need to create a wooden tablet," Peilin explained, "so that his soul will have a home. He'll no longer roam the earth rootless and hungry."

Peilin wondered if Henri thought the Chinese beliefs about the afterlife a little odd. But when she looked up at him, she only saw compassion in his eyes.

"It'll be one of the first things we tend to upon our return. Let me help you. Ping was a loyal friend and brother. I miss him, too."

The train roared toward Shanghai; its steady pulsating progress lulled both Henri and Peilin to sleep. Before long they awakened to the conductor announcing their arrival. Back in the city, Henri felt different—like a new man. He helped Peilin onto the open double-decker bus that would take them to Ezra and Rita's. He felt a renewed energy. Shanghai had been a refuge, a safe haven of last resort when he'd nowhere else to go. He'd only hoped for a temporary place to live, but it had become so much more. With medicines as scarce as they were, he'd had success in drawing patients who were willing to try alternatives. He now realized how the vast and embracing city had given him the opportunity to explore and grow beyond what he thought possible.

Henri turned and smiled. Peilin sat quietly by his side. She, too, was a part of the city that had changed him. He'd initially arrived in Shanghai tired, lonely, and disappointed in love. Now, nearly a year and a half later, the city and the woman beside him had reopened his heart and his passion.

When they reached the apartment, Ezra and Rita greeted them. They spoke fluent Chinese with Peilin and welcomed her into the apartment. Rita especially took to her, quickly grabbing her by the hand and whisking her into the kitchen. With the two women in the next room, Ezra pulled Henri aside.

"Hitler's establishing Polish ghettos," Ezra informed him. "He's prohibiting Jews from leaving."

Henri sat down at the small table.

"What about those of us here in Shanghai? Are we still safe?"

Ezra sat across from Henri.

"There's talk of a similar ghetto here for any Jew arriving after 1937."

Henri nodded silently. Since he arrived in the late fall of 1938, this new development was sure to include him. He worried what it would mean for Peilin.

Ezra must have sensed Henri's concerns. "For now, it is just a rumor. We must continue to live as we have, taking things each day in stride," he reassured him.

Henri knew that Ezra was right.

Ezra then went to his desk and pulled out a letter.

"This came for you," he said handing it over.

Henri studied the postmark. It was from his father in Berlin. He felt his heart race as he ran his hands under the crease and opened it up.

Dear Henri,

I hope this letter finds you safe and well. As I'm sure you're aware, Hitler carries on his tyrannical atrocities. Do you remember the Bloombergs? They disappeared overnight and I fear the worst. But enough about this for the moment. I'll be brief. Uncle Viktor passed away last week. As you might remember, he had long suffered from bouts of pneumonia. The winter had been especially chilling without heat in our dwelling.

Until we meet again,
—Your father

Henri wiped the tears from his eyes.

"Sad news?" Ezra asked.

"My uncle passed away."

"I'm sorry, Henri."

"Me, too."

Henri refolded the letter and tucked it back inside the envelope. Uncle Viktor was the last reason he ever would've wanted to return to Germany.

Later that night, Henri told Peilin about his uncle. Peilin looked on with a worried expression.

"Now there's no reason for me to return to Germany after the war," he admitted.

Peilin touched his head lightly. "What about America?"

"America?" Henri thought about it. "What's there for us?"

"A new place… a fresh start."

"Hope," he added, smiling. Although he hadn't thought of it before, he liked the idea.

That evening, Henri invited Peilin to take a stroll through Shanghai. The cool April found many outdoors. He took Peilin's hand in his.

"We'll have to get you a ring," Henri said, admiring the silky skin of her long fingers.

"Ring?" Peilin asked.

"Engagement ring," Henri insisted. "It's a custom where I come from—to symbolize our impending wedding."

Peilin turn shyly away.

"I don't need a ring. After all we've been through to be together, I know you love me."

Henri smiled. "I want you to have one. You're my *beshert*—my soul mate."

They turned up Bubbling Well Road and strolled amongst the familiar outdoor cafés and shops. When they reached the movie theater, they found themselves surrounded by an emerging crowd. Peilin huddled closer to him. Henri grabbed her hand and weaved through the throng of people. Just as he thought they were about to escape into the street, he found himself face to face with Brigitta and Rosen. Brigitta wore a black sequined hat. Her dark lipstick accented the fullness of her lips.

"Fancy meeting you here," Brigitta said.

He observed Brigitta's clingy arm wrapped around Rosen. Her pathetic need to be with anyone still repulsed him. Henri was careful not to say too much. He watched Brigitta's eyes as they followed Henri's extended hand down to where it met Peilin's.

"I see this Chinese woman is still hanging around," Brigitta remarked and waved her hand dismissively in the air.

Henri pulled Peilin closer to him, embarrassed that his fiancée had to bear Brigitta's sharp tongue, even if Peilin didn't understand German.

"We're engaged," Henri announced.

"*Hmph,*" Rosen huffed.

Brigitta turned to Dr. Rosen.

"You were so right to get rid of him."

Henri stood silent, trying to ignore her slight. Brigitta gripped the edge of her hat and together with Rosen pushed their way through the crowd.

"Who was that?" Peilin asked.

Henri wasn't sure how much he needed or wanted to tell.

"Some old colleagues from the hospital," he replied.

Thankfully Peilin didn't pursue the conversation further.

Henri and Peilin walked along the Bund. Neither had said a word since encountering Brigitta. Henri gazed out over the Whangpoo River; he saw ship lights blinking in the distance. He'd come so far since the day he set foot in this strange and exotic city that had now become his home. It felt exciting to tell Brigitta that he and Peilin were to marry.

When they returned to the apartment that night, Henri recognized that there was only the one small bed. He offered it to Peilin.

"I'll sleep in the living room," he told her, "on the couch."

Henri began to grab his pajamas when he felt Peilin's hand lightly touch his arm.

"Please stay," she whispered.

He turned and looked into her eyes. Her large pupils beckoned him. He opened his arms and she fell into his embrace. They kissed; a surge of energy coursed through his veins. He ran his fingers to loosen her long silky hair and across her smooth skin. He'd waited so long for this—finally he'd found true love.

Peilin lay awake next to Henri as he slept. She understood what her mother had told her about the secrets of bed play. His body gently rose and fell with each breath. The steady rhythm felt meditative, easing Peilin into a serene calmness. It was so different to wake up in bed next to a real body, rather than the cold, stiff mannequin of her ghost husband, even if last night hadn't been their wedding night.

They'd been together as friends, close friends. But for Peilin, even though she may have wanted it, she never believed this moment would've been possible. To be given this new opportunity, this new chance at love, warmed Peilin's heart.

She knew the relationship wouldn't be without its obstacles. Even if she didn't understand the language, reactions like the one from Henri's acquaintance would persist. Before meeting Henri, Peilin had witnessed a bus driver who spit on the shoes of a Chinese woman in the arms of a foreigner. At the time, Peilin remembered watching the couple as they braved the insolent narrow-mindedness of strangers. She shuddered at the memory.

For Peilin, Henri was her soul mate, just as he'd declared her as his. After all that they'd experienced together, she knew their love would endure.

Henri held the wooden tablet as Peilin took a sharp knife and carved Ping's name. According to Peilin, once the tablet was finished, Ping's wandering soul would have a home; he'd no longer remain a hungry ghost. Henri knew how important this was to Peilin. For Henri, taking care of family, even in the afterworld, was something he respected in his adopted culture. Ping had been like a younger brother to Henri. Simple yet deeply loyal, Ping worked diligently to win Henri over. Perhaps Ping sensed how much Henri needed a friend. Ping's openness to teaching Henri Chinese helped to form a bond that Henri would never forget. It was Ping who first helped Henri to feel comfortable in Shanghai. Ping gave Henri a connection to the city he now called home.

Henri wondered if it was Ping's intentions all along to bring him together with Peilin. He turned and gazed at the woman he loved. After last night, he felt bonded to her in a new way. Henri returned his thoughts to the young boy's tablet; he felt the three of them together again. Henri was sure Ping was watching from overhead, grinning with his impish smile. And even though they hadn't prepared a tablet for his uncle, Henri added a silent prayer for Viktor, too.

Peilin finished carving the tablet. She stood back for a moment, saddened but relieved of the angst over her brother's wandering soul. She nodded to Henri who took the heavy wooden piece and propped it up on the new family altar they had made in the corner of the medical clinic.

Peilin laid out a bowl of peanuts and some red *hong zao* dates. She then reached for the jasmine incense. She pulled out two of the slender sticks and handed one to Henri. Side by side, they bowed to Ping's new resting spot.

"Home at last," Henri whispered.

"We're together now," Peilin nodded contently as she sensed her entire family, including Henri, around her.

As the sweet smell of the incense filled the air, Peilin turned to Henri. Gazing into his eyes, she saw her reflection bloom before her.

Acknowledgments

With gratitude, I'd like to thank Brooke Warner, Patricia Miya, Victoria Sanders, Bernadette Baker-Baughman, Chandler Crawford, and Chris Kepner. I'd also like to thank my parents Larry and Loraine Wong, mother-in-law Harriet Eckstein, brothers Lance, Lewis, and Len, sisters Lesley, Mary, Julie, and Serena as well as my nephews and nieces, Jake, Zack, Ryan, Sydney, and Madeline. Without your love and support this novel would not have been possible.

About the Author

L ayne is a novelist and advocate for stories that infuse personal heritage into the narrative tapestry. Weaving her Chinese heritage with that of her Jewish conversion, her debut novel explores a little known historical connection when these cultures collided as a result of Hitler's rampage and World War II.

Photo © Leslie DeMeuse

Her immigrant grandfather operated an herbal store in San Francisco. Years later Layne worked as a Chinese medicine technician producing traditional herbal formulas much like her ancestors.

Layne's a native Californian. She graduated from UCLA with a degree in English Literature. She's written for television and worked as a development associate in the entertainment industry.

She's been involved in both publishing and entertainment. As a writing coach, Layne focuses on writing with an eye towards the cultural lens. She's member of the Writers Guild of America (WGA), The Authors Guild, Academy of Television Arts and Sciences (ATAS), the Coalition of Asian Pacifics in Entertainment (CAPE), Independent Writers of Southern California (IWOSC), and Asia Society. She was selected for the prestigious AFI TV writer's program and honed her craft in David Henry Hwang writing workshop at East-West Players in Los Angeles. She's also a participant in the Asian American Journalists Association's (AAJA) annual Trivia Bowl.

Layne lives in southern California with her husband. She's currently at work on her second novel. The reader is invited to visit www. Laynewong.com for more information or to contact the author.

1/15 F

CPSIA information can be obtained at www.ICGtesting.com
Printed in the USA
LVOW08s2258110115

422436LV00005B/268/P